Sexual

Assault

Quick Reference

SECOND EDITION

*For Health Care, Social Service, and
Law Enforcement Professionals*

STM **Learning**, Inc.

Leading Publisher of Scientific, Technical, and Medical Educational Resources
Saint Louis
www.stmlearning.com

Our Mission

To become the world leader in publishing and

information services on child abuse,

maltreatment, diseases, and domestic violence.

We seek to heighten awareness of these issues,

and provide relevant information to

professionals and consumers.

*A portion of our profits is contributed to nonprofit organizations
dedicated to the prevention of child abuse and the care of victims
of abuse and other children and family charities.*

Sexual Assault

Quick Reference

*For Health Care, Social Service, and
Law Enforcement Professionals*

**Diana K. Faugno, MSN, RN, CPN,
SANE-A, SANE-P, FAAFS, DF-IAFN**
Forensic Nurse Examiner
Barbara Sinatra Children's Center
Eisenhower Medical Center
Emergency Room
Rancho Mirage, California

**Patricia M. Speck, DNSc, APN,
FNP-BC, DF-IAFN, FAAFS, FAAN**
Associate Professor
University of Alabama at Birmingham
School of Nursing
Program Director for Global Affairs
Department of Family, Community,
& Health Systems
Birmingham, Alabama

Mary J. Spencer, MD
Clinical Professor of Pediatrics
University of California,
San Diego School of Medicine
Medical Director
Child Abuse Prevention and SART
Palomar Pomerado Health
San Diego, California

Angelo P. Giardino, MD, PhD
Professor and Section Chief
Academic General Pediatrics
Baylor College of Medicine
Senior Vice President/Chief
Quality Officer
Texas Children's Hospital
Houston, Texas

iii

Publishers: Glenn E. Whaley and Marianne V. Whaley
Graphic Design Director: Glenn E. Whaley
Managing Editor: Paul K. Goode, III
Print/Production Coordinator: Jennifer M. Jones and G.W. Graphics
Cover Design: Jennifer M. Jones and G.W. Graphics
Color Prepress Specialist: Kevin Tucker
Acquisitions Editor: Glenn E. Whaley
Developmental Editor: Paul K. Goode, III
Copy Editor: Paul K. Goode, III
Proofreaders: Jessica Duncan and Paul K. Goode, III

Printed in the United States of America

Publisher:
STM Learning, Inc.
Saint Louis, MO
www.stmlearning.com

The Library of Congress has cataloged the printed edition as follows:

Faugno, Diana K., 1950- , author.
    Sexual assault quick reference : for health care, social service, and law enforcement professionals / Diana K. Faugno, Patricia M. Speck, Mary J. Spencer, Angelo P. Giardino. -- Second edition.
        p. ; cm.
    Preceded by: Quick-reference sexual assault / Angelo P. Giardino ... [et al.]. c2003.
    Includes bibliographical references and index.
    ISBN 978-1-936590-44-5 (pbk. : alk. paper) -- ISBN 1-936590-44-1 (pbk. : alk. paper)
    I. Speck, Patricia M., 1948- , author. II. Spencer, Mary J., 1936 , author. III. Giardino, Angelo P., author. IV. Title.
    [DNLM: 1. Forensic Medicine--methods--Handbooks. 2. Sex Offenses--Handbooks. 3. Crime Victims--psychology--Handbooks. 4. Patient Care Team--Handbooks. 5. Physical Examination--methods--Handbooks. W 639]
    RA1151
    614'.1--dc23
                              2015027947

CONTRIBUTORS TO THE SECOND EDITION

Eileen M. Alexy,
PhD, RN, APN, PMHCNS-BC
Associate Professor
School of Nursing, Health,
and Exercise Science
Department of Nursing
The College of New Jersey
Ewing, New Jersey

Eileen M. Allen,
MSN, RN, FN-CSA, SANE-A, SANE-P
Coordinator
Monmouth County SANE/SART
Program
Freehold, New Jersey
Adjunct Faculty
Monmouth University
West Long Branch, New Jersey

Mary Katherine Dunne Atkins,
MSN, NP-C
Certified Registered Nurse Practitioner
Epilepsy Center/Department of Neurology
Registered Nurse
Surgical Intensive Care Unit
University of Alabama Birmingham
Birmingham, Alabama

Olivia S. Ashley, DrPH
Senior Public Health Scientist
Director, Risk Behavior and Family
Research Program
Associate Director, Global Gender Center
Behavioral Health and Criminal Justice
Division
RTI International
Research Triangle Park, North Carolina

Natalie Baker, DNP, ANP-BC, GNP-BC
Assistant Professor
Acute, Chronic, and Continuing Care
University of Alabama at Birmingham,
School of Nursing
Birmingham, Alabama

Imelda Buncab, BA
Social Change Agent and Consultant
Sherman Oaks, California

Kelley Catron, DNP, WHNP-BC
Instructor
Family, Child Health and Caregiver
Department
University of Alabama at Birmingham
School of Nursing
Birmingham, Alabama

Paul Thomas Clements,
PhD, RN, DF-IAFN
Associate Clinical Professor
Coordinator – Contemporary Trends in
Forensic Health Care Certificate Online
Drexel University
College of Nursing and Health Professions
Philadelphia, Pennsylvania

Elizabeth Dowdell, PhD, MS, RN
Professor
Villanova University College of Nursing
Villanova, Pennsylvania

Donna Campbell Dunn,
PhD, CNM, FNP-BC
Assistant Professor
Continuing Care
University of Alabama at Birmingham
School of Nursing
Birmingham, Alabama

Diana K. Faugno, MSN, RN, CPN,
SANE-A, SANE-P, FAAFS, DF-IAFN
Forensic Nurse Examiner
Barbara Sinatra Children's Center
Eisenhower Medical Center
Emergency Room
Rancho Mirage, California

Annie Heirendt, LCSW
Los Angeles, California

**Aimee Chism Holland,
DNP, WHNP-BC, FNP-C**
Assistant Professor
University of Alabama at Birmingham
School of Nursing
Birmingham, Alabama

**Megan Lechner,
MSN, RN, CNS, SANE-P, SANE-A**
Forensic Nurse Examiner,
Clinical Team Lead
Memorial Hospital,
University of Colorado
Adjunct Professor
University of Colorado
at Colorado Springs
Colorado Springs, Colorado

Annie McCartney, MSN, WHNP-BC
Instructor
Adult/Acute Health,
Chronic Care and Foundations
University of Alabama at Birmingham
Birmingham, Alabama

CDR Barbara Mullen (FNP), NC, USN
Family Nurse Practitioner
United States Naval Academy
Annapolis, Maryland

Tawnne O'Connor, RN, BSN
Sexual Assault Nurse Examiner
Patient Care Coordinator
Naval Medical Center San Diego
San Diego, California

**Jennifer Pierce-Weeks,
RN, SANE-P, SANE-A**
Project Director
International Association of Forensic Nurses
Elkridge, Maryland
Forensic Nurse Examiner
Emergency Department

Memorial Hospital, University of Colorado Health
Colorado Springs, Colorado

Patricia M. Speck, DNSc, APN, FNP-BC, DF-IAFN, FAAFS, FAAN
Associate Professor
University of Alabama at Birmingham
School of Nursing
Program Director for Global Affairs
Department of Family, Community, &
Health Systems
Birmingham, Alabama

Mary J. Spencer, MD
Clinical Professor of Pediatrics
University of California, San Diego
School of Medicine
Medical Director
Child Abuse Prevention and SART
Palomar Pomerado Health
San Diego, California

Amy Thompson, MD
Assistant Professor of Medicine
Department of Pediatrics
Jefferson Medical College
Philadelphia, Pennsylvania
Attending Physician
Department of Emergency Medicine
Alfred I duPont Hospital for Children/
Nemours
Wilmington, Delaware

**Ashton Tureaud Strachan,
DNP, CRNP, FNP-C**
Family Nurse Practitioner/Nurse Manager
Student Health and Wellness Clinic
University of Alabama at Birmingham
Birmingham, Alamabama

Victor I. Vieth, JD
Senior Director
Gundersen National Child Protection
Training Center
Winona, Minnesota

CONTRIBUTORS TO THE FIRST EDITION

Joyce A. Adams, MD
Clinical Professor of Pediatrics
Division of General Academic Pediatrics
and Adolescent Medicine
University of California, San Diego
Medical Center
San Diego, California

Randell Alexander, MD, PhD, FAAP
Associate Professor
Clinical Pediatrics
Morehouse School of Medicine
Forensic Pediatrician
Department of Pediatrics
Morehouse School of Medicine
Atlanta, Georgia

Eileen Allen, RN, BN, DABFN
SANE Program Coordinator
Monmouth County Prosecutor's Office
Freehold, New Jersey

Sarah Anderson, RN, MSN
University of Virginia
Department of Emergency Medicine
(Registered Nurse)
School of Nursing (Doctoral Student)
Charlottesville, Virginia

Joanne Archambault
Training Director
Sexual Assault Training and Investiga-
tions (SATI, Inc.)
Retired Sergeant
San Diego Police Department
Sex Crimes Unit

Janice B. Asher, MD
Assistant Clinical Professor
Obstetrics and Gynecology
University of Pennsylvania Medical Center
Director
Women's Health Division of Student
Health Service
University of Pennsylvania
Philadelphia, Pennsylvania

Tracy Bahm, JD
Senior Attorney
Violence Against Women Program
American Prosecutors Research Institute
(APRI)
Alexandria, Virginia

Kathy Bell, RN
Forensic Nurse Examiner
Tulsa Police Department
Tulsa, Oklahoma

Patrick E. Besant-Matthews, MD
Forensic Pathology and Forensic Medicine
Legal and Law Enforcement Consultations
Private Practice
Dallas, Texas

Sandra L. Bloom, MD
CEO, Community Works
Philadelphia, Pennsylvania

Duncan T. Brown, JD
Staff Attorney
National Center for Prosecution
of Child Abuse
American Prosecutors Research Institute
(APRI)
Alexandria, Virginia

Mary-Ann Burkhart, JD
Senior Attorney
National Center for Prosecution
of Child Abuse
American Prosecutors Research Institute
(APRI)
Alexandria, Virginia

Susan Chasson, MSN, CNM, JD
Lecturer
College of Nursing
Brigham Young University
Provo, Utah

Michael Clark, MSN, CRNP
Nurse Practitioner
Department of Emergency Medicine
Hospital of the University of Pennsylvania
Clinical Lecturer
University of Pennsylvania School of
Nursing
Philadelphia, Pennsylvania

Sharon W. Cooper, MD, FAAP
Adjunct Associate Professor of Pediatrics
University of North Carolina School of
Medicine
Chapel Hill, North Carolina
Clinical Assistant Professor of Pediatrics
Uniformed Services University of Health
Sciences
Bethesda, Maryland
Chief
Developmental Pediatric Service
Womack Army Medical Center
Fort Bragg, North Carolina

Elizabeth M. Datner, MD
Assistant Professor
University of Pennsylvania School of
Medicine
Department of Emergency Medicine
Assistant Professor of Emergency Medi-
cine in Pediatrics
Children's Hospital of Philadelphia
Philadelphia, Pennsylvania

Sue Dickinson,
RN, BSN, PHN, CEDN, SANE-A
Forensic Nurse Examiner
Palomar Pomerado Health
Escondido, California

Colette M. Eastman, DO
Obstetrics, Gynecology, and Reproduc-
tive Medicine
Physician Consultant/Instructor, Sexual
Assault Response Team
Poway, California

Thomas Ervin, RNC, FN, BSc†
Reception and Release Coordinator
California State Prison at Corcoran
Department of Corrections
State of California

Diana K. Faugno,
RN, BSN, CPN, FAAFS, SANE-A
District Director
Pediatrics/Nicu
Forensic Health Service
Palomar Pomerado Health
Escondido, California

Anne B. Finigan, RN, MScN, ACNP
Forensic Clinical Nurse Specialist/Nurse
Practitioner
Regional Sexual Assault and Domestic
Violence Treatment Centre
St. Joseph's Health Care London
London, Ontario
Canada

Martin A. Finkel, DO, FACOP, FAAP
Professor of Pediatrics
Medical Director
Center for Children's Support
School of Osteopathic Medicine
University of Medicine and Dentistry of
New Jersey
Stratford, New Jersey

Marla J. Friedman, MD
Fellow, Pediatric Emergency Medicine
Emergency Medicine
Alfred I. duPont Hospital for Children
Wilmington, Delaware

Donna Gaffney, RN, DNSc, FAAN
Associate Professor, Acute Care Nurse
Practitioner Program
College of Nursing
Seton Hall University
South Orange, New Jersey

Ann E. Gaulin, MS, MFT
Director of Counseling Services
Women Organized Against Rape
Philadelphia, Pennsylvania

Angelo P. Giardino, MD, PhD
Associate Chair – Pediatrics
Associate Physician-in-Chief
St. Christopher's Hospital for Children
Associate Professor in Pediatrics
Drexel University College of Medicine
Philadelphia, Pennsylvania

Eileen R. Giardino, PhD, RN, CRNP
Associate Professor
LaSalle University, School of Nursing
Nurse Practitioner
LaSalle University, Student Health
Center
Philadelphia, Pennsylvania

Barbara W. Girardin, RN, PhD
Forensic Health Care
Palomar Pomerado Health
Escondido, California

**Holly M. Harner,
CRNP, PhD, MPH, SANE**
Assistant Professor
William F. Connell School of Nursing
Boston College
Chestnut Hill, Massachusetts

Caren Harp, JD
Senior Attorney/ Director
National Juvenile Justice Prosecution Center
American Prosecutors Research Institute
(APRI)
Alexandria, Virginia

William C. Holmes, MD, MSCE
Assistant Professor of Medicine and
Epidemiology
Philadelphia Veterans Affairs Medical Center
Center for Clinical Epidemiology and
Biostatistics
University of Pennsylvania School of
Medicine
Philadelphia, Pennsylvania

Jeffrey R. Jaeger, MD
Assistant Professor of Medicine
University of Pennsylvania Health System
Clinical Faculty, Institute for Safe Families
Philadelphia, Pennsylvania

Susan Bieber Kennedy, RN, JD
Senior Attorney
Violence Against Women Program
American Prosecutors Research Institute
(APRI)
Alexandria, Virginia

Lisa Kreeger, JD
Senior Attorney
Violence Against Women Program Manager
DNA Forensics Program Manager
American Prosecutors Research Institute
(APRI)
Alexandria, Virginia

Susan Kreston, JD
Deputy Director
National Center for Prosecution of Child
Abuse
American Prosecutors Research Institute
(APRI)
Alexandria Virginia

Linda E. Ledray,
RN, PhD, SANE-A, FAAN
Director
Sexual Assault Resource Service
Hennepin County Medical Center
Minneapolis, Minnesota

Carolyn J. Levitt, MD
Assistant Professor of Pediatrics
Department of Pediatrics
University of Minnesota
Director
Midwest Children's Resource Center
Children's Hospitals and Clinics
St. Paul, Minnesota

Patsy Rauton Lightle
Supervisory Special Agent
Lieutenant Department of Child Fatalities
South Carolina Law Enforcement Division
Columbia, South Carolina

Judith A. Linden, MD, FACEP, SANE
Assistant Professor
Emergency Medicine
Boston University School of Medicine
Associate Residency Director
Boston University School of Medicine
Boston Medical Center
Boston, Massachusetts

John Loiselle, MD
Associate Professor of Pediatrics
Jefferson Medical College
Assistant Director, Emergency Medicine
Alfred I. duPont Hospital for Children
Wilmington, Delaware

Kathi Makoroff, MD
Mayerson Center for Safe and Healthy
Children
Cincinnati Children's Hospital Medical
Center
Cincinnati, Ohio

Jeanne Marrazzo, MD, MPH
Assistant Professor
Department of Medicine
Division of Allergy and Infectious Diseases
University of Washington
Seattle, Washington
Medical Director
Seattle STD/HIV Prevention Training
Center
Seattle, Washington

Claire Nelli, RN, SANE-A
Manager—SART Department
Villa View Community Hospital
San Diego, California

Patrick O'Donnell, PhD
Supervising Criminalist, DNA Laboratory
San Diego Police Department
San Diego, California

Jason Payne James, LLM, FRCS
(Edin & Eng), DFM, RNutr
Forensic Physician
Forensic Medical Examiner - Metropolitan
Police Service and City of London Police
Director - Forensic Healthcare Services, Ltd.
Editor-in-Chief, *Journal of Clinical*
Forensic Medicine
London, England
United Kingdom

Christine M. Peterson, MD
Director of Gynecology
Department of Student Health
Assistant Professor of Clinical Obstetrics
and Gynecolgy
University of Virginia School of Medicine
Charlottesville, Virginia

Hannah Ufberg Rabinowitz, MSN,
ARNP, FNA, NCGNP
Clinical Education
Aventura Hospital
Aventura, Florida

William J. Reed, MD, FAAP
Assistant Professor of Pediatrics
Texas A&M College of Medicine
Behavioral and Adolescent Medicine
Driscoll Children's Hospital
Corpus Christi, Texas

Iris Reyes, MD, FACEP
Assistant Professor
Emergency Medicine
Hospital of the University of Pennsylvania
Assistant Medical Director
Emergency Medicine
Hospital of the University of Pennsylvania
Philadelphia, Pennsylvania

Dawn Rice, RN, BSN, FNE
Executive Director
Fort Wayne Sexual Assault Treatment
Center
President
Indiana Chapter of the IAFN
Fort Wayne, Indiana

Laura L. Rogers, JD
Senior Attorney
National Center for Prosecution of Child
Abuse
American Prosecutors Research Institute
(APRI)
Alexandria, Virginia

Mimi Rose, JD
Chief Assistant District Attorney
Family Violence and Sexual Assault Unit
Philadelphia District Attorney Office
Philadelphia, Pennsylvania

Pamela Ross, MD
Assistant Professor of Emergency
Medicine & Pediatrics
University of Virginia Health System
Charlottesville, Virginia

Rena Rovere, MS, FNP
Sexual Assault Program Director
Clinical Nurse Specialist
Department of Emergency Medicine
Albany Medical Center
Albany, New York

Bruce D. Rubin, MD
Clinical Instructor
Department of Emergency Medicine
Hospital of the University of Pennsylvania
Philadelphia, Pennsylvania

Maureen S. Rush, MS
Vice President for Public Safety
University of Pennsylvania
Division of Public Safety
Philadelphia, Pennsylvania

Charles J. Schubert, MD
Associate Professor of Pediatrics
Division of Emergency Medicine
Cincinnati Children's Hospital Medical
Center
Cincinnati, Ohio

Diana Schunn, RN, BSN, SANE-A
SANE/SART Manager
Via Christi Regional Medical Center
Wichita, Kansas

Margot Schwartz, MD
Virginia Mason Medical Center
Infectious Diseases Section
Seattle, Washington
Clinical Instructor
Department of Medicine
University of Washington
Seattle, Washington

**Deborah K. Scott,
RN-C, BSN, ARNP, FNS**
Child Protection Team
Howard Phillips Center for
Children and Families
Orlando, Florida

Philip Scribano, DO, MSCE
Assistant Professor
Pediatrics and Emergency Medicine
University of Connecticut School of
Medicine
Director, Child Protection Program
Connecticut Children's Medical Center
Hartford, Connecticut

Christina Shaw, JD
Staff Attorney
National Center for Prosecution
of Child Abuse
American Prosecutors Research Institute
(APRI)
Alexandria, Virginia

Patricia M. Speck, APRN, MSN, BC
Coordinator of Nursing Services
and Interim Manager
City of Memphis Sexual Assault
Resource Center
Division of Public Services
and Neighborhoods
Memphis, Tennessee

Mary J. Spencer, MD
Clinical Professor of Pediatrics
University of California San Diego
School of Medicine
Medical Director
Child Abuse Prevention and
Sexual Assault Response Team
Palomar Pomerado Health
Escondido, California

Norman D. Sperber, DDS
Chief Forensic Dentist, San Diego
and Imperial County
Diplomate, American Board of Forensic
Odontology
Distinguished Fellow, American Academy
of Forensic Sciences
San Diego, California

Jeanne L. Stanley, PhD
Executive Director of Academic Services
Graduate School of Education
University of Pennsylvania
Philadelphia, Pennsylvania

Cari Michele Steele, JD
Staff Attorney
National Center for Prosecution
of Child Abuse
American Prosecutors Research Institute
(APRI)
Alexandria, Virginia

Jacqueline M. Sugarman, MD
Assistant Professor of Pediatrics
Department of Pediatrics
College of Medicine
University of Kentucky
Lexington, Kentucky

Kathryn M. Turman
Program Director
Office of Victim Assistance
Federal Bureau of Investigation
Washington, DC

Victor I. Vieth, JD
Director
National Center for Prosecution
of Child Abuse
American Prosecutors Research Institute
(APRI)
Alexandria, Virginia

Malinda Waddell, RN, MN, FNP
Director-Forensic Nurse Specialists
Long Beach, California

J.M. Whitworth, MD
Professor of Pediatrics
University of Florida
State Medical Director
Child Protection Team Program
Children's Medical Services
Department of Health
State of Florida

Dawn Doran Wilsey, JD
Senior Attorney
National Center for Prosecution
of Child Abuse
American Prosecutors Research Institute
(APRI)
Alexandria, Virginia

Janet S. Young, MD
Assistant Professor
University of North
Carolina-Chapel Hill
Department of Emergency Medicine
Chapel Hill, North Carolina

FOREWORD TO THE SECOND EDITION

Sexual assault covers a broad spectrum of unwanted sexual contact. This includes unwanted touching; forced physical contact; and forced viewing of, or involvement in, pornography. The survivor population is incredibly diverse, including both women *and* men from a variety of cultures, ethnicities, and age groups. Sexual assault may physically injure survivors and it may also exact profound, long-term emotional tolls from both primary survivors and secondary survivors, ie, in their family and friends. This problem is compounded by the low percentage of survivors who report incidents of sexual assault and, as a result, the low percentage who receives the qualified help that is so crucial to their recovery—help that should include a coordinated response from medical professionals, trained sexual assault nurse examiners, advocates, and law enforcement.

Sexual Assault Quick Reference, Second Edition is a detailed reference guide that covers a range of common and uncommon types of sexual assault, offers essential guidance and recommended treatments based on research and extensive treatment histories, and provides procedural guidelines for patient-practitioner interaction to promote best possible outcomes. It is a comprehensive, reference tool that should be considered an essential resource for professionals and volunteers serving in the sexual assault community of practice. Readers from across the full spectrum of sexual assault responders will benefit from the knowledge contained in this book. After reading *Sexual Assault Quick Reference*, Second Edition, sexual assault support service providers will be able to improve and standardize their ability to deliver consistent, high-quality care in a variety of sexual assault cases and for the survivors of those incidents.

Elisa Covarrubias
Director of Sexual Assault and Advocacy Programs
Marietta, GA

Sarah Pederson, BSN, RN, SANE
Sexual Assault Nurse Examiner Coordinator
Marietta, GA

FOREWORD TO THE FIRST EDITION

Sexual Assault is broadly defined as unwanted sexual contact of any kind. Among the acts included are rape, incest, molestation, fondling or grabbing, and forced viewing of or involvement in pornography. Drug-facilitated behavior was recently added in response to the recognition that pharmacologic agents can be used to make the victim more malleable. When sexual activity occurs between a significantly older persona and a child, it is referred to as molestation or child sexual abuse, rather than sexual assault. In children, there is often a "grooming" period during which the perpetrator gradually escalates the type of sexual contact with the child and often does not use the force implied in the term sexual assault. But it is assault, both physically and emotionally, whether the victim is a child, an adolescent, or an adult.

The reported statistics are only an estimate of the problem's scope, with the actual reporting rate a mere fraction of the true incidence. The financial costs of sexual assault are enormous; intangible costs, such as emotional suffering and risk of death from being victimized, are beyond measurement. Short-term and long-term consequences reach far into all emotional and physical aspects of a victim's life.

Trained professionals work every day to combat sexual assault in all its forms as well as the adverse aftereffects. This book offers information for all who deal with sexual assault—the crisis hotline staff, law enforcement personnel, prehospital providers, specialized detectives, medical and mental health staff, specialized sexual assault examiners, and counselors. The information is as current, accurate, and specific as it can be in a rapidly evolving field. This book seeks to provide this information in a most accessible manner for professionals needing an immediate resource; it will fill a need in many avenues where sexual victimization is seen and care is given to victims.

Robert M. Reece, MD
Director, MSPCC Institute for Professional Education
Clinical Professor of Pediatrics, Tufts University School of Medicine
Executive Editor, the *Quarterly Child Abuse Medical Update*

FOREWORD TO THE FIRST EDITION

Health care, social service, and law enforcement professionals have the unique opportunity to make a difference in how victims of sexual assault will incorporate that event into the rest of their lives. The well-prepared professional is aware of the patient's needs and sensitive to the victim's response to the examination process. This attentiveness will go a long way in beginning the emotional healing process necessary to integrate the events. Giving control back to the victim of rape is therapeutic and should be a priority throughout the examination.

The primary purpose of the sexual assault examination by the health care professional is to provide for medical diagnosis and treatment. The examiner needs to keep in mind that observations may be the result of normal development, a result of trauma caused by accident or abuse, or the result of a disease condition. Treatment may be of a clinical, psychological, or emotional nature.

The evidence-collection portion of the examination assists in linking the victim, the suspect, the crime scene, and the evidence. Documentation of this portion of the examination is just as important as documenting the history and physical assessment. This text provides easy-to-access information outline forensic, biologic, and technologic evidence collection within the discussion of the many unique situations in which a sexual assault may occur.

Necessary for any professional who deals with sexual assault, this quick reference provides a base of details essential to accomplish a thorough medical forensic examination.

Kathy Bell, RN
Forensic Nurse Examiner
Tulsa Police Department
Tulsa, Oklahoma

PREFACE TO THE SECOND EDITION

The impact of sexual assault and abuse is far-reaching and observed across social strata in communities throughout the world. Survivors are made to endure not only the injuries immediately resulting from offenses committed against them but also long-term physical, emotional, and psychological disorders that can, in some cases, last a lifetime. It is, therefore, the responsibility of those charged with caring for and representing the interests of the survivors of sexual assault to both safeguard them in the immediate aftermath of their encounters with criminal violence and, ideally, help guide them toward a path of resilient recovery, long after the end of initial treatments and investigations.

The intent of Sexual Assault Quick Reference is to support medical, social service, and legal professionals in the delivery of responsive and compassionate caregiving as well as investigative techniques tailored to the unique needs of sexual assault survivors. It ensures that readers always have an easily accessible reference on hand for a variety of topics relevant to cases of sexual assault. In recognition of the field's continual evolution, this new Second Edition revision has up-to-date standards and contemporary best practices in the medical forensic evaluation of patients across the life span, identifying and documenting physical injury, appropriately documenting and reporting cases of sexual violence, recognizing and treating sexually transmitted infections, and providing psychological and social support to survivors.

Effective response to sexual assault, as well as the best possible outcomes for survivors, depends upon the cooperative efforts of informed and dedicated professionals across disciplines, be they physicians, nurses, mental health practitioners, emergency responders, law enforcement officials, attorneys, or social service workers. This book is possible because of the commitment of nearly 100 such professionals and their combined expertise. We are happy now to offer it to you, and we sincerely hope that it will be of value and inform your efforts to mitigate the impact of sexual violence in all its forms and in the interest of the survivors seeking your care.

Diana K. Faugno, MSN, RN, CPN, SANE-A, SANE-P, FAAFS, DF-IAFN
Patricia M. Speck, DNSc, APN, FNP-BC, DF-IAFN, FAAFS, FAAN
Mary J. Spencer, MD
Angelo P. Giardino, MD, PhD

Preface to the First Edition

Sex crimes are now recognized as the precipitating event for various physical, emotional, and psychological disorders. Individuals, families, and the society as a whole suffer. Professionals are charged with working to identify and document the presence of physical injury to corroborate the victim's history, which contributes to the investigation of possible sexual abuse and assault and holds offenders accountable for their crime. Aids in this process include photographic, colposcopic, video, and narrative documentation, and the quality of these media continues to improve. Secure computer programs are being used to transmit photographs so that various professionals can consult on injuries. Research investigating assault injuries continues to support the position that the presence of injury does not prove assault, nor does the absence of injury prove consent. The interdisciplinary sexual assault response team (SART) approach, in which an expert nurse examiner or physician, a sex crimes detective, an advocate, and an experienced, specialized prosecutor work in tandem, has streamlined the process for the victim. Emotional care offered from the time of the examination has softened the impact of the process and helped the victim toward recovery. More efficient and better funded DNA profiling at the local, state, and national levels allows for more timely identification of offenders.

In this text, we see the problem of sexual assault and abuse through the eyes of many professionals: physicians, paramedics, law enforcement personnel, the judicial system, social workers, and people who work with children. The knowledge shared by these concerned and caring individuals supplies the power to intervene. This book offers current, accurate, and specific data concerning the problem of sexual assault in an easy-to-access format. With this information, we become empowered participants whose effective interventions help prevent sexual assault as well as care for its victims.

Angelo P. Giardino, MD, PhD
Elizabeth M. Datner, MD
Janice B. Asher, MD
Barbara W. Girardin, RN, PhD
Diana K. Faugno, RN, BSN, CNP, FAAFS, SANE-A
Mary J. Spencer, MD

REVIEWS

Sexual Assault Quick Reference, *Second Edition contains easy-to-read, yet comprehensive, material related to caring for the sexual assault survivor. The many professions that make up the multidisciplinary team caring for these victims, including physicians, nurses, emergency responders, social service personnel, attorneys, and law enforcement, will find that this reference includes accurate, up-to-date information and guidelines to assist in the care of these individuals. This pocket reference captures the content of the many areas of knowledge necessary to care for victims of sexual assault and has been written by a team of leaders with insurmountable knowledge and experience in this field. This text is recommended with the highest regards.*

Jessica L. Ahmann, DNP, APRN, FNP-BC
Family Nurse Practitioner
Children's Advocacy Center
Sanford
Bismarck, North Dakota

Sexual Assault Quick Reference *is a must-have reference for new SANEs to assist in their assessments, nursing diagnoses, and documentation. Chapter 5, "Differential Diagnosis," is comprehensive in identifying common normal variants and disease processes that mimic injuries seen in sexual abuse. I recommend this textbook for course coordinators when developing SANE-A/SANE-P course curricula as it covers a wide variety of subjects that should be taught in any SANE curriculum. The* Quick Reference *is also an excellent guide to SANE program coordinators to reference when developing polices, protocols, or guidelines for their institutions. All health care personnel would benefit from this textbook as it provides the most up-to-date material when working with victims of sexual violence.*

Barbra Bachmeir, JD, MSN, NP-C
Nurse Practitioner/Forensic Nurse Examiner
Emergency Department
IU Health-Methodist Hospital
Indianapolis, Indiana

This textbook would be a valuable reference for any professional or agency that provides services to sexual assault or sexual abuse survivors of any age. The chapters are written by experts in forensic medicine, forensic nursing, forensic DNA analysis, social work, and other specialties relevant to working with victims of sexual assault or sexual exploitation. Chapters include the basic legal definitions of sexual assault, sexual battery, and sexual exploitation; differentiating abuse/assault injuries from nonabuse/nonassault injuries or disease process in a victim of any age; how to form and manage a multidisciplinary team; what to include in the forensic medical report and who will view that report; the chain of custody, combined DNA index system, DNA evidence, and collecting reference samples; sexual assault by an acquaintance or intimate partner and the heavy emotional burden it places on the victim; and issues unique to elder victims living in residential care facilities or when in-home caregivers are suspects.

Thomas Collins, MA, ADN
(Certificate in Forensic Nursing), AAS (Forensic Technology)
Instructor, UCR Extension
Certificate Program in Forensic Nursing
University of California at Riverside
Riverside, California
Clinical Nurse III
University of California, San Diego
Health System
San Diego, California

The second edition of Sexual Assault Quick Reference is an excellent resource for all health care providers who see victims of sexual violence. In particular, Chapters 15-21 provide a wealth of new information on topics essential to victim care. Chapter 18,

"Sexual Assault Response in the United States Military," is a practical read for those unfamiliar with the military and how its legal system works. Chapter 20, "Strangulation in Living Patients," is nothing short of amazing with its color photos and precise breakdown of patient assessment, forensic photography, and signs and symptoms of strangulation that require further investigation and evaluation. I highly recommend this second edition as a go-to resource for professionals who respond to and care for victims of sexual assault.

Cynthia T. Ferguson, PhD, MSN, MPH, MFA, RN, CNM, AFN-BC, D-ABMDI
CDR (ret.) United States Navy
Clinical Forensics Program Consultant
Ferguson Forensics
Palmyra, Virginia

CONTENTS IN BRIEF

CONTENTS IN DETAIL

Sexual Assault

Quick Reference

SECOND EDITION

*For Health Care, Social Service, and
Law Enforcement Professionals*

STM **Learning**, Inc.

Leading Publisher of Scientific, Technical, and Medical Educational Resources
Saint Louis
www.stmlearning.com

Publisher's Note

This book contains historical time frames for physical and DNA evidence collection. Please note that previous studies are not supportive of evidence collection outside a 72-hour window postassault/post-abuse; however, the science of evidence collection is now advancing so quickly that multidisciplinary team members should consider it necessary to coordinate with a forensic laboratory in order to establish a viable time frame for evidence collection policies within the community. Whenever possible, any and all evidence should be collected and stored for the benefit of future science and justice.

Chapter 1

Principles of Sexual Assault at Any Age

Amy Thompson, MD*
Marla J. Friedman, DO
Judith A. Linden, MD, FACEP, SANE
John Loiselle, MD
Janet S. Young, MD

Child Sexual Abuse

Child sexual abuse is not a new problem but has only been accepted as a bona fide entity that deserves professional attention since the 1970s. Its definition is subject to interpretation on multiple levels. Institutional, societal, medical, and legal terminology all differ in either definition or emphasis. A broad range of developmentally inappropriate sexual behaviors is included, covering both contact and noncontact activities. The Child Abuse Prevention and Treatment Act (CAPTA) of 1974 provided a federal legal standard that all states were mandated to follow to be eligible for funds for child abuse programs. This act defined sexual abuse as "the employment, use, persuasion, inducement, enticement, or coercion of any child to engage in, or assist any other person to engage in, any sexually explicit conduct or simulation of such conduct for the purpose of producing a visual depiction of such conduct." Principles that mark most legal definitions include the following:

— A child is defined as a person under age 18 years, with some exceptions.

— Most statutes emphasize the discrepancy between the perpetrator's and victim's ages.

Revised Chapter 1 for the second edition.

— The developmental level of the child is considered.

— Laws generally distinguish who is considered a caretaker or guardian for the child.

— When the caretaker is involved in the abuse, involvement of the local child protective services (CPS) agency and law enforcement personnel is usually mandated.

— When the perpetrator is unknown, unrelated, or not considered a caretaker or involved in the child's care, the abuse may be treated as a purely criminal case.

The generally recognized forms of sexual abuse are genital fondling; masturbation; sexualized kissing; digit or object penetration of the vagina or anus; and oral-genital, genital-genital, and anal-genital contact, but the perpetrator does not need to directly contact the child physically for sexual abuse to occur, with exhibitionism; voyeurism; and viewing, producing, or distributing pornography also included in most definitions. The use of computers and the Internet to produce, compile, possesses, or disseminate child pornography as well as to seduce or attract children with the intent of sexual misuse is a recent addition to legislation. In addition, failure to protect a child is an important component of many definitions of child sexual abuse. Incest is a special category in that a different level of psychosocial problems, prognosis, and family dysfunction is involved, but the cases are handled the same with respect to reporting and meeting the legal definition of sexual abuse.

Sexual play occurs between young children of similar developmental levels and frequently involves viewing or touching, but it is considered a normal part of childhood development and curiosity. The variety and frequency of sexualized behaviors increase in both male and female children up to 5 years of age and then decreases thereafter. The distinction between sexual play and sexual abuse is generally predicated on the discrepancy in age between the 2 participants, the level of control or authority the older child holds over the younger one, the degree of coercion, and the actual activity involved.

Persons who are mandatory reporters, having a responsibility for the welfare of children, should be familiar with their own state statutes.

SCOPE

— True magnitude is unknown.

— Rates are generally considered underestimates and are based on substantial underreporting.

— Cases may never be disclosed or may be disclosed by victims but not reported to authorities.

— The Fourth National Incidence Study on Child Abuse and Neglect estimated 135 300 cases of sexual abuse in 2006, a rate of 1.8 cases/1000 children.

— Prevalence studies estimate that 17% of females and 8% of males have experienced childhood sexual abuse.

— One-third of victimized women and 40% of victimized men never disclose.

— Physicians and other mandated reporters often fail to report cases of sexual abuse, with a perceived lack of sufficient evidence, concern for disrupting the patient-physician relationship, fear of harming the family, and distrust of local CPS agencies cited as the most common reasons for not reporting.

— Recall bias may affect the prevalence data reported, with false childhood memories overestimating the true prevalence and denial, repressed memories, and a continuing unwillingness to disclose traumatic events generating an underestimate.

VICTIMS

— There is no classic profile of the sexually abused child.

— Female victims account for more than 3 times the number of male victims in reported cases of child sexual abuse. Data also show that girls are 2.5 times more likely to be victims of sexual abuse than boys.

— The risk for sexual abuse is highest during preadolescence with 9 to 11 years being the mean age, with a smaller peak in the early school-age years.

— Sexually abused boys tend to be younger than their female counterparts.

— Race and ethnicity do not differ from nonabused populations, although there is some evidence that low socioeconomics might increase risk.

— Children with behavioral health problems and physical or mental disabilities are at potentially higher risk for victimization.

— Perpetrators report that they seek children who are available, trusting, lack self-esteem, and have desirable physical attributes.

— Children living without 1 or both of their natural parents are at an increased risk of being abused. Females who live apart from their mothers or are not emotionally close to their mothers are at increased risk of sexual abuse. Abused males are more likely to live with their mothers and have no father figure at home.

— The single most important risk factor for both males and females is the presence of a nonbiologically-related male in the household.

— Other risk factors include having a mother who is ill, disabled, has less than a college education, or is extensively out of the home; substance abuse; parental conflict; violence in the home; having adolescent parents, foster parents, or parents who were sexually abused themselves; and being a sibling of an abused child.

OFFENDERS
— There is no classic profile of the abuser.

— Child sexual abusers tend to be older men, but one-quarter to one-third of male perpetrators are adolescents.

— Women are offenders in up to 5% of cases involving female children and 20% of cases involving male children.

— In 75% of cases of child sexual abuse, the perpetrator is known by the child. Stepfathers molest girls more often than boys, while biological fathers molest similar numbers of girls and boys.

— Incest victims are most likely to be female children who are molested by their fathers or stepfathers.

— The typical family where incest occurs is involved with multiple stressors, with parental conflict leading to an absence of sexual relations between the parents and that leading to the father looking to his daughter for comfort and love. The daughter may be depressed and withdrawn and have a poor self-image; she also yearns for attention and affection and may be happy to fill the need in her father's life. The mother feels completely dependent on her husband, making her see herself as powerless. She abandons her husband and daughter both emotionally and physically, allowing her daughter to assume her role as wife.

— Extrafamilial abuse is more common among boys, especially those over age 12 years. Boys under age 6 years are more likely to be abused by family and friends.

— The duration of molestation is shorter on average for male victims, but the acts themselves tend to be more severe.

— While fewer than 50% of child sex offenders are mentally ill, most have an emotional disorder that prevents them from forming intimate relationships with partners their own age. They experience both emotional and sexual gratification when the abuse of a child is complete. They often view their abuse as proof to themselves that they have the power to control at least that aspect of their lives.

— The victim-to-victimizer cycle is especially true for adolescent perpetrators and most often involves male victims of male offenders. The characteristics of the victim and the characteristics of the abuse often closely parallel the offender's own memory of abuse.

— Four preconditions must exist before the victimization of a child can occur:

1. Motivation of the perpetrator: the abuser has sexual desires surrounding children.

2. Internal inhibitions (overcoming internal inhibitions related to the abuse of children): this step is facilitated if the perpetrator experienced a traumatic childhood sexual event of his own.

3. External inhibitions: perpetrators are generally people on whom the child depends for emotional, physical, financial, educational, or religious support.

4. Overcoming the child's resistance to the sexual interaction

— Strategies to gain the child's trust involve many forms of manipulation and are termed "engagement."

1. The abuser targets the child and they begin to share nonsexual activities.

2. The abuser uses bribery, including gifts, favors, or privileges, to entice the child.

3. The abuser may shower the child with encouragement and compliments.

4. He may use persuasion to deceive the child into believing that they have a special friendship.

5. Over time, activity escalates, with each interaction becoming more sexual in nature.

6. Once sexual intimacy occurs, the perpetrator focuses on maintaining the secret, now using a different form of manipulation to intimidate the child.

7. The abuser may play on the child's guilt and threaten to stop loving the child; he may threaten physical violence to the child or a family member, and he may actually use force or violence.

— The child becomes confused, alone, and feels betrayed, perpetuating the secret.

Indicators of Sexual Abuse
— Children may not reveal a history of sexual abuse because they fear no one will believe them, they feel guilty or ashamed and worry about being blamed, they do not want to get the perpetrator into trouble, or they fear retaliation if they tell.

— The disclosure may be offered at any time and to any number of people.

1. May occur in a place that reminds the child of the event or where the child feels safe

2. May be to a parent at bath time or bedtime

3. May be to a sibling or playmate

4. May be to a teacher or guidance counselor after a sexual abuse prevention program in school

5. May be to a physician during a routine health examination

— A common early warning sign is the use of broad general statements, which the child uses to gauge the response of a trusted listener. These subtle suggestions should alert the listener to the possibility of sexual abuse.

— Observation of an accidental comment or suspicious behavior is often more common than intentional disclosure.

— About one-third of sexually abused children will exhibit sexualized behavior problems, defined as age-inappropriate knowledge of both sexual language and behaviors. Issues to consider include family sexuality, life stress, domestic violence, and sexual abuse when confronted with this indicator.

— Other broad, nonspecific indicators of child sexual abuse can be divided into 3 categories:

1. Physical signs and symptoms: presence of a sexually transmitted infection (STI) in a young child, presence of sperm in or on the body, discovery of childhood/teen pregnancy are obvious signs, but seldom found; more likely findings are chronic abdominal pain, enuresis or encopresis, constipation secondary to anal discomfort, recurrent urinary tract infections, vaginal discharge, and presence of a vaginal foreign body

2. Behavioral signs and symptoms: often the first signs noted by those close to the child, but not unique to sexual abuse, being present in other forms of severe stress; include temper tantrums or running away from home; developmentally regressive behaviors (thumb sucking or bedwetting); obsessive cleanliness or neglect; self-mutilating or self-stimulating behaviors; poor school attendance and performance; delinquency; substance abuse; premature participation in sexual relationships

3. Psychiatric signs and symptoms: depression, evidenced by social withdrawal and the inability to form or maintain meaningful peer relations; profound grief in response to losses of innocence, childhood, trust in oneself, trust in adults; sleeping disorders with fear of the dark and nightmares; changed eating habits (anorexia, overeating, avoiding certain foods); suicide

— Recantation rates range from 4% to 27% with younger children, those abused by a parent figure and who lacked the support of a nonoffending caretaker are more likely to recant.

Support Systems

— Specialty divisions, special police units, social workers, and multidisciplinary child abuse evaluation teams or Child Advocacy Centers where representatives of all the involved fields are gathered may be employed in evaluating childhood sexual abuse cases.

— Protocols have been developed to improve the accuracy and thoroughness of evaluation, the recommended management of the child, and the provision of legal services, including the appointment of a guardian ad litem as needed.

— Key roles are played by the pediatrician and family practitioner in the assessment of a child sexual abuse case. The practitioner is often the person the family feels most comfortable with and to whom they turn; he may be the person to whom the child discloses the abuse.

— Physicians are mandated reporters and must be familiar with state law regarding reportable offenses and the process to be followed in reporting suspicions.

— The primary care physician provides emotional as well as medical support for both child and family and must be aware of potential resources to which referrals can be made as well as consultants who are available.

— Primary care physicians are also responsible for parental education through anticipatory guidance, teaching young children about good touches and bad touches; alerting families to behaviors or physical signs that are cause for concern; and reassuring in cases of normal childhood play and curiosity.

OUTCOMES

Finkelhor and Browne describe 4 traumagenic dynamics as a framework for understanding the link between the experience of sexual abuse and its sequelae (the traumatogenic model).

— Traumatic sexualization: the inappropriate and dysfunctional development of a victim's sexuality as a result of the abuse; marked by confusion and misconceptions concerning sexuality, with distorted perceptions of sexual activities, sexual preoccupations (compulsive masturbation, sexualized play, sexual aggression, seductive behaviors), gender identity conflict and cross-gender behavior, prostitution, and sexual dysfunction as adults. Invasive abuse is more sexualizing than using the child to masturbate, and older children who can understand the implications of the abuse are more likely to suffer traumatic sexualization than other victims.

— Sense of betrayal: often three-fold, with (1) betrayal by the perpetrator in the form of manipulations and misconceptions about sex and love; (2) the child's betrayal by his/her own body, since his/her body responded to the sexual stimulation then he/she must have somehow wanted the abuse; and (3) betrayal of the child by the family who disbelieves the child's allegations or attempts to suppress them, further violating the child's trust. Responses to betrayal include anger expressed in risk-taking behavior or delinquency, dissociation in which the child separates himself from his body and from the world, or excessively clingy behavior in an effort to restore trust and security in redeeming relationships, which may continue into adulthood. If the sexual abuse is within the family, the sense of betrayal is heightened and remains for a much longer time; if the offender is not held accountable for the crime, the victim suffers a strong sense of betrayal by the legal system and the norms of society.

— Powerlessness: the loss of power that develops when the child's body is repeatedly misused or invaded without her consent and her attempts to end the abuse fail leads to fear and anxiety, which are then expressed in nightmares, phobias, eating disorders, and somatic complaints. Somatization is the preoccupation with bodily processes that many sexual abuse victims experience; among the manifestations are

9

headaches, nausea and vomiting, heart palpitations, dizziness, fatigue, back pain, and muscle aches. The victim may respond to the sense of powerlessness by running away, self-mutilation, or suicide attempts; aggressive and dominating behaviors; or posttraumatic stress disorder.

— Stigmatization: refers to the negative connotations that become part of the child's self-image after the abuse. These may result from demeaning comments made directly to the child by the offender; the message of badness and shame that accompanies pressure from the perpetrator to keep silent; or the child's internal stigma of guilt. Stigmatization may be magnified if the family reacts with disgust or blames the child for the abuse. Victims identify with other stigmatized groups in society and may involve themselves in substance abuse, delinquency, and prostitution, viewing themselves as damaged goods and alienating themselves from family and friends.

Coping Mechanisms

Avoidant Coping

— Involves distraction, wishful thinking, and cognitive restructuring

— Used more often by children who received greater social support after disclosure

— Produces short-term benefits but long-term problems, with victims using this strategy developing more negative attitudes and anxieties about sexuality

— Associated with fewer behavioral problems than other coping mechanisms but may be a risk factor for PTSD

Internalized Coping

— Includes social withdrawal, self-blame, and resignation

— Used more commonly by children who received negative reactions from others after disclosure; may be linked to hyperreactive behaviors that lead to the development of posttraumatic stress reactions

— Found more frequently in female victims, who display internalized behaviors (dissociation and depression), phobias, regressive behaviors, and multiple somatic complaints

— Rated the least helpful of the strategies by victims

Angry Coping

— Involves the cathartic release of emotions and the tendency to blame others; also termed externalization

— Instigated often when the perpetrator had a more distant relationship to the child

— High frequency of abuse interactions and forceful abuse also noted as antecedents to this coping strategy

— Seen more in older victims and in male victims

— Associated with the greatest number of behavioral problems, including physical as well as sexual aggression in males and sexually reactive behaviors in females (which put them at increased risk for revictimization)

Active/Social Coping

— Uses child's problem-solving abilities as well as social support resources

— Most commonly implemented by children who experienced less severe sexual experiences

— Only strategy not linked to negative abuse-related behaviors

— Does not produce measured benefits

INTERVENTIONS

— Ensure child's safety from further abuse

— Undertake family therapy to facilitate a supportive and protective environment for the child; the most significant determinant of eventual prognosis is the belief and support of a nonoffending caretaker

— Personal therapy for the child; must be developmentally appropriate

— Comparison of abuse-specific cognitive behavior therapy and nondirective supportive therapy shows both to be appropriate for posttraumatic stress symptoms, although significantly greater improvement occurred with cognitive behavior therapy

— Adult survivors of child sexual abuse are more likely to become victims of domestic violence and sexual assault; develop addictions to alcohol and drugs; and are at higher risk for developing medical problems as adults, such as STIs, obesity, irritable bowel syndrome, ischemic heart disease, autoimmune disease, and chronic obstructive pulmonary disease (COPD)

— The severity of long-term effects is affected by the duration and frequency of abuse, use of force, if penetration occurred, the relationship of the perpetrator to the child and presence of maternal support

ADOLESCENT AND ADULT SEXUAL ABUSE

Rape is generally defined as meeting 3 criteria:

1. Any vaginal, anal, or oral penetration by a penis, object, or other body part

2. Lack of consent, communicated with verbal or physical signs of resistance, or if the victim is unable to consent by means of incapacitation because of age, disability, or drug or alcohol intoxication

3. Threat of or actual use of force

Modern definitions of rape also include taking advantage of incapacitated individuals, such as children, the disabled, or the elderly. Drug-facilitated rape has also recently been addressed, with increased penalties where this takes place. Sexual assault has a broader characterization, including any unwanted sexual contact, thus encompassing rape, incest, molestation, fondling or grabbing, or forced viewing of or involvement in pornography as well as other less definable behaviors.

SCOPE

— Annual rates of sexual assault per 1000 persons (male and female) were reported in 2004 by the US Department of Justice to be 1.2 for ages 12 through 15 years, 1.3 for ages 16 through 19 years, 1.7 for ages 20 through 24 years and 1.6 for ages 24 through 29 years.

— The 2005 National Crime Victimization Survey statistics reported 176 540 rapes and sexual assaults of females 12 years or older and 15 130 rapes and sexual assault of males 12 years or older.

— Most rapes are never reported to either the police or health care providers, with adolescents and males being least likely to report.

— The majority of males who rape males are not homosexual and the majority of males who are raped are not homosexual.

— Youths and adolescents are sexually assaulted in disproportionate numbers compared to the population, with 18% of female and 12% of male middle and high school students reporting having had a prior unwanted sexual experience.

— Victims who know their assailant are less likely to report the crime or receive medical care.

— Alcohol or drug use before a sexual assault has been reported by more than 40% of adolescent victims and adolescent assailants.

Why Victims Don't Report (and Remain "Silent Victims")

— Fear of family, friends, and others finding out

— Fear of the assault being made public by the media

— Fear of being blamed

— Fear of retaliation

— Perceived shame or actual stigma associated with being the victim of a sexual assault

— Victim does not fit into the classic definition of a rape victim as a woman raped by a stranger

Victim-Assailant Relationships

While rape is an act of violence, it is also an act of opportunity. The one common link that identifies rape victims is that the rapist has access to the victim.

— Two-thirds to three-quarters of all adolescent rapes and sexual assaults are perpetrated by a person known to the victim.

— Most victims and perpetrators are of the same race.

— Many rapists prey on vulnerable victims who may be seen as less likeable or credible, eg, homeless or substance abusers.

— More attractive, provocatively dressed individuals are not more likely to be victims of rape.

— The classic rape victim is a victim of "blitz" rape, but this is actually fairly uncommon.

— "Confidence rape," in which the victim has had a previous nonviolent relationship with the assailant, occurs more commonly than "blitz" rape. This may involve the following situations:

1. Friend or acquaintance who uses deceit such as offering a ride home

2. Assailant who controls the victim by age or rank

3. Assailant who exploits someone unable to give consent

— In "stress-sex" situation, the victim initially consents to contact, but the assailant becomes abusive and violent, forcing further sexual activity without consent; this often occurs in date rape or situation rape, eg, prostitute as victim.

Public Health Implications

Most cost calculations only consider short-term "tangible" costs, which focus on property and productivity lost or medical bills. Intangible costs include pain, suffering, risk of death, disability, and long-term emotional trauma.

With regard to health care, sexual assault victims:

— Are more likely to develop mental health problems, including depression, anxiety, PTSD, low self-esteem, social phobia, and eating disorders

— Have higher rates of tobacco, alcohol, and drug use

— Use the health care system at a higher rate even for problems not related to sexual assault, with outpatient costs 2.5 times greater than for nonvictims

— Are twice as likely to experience teen childbirth

Populations at Risk

— The greatest risk factor for sexual assault is female gender; female victims exceed male victims by a ratio of 13.5:1.

— The second greatest factor is young age, with studies suggesting that 50% to 60% of victims are under age 17 years, over 80% under age 25 years, and only 6% over age 29 years.

— Adolescents and young women are most at risk for acquaintance and date rape.

— Women attending college have a risk of rape 3 times greater than the general population; they are often raped by someone they know.

— Past victimization is a strong risk factor for revictimization, with sexual assault in childhood a powerful risk factor for sexual assault as an adult.

— Women in physically and emotionally abusive relationships are more likely to experience rape and sexual assault, especially repeated rape and serious physical injuries; they are also less likely to report to health care providers and law enforcement agencies.

— Mental incapacitation is a risk factor, possibly targeted by predators because mentally incapacitated individuals are unable to perceive dangerous situations, they are vulnerable, and they are less likely to be taken seriously if they report the incident.

— The sexual assault rates of women in the military and institutionalized women are significantly higher than in the general population.

Immediate Reactions to Sexual Trauma
— Compared to adult victims, many adolescent rape victims do not seek immediate medical assistance.

— There is no "normal" or "abnormal" response to sexual victimization, but immediate reactions may include shock and disbelief, shame, and self-blame; anger toward the assailant, health care workers, advocates, or law enforcement personnel is also seen.

— Outward behaviors range from crying and sobbing to a quiet, calm demeanor; inwardly the victim may feel anxiety, helplessness, and guilt.

— Fear of death is the most intense fear during and immediately after a rape.

— Other initial concerns:

    — Fear of contracting an STI

    — Fear of pregnancy

    — Fear of serious genital injury that would affect sexual functioning

    — Fear of transmission of human immunodeficiency virus (HIV)

— The rape trauma syndrome consists of a group of "behavioral, somatic, and psychological reactions that are an acute stress reaction to a life-threatening situation." Its 2 phases are as follows:

1. Acute "disorganization phase": lasts several weeks; survivor experiences somatic reactions, such as pain from physical trauma, headaches, sleep disturbances, gastrointestinal symptoms, and genitourinary symptoms; may also continue to display initial emotional reactions of fear, humiliation, self-blame, anger, and revenge; recall of the event is often clouded by intense feelings of guilt, helplessness, and fear.

2. "Reorganization phase": lasts several weeks to years; survivor often continues to have somatic symptoms, with nonspecific anxiety that can be associated with phobias; may fear being indoors if he or she was raped inside or may fear crowds; survivor often changes addresses and phone numbers frequently.

Delayed Effects on the Survivor

— Survivors often experience posttraumatic stress disorder; depression; suicidal ideation; substance abuse; and physical complaints, eg, pelvic pain, abdominal pain, and headaches.

— Posttraumatic stress disorder (PTSD):

1. Among the most debilitating after-effects of sexual assault

2. Hallmarks: persistent reliving of event and behavioral changes to avoid stimuli associated with the trauma

3. Occurs in up to one-third of sexual assault survivors

— Major depression:

1. Extremely common, with almost 30% of survivors experiencing at least 1 episode

2. Occurs in 3 times more rape survivors than nonvictims

— Substance abuse:

1. May involve alcohol or other drugs with victims of sexual abuse 1.6 times more likely to engage in regular alcohol use and 2 times more likely to have reported recent marijuana use

2. Attempt to self-medicate the painful emotions linked to sexual victimization

3. Often places survivor at increased risk for further victimization

4. PTSD often associated with increased rates of drug- and alcohol-related problems

COMPONENTS OF AN EFFECTIVE RESPONSE

Ideal care of a sexual assault victim includes compassionate treatment by knowledgeable professionals, which encompasses rape crisis hotline personnel, police and law enforcement personnel, and prehospital providers as well as specially trained detectives, skilled medical staff, trained sexual assault examiners, and rape crisis counselors.

Rape Crisis Centers

— First established in San Francisco and Washington, D.C. as an outgrowth of the feminist movement in the 1970s

— Staff are usually lay people who may be sexual assault survivors

— Function in prevention, acute treatment, and ongoing follow-up

— Provide public education to prevent rape, confidential emergency assistance for victims and family members or friends, and short-term follow-up crisis counseling

Prehospital Personnel

— Must be aware that rape or sexual assault is not specific to one gender, race, or socioeconomic status

— Require training in evidence preservation and the importance of saving the sheet the patient is transported on as well as avoiding cutting the patient's clothes and destroying evidence whenever possible

— Need to listen to patient with empathy and remind the patient that the assault is never the victim's fault

— Establish a safe environment to transfer the patient, including removing the patient from the scene as soon as possible

Emergency Department Personnel

— Victim should be given top priority, brought back from triage immediately, and provided a safe, nonthreatening environment

— Should have immediate screening to see if serious injuries are present

— Avoid undressing the patient so that clothing can be collected during the forensic examination.

— Instruct the patient not to eat, drink, or urinate if possible.

— Offer appropriate postexposure prophylaxis for pregnancy and STIs.

— Recognize that there is no "appropriate" survivor response and be able to respond appropriately and effectively to the range of survivor reactions, providing a supportive, nonthreatening patient interaction that allows the patient to retain control, thus preventing further anxiety.

— Be able to address concerns that rape victims may not always express, such as whether the injuries will cause permanent damage and the likelihood of becoming pregnant or acquiring an STD, especially HIV.

— Focus on examining the victim, collecting evidence if the patient consents, offering support, and giving medical treatment.

Specially Trained Personnel

— Sexual assault detectives: conduct interview in nonjudgmental, sensitive, and compassionate manner while obtaining vital information

— Sexual assault nurse examiners (SANE practitioners) and rape crisis counselors: most helpful in evaluating and treating the victim, with SANEs able to counsel the patient, collect a history, examine and obtain forensic evidence compassionately, and evaluate the patient's physical and psychological injuries

— Follow-up services: should arrange for mental health care counselors, rape crisis center referral, medical follow-up including testing for pregnancy, HIV, hepatitis, and STDs

PREVENTION

Primary Prevention Programs

— Interventions aimed at decreasing the number of sexual assaults

— The most effective means of decreasing the sequelae of sexual victimization

— Must be aimed at younger population (under age 18 years), with special programs targeted toward college-age populations

— Include rape myth–based programs, victim empathy programs, lecture format courses, discussion groups, interactive improvisational theater presentations, and self-defense strategies

— Programs for women should focus on increasing women's awareness, addressing rape myths and risk perception, and decreasing risky behaviors.

— Programs for men should focus on increasing awareness, increasing respect for women, dispelling rape myths, and enhancing empathy for victims.

— Encourage parents to limit and monitor their child's access to the World Wide Web, as Internet sexual solicitation and exploitation have emerged as a risk.

Secondary Prevention Programs

— Aimed at early screening and identification of sexual assault survivors and decreasing future assaults and the sequelae of sexual assault once it has already occurred

— Include efforts to improve care of rape survivors immediately after the crime and improving follow-up services

Tertiary Prevention Programs

— Focus on interventions to treat and alleviate advanced disease or the late effects, such as the physical and mental health sequelae of sexual assault

— Include educating medical providers about the importance of asking questions about previous trauma and recognizing the signs and symptoms of previous sexual victimization and rape trauma syndrome

— Train providers to recognize signs of sexual and physical abuse, respond effectively, and refer to resources available in the area

— Train providers to recognize risk factors for and common health problems experienced by victims of child sexual trafficking

REFERENCES

1. Acierno R, Resnick HS, Kilpatrick DG, Saunders B, Best CL. Risk factors for rape, physical assault and post-traumatic stress disorder in women: examination of differential multivariate relationships. *J Anxiety Disord.* 1999;13(6):541-563.

2. American Academy of Pediatrics, Committee on Child Abuse and Neglect. Guidelines for the evaluation of sexual abuse in children. *Pediatrics.* 1999;103(1):186-191.

3. Bachman R, Saltzman LE. *Violence Against Women: Estimates From the Redesigned Survey.* Washington, DC: US Department of Justice; 1995. NCJ-154348.

4. Banyard VL, Williams LM, Siegel JA. Childhood sexual abuse: a gender perspective on context and consequences. *Child Maltreatment.* 2004;9(3):223-238.

5. Bass E, Thornton L, eds. *I Never Told Anyone: Writings by Women Survivors of Sexual Abuse.* New York, NY: Harper & Row; 1983.

6. Botash A. What office-based pediatricians need to know about child sexual abuse. *Contemp Pediatr.* 1994;11:83-100.

7. Briere J, Runtz M. Symptomatology associated with childhood sexual victimization in a nonclinical adult sample. *Child Abuse Negl.* 1988;12(1):51-59.

8. Burgess AW, Holmstrom LL. Rape trauma syndrome. *Am J Psychiatry.* 1974;131(9):981-986.

9. Butler AC. Child sexual assault: risk factors for girls. *Child Abuse Negl.* 2013;37(9):643-652.

10. Chaffin M, Wherry JN, Dykman R. School age children's coping with sexual abuse: abuse stresses and symptoms associated with four coping strategies. *Child Abuse Negl.* 1997;21(2):227-240.

11. Chartier MJ, Walker JR, Naimark B. Childhood abuse, adult health, and health care utilization: results from a representative community sample. *Am J Epidemiol.* 2007;165(9):1031-1038.

12. Child Abuse Prevention and Treatment Act (CAPTA). 1974;PL 93-247.

13. Christian CW, Schwarz DW. Child maltreatment and the transition to adult-based medical and mental health care. *Pediatrics.* 2011;127(1):139-145.

14. Cohen JA, Mannarino AP. Predictors of treatment outcomes in sexually abused children. *Child Abuse Negl.* 2000;24(7):983-994.

15. Committee on Adolescence. Care of the adolescent sexual assault victim. *Pediatrics.* 2001;107(6):1476-1479.

16. Conte JR, Schuerman JR. Factors associated with an increased impact of child sexual abuse. *Child Abuse Negl.* 1987;11(2):201-211.

17. Cosentino CE, Collins M. Sexual abuse of children: prevalence, effects, and treatment. *Ann NY Acad Sci.* 1996;789:45-65.

18. Deblinger E, Lippman J, Steer R. Sexually abused children suffering posttraumatic stress symptoms: initial treatment outcome findings. *Child Maltreatment.* 1996;1(4):310-321.

19. Dong M, Giles WH, Felitti VJ, et al. Insights into causal pathways for ischemic heart disease: adverse childhood experiences study. *Circulation.* 2004;110(13):1761-1766.

20. Erickson PI, Rapkin AJ. Unwanted sexual experiences among middle and high school youth. *J Adolesc Health.* 1991;12(4):319-325.

21. Feldhaus KM, Houry D, Kaminsky R. Lifetime sexual assault prevalence rates and reporting practices in an emergency department population. *Ann Emerg Med.* 2000;36(1):23-27.

22. Finkelhor D. Sexual abuse: a sociological perspective. *Child Abuse Negl.* 1982;6(1):95-102.

23. Finkelhor D, ed. *Child Sexual Abuse: New Theory and Research.* New York, NY: Free Press; 1984.

24. Finkelhor D. Epidemiological factors in the clinical identification of child sexual abuse. *Child Abuse Negl.* 1993;17(1):67-70.

25. Finkelhor D, Baron L. High risk children. In: Finkelhor D, ed. *Sourcebook on Child Sexual Abuse.* Beverly Hills, CA: Sage Publications; 1986:60-88.

26. Finkelhor D, Browne A. The traumatic impact of child sexual abuse: a conceptualization. *Am J Orthopsychiatry.* 1985;55(4):530-541.

27. Finkelhor D, Hotaling G, Lewis IA, Smith C. Sexual abuse in a national survey of adult men and women: prevalence, characteristics, and risk factors. *Child Abuse Negl.* 1990;14(1):19-28.

28. Friedrich WN, Urquiza AJ, Beilke R. Behavioral problems in sexually abused young children. *J Pediatr Psychol.* 1986;11(1):47-57.

29. Friedrich WN. Sexual victimization and sexual behavior in children: a review of recent literature. *Child Abuse Negl.* 1993;17(1):59-66.

30. Goad J. Understanding roles and improving reporting and response relationships across professional boundaries. *Pediatrics.* 2008;122(suppl 1):S6-S9.

31. Gorey KM, Leslie DR. The prevalence of child sexual abuse: integrative review adjustment for potential response and measurement biases. *Child Abuse Negl.* 1997;21(4):391-398.

32. Greenbaum J, Crawford-Jakubiak JE. Child sex trafficking and commercial sexual exploitation: health care needs of victims. *Pediatrics.* 2015;135(3):566-574.

33. Guidry HM. Childhood sexual abuse: role of the family physician. *Am Fam Physician.* 1995;51(2):407-414.

34. Herendeen PM. Evaluating for child sexual abuse. *Adv Nurse Pract.* 1999;7(2):54, 57-58.

35. Hilton MR, Mezey GC. Victims and perpetrators of child sexual abuse. *Br J Psychiatry.* 1996;169(4):408-415.

36. Holmes MM, Resnick HS, Kilpatrick DG, Best CL. Rape-related pregnancy rate: estimates and descriptive characteristics from a national sample of women. *Am J Obstet Gynecol.* 1996;175(2):320-324; discussion 324-325.

37. Holmes WC, Slap GB. Sexual abuse of boys: definition, prevalence, correlates, sequelae, and management. *JAMA*. 1998;280(21):1855-1862.

38. Hornor G. Child sexual abuse: consequences and implications. *J Pediatr Health Care*. 2010;24(6):358-364.

39. Horwitz AV, Widom CS, McLaughlin J, White HR. The impact of childhood abuse and neglect on adult mental health: a prospective study. *J Health Soc Behav*. 2001;42(2):184-201.

40. Hussey JM, Chang JJ, Kotch JB. Child maltreatment in the United States: prevalence, risk factors, and adolescent health consequences. *Pediatrics*. 2006;118(3):933-942.

41. Jenny C, Crawford-Jakubiak; Committee on Child Abuse and Neglect. Clinical report: the evaluation of children in the primary care setting when sexual abuse is suspected. *Pediatrics*. 2013;132(2):e558-e567.

42. Jensen TK, Gulbrandsen W. Mossige S, Reichelt S, Tjersland OA. Reporting possible sexual abuse: a qualitative study on children's perspective and the context for disclosure. *Child Abuse Negl*. 2005;29(12):1395-1413.

43. Johnson CF. Child sexual abuse. *Lancet*. 2004;364(9432):462-470.

44. Justice B, Justice R, eds. *The Broken Taboo: Sex in the Family*. New York, NY: Human Sciences; 1979:109-202.

45. Kaplow JB, Dodge KA, Amaya-Jackson L, Saxe GN. Pathways to PTSD, part II: sexually abused children. *Am J Psychiatry*. 2005;162(7):1305-1310.

46. Kaufman M; Committee on Adolescence. Care of the adolescent sexual assault victim. *Pediatrics*. 2008;122(2):462-470.

47. Kellogg N; American Academy of Pediatrics Committee on Child Abuse and Neglect. The evaluation of sexual abuse in children. *Pediatrics*. 2005;116(2):506-512.

48. Kellogg ND; Committee on Child Abuse and Neglect. Clinical report—the evaluation of sexual behaviors in children. *Pediatrics*. 2009;124(3):992-998.

49. Kempe CH. Sexual abuse, another hidden pediatric problem: the 1977 C. Anderson Aldrich Lecture. *Pediatrics*. 1978;62(3):382-389.

50. Kendall-Tackett KA, Simon AF. A comparison of the abuse experiences of male and female adults molested as children. *J Fam Violence*. 1992;7(1):57-62.

51. Kendall-Tackett KA, Williams LM, Finkelhor D. Impact of sexual abuse on children: a review and synthesis of recent empirical studies. *Psychol Bull*. 1993;113(1):164-180.

52. Kerns DL, Terman DL, Larson CS. The role of physicians in reporting and evaluating child sexual abuse cases. *The Future of Children*. 1994;4(2):119-134.

53. Kilpatrick DG, Saunders BE. *Prevalence and Consequences of Child Victimization: Results from the National Survey of Adolescents, Final Report*. Washington DC: US Department of Justice, Office of Justice Programs, National Institute of Justice; 1997.

54. Kilpatrick DG, Saunders BE, Seymour AK. *Rape in America: A Report to the Nation*. Charleston, SC: Crime Victim Research and Treatment Center; 1992.

55. Koss MP, Dinero TE, Seibel CA. Stranger and acquaintance rape: are there differences in the victim's experience? *Psychol Women Q*. 1988;12(1):1-24.

56. Koss MP, Gidycz CA, Wisniewski N. The scope of rape: incidence and prevalence of sexual aggression and victimization in a national sample of higher education students. *J Consult Clin Psychol*. 1987;55(2):162-170.

57. Leventhal JM. Epidemiology of sexual abuse of children: old problems, new directions. *Child Abuse Negl*. 1998;22(6):481-491.

58. London K, Bruck M, Ceci SJ, Shuman DW. Disclosure of child sexual abuse: what does the research tell us about the way that children tell? *Psychol Public Policy Law*. 2005;11(1):194-226.

59. Malloy LC, Lyon TD, Quas JA. Filial dependency and recantation of child sexual abuse allegations. *J Am Acad Child Adolesc Psychiatry*. 2007;46(2):162-170.

60. Mitchell KJ, Finkelhor D, Wolak J. Risk factors for and impact of online sexual solicitation of youth. *JAMA*. 2001;285(23):3011-3014.

61. Muram D, Hostetler BR, Jones CE, Speck PM. Adolescent victims of sexual assault. *J Adolesc Health*. 1995;17(6):372-375.

62. Nadelson CC, Notman MT, Zackson H, Gornick J. A follow-up study of rape victims. *Am J Psychiatry*. 1982;139(10):1266-1270.

63. National Institute of Justice. *The Extent and Costs of Crime Victimization: A New Look*. Washington, DC: US Department of Justice; 1996.

64. Negriff S, Schneiderman JU, Smith C, Schreyer JK, Trickett PK. Characterizing the sexual abuse experiences of young adolescents. *Child Abuse Negl*. 2014;38(2):261-270.

65. Nieves-Khouw FC. Recognizing victims of physical and sexual abuse. *Crit Care Nurs Clin North Am*. 1997;9(2):141-148.

66. Noll JG, Shenk CE. Teen birth rates in sexually abused and neglected females. *Pediatrics*. 2013;131(4):e1181-e1187.

67. Palusci VJ, Cox EO, Shatz EM, Schultze JM. Urgent medical assessment after child sexual abuse. *Child Abuse Negl*. 2006;30(4):367-380.

68. Pierce R, Pierce LH. The sexually abused child: a comparison of male and female victims. *Child Abuse Negl*. 1985;9(2):191-199.

69. Sanford J, Cryer L, Christensen BL, Mattox KL. Patterns of reported rape in a tri-ethnic population: Houston, Texas, 1974–1975. *Am J Public Health*. 1979;69(5):480-484.

70. Sansonnett-Hayden H, Hakey G, Marriage C, Fine S. Sexual abuse and psychopathology in hospitalized adolescents. *J Am Acad Child Adolesc Psychiatry*. 1987;26(5):753-757.

71. Sedlak AJ, Broadhurst DD. *Third National Incidence Study of Child Abuse and Neglect: Final Report*. Washington, DC: US Department of Health and Human Services; 1996.

72. Sedlak AJ, Mettenburg J, Basena M, et al. *Fourth National Incidence Study on Child Abuse and Neglect (NIS-4): Report to Congress*. Washington, DC: US Department of Health and Human Services, Administration for Children and Families; 2010.

73. Seifert SA. Substance use and sexual assault. *Subst Use Misuse.* 1999;34(6):935-945.

74. Sorenson T, Snow B. How children tell: the process of disclosure in child sexual abuse. *Child Welfare.* 1991;70(1):3-15.

75. Stoltenborgh M, van IJzendoorn MH, Euser EM, Bakermans-Kranenburg MJ. A global perspective on child sexual abuse: meta-analysis of prevalence around the world. *Child Maltreatment.* 2011;16(2):79-101.

76. Sullivan PM, Knutson JF. The association between child maltreatment and disabilities in a hospital-based epidemiological study. *Child Abuse Negl.* 1998;22(4):271-288.

77. Tjaden P, Thoennes N. *Prevalence, Incidence, and Consequences of Violence Against Women: Findings from the National Violence Against Women Survey.* Washington, DC: National Institute of Justice; 1998. NCJ-172837.

78. Tjaden P, Thoennes N. *Full Report of the Prevalence, Incidence, and Consequences of Violence Against Women.* Washington, DC: National Institute of Justice and Center for Disease Control; 2000. NCJ-183781.

79. Ullman SE, Filipas HH. Gender differences in social reactions to abuse disclosures, post-abuse coping, and PTSD of child sexual abuse survivors. *Child Abuse Negl.* 2005;29(7):767-782.

80. US Department of Health and Human Services; Administration on Children, Youth and Families. *Child Maltreatment 1998: Reports From the States to the National Child Abuse and Neglect Data System.* Washington, DC: US Government Printing Office; 2000.

81. US Department of Health and Human Services; Administration for Children and Families; Administration on Children, Youth and Families; Children's Bureau. *Child Maltreatment 2004.* Washington, DC: US Government Printing Office; 2006.

82. Walker EA, Gelfand AN, Gelfand MD, Koss MP, Katon WJ. Medical and psychiatric symptoms in female gastroenterology clinic patients with histories of sexual victimization. *Gen Hosp Psychiatry.* 1995;17(2):85-92.

83. Walker EA, Katon WJ, Roy-Byrne PP, Jemelka RP, Russo J. Histories of sexual victimization in patients with irritable bowel syndrome or inflammatory bowel disease. *Am J Psychiatry.* 1993;150(10):1502-1506.

84. Whetsell-Mitchell J. Indicators of child sexual abuse: children at risk. *Issues Compr Pediatr Nurs.* 1995;18(4):319-340.

85. Whetsell-Mitchell J. The many faces of child sexual abuse. *Issues Compr Pediatr Nurs.* 1995;18(4):299-318.

Chapter 2

ANOGENITAL ANATOMY

Eileen M. Allen, MSN, RN, FN-CSA, SANE-A, SANE-P*
William J. Reed, MD, FAAP
Diana K. Faugno, MSN, RN, CPN, SANE-A, SANE-P, FAAFS, DF-IAFN
Patricia M. Speck, DNSc, APN, FNP-BC, DF-IAFN, FAAFS, FAAN

Recognition and understanding of genital and anal anatomy is essential when evaluating patients for sexual assault. The examiner must be familiar with the appearance of normal anatomy in order to recognize injury and/or medical conditions that can influence the physical appearance of the tissue and mimic sexual assault injury. This chapter will identify the genital and anal anatomy of children, adolescents, and adults as well as review the terminology of injury.

MEDICAL EMBRYOLOGY OF THE EXTERNAL GENITALIA

— Genetic sex is determined at the time the ovum is fertilized, but during the first 12 weeks of embryonic life, both male and female primordial tracts are present and develop in unison.

— In the female: cortex develops into the ovary at 10 to 11 weeks, with medullary regression.

— In the male: medulla differentiates into the testis, with regression of the cortex.

— Gonadal primordia are influenced by the sex-determining region (SRY) on the Y chromosome.

If a functioning testis is present, the phenotype is male, whereas in the absence of the sex-determining region, with or without the presence of an ovary, the phenotype is female.

Revised Chapter 2 for the second edition.

DEVELOPMENT OF EXTERNAL GENITALIA IN BOYS

— External genital development occurs between 10 and 16 weeks of gestation. The genital tubercle grows into a penis and the urogenital folds fuse to enclose the penile urethra.

— At 28 weeks, the inguinal scrotal stage of descent begins, with the testis descending into the scrotal sack between 28 and 32 weeks of gestation.

— Testosterone is responsible for the evolution of the vas deferens, epididymis, ejaculatory ducts, and seminal vesicle. Dihydrotestosterone results in the development of the male external genitalia, including the prostate gland, and the bulbourethral glands, or Cowper's glands.

— At puberty, testosterone leads to spermatogenesis and the development of the secondary sexual characteristics as well as a five- to seven-fold enlargement of the prostate gland, epididymis, and testes.

ANATOMIC VARIATIONS IN BOYS

Many variations of normal and some previously unrecognized problems may be noted in the examination of the male from infancy through puberty stage Tanner G5. The more common variations in genital findings are as follows:

— Leydig cell aplasia or hypoplasia

— Partial androgen insensitivity

— Phimosis

— Paraphimosis

— Hypospadias

— Circumcision adhesions

— Erythema or hyperpigmentation

— Smegma

— Uric acid crystals

— Pink pearly papules of the penis

— Urethral meatal stenosis

— Epispadias

— Shawl defect

— Micropenis

— Diphallia

DEVELOPMENT OF EXTERNAL GENITALIA IN GIRLS

— Female external genitalia develop from the genital groove and urogenital sinus between 6 and 11 to 12 weeks of gestation.

— Among the principal structures are the mons pubis, labia minora and majora, symphysis pubis, clitoral prepuce, vulva, vagina, and hymen.

ANATOMIC VARIATIONS IN GIRLS

Some congenital abnormalities in females pass undetected in the newborn, becoming clinically apparent only later or remaining partially expressed and found only incidentally during surgery or other procedures. The more prevalent variants are:

— Labial agglutination or fusion

— Premenarchal lichen sclerosis

— Labial hypertrophy

— Midline perineal fusion defect

— Vaginal prolapse

— Vaginal atresia

— Vaginal duplication

— Linea vestibularis

— Skene's duct cysts

— Prolapse of the urethral meatus

— Paraurethral cysts

Female external genitalia vary in size, shape, and color. The term "external genitalia" can be confusing to those outside the health care professions and has been used in court to argue that external genitalia are actually outside structures. In reality the introitus contains structures only visible with separation of the labia majora. These anatomical structures are covered with nonkeratinized epithelium making them internal structures. The exposed skin structures, including the mons pubis and the external surfaces of the labia majora, are covered with keratinized cellular structures, hair, and glands. The introitus extends from the mons to the perianal areas and has 3 vulvar openings that are visible. (See **Figure 2-1** for a visual reference of female genital anatomy.)

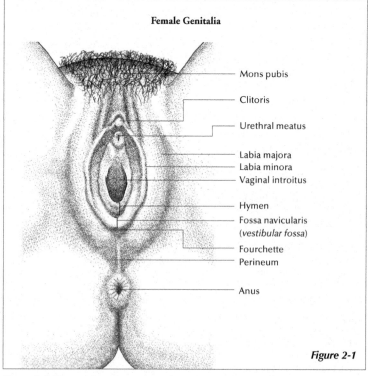

Female Genitalia

Mons pubis

Clitoris

Urethral meatus

Labia majora
Labia minora
Vaginal introitus

Hymen
Fossa navicularis
(*vestibular fossa*)
Fourchette
Perineum

Anus

Figure 2-1

Figure 2-1. *The genital structures of the adult female.*

FEMALE GENITAL STRUCTURES

The *vulva* is a general term for an area that includes the mons pubis; labia majora; clitoral hood, or prepuce; clitoris; labia minora; vestibule, or introitus, and its contents; posterior fourchette; and fossa navicularis.

The *mons pubis* is the rounded fleshy prominence created by underlying adipose tissue that lies over the pubic symphysis bone. The area is covered in keratinized skin and, at puberty, with hair that persists throughout life.

The *labia majora* are the 2 folds of skin on either side of the labia minora. The lateral aspect of this area is usually covered with hair that appears during puberty. The skin of the labia majora forms the lateral boundaries of the vulva and vestibule and includes all surfaces covered by mucous membrane, including the inner aspects of the labia majora. The anterior aspect of the labia majora meet at the midline below the mons pubis, providing a mechanical barrier that protects the internal structures of the genitalia.

The *clitoral hood*, or prepuce, is a fold of skin covering the clitoris and found in the vestibule. It is homologous with the male foreskin. The hood varies in size and must be retracted to observe the underlying clitoral tissue.

The *clitoris* is a small, cylindrical, bulbous structure capable of erection, found at the anterior portion of the vulva, and covered by the clitoral hood, or prepuce. The size of the entire clitoris is 3 to 5 cm, with the visible portion less than 1 cm, and is dependent on erection. It is the most sensitive part of the female genital anatomy.

The *labia minora* are the longitudinal, thin folds of skin medial to the labia majora. The labia minora are hairless but have many sensory nerve endings. The labia minora are located in the vestibule and meet at the midline anteriorly to form the clitoral hood and posteriorly to form the posterior fourchette in the adult female. In children and infants, the labia minora often terminate at the 3 o'clock and 9 o'clock positions of the vestibule, only to enlarge during puberty, meeting at the midline of the posterior fourchette. Labia minora may be unequal in size with either the right or left protruding further from the attachment. The labia minora may regress in the menopausal female.

The function of the labia minora is twofold. First, the location and position during normal activity protect the inner structures of the vestibule. Second, the tissue becomes erect with stimulation. During sexual response, the labia minora become engorged and elevated, opening the lumen of the vagina in preparation for penetration of the vaginal vault.

The *vestibule* is the area of the female genitals without hair. Although the area is labeled external genitalia* in many texts, the vestibule is actually internal to the visible structures of the labia major. The structures of the vestibule are covered with mucous membrane, and the area contains the openings of the vagina, urethra, and the Skene's and Bartholin's glands.

Vestibular bands, or urethral ligaments, are structures that support the urethra. When unrecognized, some examiners have labeled the finding as scars from sexual abuse. These bands are more visible in prepubertal children and can be difficult to see if there is significant estrogen effect. When seen, these bands are usually symmetrical, found in pairs, and attached to the pubic symphysis area.

The *posterior fourchette*, or posterior commissure, is an area that represents the union of the 2 labia minora posteriorly, and it is the most frequently injured site in females reporting rape. It is often injured in straddle injury in children and in consensual sexual penetration in adults. It is typically the point of first contact with the penis or foreign object when the female is on her back. Tears with consenting or nonconsenting sex are common and are sometimes referred to as "mounting injury."

The *fossa navicularis* is a concavity of the lower vestibule posterior and inferior to the hymenal attachment. It covers the surface of the introitus area that extends from the base of the hymen to the posterior fourchette between the 5 o'clock and 7 o'clock positions in the supine position (see **Figure 2-2**).

The *urethral meatus* is a location on the urethra at the external opening of the urethral tube. The urethra connects the urinary bladder to the urethral meatus for the purpose of releasing urine. In the female, this opening is located in the anterior vestibule, external to the hymen.

---

*It is important to point out that the term "external genitalia" is a misnomer that includes all the distal internal structures of the genitalia (as noted above) and that the only true external portions of the genitalia are the mons pubis and the lateral aspects of the labia majora covered by mucous membrane and visible without separation of the labia majora.

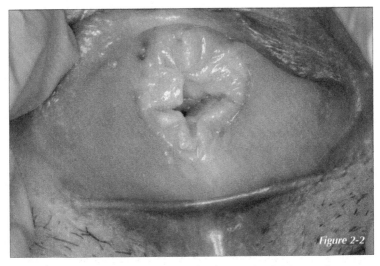

Figure 2-2. *This image highlights the posterior fourchette, or the posterior commissure or Hart's line.*

Urethral prolapse is a condition with unknown causes sometimes seen in preschool-aged African American girls and less often observed in other ages and races. The urethral lining protrudes from the urethral meatus resulting in a "donut-shaped" circle of tissue around the meatus which can appear deep red and may become excoriated and sometimes bloody from irritation. This finding may be mistaken for genital trauma. Treatment with exogenous estrogen will assist with rapid resolution.

THE HYMEN

The hymen is a recessed structure at the entrance to the vaginal opening. It is described as a collar or semicollar of tissue surrounding the vaginal orifice comprised of fibrous bands covered by epithelium composed of squamous cells. The hymen structure is the least understood of the genital structures.

Evidence reveals that the hymen is not an indicator of virginity nor can an examiner tell if an individual is a "virgin." Myths about the hymen abound, and it is a common, albeit mistaken, belief that once the female genitals have been penetrated by a penis during intercourse the hymen is "broken" or no longer exists.

— The hymen separates the vulva from the distal vaginal vault. The physical appearance changes with (1) age, (2) positioning during evaluation, and (3) degree of patient relaxation. When exposed, the tissue responds to estrogen with hypertrophic, ie, larger cells, and hyperplastic, ie, more cells growth, producing a structure that may be larger than the vulvar space available, which results in folding and redundancy of appearance, making evaluation of the margins difficult.

— The effects of estrogen on the hymen are first noted in the newborn female and result from maternal estrogen that has crossed the placenta. The labia minora, clitoris, and paraurethral tissue are prominent; hymenal tissue is thickened, pale, and has few surface capillaries.

— At birth and during puberty, changes occur in the morphology, size, mucosa, secretions, environmental pH, and bacterial flora of the hymen.

— In the first 4 to 6 weeks of life, about 10% of newborn girls have pigmentation of the external genitalia, a thick white creamy discharge, and withdrawal vaginal bleeding.

— By age 7 to 10 years, early changes in the hymen show estrogen effects again. The labia minora mature and elongate, periurethral tissue increases, and the hymen thickens.

The hymen's appearance also changes throughout the life span. The effects of estrogen on the tissue are predictable, caused by a response in the physical receptors in the hymen and surrounding tissue (see **Table 2-1**).

Table 2-1. Hymen Tissue Response to Estrogen
— *Estrogen effect* is clinically absent at certain developmental ages.
— Maternal estrogen effect is present at birth until age 2-3 in hymenal, vaginal, and uterine tissue.
— A reduction in estrogen results in thinning of the hymenal tissue circumferentially and narrowing of the hymen laterally.
— Estrogen creates a response in the tissue resulting in hypertrophy and hyperplasia of the hymen, vagina, and vestibular tissues.
(continued)

Table 2-1. Hymen Tissue Response to Estrogen *(continued)*

— Estrogen reduces sensitivity to palpation of the vestibular structures, hymen, and vagina.

— Physiological discharge (leukorrhea) is present with estrogenized tissue.

— Estrogen levels decrease after birth and increase during puberty throughout the childbearing years only to diminish with aging.

— Exogenous estrogens have been used medically to enhance the healing process.

— Vagina pH becomes more acidic with estrogen and more basic in the absence of estrogen.

— The acid base of the vestibule and vagina change from acidic at birth to basic in early childhood, acidic in puberty and throughout reproductive years, and finally to basic in menopause.

— Bacterial and glycogen counts increase with estrogen and decrease in the absence of estrogen.

The hymen may occur in at least 6 well-described and anatomically differing configurations, and its appearance may be influenced by estrogenization, aging, and development as well as the patient's position during the examination, the examiner's experience and/or bias, the patient's degree of relaxation, and the use of labial traction or labial separation. Three basic hymenal types are recognized:

1. Fimbriated: denticulate, sleeve-like, or scalloped (**Figures 2-3** and **2-4**)

2. Annular: concentric or symmetrical (**Figure 2-5**)

3. Posterior rim: crescentic or semilunar (**Figures 2-6** and **2-7**)

These may be seen in 7 configurations:

1. Fimbriated	3. Redundant	5. Septate	7. Imperforate
2. Annular	4. Crescentic	6. Cribriform	

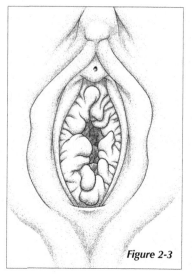

Figure 2-3

Figure 2-3. A fimbriated, or denticulate, hymen.

Figure 2-4. The redundant, or sleeve-like, hymen.

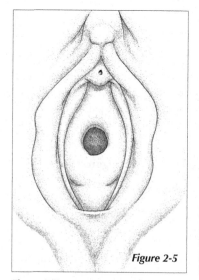

Figure 2-5

Figure 2-5. The annular hymen.

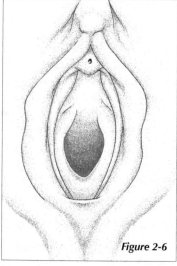

Figure 2-6

Figure 2-6. The crescentic hymen.

— Annular or fimbriated configuration is most common at birth. Fimbriated hymen is more often noted in African American infants and decreases with age. The incidence of crescentic hymen increases with age and is the most prevalent by age 3 years. Septal remnants are common, and imperforate hymen occurs in over 1 in 1000 live female births.

— Nonspecific clinical features of the normal and recognized variants of hymenal anatomy include:

— Variations in morphology

— Presence of an external vaginal ridge

— Presence of a hymenal tag

— Presence of a longitudinal intravaginal ridge

— Hymenal notches or clefts

— Vaginal rugae

— Periurethral and perihymenal vestibular bands

— Labial agglutination/adhesions

— Erythema of the vestibular sulcus

— Linea vestibularis

— Hymenal bumps or mounds

— Lymphoid follicles

— The Hymen Estrogen Response Scale (HERS) is a useful tool in evaluating changes to the hymen and surrounding structures related to developmental and cyclic changes throughout the life span (see **Table 2-2**).

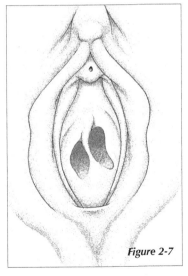

Figure 2-7

Figure 2-7. *The septate hymen.*

Table 2-2. Hymen Estrogen Response Scale and Scoring

Variable	0	1	2	Score
Color	Red	Pink	White	
Thickness	Translucent	Partial translucency	No translucency	
Lubrication	None/scant clear	Scant white caked	Clear to white mucous	
Distensibility	None – flat	Some folds/ scallops	Redundancy/ layers	
Sensitivity	Painful to touch	Sensitive to touch	No pain to touch	
HERS Score Total				

Score	HERS Interpretation
0-1	No estrogen effect (NEE)
2-4	Early transition (ET)
5-7	Late transition (LT)
8-10	Full estrogen effect (FEE)

Reprinted with permission from PM Speck © 1998, rev. 2002, 2007.

Inspection of the Hymen

The hymen can sometimes be visualized using labial separation. Labial separation is best used to initially evaluate the flat and minimally folded structures of the introitus (**Figures 2-8** and **2-9**).

Labial traction, or labial tunneling, allows the examiner to visualize the area containing the structures of the introitus (**Figure 2-10**). Labial traction flattens the posterior fourchette, fossa navicularis, perineum, and other introital vestibular areas when the patient is in the supine lithotomy position with her legs in stirrups.

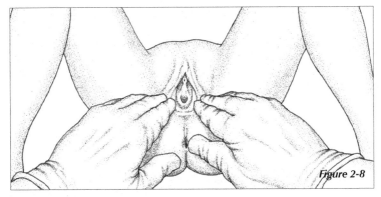

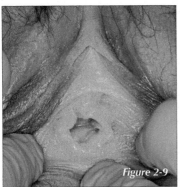

Figure 2-8. Genital examination of the female in the supine frog-leg position with labial separation and traction.

Figure 2-9. This figure demonstrates the labial separation technique. Labial separation is a technique used to flatten tissue to expose an area of interest. It is not, however, the best technique for visualization of the entire vestibular and hymenal structures.

Figure 2-10. Labial traction exposes an estrogenized, pale, and thick annular hymen and surrounding tissue.

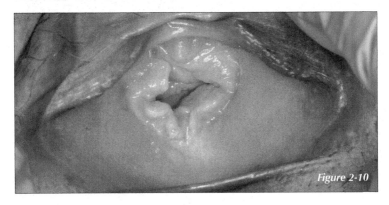

During documentation, the genital structures are described and the position is stated using a fixed imaginary clock for locations of injury, noninjury, or structures. While nurses may vary in the positioning of the clock, a full description will clearly tell those reading or reviewing the report where the injury is located; for example, one may describe the hymen as missing from the 5 o'clock to 7 o'clock position in the supine position using the lateral traction method (**Figure 2-11**).

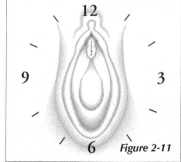

Figure 2-11

FEMALE REPRODUCTIVE PARTS
The reproductive organs in the fe-male include the vagina, the cervix, the uterus, the fallopian tubes, and the ovaries.

The *vagina* is a muscular, hollow tube that extends from the vaginal opening to the cervix. It is lined by nonkeratinizing, stratified, squa-mous epithelium that undergoes

Figure 2-11. *Diagram with clock overlay.*

hormone-related cyclical changes. The vagina does not contain secretion glands, but it is rich with capillaries and veins. It is about 8 cm to 12 cm (3 inches to 5 inches) long in an adult female.

The *vaginal introitus* is an anatomical area where the pubo-vanalis muscle forms the entrance to the vagina bound by the internal border of the mons to the perianal areas. It has 3 visible openings.

Vaginal rugae develop as a result of estrogen receptor stimulation and produce a redundancy of normal folds of the epithelium. After menopause the vaginal walls will thin significantly and flatten again unless estrogen is replaced. Vaginal columns support the vaginal canal and may be visible.

The *posterior fornix* is a location adjacent to where the cervix attaches inferiorly to the vagina. This area allows for pooling of discharge and is where the cervix rests in seminal products after intercourse.

The *uterus* is a hollow, thick-walled, pear-shaped, muscular organ between the bladder and rectum. The uterus is held loosely in place by 6 ligaments, and its position varies. The uterus changes size throughout the life span. It is the site of implantation of the fertilized ovum, where the fetus develops during pregnancy, and the structure that sheds its lining monthly during menstruation.

The *cervix* (**Figures 2-12-a** through **2-12-g**) is located at the neck of the uterus, between the isthmus and the vagina. It should be pink, smooth, and evenly colored. The cervix protrudes 1 cm to 3 cm into the vagina and has no nerve endings. The ectocervix, or the part that protrudes into the vagina, is lined with squamous epithelium.

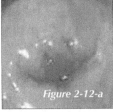

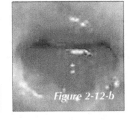

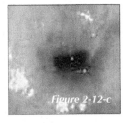

Figure 2-12-a. *Normal cervix.*

Figure 2-12-b. *Normal cervix.*

Figure 2-12-c. *Postmenopausal cervix.*

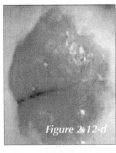

Figure 2-12-d. *Ectopy (erythroplasia). Normal physiological change seen during pregnancy and puerperium.*

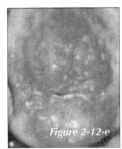

Figure 2-12-e. *Abnormal cervix. Refer patient for follow-up.*

Figure 2-12-f. *Nabothian follicles (chronic cervicitis). Refer the patient to the primary health clinic.*

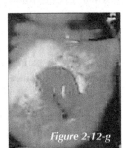

Figure 2-12-g. *Cervical polyp (benign). Refer patient for follow-up.*

The *cervical os* is the opening of the cervix. This area consists of unstratified, columnar epithelium cells. There may be a circumscribed area around the cervical os consisting of exposed columnar epithelium extending out from the cervical os. This is called *extropion* or *eversion* and is prominent in young adolescents that present with an immature physical appearance. Cervical eversion is common in women of all ages, depending on the stage or day in their menstrual cycle. An inexperienced examiner may confuse cervical eversion with injury.

The *fallopian tubes*, or oviducts, are a pair of tubes that extend about 10 cm (4 inches) from the upper uterus out toward, but not to, the ovaries through which ova travel from the ovaries to the uterus, where fertilization of the ovum takes place.

The *ovaries* are 2 almond-sized organs located at the end of each fallopian tube. The ovaries have 2 functions: (1) to produce ova (releasing 1 per month from puberty to menopause) and (2) to produce *estrogen* and *progesterone*.

The *perineum* is the external surface or base of the perineal body, lying between the vulva and the anus. The perineal body consists of the central tendon of the perineum that separates the lower end of the vagina from the rectum in the female and the anus and scrotum in the male. This area has an injury rate of 11% in sexual assault.

MALE GENITAL ANATOMY

The visible male genitals consist of the penis and the scrotum, both of which are covered with skin (see **Figures 2-13** and **2-14**).

The *penis* is the male sex organ composed of 3 chambers of elastic erectile tissue through which the urethra passes. It is a cylindrical structure with the capacity to be flaccid or erect. The average length of a nonerect penis is 8.5 cm to 10.5 cm. The length of an erect penis averages 16 cm to 19 cm with an average diameter of 3.5 cm. An erection occurs when the 3 chambers of elastic tissue expand as blood flows into them. Two chambers are called corpora cavernosa, which absorb most of the blood. The third chamber, the corpus spongiosum, covers the urethra.

The *glans penis*, or balanus, is the cap-shaped expansion of corpus spongiosum at the head of the penis, which is covered by loose skin, ie, foreskin or prepuce, that enables it to expand freely during an erection.

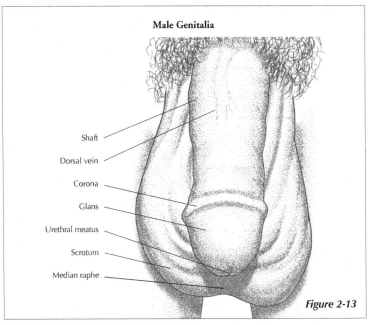

Male Genitalia

Shaft

Dorsal vein

Corona

Glans

Urethral meatus

Scrotum

Median raphe

Figure 2-13

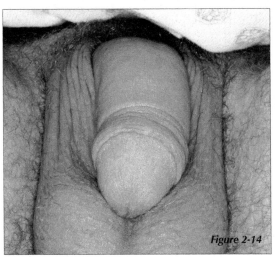

Figure 2-14

Figure 2-13.
Frontal view of the external male genitalia.

Figure 2-14.
Tanner V flaccid circumcised penis. The urethra is midline, and there is no erythema or discharge present.

The c*orona of the glans* is the rounded and prominent border of the glans on the distal portion of the penile shaft. It is the most sensitive part of the glans. The frenulum is a small fold of membrane attaching prepuce to the central ventral surface of corona.

The ***urethral meatus*** is a slit-like opening primarily located at the tip of the glans. This is where the urine and seminal products, including spermatozoa, will exit the body. Recent evidence has suggested that the location of the urethral meatus on the glans is variable and represents a normal presentation among the populations, where surgical repair for functional outcomes remains the intervention of choice.

The *foreskin*, also called the prepuce, is analogous to the prepuce in the female, which covers the clitoris. All males are born with foreskin that completely covers the glans. The foreskin adheres to the glans until a boy is between age 5 to 15 years, and any attempt to force it back before it separates naturally can result in painful tearing and scar tissue formation. Some cultures will circumcise the foreskin so that the glans is exposed for religious reasons. In the United States in the early 1990s, circumcisions were done more for health and hygiene, but the practice is becoming less common today.

The ***scrotum*** is the pouch that contains the testicles and their accessory organs. It is located inferiorly to the penis and is covered with hair in the reproductive-aged male.

MALE REPRODUCTIVE PARTS
The male reproductive parts are the testes, epididymides, vasa deferentia, seminal vesicles, prostate gland, and Cowper's glands.

The ***testes*** are paired, oval-shaped organs that produce sperm and male sex hormones; they are located in the scrotum. At age 1 year, about 1% of boys have undescended testes (cryptorchidism).

The ***epididymides*** are the 2 highly coiled tubes against the posterior side of the testes where sperm mature and are stored until they are released during ejaculation.

The ***vasa deferentia*** (singular: vas deferens) are the paired tubes that carry the mature sperm from the epididymides to the urethra.

The ***seminal vesicles*** are a pair of glandular sacs that secrete about 60% to 70% of the fluid that makes up the semen in which sperm are transported. After a vasectomy, sperm is no longer present in the ejaculate, but the quantity of seminal fluid remains the same.

The ***prostate gland*** is a walnut-sized glandular structure that secretes about 30% of the fluid that makes up semen.

The ***Cowper's glands*** are 2 pea-sized glands at the base of the penis under the prostate that secrete a clear alkaline fluid into the urethra during sexual arousal and before orgasm and ejaculation.

FEMALE PUBERTY

— Breast budding (thelarche) is, traditionally, the first sign of puberty, although hymenal changes may occur earlier.

— Lack of breast development by age 14 years or lack of any development by age 13 years is considered abnormal and deserves further evaluation.

— Pubic hair appears (pubarche) at the same time as breast development or within 5 to 6 months thereafter.

— In the prepubertal female the uterus/cervix ratio is 1:2 or 1:3, but this reverses to 2:1 after puberty. Other internal genital changes are as follows:

1. Myometrium thickens markedly.

2. Uterine lining becomes multilayered, columnar, and mucocolumnar.

3. Uterine length becomes 3.5 cm on average.

4. Ovaries increase in size.

5. The cervix undergoes anteflexion, placing it into the posterior vaginal vault.

6. Ectopy of the columnar epithelium into the vaginal vault occurs.

— Changes in the external genitalia include the following:

1. Thickening of the hymen and tissue in the periurethral area.

2. Vagina lengthens and epithelium lining thickens.

3. Mucus-secreting cells and Skene's and Bartholin's glands produce watery mucus.

4. Vaginal epithelium becomes lighter pink in color and tissue rugation and protrusion increase.

5. Elasticity increases and sensitivity to pain decreases.

6. The vaginal pH becomes 3.5 to 5, which may be protective against vulvovaginitis.

7. Labia majora and labia minora enlarge.

SEXUAL MATURITY RATING

— The Tanner stages of maturity are guidelines used in assessing the progression of pubertal development in adolescents (**Table 2-3**). They are not criteria for use in video review of probable chronological age.

Table 2-3. Tanner Stages of Maturity

BREAST SEXUAL MATURITY RATING

Stage 1 (prepubertal): Elevation of the papilla

Stage 2: Breast budding with areolar enlargement and, later, tenderness

Stage 3: Enlargement with no separation of breast/nipple contour

Stage 4: Projection of the areola and papilla to form a clear mound (nipple)

Stage 5: The mature stage with areolar recession

PUBIC MATURITY RATING

Stage 1 (preadolescent): Only vellus over the pubes, no pubic hair

Stage 2 (pubarche): Sparse growth, downy hair, straight, little curl, hairs easily counted

Stage 3: Hair darker, coarser, curlier, mainly over the pubes, still countable

Stage 4: Adult type hair over the mons and labia, counting now requires compulsive behavior

Stage 5: Mature stage spreads to medial thighs and forms the female escutcheon (inverted triangle)

(continued)

Table 2-3. Tanner Stages of Maturity *(continued)*

BOYS SEXUAL MATURITY RATING

Stage G1 (preadolescent): Infantile, no enlargement of penis, testicular volume 1.5 mL

Stage G2: Testes enlarge (volume 1.6 mL-6 mL), early sparse pubic hair

Stage G3: Hair increases, both testes (volume 6-12 mL) and penis grow

Stage G4: Hair now thickened, scrotum more rugated, volume of testes 12-20 mL

Stage G5: Adult male hair on the thighs; penis and testes (volume >20 mL) full size; male escutcheon is triangular shaped

Testicular size may be measured by comparing the graduated testes on the orchidometer developed by Swiss ephebiatrician and endocrinologist Dr. Andrea Prader.

MALE PUBERTY AND VARIATIONS IN MALE SEXUAL DEVELOPMENT

— The first sign of puberty in the male is enlargement of the testes at a mean age of 9.5 years, accompanied by tenderness with referred pain to the ipsilateral lower quadrant. Testicular size is the most accurate method of assessing male puberty.

— The average length of puberty is 2.5 to 3 years, with progression from spermarche to ejaculation to fertility.

— At a mean age of 11.6 years, the penis grows in length and pubic hair appears at its base. Next axillary hair grows, bony growth occurs, and finally muscle mass increases.

— Variations found at physical examination include the following:

— Gynecomastia

— Spermatocele

— Varicocele

— Pink pearly papules of the penis

FEMALE AND MALE ANAL ANATOMY

The *anus orifice* is at the lower opening of the digestive tract that lies in the fold between the buttocks. Functionally the anus dilates routinely to allow the passage of feces and could readily admit an object the size of a penis with minimal or no residual findings.

Perianal skin folds are wrinkles of perianal skin created by the contraction of the anal sphincter. These skin folds are also called *rugae* and are symmetrical, circumferentially radiating folds formed by relaxation of corrugator cutis ani muscle.

The *anus* is viewed as a linear slit-like opening visible with retraction of the buttocks; however, in adults the anus is a 3-cm to 4-cm tubular canal. The anal opening is surrounded by and kept closed with 2 sphincter muscles (**Figure 2-15**). The internal sphincter is located at the internal end of the anal canal. The external anal sphincter surrounds the anus posterior to the perineum. There is no lubricating glans around the anus. The anal tone is relaxed and will readily dilate after gentle traction on the buttocks if feces are present. This is a normal physiological finding that should not be confused with recent or past injury.

The *anal verge* overlies the subcutaneous tissue of the external anal sphincter at distal end of the anal canal and extends exteriorly to the margin of anal skin. It is a transitional area between the mucous membrane of the anal canal and the perianal skin. The external hemorrhoidal plexus of perianal space is within the loose connective tissue surrounding proximal anal orifice. This vein frequently becomes engorged when the patient is in supine or prone position and may be mistaken for a bruise. The examiner can differentiate a contusion from

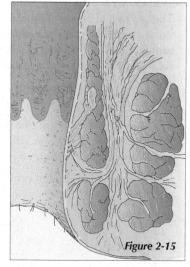

Figure 2-15

Figure 2-15. *Cross section of anus (normal).*

an engorged vein by changing the position of the patient or with claudication through active pressure.

The *pectinate*, or dentate, line is the saw-toothed line of demarcation between the lower portion of the anal valves and the pectin, a smooth zone of stratified squamous epithelium extending to the anal verge that separates the anus from the rectum and reveals the sinuses and columns.

The *rectum* is defined as the distal portion of the large intestine (**Figure 2-16**). It lies superior to the pectinate line. It is about 13 cm in length. The walls are glandular mucosa with an autonomic nerve supply that is pain insensitive.

NORMAL PERINEUM AND ANORECTUM
— The anus is normally located in the middle of any pigmentation and has circumferential rugal folds.

— Perianal tissue overlying the external anal sphincter at the most distal part of the anal canal is the anal verge. The anoderm meets the rectal ampulla at the pectinate line.

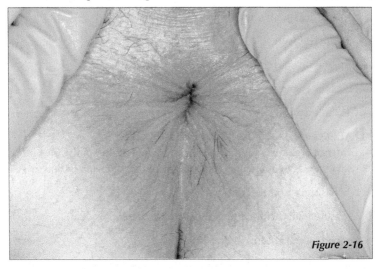

Figure 2-16

Figure 2-16. *Anal folds are generally visible with limited traction. In a preinjury state, they are symmetrical and form a slit-like opening. With relaxation of the external anal sphincter, the anus opens to form a cylindrical tube that allows visibility of the rectum.*

— Circumferentially and deep to this tissue in the perianal space are the inferior or external hemorrhoidal veins. Because they have no valves, they are easily distended and obstructed.

— Color variations and changes that may be noted in children but are within norms are as follows:

1. Red = erythema

2. Brown = hyperpigmentation

3. Blue = venous congestion

4. White = lichen sclerosis or autoimmune disorders

ANATOMIC VARIATIONS
Among the noninjury-related variations that are noted are the following:

— Diastasis ani

— Anal tags

— Symmetrical or asymmetrical anal opening

— Superficial fissures

— Imperforate anus

— Fistulous formation

— Cloacal exstrophy

HEALING AFTER ANOGENITAL INJURY
— Evidence of tissue injury in anogenital trauma heals rapidly; therefore, sexual assault or abuse may result in any of the following findings:

1. No injury to the victim

2. Acute injury with rapid healing and no evident residual

3. Evidence of chronic and recurrent abuse

— Serious tissue injury or deformation is more often seen in sexual assault cases than in child sexual abuse.

— Scarring can distort predicted clinical prognosis and lead to a faulty conclusion.

— Pain and bleeding correlate with an increased probability of finding evidence of significant injury in child sexual abuse.

— The more protection from estrogenization, glycogen production, and secretion content, the less clinically observable the injury becomes over time.

— Wound resolution is the reverse action of original structure and function and involves 2 overlapping phases, taking place only if tissue damage is minor, complications do not ensue, and damaged or destroyed tissue has the ability to proliferate the remaining cells. Resolution may require up to 2 years, depending on the tissue injured.

— Healing occurs in 2 ways:

  1. Regeneration

    a. Generation of cellular debris as thrombosis, platelet degradation, and inflammation occur rapidly (noticeable within 24 hours).

    b. Regeneration of denuded epithelial cells (48 to 72 hours).

    c. Production of new immature cells (5 to 7 days).

    d. Differentiation and maturation of new cells (several weeks).

    e. Most superficial anogenital injuries cannot be seen with the unaided eye by 4 to 5 days (**Figure 2-17**).

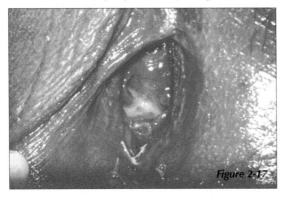

Figure 2-17.
Subacute trauma (9 days postinjury).

2. Repair

   a. Angiogenesis of new capillaries.

   b. Migration and proliferation of fibroblasts.

   c. Synthesis of extracellular matrix by fibroblasts.

   d. Maturation and remodeling of fibrous tissue scar.

   e. The wound appears reddened from neovascularization then contracts and pales as the scar matures, at about 60 days. Very little repair healing occurs in the anogenital area, possibly because of mucosal surface qualities, but narrowing of the hymenal rim at the point of injury is not uncommon. A V-shaped cleft or notch occurs when the elastic tissue in the separating edges of the hymen retracts during injury.

   f. Healing varies from person to person and is dependent on age, medications, physical environments, and health status of the individual.

REFERENCES

1. Adams JA, Knudson S. Genital findings in adolescent girls referred for suspected sexual abuse. *Arch Pediatr Adolesc Med.* 1996;150(8):850-857.

2. Anderson S, McClain N, Riviello RJ. Genital findings of women after consensual and nonconsensual intercourse. *J Int Forensic Nurs.* 2006;2(2):59-64.

3. Berenson AB, Heger AH, Hayes JM, Bailey RK, Emans SJ. Appearance of the hymen in prepubertal girls. *Pediatrics.* 1992;89(3):387-394.

4. Biggs M, Stermac LE, Divinsky M. Genital injuries following sexual assault of women with and without prior sexual intercourse experience. *CMAJ.* 1998;159(1):33-37.

5. Biro FM, Falkner F, Khoury P, Morrison JA, Lucky AW. Areolar and breast staging in adolescent girls. *Adolesc Pediatr Gynecol.* 1992;5(4):271-272.

6. Cardozo L, Bachmann G, McClish D, Fonda D, Birgerson L. Meta-analysis of estrogen therapy in the management of urogenital atrophy in postmenopausal women: second report of the Hormones and Urogenital Therapy Committee. *Obstet Gynecol.* 1998;92(4 pt 2):722-727.

7. Cold CJ, Taylor JR. The prepuce. *Br J Urol Int.* 1999;83(suppl 1):33-34.

8. Crowley CA. The gynecological examination of infants, children, and young adolescents. *Pediatr Clin North Am.* 1981;28:247-266.

9. de la Taille A, Delmas V, Lassau JP, Boccon-Gibod L. Anatomic study of the pubic-urethral ligaments in women: role of urethral suspension. *Progr Urol.* 1997;7(4):604-610.

10. Emans SJ, Woods ER, Allred EN, Grace E. Hymenal findings in adolescent women: impact of tampon use and consensual sexual activity. *J Pediatr.* 1994;125(1):153-160.

11. Emans SJ, Woods ER, Flagg NT, Freeman A. Genital findings in sexually abused, symptomatic and asymptomatic, girls. *Pediatrics.* 1987;79(5):778-785.

12. Finkel M. Physical Examination. In: Finkel M, Giardino A, eds. *Medical Evaluation of Child Sexual Abuse.* 3rd ed. Elk Grove, IL: American Academy of Pediatrics; 2009:53-132.

13. Finkel MA. Anogenital trauma in sexually abused children. *Pediatrics.* 1989;84(2):317-322.

14. Gaffney D. Genital injury and sexual assault. In: Giardino A, Datner E, Asher J, Girardin BW, Faugno D, Spencer M, eds. *Sexual Assault: Victimization Across the Life Span: A Clinical Guide.* Saint Louis, MO: GW Medical; 2003:223-239.

15. Giardino A, Alexander R, eds. *Child Abuse: Quick Reference for Healthcare, Social Service, and Law Enforcement Professionals.* 2nd ed. Saint Louis, MO: GW Medical Publishing; 2006.

16. Giardino A, Datner E, Asher J, eds. *Sexual Assault: Victimization Across the Life Span: A Clinical Guide.* Saint Louis, MO: GW Medical Publishing; 2003.

17. Girardin B, Faugno D, Seneski P, Slaughter L, Whelan M. *The Color Atlas of Sexual Assault.* Saint Louis, MO: Mosby; 1997.

18. Girardin BW, Faugno DK, Spencer MJ, Giardino AP, eds. *Sexual Assault: Victimization Across the Life Span: A Color Atlas.* Saint Louis, MO: GW Medical Publishing; 2003.

19. Goto K, Yoshinari H, Tajima K, Kotsuji F. Microperforate hymen in a primigravida in active labor: a case report. *J Reprod Med.* 2006;51(7):584-586.

20. Heger A, Emans S, Muram D, eds. *Evaluation of the Sexually Abused Child.* 2nd ed. New York, NY: Oxford University Press; 2000.

21. Heger AH, Ticson L, Guerra L, et al. Appearance of the genitalia in girls selected for nonabuse: review of hymenal morphology and nonspecific findings. *J Pediatr Adolesc Gynecol.* 2002;15(1):27-35.

22. Hutton KAR, Babu R. Normal anatomy of the external urethral meatus in boys: implications for hypospadias repair. *BJU Int.* 2007;100(1):161-163.

23. Jenny C. *Medical Evaluation of Physically and Sexually Abused Children.* Thousand Oaks, CA: Sage Publications; 1996.

24. Linden J, Lewis-O'Connor A, Jackson M. Forensic examination of adult victims and perpetrators of sexual assault. In: Olshaker J, Jackson M, Smock W, eds. *Forensic Emergency Medicine.* 2nd ed. Philadelphia, PA: Lippincott, Williams and Wilkins; 2006:85-125.

25. Masters W, Johnson V, Kolodny R. *Human Sexuality.* 5th ed. New York, NY: Harper Collins Publishers; 1995.

26. McCaan J, Miyamoto S, Boyle C, Rogers K. Healing of hymenal injuries in prepubertal and adolescent girls: a descriptive study. *Pediatrics.* 2007;119(5):e1094-e1106. doi: 10.1542/peds.2006-0964.

27. McCann J, Voris J, Simon M, Wells R. Comparison of genital examination techniques in prepubertal girls. *Pediatrics.* 1990;85(2):182-187.

28. Moore KL, Persaud TVN, Torchia MG. Urogenital system. In: Moore KL, Persaud TVN, Torchia MG, eds. *The Developing Human: Clinically Oriented Embryology.* 9th ed. Philadelphia, PA: Saunders; 2013:245-288.

29. Myher AK, Berntzen K, Bratlid D. Genital anatomy in non-abused preschool girls. *Acta Pediatr.* 2003;92(12):1353-1462.

30. Olshaker J, Jackson M, Smock W. *Forensic Emergency Medicine.* 2nd ed. Philadelphia, PA: Lippincott, Williams and Wilkins; 2006:119.

31. Pokorny SF. Configuration of the prepubertal hymen. *Am J Obstet Gynecol.* 1987;157(4 pt 1):950-956.

32. Pokorny SF, Kozinetz CA. Configuration and other anatomic details of the prepubertal hymen. *Adolesc Pediatr Gynecol.* 1988;1(2):97-103.

33. Simpson JL. Disorders of sexual differentiation. In: Sanfilippo JS, Muram D, Dewhurst J, Lee PA, eds. *Pediatric and Adolescent Gynecology.* 2nd ed. Philadelphia, PA: WB Saunders; 2000:87-115.

34. Slaughter L, Brown CR, Crowley S, Peck R. Patterns of genital injury in female sexual assault victims. *Am J Obstet Gynecol.* 1997;176(3):609-616.

35. Speck PM, Lee ED. Hymen estrogen response scale (HERS) reliability study. *End Violence Against Women International and Office for Victims of Crime Notebook.* Addy, WA: End Violence Against Women International; 2011:28-29.

36. Stedman TL. *American Heritage Stedman's Medical Dictionary.* 2nd ed. Boston, MA: Houghton Mifflin Company; 2004.

37. Styne DM. Normal growth and pubertal developmental. In: Sanfilippo JS, Muram D, Dewhurst J, Lee PA, eds. *Pediatric and Adolescent Gynecology.* 2nd ed. Philadelphia, PA: WB Saunders; 2000:31.

38. Swartz M. *Textbook of Physical Diagnosis: History and Examination.* 5th ed. Philadelphia, PA: Saunders/Elsevier; 2006.

39. Tortora GJ, Anagnostakos N. *Principles of Anatomy and Physiology.* 6th ed. Harper Collins; 1990:736-738.

40. Velazques EF, Bock A, Soskin A, Codas R, Arbo M, Cubilla AL. Preputial variability and preferential association of long phimotic foreskins with penile cancer: an anatomic comparative study of types of foreskin in a general population and cancer patients. *Am J Surg Pathol.* 2003;27(7):994-998.

41. White C, McLean I. Adolescent complaints of sexual assault: injury patterns in virgin and non-virgin groups. *J Clin Forensic Med.* 2006;13(4):172-180.

42. Wilson PD, Dixon JS, Brown AD, Gosling JA. Posterior pubo-urethral ligaments in normal and genuine stress incontinent women. *J Urology.* 1983;130(4):802-805.

43. Yang CC, Bradley WE. Innervation of the human glans penis. *J Urology.* 1999;161(1):97-102.

Chapter 3

Physical Evaluation of Children

Diana Faugno, MSN, RN, CPN, SANE-A, SANE-P, FAAFS, DF-IAFN*
Jacqueline M. Sugarman, MD

The child who comes to medical attention in the medical setting—either acute or chronic—because he or she made a specific disclosure of developmentally inappropriate sexual contact or who has either physical or behavioral symptoms that cause concern for such contact should undergo a history, physical examination, diagnostic and forensic testing as needed, and referrals as appropriate.

History

— Research continues to show that most children who are sexually abused have normal examinations, so the diagnosis of sexual abuse usually rests solely on the history given by the child.

— Obtaining and documenting an accurate account of what happened is crucial in diagnosing sexual abuse.

— Make every attempt to interview the child separate from the parents, guardians, or accompanying caregivers so his or her full disclosure of the events is not hindered.

— Do not assume that the child's caregiver believes the child and will protect the child from further abuse.

— First, interview the accompanying caregiver separate from the child so you can obtain a history and better understand the child's world. Obtain from the caregiver:

*Revised Chapter 3 for the second edition.

1. The child's names for body parts

2. How long ago the abuse took place and the possible extent of the abuse

3. Any unusual living situations

4. The child's past medical history

5. Changes in the child's behavior

6. Medications that the child is taking

7. Any concerns from the guardian

8. Written consent for the examination

— If the child has been brought to medical attention because of behavior or physical symptoms that seem suspicious for sexual abuse, ask specifically what is being questioned. Be aware that most signs and symptoms in abused children are nonspecific (see **Table 3-1**).

Table 3-1. Common Complaints of Sexually Abused Children and Adolescents Upon Arrival for Care

PHYSICAL SIGNS AND SYMPTOMS

— Genital discharge and bleeding	— Genital or urethral trauma
— Genital itching	— Other genital infections
— Pregnancy	— Fatigue or exhaustion
— STIs	— Sleep disturbance
— Abdominal pain	— Drug overdose
— Appetite disturbance	— Recurrent urinary tract infections (UTIs)
— Genital skin lesions	

PSYCHOSOMATIC DISORDERS

— Diffuse somatic complaints	— Abdominal pain
— Anorexia	— Headaches
— Hysterical or conversion reactions	*(continued)*

Table 3-1. Common Complaints of Sexually Abused Children and Adolescents Upon Arrival for Care *(continued)*

SEXUAL PROBLEMS

— Promiscuity or prostitution
— Sexual perpetration on others
— Sexual revictimization

— Sexual dysfunction
— Fear of intimacy

SOCIAL OR BEHAVIORAL PROBLEMS

— School adjustment problems
— Mood swings
— Phobias, avoidance behaviors
— Aggressive behavior
— Truancy or runaway behavior
— Self-mutilating behavior
— Family conflicts

— Neurotic or conduct disorders
— Social withdrawal
— Impulsive behavior
— Substance abuse
— Suicidal ideation, gestures, or attempts

PSYCHOLOGICAL PROBLEMS

— Anxiety
— Depression
— Self-hate, self-blame
— Mistrust

— Hyperalertness
— Terrified of rejection
— Flashbacks
— Dissociation

OTHER

— Asymptomatic sibling of a victim
— Association with a known perpetrator

Adapted from Hunter RS, Kilstrom N, Loda F.[23]

1. Sexual behaviors that appear most frequently in nonabused children include self-stimulating behaviors, exhibitionism, and behaviors related to personal boundaries.

2. Infrequent behaviors in nonabused children are more intrusive, such as putting the mouth on sex parts or putting objects into the vagina or rectum.

3. Compulsive masturbation and behavior that suggests a child's explicit or inappropriate knowledge of adult sexual behavior warrant further investigation.

Form an impression as to whether the caregiver is protective of the child and if the child is at risk for being abused in the future. Ask if the perpetrator resides in the home and if there are other children at risk.*

— Conduct the interview of the child in an unhurried manner and an unthreatening environment (**Table 3-2**). Be sensitive to the child's desire for an impartial third party to be present. Follow your organizational procedures.

— It is often best to talk to the child/adolescent without parents/guardians. Many times there is more disclosure or description of the acts when the child is able to connect with the medical provider.

— Tailor your attempts to establish rapport to the child's developmental status.

— Avoid long, complex questions and the use of pronouns instead of names. Be direct.

— In building rapport, gauge the child's developmental level.

— Ask about daily living and intimate relationships.

— Ask the child to identify body parts by either pointing to them on a diagram or drawing a crude stick figure, usually starting with the head and working downward.

---

*Child protective services (CPS) will determine if the child is safe to send home.

Table 3-2. Interview Protocol

Initial procedure	— Obtain information from caretaker or social worker.
	— Determine child's terminology for genitalia.
— Interview child alone in nonthreatening environment.	— What's your name?
	— How old are you?
	— Who lives at your house?
— Establish rapport with child.	— Do you have any pets?
	— What school do you attend?
— Ask about daily living and intimate relationships.	— Where do you sleep?
	— Who gives you a bath?
— Ask child to identify body parts/ascertain names for genitalia.	— Identify hair, eyes, nose, belly button, private parts.
— Try to determine what happened.	— Why did you come to see the doctor?
	— Did something happen to you?
— Begin with open-ended questions (may need to ask more specific questions for younger children).	— Did something happen to your bottom?
More specific questions	— Where were you when it happened?
	— Where was Mommy? Daddy?
	— Who did it? What did he/she do?
	— Where were your clothes?
	— Did you tell anyone?
	— Who did you tell?
	— What did he or she say when you told?

(continued)

Table 3-2. Interview Protocol *(continued)*	
Conclude the interview.	— Tell the child she did a good job. — Reassure her that it was not her fault and nobody blames her.
Explain the examination.	— "Now I'm going to check you out, listen to your heart and lungs, feel your tummy, and look at your private parts."
Document	— Document questions asked and answers given. — Record exact words and phrases.
Modifications for adolescents	— Obtain more specific information: date and time of assault, history of assault (oral, rectal, or vaginal penetration; oral contact by the offender; ejaculation [if known by the patient], digital penetration, or penetration with foreign object). — Obtain history of any self-cleaning activities (bathing, teeth brushing, urination, douching, changing clothes). — Obtain menstrual history and whether the patient uses contraceptives. Were any lubricants or a condom used?

Adapted with permission from Midwest Children's Resource Center Interview Protocol, Carolyn Levitt, MD, Director, Midwest Children's Resource Center.

— Once rapport has been established, ask about abuse using open-ended or nondirective questions (see **Table 3-3**).

— Note spontaneous responses regarding sexual details, such as ejaculation, because most children have no knowledge of them and often use other words to describe them, eg, "drippy stuff."

— Be aware that not every child will be cooperative. Some have been threatened by the perpetrator, some may feel guilty because they believe the abuse was their fault, some may not want to betray the perpetrator, some may fear no one will believe them, and some may be too embarrassed or shy. Some simply don't want to talk at that particular time. Reporting child sexual abuse is often a process.

1. It may be necessary to defer further interviewing and proceed with the examination or reschedule both.

2. If the abuse occurred in the past 72-120 hours,* physical findings or forensic evidence may be found, so it may be necessary to proceed despite the child's reluctance.

— At the conclusion of the interview, tell the child that he or she did well and did the right thing by telling. Reassure children that the abuse was not their fault and they are not in trouble—they are very brave. Finally, tell the child what will happen next, ie, the physical examination.

Table 3-3. Types of Questions Used in Interviews of Suspected Child Abuse Victims		
TYPE OF QUESTION	CHARACTERISTICS	EXAMPLES
Open-ended	— Draws mainly upon recall memory — Accuracy is thought to be maximized — Optimal starter questions; follow with clarifiers	— "Tell me why you came in to see me today." — "Tell me all about it." — "And then what happened?"
Specific or focused	— Both recall and recognition memory are tapped — Reasonable accuracy — Appropriate when used to clarify responses to open-ended questions	— "Who hit you there?" — "Where did he touch you?" *(continued)*

*Refer to Publisher's Note on page xliv.

Table 3-3. Types of Questions Used in Interviews of Suspected Child Abuse Victims *(continued)*

Type of Question	Characteristics	Examples
Multiple choice	— Draws mainly upon recognition memory — Accuracy may be improved if an unspecified alternative is included — Appropriate as a clarifying question	— "Did that happen in the bedroom, the bathroom, or somewhere else?" — "Did she hit you one time or more than one time?"
Yes/No	— Forces a choice. Younger children may simply choose first or last option. — May be less reliable — Best used for clarification or in head-to-toe review of systems, returning to open-ended query, if child gives affirmative response	— After child has stated that she had been touched on her "private parts": "When you were touched on your private parts, did that hurt you?" — "Have you even been hurt on your back?"
Leading	— Suggests that there is only one acceptable response — Format of question generally includes an act, an actor, and a tag — Accuracy questionable — Should never be used	— "Your dad hit you, didn't he?" — "No one has ever done anything to hurt your bottom, have they?"
Coercive	— Evokes emotions, secondary gain, not necessarily memory retrieval — Accuracy severely compromised — Inappropriate, should never be used	— "Tell me who did that to you, and I'll let you go back to see your mommy in the playroom."

The Physical Examination

Purposes

1. Document the condition of the patient.

2. Diagnose and treat injuries and STIs.

3. Collect and preserve evidence.

4. Reassure the patient and address concerns about his or her physical and psychologic well-being.

Procedure
(**Table 3-4**)

Table 3-4. Equipment for Sexual Assault Examination	
EQUIPMENT	COMMENTS
Drapes, gowns	Preserve patient's modesty
Books, videos, pictures	Distract young patient while examination is being performed
Sterile saline	May be needed to "float" hymen
Urine container to collect dirty urine for NAAT testing	(See *Chapter 11* for more information.)
Culture tubes for vaginal/ urethral, anal, and pharyngeal specimens	— Culture is the gold standard for detecting *C. trachomatis* and *N. gonorrhoeae* in children if the NAAT is positive. — (See *Chapter 11* for more information.)
Saline solution for wet prep, microscope slides	When vaginal discharge needs to be tested for *T. vaginalis*
Viral culture media	Per lab protocol

(continued)

Table 3-4. Equipment for Sexual Assault Examination *(continued)*

EQUIPMENT	COMMENTS
Forensic evidence collection kit	— If abuse occurred within the last 72-120 hours and medical discretion determines need — Available from police
Additional swabs	May be necessary to collect additional forensic evidence
Digital camera or colposcope with camera	— Optional; magnification is helpful, not required. — Photographs will help the examiner describe findings.
Blood drawing supplies	— If blood for serology or rape kit is to be obtained — In all children/adolescents, obtain a buccal swab for reference. You may not need to draw blood for DNA and subject the patient to this painful procedure.
Measuring tape and L ruler	Should any lesions need to be measured

— Integrate any forensic evidence collection with the medical testing and examination.

— Ensure that the patient feels comfortable with you and can anticipate what the examination will entail. This will be based on the child's age and developmental level.

— Respect the patient's modesty and allow them to feel that they have some control over the examination.

— Begin with overall inspection of the patient, usually those areas that are least anxiety provoking, and progress to the most sensitive areas.

— Note nongenital as well as genital injuries.

— Determine when the alleged abuse occurred, if possible.

— Examine genital areas, taking photographs. Use the Tanner stage to communicate sexual maturity. Follow your documentation form.

— Prepubertal female genitalia are examined without a speculum; if there is unexplained vaginal bleeding, the examination should usually be accomplished under anesthesia by a pediatric gynecologist or surgeon.

— Generally, thorough visual inspection of the external genitalia, vaginal vestibule, and hymenal structures should be completed in all examinations.

1. Visual inspection in the prepubertal female typically occurs when the child is lying in a supine position and in the knee-chest position as well (**Figure 3-1**).

2. In the supine frog-leg position, the hymen is best visualized using gentle traction on the labia majora (**Figures 3-2-a** and **3-2-b**). Pull the labia majora outward and downward.

3. In the knee-chest position, the labia majora is lifted upward and outward to visualize the hymen; this allows you to see the posterior hymen, vagina, anus, and often the cervix as well (**Figure 3-3**).

4. For estrogenized, redundant, or folded hymenal tissue, use a swab moistened with saline solution to tease the tissue apart (**Figure 3-4**) or apply a few milliliters of warm saline solution to make the hymenal edges float (**Figures 3-5-a** through **3-5-d**).

5. Describe findings related to the hymen in relation to the face of a clock (**Figure 3-6**), always noting whether the patient is prone or supine.

6. Male genitalia are examined while the patient is sitting or standing. Retract the foreskin if possible and examine the glans. Also examine the scrotum and testes.

7. For either sex, the anus can be examined while the child is in a lateral decubitus position; in the prone knee-chest position, which children often know as a cannonball position; or supine with the knees drawn up to the chest. The anus is seen by spreading the gluteal folds. Note rectal sphincter tone. Digital rectal examination is not needed, but endoscopic examination is indicated if deeper rectal injury is suspected because of severe or unexplained bleeding.*

---

*The child may have to be taken to the operating room (OR) for this examination, depending on the child's age.

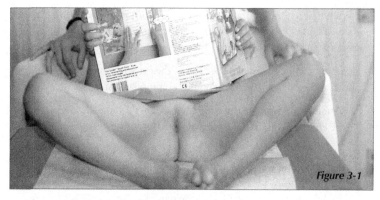

Figure 3-1

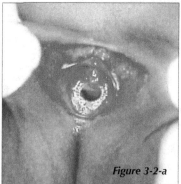

Figure 3-2-a

Figure 3-1. Child in a frog-leg supine position with a book on her abdomen to distract her attention from the exam.

Figure 3-2-a. Labial traction for a child in the supine frog-leg position. Examiner is gently pulling outward and downward on labia majora with gloved hands. In view is a normal crescentic hymen of a Tanner stage 1 girl. Hymen has attachments at the 11 and 1 o'clock positions without tissues being present between the 2 attachments.

Figure 3-2-b. Labial traction of an adolescent estrogenized hymen.

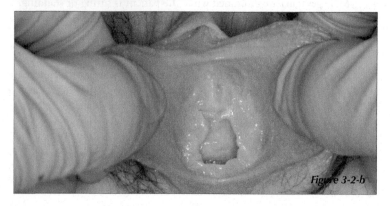

Figure 3-2-b

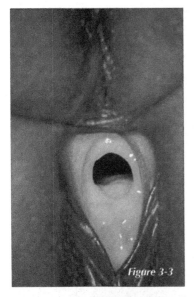

Figure 3-3. *Knee -chest position with annular hymen present.*

Figure 3-4. *Big swab lifting the estrogenized hymen for evaluation during the medical examination of an adolescent.*

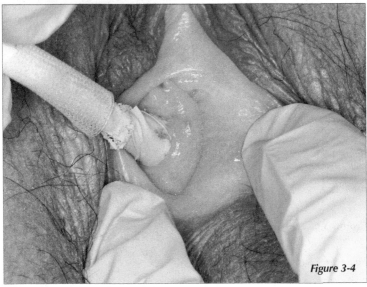

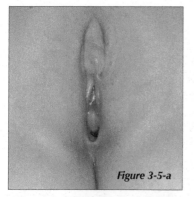

Figure 3-5-a

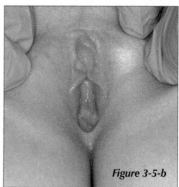

Figure 3-5-b

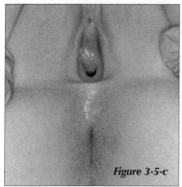

Figure 3-5-c

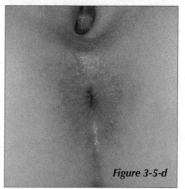

Figure 3-5-d

Figure 3-5-a. *Supine position with no traction. Photograph taken before starting genital examination.*

Figure 3-5-b. *Supine position with labial traction. Hymen is closed.*

Figure 3-5-c. *Crescentic hymen is open, and no evidence of injury is present.*

Figure 3-5-d. *Supine position of the anus. No visible injury noted.*

Figure 3-6. *Face of a clock.*

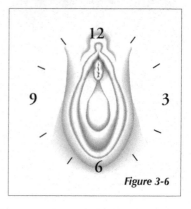

Figure 3-6

Findings of Concern in Sexual Abuse Evaluations
— Refer to Adams et al's "Updated Guidelines for the Medical Assessment and Care of Children Who May Have Been Sexually Abused" (available online at http://www.sciencedirect.com/science/article/pii/S1083318815000303) for detailed information on normal findings, findings requiring differential diagnosis, and findings supportive of a disclosure of sexual abuse.

— If a sexually transmitted infection is suspected, follow the STI screening recommendations given in *Chapter 11*.

Forensic Evidence
A sexual assault examination kit provides an organized means of collecting forensic evidence. While they vary from state to state, generally they provide the means to collect clothing worn by the patient, debris from the assaulted genital area, pubic hair (if the patient is pubertal), swabs for collecting dried secretions left on the patient's genital area, head hair, buccal swabs, and blood from the patient. **Table 3-5** outlines the procedure to be followed.

Table 3-5. Sexual Assault Examination Protocol and Evidence Collection for Children and Adolescents

— Examine for nongenital trauma.	— Search hair for foreign material and blood.
— Inspect buccal cavity.	
— Inspect for bite marks.	— Inspect for bruises.

— Collect relevant clothing and underwear in a paper bag. Each piece of clothing goes in its own paper bag.
Comments:

    — Avoid plastic bags because mold can form.

    — Damaged or torn clothing may be significant; take a photograph of the variance.

    — Clothing provides surface on which traces of foreign material may be found.

    — Each garment should be placed in a separate bag to prevent cross-contamination.

Modifications for Prepubertal Children:

    — Collect underwear or diaper in a paper bag.

(continued)

Table 3-5. Sexual Assault Examination Protocol and Evidence Collection for Children and Adolescents *(continued)*

— Examine genital area.

Modifications for Prepubertal Children:
— A speculum examination is not performed.

— If the examiner suspects a vaginal laceration or tear because the patient has unexplained vaginal bleeding, a speculum examination will need to be done, most likely under anesthesia.

— Comb hair from pubic area.

Comments:
— May contain specimens from assailant and may, in some cases, help to identify race, sex, blood type, and hair color of suspect

Modifications for Prepubertal Children:
— No pubic hair to comb

— Debris can be collected from pubic area.

— Cut or pluck head and pubic hair from patient.*

Comments:
— Follow your protocol. Collect all debris found in the head hair.

— In pubertal examinations where there is vaginal fluid, follow your protocol. Do a wet mount of material from posterior fossa for motile sperm.

— Fixed smear from the vagina and cervical os if speculum has been inserted.

Comments:
— Wet mount may not be required in all states.

— If penetration to the anus or mouth occurred, anal and/or oral swabs should be collected.

— For male patient or penile trauma, the external shaft and glans of the penis should be swabbed with swabs that are slightly moistened with distilled water or saline solution.

(continued)

Table 3-5. Sexual Assault Examination Protocol and Evidence Collection for Children and Adolescents *(continued)*

— Swab from any area that fluoresces with UV lamp (Wood's lamp) or appears to have dried secretions on it (vulva, rectum, inner thighs).

Comments:

— State crime laboratory can analyze for acid phosphatase, ABO(H) antigen, and sperm precipitins.

Modifications for Prepubertal Children:

— Speculum must not be inserted unless under anesthesia.

— Collect debris from beneath fingernails.

— Note dried secretions on skin by examination or fluorescing on Wood's lamp examination.

Comments:

— State crime laboratory can analyze for acid phosphatase, ABO(H) antigen, and sperm precipitins.

SERUM

— Serology for hepatitis B, syphilis, and HIV

— Beta HCG

— Blood typing

Comments:

— Sample will determine if the patient secretes blood group antigens in body fluids other than blood.

— Follow your community protocol.

---

*Many kits no longer include this as a standard. Follow your community protocol.
Adapted from American College of Obstetricians and Gynecologists.[9]

DEFINITIVE CARE

— Refer to CDC guidelines for antibiotic prophylaxis for STIs to selected pubertal children and adolescents (available online at http://www.cdc.gov/std/tg2015/tg-2015-print.pdf and http://www.cdc.gov/std/tg2015/sexual-assault.htm#pep).

— For acute assaults, human immunodeficiency virus (HIV) prophylaxis may be required (see *Chapter 5*). Follow your community standard.

— Medical follow-up is generally recommended for all patients at 2 weeks and 12 weeks after an assault. Follow the Centers for Disease Control and Prevention (CDC) guidelines for follow-up and your community standard.

— Emotional and mental well-being needs to be addressed. Stress that healing will come over time and ensure that adequate follow-up with the resources available in the community is in place before the patient leaves the examination site.

— **Table 3-6** offers an assault examination checklist to follow in approaching a child sexual assault examination.

Table 3-6. Sexual Assault Examination Checklist

— History documented

— Physical examination documented (documentation that photographs were taken; sexual assault evidence collection kit obtained, correctly labeled, and sealed, and that chain of evidence maintained)

— Testing for STIs obtained per CDC guidelines

— Prophylaxis for STIs and pregnancy per CDC guidelines, discussed with patient and provided

— Mental health counseling follow-up arranged

— Appropriate authorities (law enforcement, CPS) notified

— Documentation of person to whom child was released

REFERENCES

1. Adams JA, Harper K, Knudson S, Revilla J. Examination findings in legally confirmed child sexual abuse: it's normal to be normal. *Pediatrics.* 1994;94(3):310-317.

2. Adams JA, Kellogg ND, Farst KJ, et al. Updated guidelines for the medical assessment and care of children who may have been sexually abused. *J Pediatr Adolesc Gynecol.* In press. doi: 10.1016/j.jpag.2015.01.007.

3. Adams JA, Starling SP, Frasier LD, et al. Diagnostic accuracy in child sexual abuse medical evaluation: role of experience, training, and expert case review. *Child Abuse Negl.* 2012;36(5):383-392. doi: 10.1016/j.chiabu.2012.01.004.

4. American Academy of Pediatrics, Committee on Child Abuse and Neglect. Guidelines for the evaluation of sexual abuse of children. *Pediatrics.* 1999;103(1):186-191.

5. American Academy of Pediatrics, American Academy of Pediatric Dentistry. Oral and dental aspects of child abuse and neglect. *Pediatrics.* 1999;104(2):348-350.

6. American College of Emergency Physicians. *Evaluation and Management of the Sexually Assaulted or Sexually Abused Patient.* 2nd ed. Dallas, TX: American College of Emergency Physicians; 2014.

7. American College of Obstetricians and Gynecologists. *Guidelines for Women's Health Care: A Resource Manual.* 3rd ed. Washington, DC: American College of Obstetricians and Gynecologists; 2007.

8. American College of Obstetricians and Gynecologists. *Technical Bulletin, Sexual Assault.* 1987;101:1-5.

9. American Professional Society on the Abuse of Children. *Practice Guidelines, Descriptive Terminology in Child Sexual Abuse Evaluations.* San Diego, CA: American Professional Society on the Abuse of Children; 1995.

10. Bays J, Chadwick D. Medical diagnosis of the sexually abused child. *Child Abuse Negl.* 1993;17(1):91-110.

11. Berenson AB, Chacko MR, Wiemann CM, Mishaw CO, Friedrich WN, Grady JJ. A case-control study of anatomic changes resulting from sexual abuse. *Am J Obstet Gynecol.* 2000;182(4):820-831; discussion 831-834.

12. Berkoff MC, Zolotor AJ, Makoroff KL, Thackeray JD, Shapiro RA, Runyan DK. Has this prepubertal girl been sexually abused? *JAMA.* 2008;300(23):2779-2792.

13. Centers for Disease Control and Prevention. Sexually transmitted diseases treatment guidelines, 2015. *MMWR Recomm Rep*. 2015;64(3):1-137.

14. Christian CW. Timing of the medical examination. *J Child Sex Abus*. 2011;20(5):505-520. doi: 10.1080/10538712.2011.607424.

15. Christian CW, Lavell JM, De Jong AR, Loiselle J, Brenner L, Joffee J. Forensic evidence findings in prepubertal victims of sexual assault. *Pediatrics*. 2000;106(1):100-104.

16. Cosentino LA, Campbell T, Jett A, et al. Use of nucleic acid amplification testing for diagnosis of anorectal sexually transmitted infections. *J Clin Microbiol*. 2012;50(6):2005-2008. Doi: 10.1128/JCM.00185-12.

17. DeLago C, Deblinger E, Schroeder C, Finkel MA. Girls who disclose sexual abuse: urogenital symptoms and signs after genital contact. *Pediatrics*. 2008;122(2):e281-e286. doi: 10.1542/peds.2008-0450.

18. Finkel MA, Alexander RA. Conducting the medical history. *J Child Sex Abus*. 2011;20(5):486-504. doi: 10.1080/10538712.2011.607406.

19. Finkel MA, Giardino AP. *Medical Evaluation of Child Sexual Abuse: A Practical Guide*. 3rd ed. Elk Grove Village, IL: American Academy of Pediatrics; 2009.

20. Frasier LD. The pediatrician's role in child abuse interviewing. *Pediatr Ann*. 1997;26(5):306-311.

21. Frasier LD, Thraen I, Kaplan R, Goede P. Development of standardized clinical training cases for diagnosis of sexual abuse using a secure telehealth application. *Child Abuse Negl*. 2012;36(2):149-155.

22. Hornor G. Medical evaluation for child sexual abuse: what the PNP needs to know. *J Pediatr Health Care*. 2011;25(4):250-256.

23. Hunter RS, Kilstrom N, Loda F. Sexually abused children: identifying masked presentation in a medical setting. *Child Abuse Negl*. 1985;9(1):17-25.

24. Gavril AR, Kellogg ND, Nair P. Value of follow-up examinations of children and adolescents evaluated for sexual abuse and assault. *Pediatrics*. 2012;129(2);282-289. doi: 10.1542/peds.2011-0804.

25. Giardino AP, Finkel MA, Giardino ER, Seidl T, Ludwig S. *A Practical Guide to the Evaluation of Sexual Abuse in the Prepubertal Child.* Thousand Oaks, CA: Sage Publications; 1992.

26. Girardet R, Bolton K, Lahoti S, et al. Collection of forensic evidence from pediatric victims of sexual assault. *Pediatrics.* 2011;128(2):233-238.

27. Hymel KP, Jenny C. Child sexual abuse. *Pediatr Rev.* 1996;17(7):236-250.

28. Jenny C. Medical issues in sexual abuse. In: Briere J, Berliner L, Buckley JA, Jenny C, Reid T, eds. *The APSAC Handbook on Child Maltreatment.* Thousand Oaks, CA: Sage Publications; 1996:197-199.

29. Jenny C, Crawford-Jakubiak JE; Committee on Child Abuse and Neglect; American Academy of Pediatrics. The evaluation of children in the primary care setting when sexual abuse is suspected. *Pediatrics.* 2013;132(2):e558-e567. doi: 10.1542/peds.2013-1741.

30. Kellogg ND, Lamb JL, Lukefahr JL. The use of telemedicine in child sexual abuse evaluations. *Child Abuse Negl.* 2000;24(12):1601-1612.

31. Meyers JE. Role of physician in preserving verbal evidence of child abuse. *J Pediatr.* 1986;109(3):409-411.

32. Myhre AK, Bemtzen K, Bratlid D. Perianal anatomy in non-abused preschool children. *Acta Paediatr.* 2001;90(11):1321-1328.

33. Siegel RM, Schubert CJ, Meyers PA, Shapiro RA. The prevalence of sexually transmitted diseases in children and adolescents evaluated for sexual abuse in Cincinnati: rationale for limited STD testing in prepubertal girls. *Pediatrics.* 1995;96(6):1090-1094.

34. Starling SP, Jenny C. Forensic examination of adolescent female genitalia: the Foley catheter technique. *Arch Pediatr Adolesc Med.* 1997;151(1):102-103.

35. US Department of Justice, Office of Violence Against Women. *A National Protocol for Sexual Assault Medical Forensic Examinations: Adults/Adolescents.* 2nd ed. Washington, DC: US Department of Justice; 2013. NCJ 228119.

Chapter 4

Forensic Evaluation of Children*

Diana Faugno, MSN, RN, CPN, SANE-A, SANE-P, FAAFS, DF-IAFN‡
Sarah Anderson, RN, MSN
Pamela Ross, MD

The forensic evaluation of a prepubescent child is designed to collect, document, and preserve evidence in a law enforcement investigation of a crime or possible crime. In the event of a crime, the systematic manner of collecting, documenting, and preserving evidence is referred to as *processing the scene* (**Figure 4-1**).

Figure 4-1. Crime scene photograph. Note the yellow place card numbers depicting evidence in the photograph, such as clothing lying on the floor.

*Inherent in the published material is the responsibility of the licensed provider to seek emerging research for evidence-based practice.

‡*Revised Chapter 4 for the second edition.*

PRINCIPLES OF EVIDENCE COLLECTION
DETERMINATION OF TEAM COMPOSITION

— Establish a team to provide contamination control; accurately document; prioritize evidence collection; and to collect, preserve, package, transport, and submit evidence by established protocols.

— Team members may be law enforcement, child protective services (CPS), social workers, medical personnel, psychologists, forensic interviewers, and district attorneys.

— All team members need specialized training in pediatric sexual abuse.

CONTAMINATION CONTROL

— Ensure that the integrity of the evidence is maintained.

— Use nonreusable items to collect specimens and observe universal precautions.

DOCUMENTATION

— Assess what needs to be documented and establish the types of equipment needed, considering photography, video, diagrams, measurements, and notes.

1. Take photographs with and without scale and evidence identifiers.

2. Photograph or videotape to provide a broader perspective and demonstrate correct technique during evidence collection and examination.

3. Document variances with measurements and document location of injuries and evidence collected in relation to the body.

4. Note location of the examination; times of arrival and completion of the examination; general information before evidence collection begins; transient evidence, ie, smells, sights, conditions; and deviations from usual standards of practice or care.

PRIORITIZATION OF EVIDENCE COLLECTION

— Prevent loss, destruction, and/or contamination of evidence.

1. Conduct a careful, methodical evaluation, considering all physical evidence possibilities.

2. Focus on easily accessible areas in open view before proceeding to out-of-view locations.

3. Follow a systematic search pattern based on size, type, and location of evidence.

4. Move from least intrusive to most intrusive processing and collection methods.

5. Continually assess environmental factors and other factors that might affect evidence.

COLLECTION AND PRESERVATION OF EVIDENCE
— Maintain evidence security throughout the process.

1. Note location of collected evidence, date and time collected, who collected it, and who had access to it.

2. Establish a chain of custody—document handling and account for all specimens through each step of the evidence processing. Begin with initial collection and follow all the way to the courtroom, thereby ensuring validity and admissibility of forensic evidence in court.

3. Obtain reference samples. Secure any electronically recorded evidence immediately.

4. Establish policies and procedures relating to evidence collection and the release of evidence and maintain them, updating periodically.

LIMITATIONS OF THE FORENSIC EVALUATION

Most nonacute examinations of children who have been sexually abused will show less than 5% visible evidence of findings. There are many reasons for this such as delayed reporting so if there was an injury it has had time to heal. Often the most important evidence will be the child's history of the event.

WHEN TO COLLECT EVIDENCE*

Forensic evidence is only collected after initiating law enforcement or CPS investigation. The American Academy of Pediatrics recommends forensic evidence collection when sexual abuse is believed to have occurred within the previous 72 hours or when there is bleeding or acute injury. Many

---

*The child may have to be taken to the operating room (OR) for this examination, depending on the child's age.

programs now recommend 120 hours post assault because DNA analysis technology is more sensitive and continues to change.

PROCESS OF COLLECTION

— A head-to-toe physical examination, including a detailed genital examination, should be done with the patient in the frog-leg position, either supine or on the caregiver's lap, and in the prone knee-chest position. Written documentation of evidence, diagrams, and photographs are recommended.

— Physical evidence recovery kits specifically for sexual assaults are usually supplied by law enforcement agencies or can be obtained through a state forensics laboratory (**Figure 4-2-a** and **Figure 4-2-b**). Most are designed for adults but are routinely modified for pediatric use. Follow the kit's instructions on how the evidence should be collected and how to handle used and unused supplies (**Table 4-1**).

— Collect evidence using normal saline solution, distilled water, or sterile water, based on the recommendations of the local forensic laboratory. Collect and separately package each piece of clothing worn during and immediately after the assault.

1. If the child is still wearing the original clothes, undress the child over a paper sheet placed on a clean hospital bed sheet or another sheet of paper.

2. If the clothing is damp or wet, place examination table paper between the layers and notify the police so the articles of clothing are dried and stored properly.

3. Label each package to identify the child, date, time, and your signature and seal it securely.

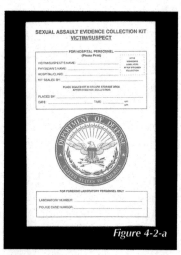

Figure 4-2-a

Figure 4-2-a. Example of an evidence collection kit. This kit can be modified by the examiner based on the history of the event.

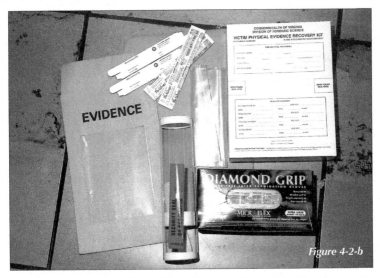

Figure 4-2-b. *The contents of a physical evidence recovery kit.*

4. Initial the seal.

5. Collect linens and bedding, whether they are brought to the emergency room or are at the scene, packaging them individually in paper bags, sealing them, and turning them over to the police.

6. Instruct the child's caregivers to minimize bathing, teeth brushing, voiding, defecating, vomiting, eating, drinking, and changing clothes after an assault if at all possible.

PROCESS OF FORENSIC EVALUATIONS
MORE THAN 72-120 HOURS AFTER INCIDENT OR IN CHRONIC ABUSE BASED ON YOUR COMMUNITY STANDARD
— Do not use a forensic evidence collection kit.

— Perform a head-to-toe physical examination and detailed anogenital examination, as for acute abuse.

— Document findings and provide diagrams and photographic evidence.

Table 4-1. Forensic Evidence Collection and Preservation

SPECIMEN: CLOTHING

— Garments
— Bedding (includes sheets and paper drapes used to lay clothing on)
— Diaper

Evidence Collection Items
— Paper envelopes (various sizes)   — Permanent marker
— Evidence tape   — Examination table paper

Method of Preservation
— Remove clothing one piece at a time.

— Avoid cutting through any holes, tears, or stained areas.

— If clothing is damp or wet, place a piece of paper between the layers.

> *Rationale: If clothing is packaged together, the trace evidence may be transferred to other items.*

— Place each item in its own paper envelope or package.

> *Rationale: If clothing is packaged together, the trace evidence may be transferred to other items.*

— Seal with a piece of evidence tape labeled with the date, time, and initials.

— If items are saturated and are soaking through the package, the package can be placed in a plastic bag, but it must be left open.

> *Rationale: If the items are placed in a sealed plastic bag, bacteria and fungus growth will be increased.*

SPECIMEN: DEBRIS

— Hair   — Grass, leaves, vegetation
— Paint chips   — Fibers

Evidence Collection Items
— Paper envelopes (various sizes)
— Evidence tape
— Permanent marker

(continued)

Table 4-1. Forensic Evidence Collection and Preservation *(continued)*

Method of Preservation
— Collect and place in separate envelopes.

    Rationale: These items may connect the suspect with the child or the child and/or suspect with the crime scene.

— Write a description of the item and where it was collected on the outside of the envelope before placing the item inside.

— Seal the envelope with evidence tape labeled with the date, time, and initials.

SPECIMEN: BODY FLUIDS

— Seminal fluid	— Urine
— Blood	— Gastric contents

Evidence Collection Items

— Specimen containers and tubes	— Paper envelopes (various sizes)
— Sterile cotton swabs	— Evidence tape
— Sterile water	— Permanent marker

Method of Preservation
— If large quantities, collect in specimen containers or tubes. The containers should be sealed with evidence tape that has been initialed with date, time, location collected. The container should be placed in a plastic bag. The fluid specimens must be refrigerated.

    Rationale: These items may connect the suspect with child or the child and/or the suspect with the crime scene.

— Areas of suspected body fluids or stains should be collected using the double swab technique. Swabs need to be either dried before packaging or placed in air-dry boxes. The swabs are placed in a paper envelope sealed with evidence tape, labeled with date, time and initials.

— If clothing is damp or wet, place a piece of paper between the layers.

CHRONIC ABUSE WITH THE MOST RECENT
ACUTE OCCURRENCE WITHIN 72-120 HOURS
— Perform forensic evidence collection and a full evaluation.

— Look for evidence of acute injuries as well as old injuries.

INTERVIEW PROCESS
— (See *Chapter 3* for specifics of the interview.)

PHYSICAL EXAMINATION
— (See *Chapter 3* for a general overview of the physical examination.)

— The physical examination and evidence collection are performed at the same time.

— Look for signs of injury from abuses that are acute, healing, or chronic.

— Perform the genital examination with the child as directed in *Chapter 3*. In the female child, the genital examination should include direct visualization initially, gentle labial separation, and finally labial traction.

— During visualization identify and inspect the following: medial thighs, mons pubis, labia minora, labia majora, clitoris, urethra, peri-urethral area, fossa navicularis, and posterior commissure/fourchette and hymen.

— View the anus with and without traction. Use the supine knee-chest or knee-chest position for this examination.

— Note the presence or absence of stool in the rectal vault if able.

— In the male child, carefully inspect the medial thighs, scrotum, testicles, penis, and urethra along with the anal examination.

— Unless they facilitate the removal of a foreign body, speculum and digital examinations of prepubertal children are not needed. Any speculum examination on children should only be done under conscious sedation, in the operating room, or if the child has had menses.

SPECIAL EVIDENCE COLLECTION
TECHNIQUES IN THE EVALUATION OF SEXUAL ABUSE
— Forensic photography

1. A digital camera with 10 pixels or greater and a macro lens gives the best resolution. Digital cameras allow immediate review and reduce the risk of obtaining inadequate photographs or none at all.

2. Take an overview or full body picture, an orientation picture and medium range shot, and then a close-up of all areas to be emphasized; all close-ups should be taken with and without a scale, which should be held parallel to and in the same plane as the injury and camera. This is called the rule of 4s and 5s.

3. Repeat photographs may be required in a few days when bruises are more pronounced and patterns easier to identify; these can also help discern whether anomalies seen in the initial examination have changed or remained the same.

4. Digital photography or the use of colposcopy will magnify the genitalia and can increase the ability to see genital and perineal abnormalities. Photographs of findings facilitate consultation between examiners in peer review, discussion with child abuse experts, and presentation in court. Photographs should be taken with and without a scale.

5. A Wood's lamp/Alternative Light Source (ALS) may be used to identify suspicious areas for more definitive testing. Semen, urine, and other oily substances may fluoresce a blue-green to orange color. Examine the child's body under a Wood's lamp/ALS in a darkened room and swab, package, and send any areas of fluorescence to the laboratory. Often time there is no fluorescence and it is best to always swab based on the history given.

— Double swab technique

1. The double swab technique should be used for any areas that fluoresce under the alternate light source or where you suspect that a body fluid is present.

2. The first swab is obtained with a damp cotton-tipped applicator, and the second with a dry cotton-tipped applicator.

3. Follow the directions given by your local crime lab.

— Saline float/irrigation of hymenal tissue

1. If hymenal tissue is folded over and the edges not easily identified, even with positioning of the child, gently dribble saline solution over the edges of the hymen and reexamine the child.

2. Be sure to inform the child that this will be done beforehand because of the extreme sensitivity of the prepubescent hymen.

— Foley catheter technique vs Big Blue Swab

1. Only used in pubertal and postpubertal girls, the Foley catheter technique allows the identification of forensically significant abnormalities in the hymenal tissue by allowing the examiner to see the floppy, redundant edges.

2. A Foley catheter is inserted just past the vaginal opening, the balloon is inflated with 10 mL of sterile water, and traction is gently applied to help spread hymenal tissue edges

3. The Big Blue Swab is inserted just past the vaginal opening and is used to run the hymen or lift the hymen while looking for any injury, fresh or old. This technique is less intrusive than the Foley catheter. (See **Figure 4-3-a** through **d**)

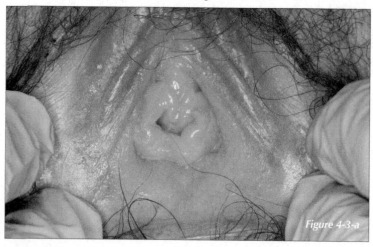

Figure 4-3-a

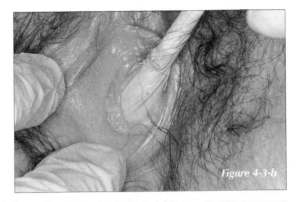

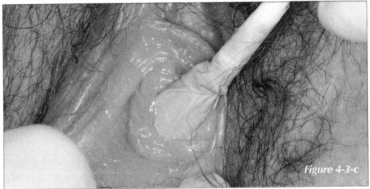

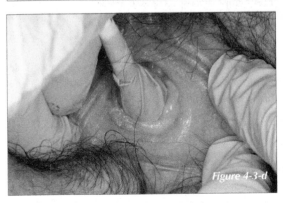

Figure 4-3-a through d. *Big Blue Swab inserted past the hymen to lift and evaluate the hymen for any tears, old or acute.*

— Toluidine blue (used only in acute examination)

1. Perform all DNA swabs of the external genitalia *before* applying toluidine blue dye.

2. Toluidine blue dye is applied to the external genitalia to identify acute lacerations and abrasions.

3. Use the dye sparingly, applying it with a cotton swab.

4. Remove the dye after a few seconds using lubricating jelly, baby wipes, etc and examine the area for lacerations. Only damaged skin cells take up the dye. A positive dye outlines the injury.

— Bite mark impressions

1. Bite marks can be mistaken as a bruise or normal childhood mishap.

2. Breaks in the skin should be noted. Shape can vary depending on amount of force, surface area, and amount of contact made with the area involved.

3. If the bite mark is suspected to be acute, test the area using the double swab technique and dry or package the specimen in a self-drying box.

4. If indentations are noted in the skin, a bite mark impression can be made using a casting compound. (This is usually done by forensic odontology.) Photograph all suspected bite marks with and without a scale.

— Documentation

1. Use a form that allows for the following information: basic demographic information, history from the child, data from the physical examination, and evidence collected in written form plus schematic diagrams of the whole child and genitalia.

2. All digital photographs are numbered. It is not necessary to keep a photo log. Place book mark cards/identification labels at the start of the photographs and at the end of the photographs, denoting that all pictures in between are of that patient.

— Peer review of cases

1. All cases should be reviewed by the team members to ensure consistency in the interpretation of findings and as a continued learning experience.

2. Feedback is also given regarding the written/electronic and photographic documentation of examinations.

— Testing for sexually transmitted infections (STIs). (See *Chapter 6*)

REFERENCES

1. American Academy of Pediatrics. Guidelines for the evaluation of sexual abuse of children. *Pediatrics.* 1991;87:254-260.

2. American Academy of Pediatrics Committee on Child Abuse and Neglect. Guidelines for the evaluation of sexual abuse of children: subject review. *Pediatrics.* 2005;116(2):506-512.

3. Centers for Disease Control and Prevention. Sexually transmitted diseases treatment guidelines, 2010. Centers for Disease Control and Prevention Web site. http://www.cdc.gov/mmwr/pdf/rr/rr5912.pdf. Published December 17, 2010. Accessed March 2, 2015.

4. Christian CW, Lavell JM, De Jong AR, Loiselle J, Brenner L, Joffee J. Forensic evidence findings in prepubertal victims of sexual assault. *Pediatrics.* 2000;106(1):100-104.

5. Ferrell J. Foley catheter balloon technique for visualizing the hymen in female adolescent sexual abuse victims. *J Emerg Nurs.* 1995;21(6):585-586.

6. Gabby T, Winkleby MA, Boyce WT, Fisher DL, Lancaster A, Sensabaugh GF. Sexual abuse of children: the detection of semen on skin. *Am J Dis Child.* 1992;146(6):700-703.

7. Girardet R, Bolton K, Lahoti S, et al. Collection of forensic evidence from pediatric victims of sexual assault. *Pediatrics.* 2011;128(2):233-238.

8. Jessee SA. Recognition of bite marks in child abuse cases. *Pediatr Dent.* 1994;16(5):336-339.

9. Jones JS, Dunnuck C, Rossman L, Wynn BN, Nelson-Horan C. Significance of toluidine blue positive findings after speculum examination for sexual assault. *Am J Emerg Med.* 2004;22(3):201-203.

10. Lauber AA, Souma ML. Use of toluidine blue for documentation of traumatic intercourse. *Obstet Gynecol.* 1982;60(5):644-648.

11. McCauley J, Gusinski G, Welch R, Gorman R, Osmers F. Toluidine blue in the corroboration of rape in the adult victim. *Am J Emerg Med.* 1987;5(2):105-108.

12. National Forensic Science Technology Center. Crime Scene Investigation: A Guide for Law Enforcement. Largo, FL: National Forensic Science Technology Center; 2013. National Forensic Science Technology Center Web site. http://www.nfstc.org/bja-programs/crime-scene-investigation-guide/. Accessed March 2, 2015.

13. Pretty IA. The barriers to achieving an evidence base for bitemark analysis. *Forensic Sci Int.* 2006;159(suppl 1):S110-S120.

14. Starling SP, Jenny C. Forensic examination of adolescent female genitalia: the Foley catheter technique. *Arch Pediatr Adolesc Med.* 1997;151(1):102-103.

15. Stavrianos C, Vasiliadis L, Papadopoulos C, Kokkas A, Tatis D, Samara E. Loss of the ear cartilage from a human bite. *Res J Med Sci.* 2011;5(1):20-24.

16. Sweet D, Lorente JA, Valenzuela A, Lorente M, Villanueva E. PCR-based DNA typing of saliva stains recovered from human skin. *J Forensic Sci.* 1997;42(3):320-322.

17. Williams S, Panacek E, Green W, Kanthaswamy S, Hopkins C, Calloway C. Recovery of salivary DNA from the skin after showering. *Forensic Sci Med Pathol.* 2015;11(1):29-34.

18. Wawryk J, Odell M. Fluorescent identification of biological and other stains on skin by the use of alternative light sources. *J Clin Forensic Med.* 2005;12(6):296-301.

Chapter 5

DIFFERENTIAL DIAGNOSIS

Diana K. Faugno, MSN, RN, CPN, SANE-A, SANE-P, FAAFS, DF-IAFN*
Philip Scribano, DO, MSCE
Barbara W. Girardin, RN, PhD
Carolyn J. Levitt, MD
Malinda Waddell, RN, MN, FNP
Mary J. Spencer, MD

Examination findings may result from any of the following:

— A variation in the normal anatomy of a prepubertal child

— Nonabusive traumatic injury resembling an abusive injury

— Medical conditions

VARIATIONS OF NORMAL ANATOMY
GENITALIA
— Vestibular bands (**Figure 5-1**)

1. Includes skin tags, septa, notches, and clefts of the hymen

2. Congenital absence of the hymen

3. Superficial notches on the inferior half of the hymen; however, notches extending through more than 50% of the membrane may be found in abused children based on their histories

4. Vaginal columns

— Linea vestibularis

— Median raphae

— Failure of midline fusion

Revised Chapter 5 for the second edition.

Anus

— Skin tags, particularly midline tags; lateral skin tags may be viewed with concern

— Smooth midline external sphincter with a fan-shaped area in the posterior midline

— Perianal erythema

— Degree of anal dilation; significant dilation can result from retained stool or chronic constipation or neurogenic patulous anus; post-mortem dilation may also confuse the issue

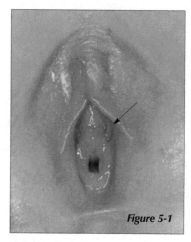

Figure 5-1

Figure 5-1. *Vestibular Bands. (Contributed by Diana Faugno, MSN, RN.)*

Nonabusive Trauma

— Straddle injury (**Figure 5-2** and **Figures 5-3**); however, these are extremely unlikely mechanisms of injury in children under age 9 months

— Penetrating injuries caused by falls onto pointed objects

— Excessive bleeding with a minor injury; occurs because of the rich blood supply to the external genitalia

— Vulvar hematomas, which result from straddle injuries and are very painful, preventing the child from urinating and causing swelling

— Vaginal injuries resulting from impalement by a sharp object or high-pressure water that insufflates the vagina; however, most of these injuries are probably abusive

— Urogenital injuries in females are generally nonabusive.

— Scrotal trauma in males

— Penile ecchymoses and/or lacerations

— Acute anal trauma with a history of penetration or attempted penetration of the anus

— Zipper entrapment

— Motor vehicle crashes that produce pelvic fracture, wherein a sharp bony fragment may penetrate the vagina and lower urinary tract

— Fissures of the posterior fourchette or anus produced during an examination that causes traction of the labia or buttocks

— A sharp foreign body that traverses the gastrointestinal tract and causes trauma on passage from the anus (rare)

— Childhood masturbation does not generally cause genital injury.

— Injury to the perineum with perianal bruising, rectal prolapse, or evisceration of the bowel from sitting on suction drain vents in swimming pools

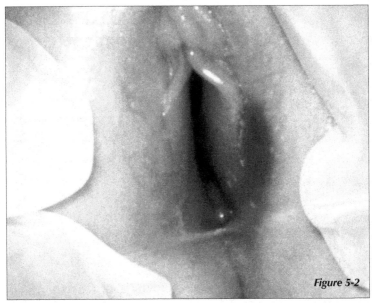

Figure 5-2. Straddle injury. (Contributed by Lori D. Frasier, MD; Salt Lake City, Utah.)

Case Study 5-1.

This 2-year-old Caucasian was jumping on the bed when she fell, straddling the side rail. Her mother's boyfriend was watching her while the mother was out running errands. The child was dressed and wearing a diaper while jumping on the bed. She was brought in within 12 hours of the accident.

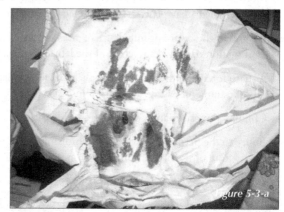

Figure 5-3-a. The diaper she wore on arrival for the exam (35mm).

Figure 5-3-b. A laceration of the posterior fourchette (35mm).

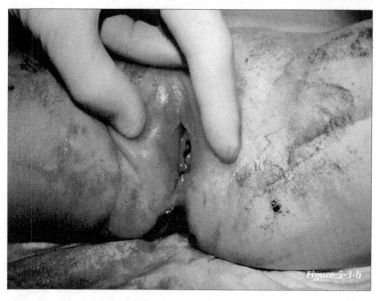

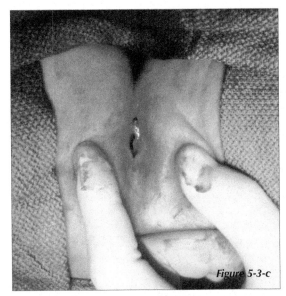

Figure 5-3-c. *The child is draped for a surgical repair (35mm).*

Figure 5-3-d.
A deep posterior fourchette laceration. There is focal erythema of the hymen at 3 to 5 and 7 to 10 o'clock. The labia majora and minora are free of injury that might be expected from a straddle fall. This case was canceled because it lacked elements of a crime.

Figure 5-3-c

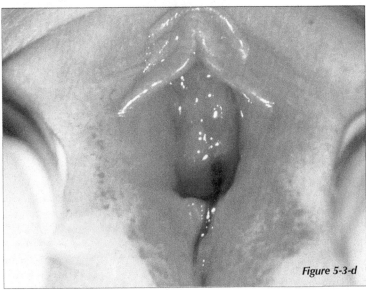

Figure 5-3-d

DERMATOLOGIC DISORDERS
— Lichen sclerosus et atrophicus (**Figure 5-4**)

1. Hemorrhagic, bullous lesions, fissures, or ulcers lead to confusion with traumatic injuries caused by a sexual assault.

2. Anogenital itching, pain, and bleeding are typical symptoms.

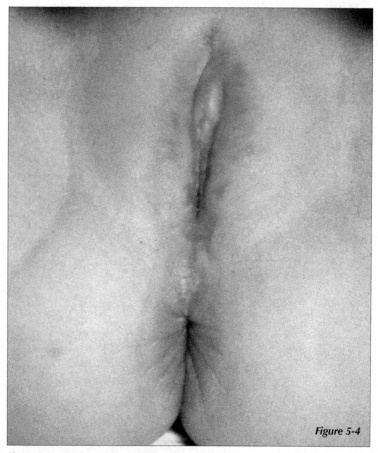

Figure 5-4

Figure 5-4. *Lichen sclerosus et atrohicus.*
(Contributed by Lori D. Frasier, MD; Salt Lake City, Utah.)

— Seborrheic dermatitis (diaper rash): severe cases may involve postinflammatory hypopigmentation and possible fissures.

— Allergic reactions that cause contact dermatitis on any region of the body

— Bedwetting: the use of a bedwetting alarm has produced a genital rash that was vesicular over the labia and inner thigh.

— Psoriasis of the diaper area: examine the nails and other skin areas to assist in diagnosis.

— Cavernous or strawberry hemangiomas (**Figure 5-5**)

  1. The most common benign vascular tumors of infancy

  2. Present at birth, these tumors grow in proportion to the growing infant and appear as small, red masses with an irregular border.

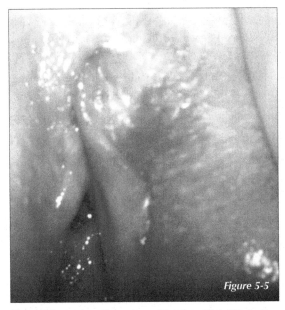

Figure 5-5. Strawberry hemangioma. (Contributed by Lori D. Frasier, MD; Salt Lake City, Utah.)

— Pemphigus disorders

1. Bullous pemphigoid is rare in children but can appear as large, tense bullae on normal-appearing or erythematous skin.

2. Associated bullae may be seen in the mouth, lower abdomen, and thighs.

3. Symptoms include mild pruritus, pain, and occasionally bleeding.

4. Pemphigus vulgaris: autoimmune disorder with flaccid vesiculobullous lesions measuring 1 to 3 cm with persistent erosions on the face, scalp, neck, and anogenital regions

INFECTIOUS DISORDERS
— Vulvovaginitis

1. Most often caused by *Staphylococcus aureus* (which may also cause impetigo in the anogenital region), group A streptococcus, *Enterococcus*, and *Shigella*)

2. Even if there are no identified risk factors and no disclosure of sexual abuse, consider *Neisseria gonorrhea* in the differential diagnostic evaluation of bacterial vaginitis.

— Group A streptococcal infection can also manifest as intense perianal erythema or, in males, balanitis, generally in early childhood.

— Vulvar or anal human papillomavirus (HPV) warts

1. Typically soft, less than 0.5 mm and have a papular or more verrucous shape (**Figure 5-6**)

2. In males the scrotal region is the predominant site of infection.

3. Children are usually asymptomatic but may complain of itching or bleeding.

4. Disease has extremely high frequency in adults (10% to 80% of asymptomatic, sexually active young women), so increasing prevalence of HPV infection in children is predictable, but concern for sexual transmission should exist.

5. Anogenital condyloma accuminata may result from infection with HPV types 6 and 11.

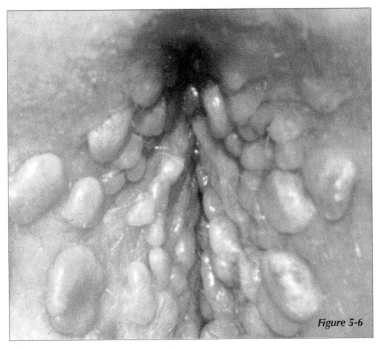

Figure 5-6

Figure 5-6. *Human papillomavirus (anal).*
(Contributed by Lori D. Frasier, MD; Salt lake City, Utah.)

— Varicella infection

— Epstein-Barr infection has been associated with genital ulcers.

— Herpes simplex virus (HSV) infection may be the result of autoinoculation from oral lesions with gingivostomatitis or infection of the digit (herpetic whitlow); a child presenting with genital herpes requires a child protection investigation in most cases.

— *Molluscum contagiosum* (**Figure 5-7**)

  1. Produces characteristic pale, umbilicated papules and is self-limiting

  2. Rarely seen on palms, soles, and mucous membranes, but can be localized to the inner thighs and perineum, causing concern for sexual abuse

— Schistosomiasis

103

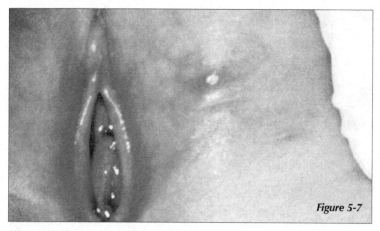

Figure 5-7. Molluscum contagiosum. *(Contributed by Lori D. Frasier, MD; Salt Lake City, Utah.)*

— Pinworm infestation (*Enterobius vermicularis*)

1. May cause vulvar bleeding or vulvar and/or anal itching

2. Diagnosed by characteristic small, white adult worms easily visualized on examinations

— Scabies

1. May be localized to anogenital region in addition to more common areas of web spaces of fingers, wrists, elbows, axillae, abdomen, and waist

2. Characterized by pruritic, erythematous, papular rash, usually worst at night when adult female mites are most active

— Retained foreign body, while uncommon, may cause recurrent urinary tract infection.

— Candidal diaper dermatitis

INFLAMMATORY DISORDERS
— Perianal lesions of Crohn's disease

1. Skin tags, fissures, thickened perianal skin, fistulas and abscesses, and scarring can result from complications of Crohn's disease.

2. Intestinal manifestations of Crohn's disease may be absent, with vulvar lesions (erythema, edema, and ulceration) being the first presentation of the disease in children.

— Kawasaki syndrome (mucocutaneous lymph node syndrome)

1. Vasculitis characterized by fever for 5 or more days and cervical adenopathy, bilateral conjunctival infection, changes to the mucus membrane (dry, cracked lips and strawberry anal skin), changes to the extremities (edema, erythema, and desquamation)

2. Erythematous rash of the perineum that progresses to desquamation of the region can precede the onset of the more diagnostic findings.

— Behçet's syndrome

1. Triad of oral aphthous stomatitis, ulcers of the external genitalia, and inflammatory disease of the eye structures (uveitis, iritis, iridocyclitis) is characteristic.

2. Genital ulcers occur in 10% of patients and are often painless and may heal with scarring by 7 to 14 days; recurrence is common.

MISCELLANEOUS DISORDERS

— Idiopathic calcinosis cutis

— Erythema multiforme

— Idiopathic thrombocytopenic purpura and other bleeding diatheses

— Henoch-Schönlein purpura

— Mongolian spots

— Disorders causing urethral bleeding or abnormalities of the urethra (hemangioma, polyps, ureterocele, prolapse of the urethra)

— Rectal prolapse: predisposing medical conditions include cystic fibrosis, myelomeningocele, prune belly syndrome, or other conditions that require straining (chronic constipation or excessive cough; see **Figures 5-8**).

— Hair tourniquet syndrome

— Labial agglutination or fusion of the labia minora (**Figure 5-9**)

1. Occurs commonly in infants and results from any inflammatory condition of the vulvar region

2. Denuded labial epithelium becomes agglutinated as the labia closely appose in the diapered child.

Case Study 5-2.

This 9-month-old male was cared for by an uncle while the mother went away for 3 days. When the mother returned, she found blood in the child's diaper. It was determined that this child had perianal fissures from a combination of diaper dermatitis and constipation. The mother brought in the large (4cm diameter) "rock-hard" ball of stool that the child passed, while he was screaming in pain.

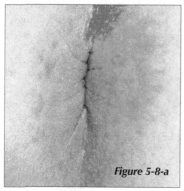

Figure 5-8-a. Perianal erythema, an abrasion at 12 o'clock, and macular lesions along the edge of the erythema.

Figure 5-8-b. This is the same area as in Figure 5-8-a, but the edges of the fissures are separated. There are 3 fissures at the superior end of the anus and at least 3 fissures around the 6 o'clock area.

Figure 5-8-c. This is the uptake of toluidine blue dye by some of the fissures.

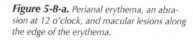

Figure 5-8-a

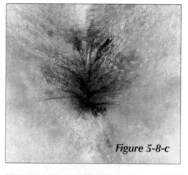

Figure 5-8-c

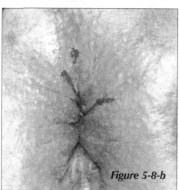

Figure 5-8-b

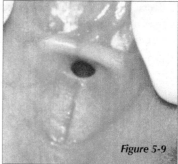

Figure 5-9

Figure 5-9. Labial agglutination. (Contributed by Lori D. Frasier, MD; Salt Lake City, Utah.)

REFERENCES

1. Agnarsson U, Warde C, McCarthy G, Evans N. Perianal appearances associated with constipation. *Arch Dis Child.* 1990;65(11):1231-1234.

2. Aho T, Upadhyay V. Vaginal water-jet injuries in premenarcheal girls. *N Z Med J.* 2005;118(1218):U1565.

3. Bays J. Conditions mistaken for child sexual abuse. In: Reese M, ed. *Child Abuse: Medical Diagnosis and Management.* 2nd ed. Philadelphia, PA: Lippincott Williams & Wilkins; 2001:287-306.

4. Bogaerts J, Lepage P, De Clercq A, et al. Shigella and gonococcal vulvovaginitis in prepubertal central African girls. *Pediatr Infect Dis J.* 1992;11(10):890-892.

5. Cain WS, Howell CG, Ziegler MM, Finley AJ, Asch MJ, Grant JP. Rectosigmoid perforation and intestinal evisceration from transanal suction. *J Pediatr Surg.* 1983;18(1):10-13.

6. Centers for Disease Control and Prevention. Suction drain injury in a public wading pool—North Carolina, 1991. *MMWR.* 1992;41(19):333-335.

7. Chi CC, Kirtschig G, Baldo M, Brackenbury F, Lewis F, Wojnarowska F. Topical interventions for genital lichen sclerosus. *Cochrane Database Syst Rev.* 2011;(12):CD008240. doi:10.1002/14651858.CD008240.pub2.

8. DeLago C, Deblinger E, Schroeder C, Finkel MA. Girls who disclose sexual abuse: urogenital symptoms and signs after genital contact. *Pediatrics.* 2008;122(2):e281-e286.

9. Dodds ML. Vulvar disorders of the infant and young child. *Clin Obstet Gynecol.* 1997;40(1):141-152.

10. Dowd MD, Fitzmaurice L, Knapp JF, Mooney D. The interpretation of urogenital findings in children with straddle injuries. *J Pediatr Surg.* 1994;29(1):7-10.

11. Eyvazzadeh AD, Smith YR, Lieberman R, Quint EH. A rare case of vulvar endometriosis in an adolescent girl. *Fertil Steril.* 2009;91(3):929. e9-929.e11.

12. Fernandez-Pineda I, Spunt SL, Parida L, Krasin MJ, Davidoff AM, Rao BN. Vaginal tumors in childhood: the experience of St. Jude Children's Research Hospital. *J Pediatr Surg.* 2011;46(11):2071-2075.

13. Frankkowski BL, Bocchini JA Jr; Council on School Health and Committee on Infectious Disease. *Pediatrics.* 2010;126(2):392-403.

14. Gibbon KL, Bewley AP, Salisbury JA. Labial fusion in children: a presenting feature of genital lichen sclerosus? *Pediatr Dermatol.* 1999;16(5):388-391.

15. Goldberg J, Horan C, O'Brien LM. Severe anorectal and vaginal injuries in a jet ski passenger. *J Trauma.* 2004;56(2):440-441.

16. Goldstein AT, Thaçi D, Luger T. Topical calcineurin inhibitors for the treatment of vulvar dermatoses. *Eur J Obstet Gynecol Reprod Biol.* 2009;146(1):22-29.

17. Grisoni ER, Hahn E, Marsh E, Volsko T, Dudgeon D. Pediatric perineal impalement injuries. *J Pediatr Surg.* 2000;35(5):702-704.

18. Gryngarten MG, Turco ML, Escobar ME, Woloj MG, Bergada C. Shigella vulvovaginitis in prepubertal girls. *Adolesc Pediatr Gynecol.* 1994;7(2):86-89.

19. Hillyer S, Mooppan U, Kim H, Gulmi F. Diagnosis and treatment of urethral prolapse in children: experience with 34 cases. *Urology.* 2009;73(5):1008-1011.

20. Hoffman L, Ma OJ, Gaddis G, Schwab RA. Cervical infections in emergency department patients with vaginal bleeding. *Acad Emerg Med.* 2002;9(8):781-785.

21. Hoffman RJ, Ganti S. Vaginal laceration and perforation resulting from first coitus. *Pediatr Emerg Care.* 2001;17(2):113-114.

22. Hostetler BR, Jones CE, Muram D. Capillary hemangiomas of the vulva mistaken for sexual abuse. *Adolesc Pediatr Gynecol.* 1994;7(1):44-46.

23. Hurwitz S, ed. *Clinical Pediatric Dermatology: A Textbook of Skin Disorders of Childhood and Adolescence.* 2nd ed. Philadelphia, PA: WB Saunders Co; 1993.

24. Isaac R, Lyn M, Triggs N. Lichen sclerosus in the differential diagnosis of suspected child abuse cases. *Pediatr Emerg Care.* 2007;23(7):482-485.

25. Jackson MG, Simms-Cendan J, Sims SM, et al. Vaginal bleeding due to an infantile hemangioma in a 3-year-old girl. *J Pediatr Adolesc Gynecol.* 2009;22(4):e53-e55.

26. Kadish HW, Schunk JE, Britton H. Pediatric male rectal and genital trauma: accidental and nonaccidental injuries. *Pediatr Emerg Care*. 1998;14(2):95-98.

27. Maronn ML, Esterly NB. Constipation as a feature of anogenital lichen sclerosus in children. *Pediatrics*. 2005;115(2):e230-e232.

28. McCann J, Voris J, Simon M, Wells R. Perianal findings in prepubertal children selected for non-abuse: a descriptive study. *Child Abuse Negl*. 1989;13(2):179-193.

29. McCann J, Wells R, Simon M, Voris J. Genital findings in prepubertal girls selected for nonabuse: a descriptive study. *Pediatrics*. 1990;86(3):428-439.

30. Merritt DF. Evaluation of vaginal bleeding in the preadolescent girl. *Semin Pediatr Surg*. 1998;7(1):35-42.

31. Mogielnicki NP, Schwartzman JD, Elliott JA. Perineal group A streptococcal disease in a pediatric practice. *Pediatrics*. 2000;106(2 pt 1):276-281.

32. Paradise JE. Vaginal bleeding. In: Fleisher GR, Ludwig S, eds. *Textbook of Pediatric Emergency Medicine*. 6th ed. Philadelphia, PA: Lippincott Williams & Wilkins; 2010:606-612.

33. Patrizi A, Gurioli C, Medri M, Neri I. Childhood lichen sclerosus: a long-term follow-up. *Pediatr Dermatol*. 2010;27(1):101-103.

34. Perlman SE. Management quandary. premenarchal vaginal bleeding. *J Pediatr Adolesc Gynecol*. 2001;14(3):135-136.

35. Perlman SE, Hertweck SP, Wolfe WM. Water-ski douche injury in a premenarcheal female. *Pediatrics*. 1995;96(4 pt 1):782-783.

36. Poindexter G, Morrell DS. Anogenital pruritus: lichen sclerosus in children. *Pediatr Ann*. 2007;36(12):785-791.

37. Powell J, Wojnarowska F. Childhood lichen sclerosus and sexual abuse are not mutually exclusive diagnoses. *BMJ*. 2000;320(7230):311.

38. Sanjeevaiah AR, Sanjay S, Deepak T, et al. Precocious puberty and large multicystic ovaries in young girls with primary hypothyroidism. *Endocr Pract*. 2007;13(6):652-655.

39. Scheidler MG, Schultz BL, Schall L, Ford HR. Mechanisms of blunt perineal injury in female pediatric patients. *J Pediatr Surg.* 2000;35(9):1317-1319.

40. Siegfried EC, Frasier LD. Anogenital skin diseases of childhood. *Pediatr Ann.* 1997;26(5):322-331.

41. Smith YR, Quint EH. Clobetasol propionate in the treatment of premenarchal vulvar lichen sclerosus. *Obstet Gynecol.* 2001;98(4):588-591.

42. Smorgick N, Padua A, Lotan G, Halperin R, Pansky M. Diagnosis and treatment of pediatric vaginal and genital tract abnormalities by small diameter hysteroscope. *J Pediatr Surg.* 2009;44(8):1506-1508.

43. Stratakis CA, Graham W, DiPalma J, Leibowitz I. Misdiagnosis of perianal manifestations of Crohn's disease. *Clin Pediatr.* 1994;33(10):631-633.

44. Stricker T, Navratil F, Sennhauser FH. Vaginal foreign bodies. *J Paediatr Child Health.* 2004;40(4):205-207.

45. Striegel AM, Myers JB, Sorensen MD, Furness PD, Koyle MA. Vaginal discharge and bleeding in girls younger than 6 years. *J Urol.* 2006;176(6 pt 1):2632-2635.

46. Sugar NF, Feldman KW. Perineal impalements in children: distinguishing accident from abuse. *Pediatr Emerg Care.* 2007;23(9):605-616.

47. Valerie E, Gilchrist BF, Frischer J, Scriven R, Klotz DH, Ramenofsky ML. Diagnosis and treatment of urethral prolapse in children. *Urology.* 1999;54(6):1082-1084.

48. Verstraelen H, Verhelst R, Vaneechoutte M, Temmerman M. Group A streptococcal vaginitis: an unrecognized cause of vaginal symptoms in adult women. *Arch Gynecol Obstet.* 2011;284(1):95-98.

49. Wood PL, Bevan T. Lesson of the week: child sexual abuse enquiries and unrecognised vulvar lichen sclerosus et atrophicus. *BMJ.* 1999;319(7214):889-890.

Chapter 6

EVALUATIONS IN SPECIAL SITUATIONS

Mary J. Spencer, MD, FAAP*
Charles J. Schubert, MD
Kathi Makaroff, MD
William C. Holmes, MD, MSCE
Sharon W. Cooper, MD, FAAP

SEXUALLY TRANSMITTED INFECTIONS

As implied by the term, sexually transmitted infections (STIs) are usually transmitted by sexual contact, although other routes of transmission are possible (**Table 6-1**). The overall incidence of STIs in victims of child abuse is relatively low (<10%). Even if a perpetrator of a sexual assault has an STI, the victim may not be infected because of the following:

— Perpetrators have a high incidence of sexual dysfunction and, therefore, may not perform the intimate contact required to transmit an STI.

— The organism carried by the perpetrator may not be easily transmitted.

— The environment of the prepubertal vagina is not as conducive to the survival of STI organisms.

— Disclosure of an episode of sexual abuse often occurs months to years after the abuse, which means that some STIs will resolve spontaneously or be asymptomatic.

The following factors should be considered in determining what workup is needed:

— Community prevalence

— Presence of STI in family member or sibling

— Presence of vaginal discharge in victim

— Probability of preexisting disease in the perpetrator

Revised Chapter 6 for the second edition.

— How recently the episode occurred

— Patient or family member requests testing

— Type of abuse

— Child's age or Tanner stage

— The specific organism

If an STI is found, an evaluation for sexual abuse must be undertaken (**Table 6-2**). For treatment, see **Table 6-3**.

Table 6-1. Modes of Transmission of STIs in Children				
ORGANISM BODY	SEXUAL ASSAULT	AUTOINOCULATION/ HETEROINOCULATION	FOMITES	INFECTED FLUIDS*
Bacterial vaginosis	X			
Chlamydia trachomatis	X			
Gonorrhea	X		?‡	
Hepatitis B	X			X
HIV	X			X
HPV	X	X	?‡	
HSV	X	X		
Syphilis	X			
Trichomonas vaginalis	X		?‡	

*Excluding genital secretions.
‡No study has directly documented this in children.
Abbreviations: human immunodeficiency virus (HIV), human papillomavirus (HPV), herpes simplex virus (HSV).

Table 6-2. Laboratory Investigations for STIs in the Evaluation of Sexually Abused Children

SEXUALLY TRANSMITTED INFECTION	DIAGNOSTIC TEST
Gonorrhea	— NAATS on urine more sensitive than culture — Confirm positive NAATS with a bacterial culture — Prepubertal males, oropharyngeal or anal contact require culture
Chlamydia infection	— NAATS on urine more sensitive than culture — Confirm positive NAATS with bacterial culture — Prepubertal males, oropharyngeal or anal contact require culture

Syphilis	— Serological blood tests
	  — Positive nontreponemal test: RPR, VDRL, ART
	— Positive nontreponemal tests require confirmation with approved treponemal tests
	  — Positive treponemal tests
	  — Fluorescent treponemal antibody
	  — Microhemagglutination test for *T. pallidum*

HPV	— Usually made by appearance on physical examination — Virus type can be determined, but identification of virus type does not differentiate sexual from nonsexual transmission
***Trichomonas* infection**	— Microscopic identification by wet mount — Bacterial culture of vaginal secretions — Must differentiate from other types of Trichomonas organisms if identified in urine or stool — New NAATs method available — Point of care vaginal swab

(continued)

Table 6-2. Laboratory Investigations for STIs in the Evaluation of Sexually Abused Children

SEXUALLY TRANSMITTED INFECTION	DIAGNOSTIC TEST
HSV	— Usually made by appearance on physical examination — Virus can be cultured early scraping base of fresh vesicle — Virus type can be determined, but identification of virus type does not differentiate sexual from nonsexual transmission
HIV	Serologic blood tests — EIA — If EIA is positive: Western blot or immunofluorescence antibody test is used for confirmation
Bacterial vaginosis	Diagnosis made clinically by presence of 3 of following symptoms or signs: — Homogeneous gray or white discharge on examination — Vaginal fluid pH > 4.5 — Positive amine test: mixing vaginal fluid with 10% potassium hydroxide results in a fishy odor — Presence of "clue cells": vaginal epithelial cells massively coated with coccobacilli — Bacterial culture
Hepatitis B	Serologic blood tests — Hepatitis B surface antigen (HBsAg) detects acutely or chronically infected individuals — Anti-HBc identifies individuals with acute past HBV infection; — Is not present after immunization

Abbreviations: automated regain test (ART), enzyme immunoassay (EIA), hepatitis B virus (HBV), human immunodeficiency virus (HIV), human papillomavirus (HPV), herpes simplex virus (HSV), ligase chain reaction (LCR), nucleic acid amplification tests (NAAT), polymerase chain reaction (PCR), rapid plasma regain test (RPR), Venereal Disease Research Laboratory (VDRL).

Table 6-3. Treatment Options for STIs in Children

Organism	Treatment Options*
Gonorrhea[†] Uncomplicated vulvovaginitis, cervicitis, urethritis, proctitis, or pharyngitis	— Prepubertal children who weigh <45kg: ceftriaxone 125 mg IM in a single dose. Children and adolescents who weigh> 45 kg and are 8 years old or older: ceftriaxone 250 mg IM in a single dose plus azithromycin 1 g orally or doxycycline 100 mg bid x 7 days
Chlamydia Uncomplicated genital tract infection	— Prepubertal children: erythromycin base 50 mg/kg orally in divided doses for 14 days (maximum daily dose 2 g) or azithromycin 20 mg/kg orally as a single dose (maximum 1 g) — Child >45 kg azithromycin 1 g po x1 — Adolescents: doxycycline 100 mg orally twice daily for 7 days or azithromycin 1 g orally as a single dose
Syphilis	— Primary, secondary, and early latent disease in children: benzathine penicillin G 50000 U/kg IM in a single dose (not to exceed the adult dose of 2.4 million U) — Late latent syphilis in children: benzathine penicillin G 50000 U/kg IM weekly for 3 weeks (not to exceed the adult dose of 7.2 million U)
Trichomonas **infection**	— Prepubertal children: metronidazole 15 mg/kg orally in 3 divided doses for 7 days (maximum daily dose 2 g) — Adolescents: metronidazole 2 g orally as a single dose or 250 mg 3 times a day for 7 days
HPV	— Consultation with a dermatology specialist is recommended — Laser or surgical ablation — Spontaneous remission does occur

(continued)

Table 6-3. Treatment Options for STIs in Children *(continued)*

ORGANISM	TREATMENT OPTIONS*
HSV	— Consultation with an infectious disease specialist is recommended — Acyclovir 80 mg/kg/day divided 4 times a day for 7 to 10 days — Other antivirals
HIV	— Consultation with an infectious disease specialist is recommended
Bacterial vaginosis	— Metronidazole 1 g orally in 2 divided doses for 7 days or 15 mg/kg/day 3 times a day for 7 days
Hepatitis B	— No specific therapy for acute HBV infection is available

*Drug dosages recommended by Pickering LK, Baker CJ, Kimberlin DW, eds. Red Book: 2012 Report of the Committee on Infectious Diseases. 29th ed. Elk Grove Village, IL: American Academy of Pediatrics; 2012.

‡Patients should also receive concurrent treatment for presumptive chlamydial infection.

Adapted from Centers for Disease Control and Prevention. Sexually transmitted diseases treatment guidelines, 2010. MMWR Recomm Rep. 2010;59(RR12):1-110.

Adapted from Papp JR, Schachter J, Gaydos CA, Van Der Pol B. Recommendations for the laboratory-based detection of Chlamydia trachomatis and Neisseria gonorrhoeae – 2014. MMWR Recomm Rep. 2014;63(RR02):1-19.

CHLAMYDIA TRACHOMATIS

— Bacterial agent, obligate intracellular parasite with multiple variants

— Currently the most common reportable STI in the United States; highest rates are in sexually active adolescents and young adults (15-24 years age group)

— Infants acquire via vertical transmission, with 50% to 75% of children of infected women becoming infected usually with conjunctivitis or pneumonia

— Incubation period variable (at least a week)

— Sites: conjunctiva, nasopharynx, rectum, vagina

— If not perinatally acquired, considered a marker for sexual abuse because no evidence supports a postnatal nonsexual acquisition

— Symptoms/signs: rectal and vaginal cases are often asymptomatic in children; epididymitis, urethritis, and vaginitis noted in postpubertal individuals; women may have pelvic inflammatory disease, ectopic pregnancy, or infertility

— Diagnosed by history, physical examination, and laboratory findings. NAATs first catch urine or vaginal swabs for vaginal or urethral infection. Tissue culture is not as sensitive. Self-collected rectal swabs and site-specific swabs for oropharyngeal exposure for NAATs are more sensitive and specific than culture but not approved by the FDA as yet.

— Recommend annual screening for sexually active women < 25 years and for older women at increased risk of infection, eg, those with a new sex partner, multiple, or concurrent partners and those with partners with STIs.

NEISSERIA GONORRHOEAE
— Gram-negative diplococcus

— Second most common sexually transmitted infection, often coexisting with *Chlamydia trachomatis*

— Acquired vertically by newborn infant; when found in prepubertal children beyond the newborn period, strongly consider sexual abuse

— Usually affects eye but can involve disseminated disease and result in bacteremia, meningitis, endocarditis, or arthritis

— Transmission occurs from intimate contact with the organism found in secretions of infected mucosal surfaces; survives up to 24 hours on toilet seats and towels but is very susceptible to drying and cool temperatures, making transmission from fomites unlikely.

— Signs/symptoms: children are usually symptomatic, having vaginal discharge; adolescents can have more ascending disease, such as Fitz-Hugh-Curtis syndrome (perihepatitis) or be asymptomatic.

— Diagnosis is based on NAATs (urine) or bacterial culture. Culture requires endocervical (women) or urethral (men) swabs, and NAATs can be performed on urine or above swabs. Grams stain of urethral secretions in infected males is sensitive and specific when polymorphonuclear leukocytes and gram-negative intracellular diplococci are seen.

— Recommend annual testing of sexually active women < 25, older high-risk women, and high-risk males (MSM).

HUMAN IMMUNODEFICIENCY VIRUS (HIV)

— A cytotrophic retrovirus that causes acquired immunodeficiency syndrome (AIDS) and is found in 2 types; type 1 is the most common in the United States.

— Transmission by 4 means: vertical, breastfeeding, percutaneous or mucous membrane exposure to infected blood or body fluids, or sexual contact

— Signs/symptoms: in children include failure to thrive, generalized lymphadenopathy, hepatomegaly, splenomegaly, diarrhea, oral candidiasis, central nervous system (CNS) disease, cardiomyopathy, hepatitis, and recurrent invasive infections; opportunistic infections are common

— Consider testing for HIV in the following circumstances:

1. The perpetrator has known HIV infection or known risk factors for HIV infection

2. The victim has had multiple assailants, another STI, a history of vaginal or rectal penetration, or known risk factors for HIV infection

3. The child/adolescent or parent requests testing

— The initial testing is a screening test, and being as the test needs follow-up, a referral to the victim's personal physician is indicated.

— Tests must be repeated at 6 weeks and 3 and 6 months after the initial visit.

— Arrange for pretest and posttest counseling.

SYPHILIS

— Caused by a thin, mobile spirochete, *Treponema pallidum*

— Incidence has increased, with neonates and children affected to a degree similar to that found in adults.

— Common in men who have sex with men; recent increase in adult females

— Transmitted to children in utero (congenital syphilis) or through intimate contact (acquired syphilis); *T. pallidum* is fragile and survives only briefly outside the host

— Signs/symptoms: at birth, infected infants may or may not show signs of disease, but these may occur after as long as 2 years and include hepatosplenomegaly, snuffles, lymphadenopathy, rash, and hemolytic anemia; after age 2 years, late manifestations may develop (40% of untreated cases), involving the CNS, bones, teeth, skin, and eyes; symptoms occur in 3 stages:

1. Primary syphilis: 1 or multiple indurated painless ulcers or chancres at the site of inoculation and lasting 1 to 5 weeks

2. Secondary syphilis: generalized maculopapular rash of the palms and soles, with condyloma lata (flat, gray-white coalescent papular lesions of the vulva or anus) possible

3. Latent period and then tertiary syphilis, which involves dermal and cardiovascular manifestations

— Diagnosed by serologic testing, with definitive diagnosis by microscopic darkfield examination of the primary chancre

— Testing may be done for the following situations:

1. Child has evidence of other STIs

2. Adolescent victim

3. Child lives with a family member or the perpetrator who has syphilis

4. Child lives in an area with a high incidence of syphilis

5. Infant of mother with active syphilis

HERPES SIMPLEX VIRUSES (HSVs)

— Double-stranded DNA viruses that occur in 2 types, with HSV-1 usually involving the face and skin above the waist and HSV-2 the genitalia and skin below the waist; however, either type may be found in either location

— Transmitted to infants during birth through an infected maternal genital tract or by ascending infection; may also be transmitted post-natally from a caregiver via nongenital contact; transmitted to children via contact with infected lesions either sexually or nonsexually

— Signs/symptoms: for newborns, localized CNS disease, disseminated disease, or localized skin disease; for children and infants beyond the neonatal period, genital herpes involves tender vesicular or ulcerative lesions of the genitalia, perineum, or both plus systemic symptoms (fever, malaise) and tender inguinal adenopathy

— Diagnosed by visual inspection of the lesions and confirmed by cell culture and serology (acute and convalescent serum drawn 30 days apart). Both type-specific virologic and type-specific serologic tests for HSV are currently available.

TRICHOMONAS INFECTION

— Caused by *Trichomonas vaginalis*, a flagellated protozoa; common STI in adolescents and adults but uncommon in prepubertal girls beyond the first few weeks of life due to the hostile vaginal environment of this age group

— Acquired during birth or through sexual contact in adults; therefore, the presence in a prepubertal girl is strongly suspicious for sexual abuse

— Signs/symptoms: may be asymptomatic; in infants, a vaginal discharge; in prepubertal girls, vaginitis; in adolescent and adult females, a pale yellow or green vaginal discharge, vulvovaginal itching, dysuria or abdominal pain; in infected males, urethritis, epididymitis, or prostatitis

— Diagnosis in women is made using NAATs from vaginal, endocervical, or urine specimens. The OSOM Trichomonas Rapid Test at point of care specimens is specific (97%-100%) and sensitive (82%-95%). Culture can also be done on vaginal swabs.

HUMAN PAPILLOMAVIRUS (HPV) INFECTION

— A nonenveloped, icosahedral, double-stranded DNA virus comprising over 100 virus types, at least 40 of which can infect the genital area.

— Signs/symptoms: anogenital warts in adults and children (condylomata acuminata), associated with itching, burning with urination, pain, or bleeding

1. May range from clinically unapparent infection to obvious symptoms

2. Males have lesions on the shaft of the penis, urethral meatus, scrotum, or perianal area.

3. Females have lesions on the labia and perianal area and less commonly in the vagina and cervix.

— Among adults, almost exclusively transmitted sexually, but children may acquire vertically or perinatally, through digital autoinoculation or heteroinoculation, via fomites or casual contact, or through sexual abuse

— Diagnosis must be based on history as well as clinical findings:

1. Check for history of cutaneous warts in caregivers or maternal history of genital warts or abnormal Papanicolaou (Pap) smears.

2. Do complete forensic interview and physical examination of the child to help determine if the HPV infection was acquired via sexual or nonsexual contact.

3. Confirmation is made with tissue biopsy, but biopsy is only required when the diagnosis is in doubt.

— Because evidence supports a link between anogenital HPV infection and anogenital neoplasm, regular follow-up on a long-term basis is recommended.

— Vaccine is available for females 9 to 26 years of age and boys at 13-21 years of age, can be administered regardless of previous history of HPV, and may prevent most neoplastic disease.

Bacterial Vaginosis

— An abnormal condition of the vagina characterized by a shift in the vaginal flora from the normally predominant *Lactobacillus* to an overgrowth of *Gardnerella vaginalis*, *Mycoplasma hominis*, and anaerobic bacteria

— Signs/symptoms: vaginal discharge that is nonviscous, homogeneous, white, and malodorous (fishy) without abdominal pain, dysuria, or significant pruritus; may also be asymptomatic

— Transmission is controversial but its presence should prompt testing for other sexually transmitted pathogens.

— Diagnosis of Gardnerella vaginalis by bacterial culture

— Diagnosed on clinical grounds based on the presence of 3 of the following 4 symptoms or signs (Amsel's criteria):

1. Homogeneous gray or white discharge

2. Vaginal fluid pH over 4.5

3. Positive amine test

4. Presence of vaginal epithelial cells that appear moth eaten or massively coated with coccobacilli on gram stain ("clue cells")

5. Diagnosed by clinical presentation correlated by Gram stain. Other tests include Affirm VP 111 (Becton Dickinson, Sparks, MD), a DNA hybridization probe test for high concentrations of Gardnerella vaginalis, and the OSOM BVBlue test (Sekisui Diagnostics).

Hepatitis B (HBV) Infection
— Caused by a DNA-containing hepadenovirus

— Transmitted through blood or body fluids, including semen, cervical secretions, and saliva; may be transmitted through infusion of blood or blood products, percutaneous or mucous membrane exposure to blood or body fluids, or sexual activity; mother-to-infant transmission occurs to infants born to hepatitis B-infected mothers; when prevalence of HBV is high, horizontal transmission during early childhood is possible

— Signs/symptoms: range from asymptomatic to nonspecific (anorexia or malaise) to clinical hepatitis with jaundice; about 10% of individuals develop chronic infection, which increases the risk of chronic liver disease or primary hepatocellular carcinoma

— Diagnosis based on serologic antigen tests for the hepatitis B surface antigen; incubation period is 45 to 120 days, so testing should be repeated 3 and 6 months after exposure

— When found in a child beyond the perinatal period, should prompt suspicion for sexual abuse

— Hepatitis B vaccine in childhood can prevent the infection.

SEXUAL ABUSE IN BOYS AND MALE ADOLESCENTS

Understanding the cultural norms of masculine gender socialization is the first task to pursue when evaluating issues specific to sexually abused boys and male adolescents.

— One of the core moves in male development is the movement away from the feminine.

— If the abuse occurs at the hands of a male perpetrator, the boy faces having to disclose participating in a homosexual act while avoiding homosexuality as an overriding concern of the "Boy Code"; thus, he often hides the truth.

— Incidence rates of sexual abuse among males range from 4% to 16% or higher.

— Understanding the types of acts that happen to a boy and being able to discuss this information frankly in front of the boy or adolescent who has experienced the activity is important in beginning care. Types of abuse include the following:

    — Noncontact interactions: exhibitionism, masturbation in front of the boy, asking the boy to expose himself, verbally or visually stimulating the boy sexually via pornography

    — Contact interactions: in addition to the obvious (deep kissing, sexualized touch, manual-genital contact, orogenital contact, oroanal contact, anal penetration, or vaginal penetration), contact interactions do not necessarily involve actual touching of the skin but may include any noncontact interaction that culminates in the perpetrator touching the boy's genitals or other eroticized body parts through clothing

Because boys are unlikely to disclose abuse, a screening strategy is important to identify abuse histories and manage them clinically. Steps to consider are as follows:

— Create an environment that demonstrates willingness to consider male sexual abuse as a common reality, eg, by providing reading material in the waiting room.

— Employ direct, verbal screening within the safety of a private clinical interaction; do not use a paper screening form.

— Provide an explanatory and normalizing introduction to all abuse- and/or violence-related screening questions.

— Recognize that the boy may prefer silence and nondisclosure.

— Ask screening questions at each visit.

If the boy and/or male adolescent discloses an abusive history in response to screening:

— The provider's first response should be a nonjudgmental, validating, empowering, and advocating comment or series of comments. Examples are as follows:

1. "I think you are a brave person to have told me what you did. It's like what a superhero would do, and I'm particularly glad you did because I can help you."

2. "I'm sorry this happened to you."

3. "It was not your fault."

4. "I'm here to help you."

5. "It's my job, along with your family member, [family member's name], to make sure that you are safe from now on."

These initial comments affirm the boy's decision to tell and the provider's willingness to help and they provide a supportive environment.

— The boy may experience extreme ambivalence with fear, regret, anticipation, exhilaration, worry, loss, relief, happiness that someone finally knows, and anxiety about the future. These feelings may manifest as bodily symptoms: tachycardia, sweating, dizziness, or blushing.

— If the boy is uncomfortable, proceed with simple questions concerning other topics, staying attuned to reported changes in all areas of the boy's life that may raise red flags for abuse or its aftermath.

— When you return to the topic of abuse, acknowledge the boy's feelings and reassure him to initiate a sense of trust.

— Establish common ground with regard to the use of names for different body parts. It is also possible to show the boy anatomical dolls or draw pictures and use these guides for him to explain what happened.

— Remember that the process of disclosure often occurs in stages and be patient.

— Keep the focus on acknowledging the boy's experience and exhibit empathy without visible emotion.

— Be aware that females may also be perpetrators and be sensitive to this possibility.

— Make it clear that you are required by law to report known sexual abuse of a minor. Any plan for reporting must ensure the safety of the boy and allow no further abuse to occur.

— An examination is an important component of the evaluation of sexual abuse. Guidelines include the following:

1. Have both male and female providers available from which the victim may choose.

2. If you are not prepared to complete this part of the assessment, refer the patient to a site where the needed expertise is available.

3. Broadly describe what he will experience at the specialty site.

4. Keep a sexual assault examination kit available.

5. Refer the boy to a therapist with expertise in treating sexually abused boys as well as girls.

— If you must refer the boy elsewhere, assure him that he can and should continue to see you after he receives care at the other site. It is also helpful to mention the individuals who will complete the examination there.

— Family members/parents of the sexually abused boy play an important role (**Table 6-4**).

Table 6-4. Recommendations for Parents/Family Members of Sexually Abused Boys

DO NOT

1. Pry into physically intimate details of experience, but be fully accepting of these details should victim choose to divulge them.

2. Ask questions that begin with "Why?" These can easily be misconstrued as blaming questions.

3. Minimize the gravity of what has happened, such as making jokes about abuse events.

4. Encourage threats of revenge against perpetrator. Victim may worry about the safety of those exacting revenge, and threats may affect legal remedies.

5. Seek the "remedy" of distraction, or "taking his mind off it." The victim should be the one to request distraction. However, distraction should not be the primary mode of resolving abuse history.

6. Assume that because the victim is quiet, stoic, and seemingly unharmed by the abuse that he is not upset, angry, hurt, confused, and in other ways harmed by the abuse.

7. Take personally increased concerns by the male victim surrounding communication about either the event, the confusion after the event, or even generalizing this to all things in the relationship. He may be establishing boundaries.

8. Become demeaning if school performance declines. Inform school personnel on a "need to know" basis and then only with discussion about this with victim.   *(continued)*

Table 6-4. Recommendations for Parents/Family Members of Sexually Abused Boys *(continued)*

Do

1. Allow victim to talk about details he would like to talk about.

2. Reassure him that he isn't responsible for what happened, you don't blame him, and you don't think that he is weak. At the same time, encourage discussion of self-blaming beliefs and other self-doubts.

3. Be careful about attempts to reduce tension (humor that reflects one's own discomfort is inappropriate).

4. Respect victim's wishes with regard to disclosure. He should determine, when possible, who is and is not told, how, when, why, and so forth.

5. Remind family and friends to be careful in comments they make that could be understood, misunderstood, or purposefully meant to imply blame.

6. Remind family/friends that the victim has privacy needs. At the same time, don't isolate the victim because this can confirm beliefs he is damaged.

7. Be careful about how the victim is "protected." Disclosure can be regretted if it leads to restrictive rules having more to do with fears than real threats. Encourage him to resume his normal life.

8. Be aware of behavioral change, such as loss of appetite, withdrawal, sleep disturbance, fears of being alone or being touched, excessive crying, bedwetting, sexual preoccupations, or alcohol and drug use, that may indicate difficulties victim is unable to articulate.

Adapted from McEvoy AW, Rollo D, Brookings JB. If He Is Raped: A Guidebook for Parents, Partners, Spouses, and Friends. *Holmes Beach, FL: Learning Publications, Inc; 1999.*

DISABILITY AND SEXUAL VIOLENCE

The child or adult with a disability is a special patient when sexual assault is the concern. Often disclosure of the event is delayed or expressed behaviorally or with physical evidence rather than orally. As in the case of victims without disabilities, the most likely offender is known to the victim. The largest offenders of the developmentally delayed are caretakers (28%), natural and stepfamily members (19%), neighbors and friends (15%), babysitters (9.8%), and dates (3.8%).

WHY ABUSE OF THE DISABLED OCCURS

— Disability-related abuse occurs when the perpetrators withhold needed equipment and assistance to coerce sexual conduct.

— The effects of sexual assault are the same for victims with disabilities as with other patients, although reporting is less likely to be believed or investigated.

— Lack of primary prevention efforts

— Laws protecting the developmentally delayed are vague, inconsistent and inadequate.

— The incidence of abuse and assault among persons with disabilities is significantly higher than in the general population.

— Children may be at higher risk because of the increased burden of care associated with their condition. The presence of a physical or mental disability is a recognized risk for victimization by hate crime.

— Myths that propagate the psychological justification of hate crimes include the following:

1. The *dehumanization* myth: perpetrators may feel their abusive behavior is not really injuring another person because the person with a disability is less than a full member of society.

2. The *damaged merchandise* myth: the individual with a disability is worthless and has nothing to lose.

3. The *feeling no pain* myth: people with disabilities have no feelings or are immune to pain and suffering.

4. The ***disabled menace*** myth: individuals with disabilities are different, unpredictable, and dangerous, promoting fear in others.

5. The ***helpless*** myth: individuals with disabilities are helpless and, therefore, unable to take care of themselves, making them vulnerable to abuse and manipulation.

NURSING HOME AND GROUP HOME RESIDENTS

— Sexual abuse and physical abuse allegations of institutionalized persons are not reported promptly and law enforcement personnel are rarely summoned to investigate. Even when allegations are substantiated, minimal disciplinary action occurs, with extremely rare cases leading to criminal prosecution despite severe abuse.

— Often the incidents are witnessed but not reported, or residents informed a family member who did not follow through.

— Examination of a nursing home resident may be hampered by joint contractures, victim resistance because of the pain of the assault, or difficulty communicating with a patient who has dementia and cognitive impairment.

— Nursing home residents are often immunocompromised and may have had minimal sexual experiences. The onset of symptoms (fever, malaise, changes in blood pressure, skin rashes) in a patient suspected to have been abused or assaulted requires a thorough medical assessment.

EVALUATION OF THE CHILD OR ADULT WITH A DISABILITY

If a victim with a disability comes for health care with evidence of severe physical bodily harm and genital trauma, the practitioner must provide a concise but extremely detailed account of both the history as related by the victim and that offered by any other reliable observer. Interviews of multiple caregivers may be required.

— Make a call to law enforcement immediately to secure the crime scene before intentional or unintentional tampering of evidence occurs.

— Obtain verbal evidence from the victim whenever possible, using such aids as photographs of various rooms in the facility, interpreters, or family members or other persons familiar with the disabled victim.

— Document the method and content of any forthcoming disclosure.

— Note any extremely sexually explicit information that is well outside the normal range of the victim's psychosexual development and knowledge.

— Carefully document tactile descriptions and/or sensory information, such as tastes, smells, sounds, made by the perpetrator.

— Be aware that individuals with disabilities are at risk to behave in a more compliant manner than nondisabled individuals in attempts to ensure that they will be liked and included by others. Carefully explore and document all aspects of your interaction.

— Tailor your evaluation to the individual's disability:

1. Hearing-impaired victim: try to obtain a cursory history even if a certified sign language interpreter is not readily available. Even with an interpreter, make eye contact with the victim and follow the standard method of interviewing (build rapport, allow free association conversation, then embark on the sexual assault history). Review the behaviors of the victim with a supportive family member or care provider as well as with the victim.

2. Visually impaired victim: be aware that most of the data will be nonvisual sensory information. Details such as time of day or place of assault will require greater explanation, proceeding in a step-by-step fashion. Children and adolescents with visual impairment may also have language delay. Screen the child for language concepts and ensure that the child is responding reliably, consistently, and with expressive understanding. Tactile defensiveness is a common response in multiply impaired individuals after a sexual assault; it should not be assumed that no sexual assault could have occurred based on this behavior.

3. Cognitively or behaviorally impaired victim: be aware that nonverbal documentation may constitute the essence of the history, requiring the assistance of a care provider who is familiar with the habits and behaviors of the victim. The change in behavior is the

most important time line event. Among the behavioral changes being observed are the following:

— Irrational fearfulness of a person, place, or object

— Emotional liability

— Problems with arousal, such as hypersomnolence or insomnia

— Changes in activity level, eg, hyperactive or withdrawn

— Distractibility

— Angry outbursts

— Separation anxiety behaviors

— Increased masturbation

— Sexualized behaviors

4. Motor-impaired victim: depending on the etiology of the motor delay, cognition may be spared, with the exception of the traumatic brain injury victim, who may have significant gaps in motor, cognitive, and behavioral function. A family member or individual accustomed to the victim's communication style is invaluable to assist in understanding what is being communicated.

Interview Techniques

— Once a rapport has been established, frame questions with a certain topic, enabling the victim to focus on specific facts.

— Once the individual has described various locations in or around the scene of the crime, specify that you want to discuss "the place where you got hurt, at school."

— Be aware that redundancy in questioning for children and adults with disabilities increases the chance that both examiner and victim will be talking consistently about the same thing at the same time.

— Talk slowly and choose your words carefully. Clarify what terms the victim uses for anatomic parts of the body.

— Use simple picture board symbols or allow the victim to draw what happened.

— Allow the victim to describe the perpetrator within the context, for example, "the man who always takes us to the lunchroom."

— Consider a gradual approach to seeking information.

— Perform a brief test of mental status and short-term memory as part of the evaluation.

— Ask questions about daily routines to encourage free association conversation in building rapport.

PHYSICAL EXAMINATION

— Examinations in institutionalized settings may be very difficult and require sedation to complete evidence collection. Examination under anesthesia is also an option.

— If it is necessary to move the victim to another facility for the physical examination, be aware that several barriers may limit access for the victim with a disability and make adjustments or accommodations as required.

— Note that disabled women are less likely to have regular pelvic examinations than other women and provide for dignified and independent access to the examination.

1. Make accommodations to avoid injury to the staff or victim during transfer onto the examination table.

2. Ask women what would make the examination more comfortable and respond accordingly.

— A more comfortable examination experience can be achieved by considering the following:

1. Positioning of the patient's legs

2. Warming the temperature of the room and table

3. Positioning the table in a 45-degree angle to avoid pulmonary compromise

4. Administering oxygen

5. Examining the patient on a bed rather than a firm examination table if that is desired

6. Employing extra personnel to assist with the examination

— Use a rape kit to collect evidence and consider the possibility of the victim having acquired an STI.

— Violence associated with sexual assault requires close surveillance for head and neck injury, facial trauma, and other bodily injuries. Be very thorough, as if examining a young child, to be assured of discovering every affected site.

DNA Testing
A DNA result falls into 1 of the 3 categories:

1. Inclusion: the DNA profile of a known individual matches the DNA profile from the crime scene.

2. Exclusion: there is no DNA match between the suspect and the crime scene.

3. Inconclusive: DNA testing did not produce information that would allow the individual to be either included or excluded as the source of the biological evidence.

Sexual Assault and Homicide
Generally the cause of death in a homicide of a disabled child or youth is strangulation, often associated with blunt trauma to the head and/or stabbing. Other findings are as follows:

— Severe tearing through the vagina, rectum, or both in children

— Less severe genital trauma in youths, with abrasions, superficial lacerations, or contusions at the introitus of the vagina, usually the 6 o'clock position; bruising of the inner thighs; and bite marks on the breasts

— Anal injuries are generally minor and on the anal verge.

— Seminal deposits may be noted on the perineum, perianal area, and the thighs; these are nonspecific but require further analysis.

— Preexisting medical problems often contribute to the victim's death.

Multidisciplinary Considerations
— A team decision-making process is indicated, particularly when the victim has a disability.

— The sexual assault response team (SART) is composed of specially trained sexual assault investigators, a sexual assault nurse examiner (SANE), and possibly a prosecutor with advanced training in sexual assault cases.

— With a nonverbal or verbal child victim, review of custody or other extenuating concerns that might support a coerced or spontaneous false allegation should be considered. If it is discounted, it lends support to the credibility of the final decision.

— All should be documented in the medical record, according to jurisdictional considerations.

— In an institutional setting, the caregiver histories may be contaminated; law enforcement questioning is important to determine what is rumor and what acts actually occurred.

— The most important factors to be documented for legal considerations in a case involving a sexual assault survivor are as follows:

1. The child's method and content of disclosure

2. A history of changes in the child's behavior

3. Physical examination findings, including the child's behavior during the examination

— Establish that you are a health care professional and the encounter is a check-up. Document that the patient expresses the understanding that he or she is present to "see the doctor and make sure that their body is all right."

— Establish that the victim is competent to give a medical history; this is possible if the person's cognitive developmental level is at least age 4 years or is an adult capable of self-care and has mastered activities of daily living.

— Gather information from a familiar care provider regarding the child's or the youth's short-term and long-term memory, reliability to recount normal facts, and expressive and receptive language abilities.

— Recognize the importance of the social worker's role in the emergency room setting; he or she can offer information regarding the victim's functional levels and language comprehension, allowing the practitioner to craft appropriate questions.

— Note if sexually explicit language is used in describing events, which indicates environmental exposure of a chronic nature or sexual experiences that have been explained in this way.

— Note the individual's behavior (as listed earlier).

— Address the issue of consent:

1. Includes not just volition but also the victim's ability to understand the nature of the sexual act and its consequences.

2. Without confirmation of an understanding of these areas, the individual cannot satisfy the legal criteria for distinguishing between a consensual sex act and sexual abuse.

— Be aware that competency to testify in court has legal ramifications and includes the following 4 factors:

1. A present understanding of the difference between a truth and a lie as well as an indication that the person feels compelled to speak the truth

2. The mental capacity at the time of the event to observe or receive accurate impressions of the event

3. Memory sufficient to retain an independent recollection of the observations

4. The capacity to communicate into words that memory and to understand questions about the event

References

1. American Academy of Pediatrics. Bacterial vaginosis. In: Pickering LK, Baker CJ, Kimberlin DW, eds. *Red Book: 2012 Report of the Committee on Infectious Diseases.* 29th ed. Elk Grove Village, IL: American Academy of Pediatrics; 2012:149-150.

2. American Academy of Pediatrics. Hepatitis B. In: Pickering LK, Baker CJ, Kimberlin DW, eds. *Red Book: 2012 Report of the Committee on Infectious Diseases.* 29th ed. Elk Grove Village, IL: American Academy of Pediatrics; 2012:369-390.

3. American Academy of Pediatrics. Human immunodeficiency virus infection. In: Pickering LK, Baker CJ, Kimberlin DW, eds. *2012 Red Book: Report of the Committee on Infectious Diseases*. 29th ed. Elk Grove Village, IL: American Academy of Pediatrics; 2012:418-439.

4. Bagley C, Bolitho F, Bertrand L. Mental health profiles, suicidal behavior, and community sexual assault in 2112 Canadian adolescents. *Crisis*. 1995;16(3):126-131.

5. Bays J, Chadwick D. Medical diagnosis of the sexually abused child. *Child Abuse Negl*. 1993;17(1):91-110.

6. Boney-McCoy S, Finkelhor D. Prior victimization: a risk factor for child sexual abuse and for PTSD-related symptomatology among sexually abused youth. *Child Abuse Negl*. 1995;19:1401-1421.

7. Centers for Disease Control and Prevention. Sexually transmitted diseases treatment guidelines, 2015. *MMWR Recomm Rep*. 2015;64(3):1-137.

8. Crowe C, Forster GE, Dinsmore WW, Maw RD. A case of acute hepatitis B occurring four months after multiple rape. *Int J STD AIDS*. 1996;7(2):133-134.

9. DiMaio VJM, Dana S. *Handbook of Forensic Pathology*. Austin, TX: Landes Bioscience; 1998.

10. Faller KC. Characteristics of a clinical sample of sexually abused children: how boy and girl victims differ. *Child Abuse Negl*. 1989;13(2):281-291.

11. Federal Bureau of Investigation. *Summary of Hate Crime Statistics*. Washington, DC: Federal Bureau of Investigation; 2000.

12. Finkelhor D, Hotaling G, Lewis IA, Smith C. Sexual abuse in a national survey of adult men and women: prevalence, characteristics, and risk factors. *Child Abuse Negl*. 1990;14(1):19-28.

13. Frasier LD. Human papillomavirus infection in children. *Pediatr Ann*. 1994;23(7):354-360.

14. Gardner M, Jones JG. Genital herpes acquired by sexual abuse of children. *J Pediatr*. 1984;104(2):243-244.

15. Gil E, Johnson C. *Sexualized Children: Assessment and Treatment of Sexualized Children and Children Who Molest.* Rockville, MD: Launch Press; 1993.

16. Groth AN, Burgess AW. Sexual dysfunction during rape. *New Engl J Med.* 1977;297(14):764-766.

17. Girardet RB, Lahoti S, Howard LA, et al. Epidemiology of sexually transmitted infections in suspected child victims of sexual assault. *Pediatrics.* 2009;124(1):79-86.

18. Hammerschlag MR. Chlamydia trachomatis in children. *Pediatr Ann.* 1994;23(3):349-353.

19. Jenny C. Sexually transmitted diseases and child abuse. *Pediatr Ann.* 1992;21(8):497-503.

20. Harrison PA, Fulkerson JA, Beebe TJ. Multiple substance use among adolescent physical and sexual abuse victims. *Child Abuse Negl.* 1997;21(6):529-539.

21. Hernandez JT, Lodico M, DiClemente RJ. The effects of child abuse and race on risk-taking in male adolescents. *J Natl Med Assoc.* 1993;85(8):593-597.

22. Hibbard RA, Ingersoll GM, Orr DP. Behavioral risk, emotional risk, and child abuse among adolescents in a nonclinical setting. *Pediatrics.* 1990;86(6):896-901.

23. Jones JG, Yamauchi T, Lambert B. Trichomonas vaginalis infestation in sexually abused girls. *Am J Dis Child.* 1985;139(8):846-847.

24. Kohan MJ, Pothier P, Norbeck JS. Hospitalized children with history of sexual abuse: incidence and care issues. *Am J Orthopsychiatry.* 1987;57(2):258-264.

25. Levitt CJ. Sexual abuse of boys: a medical perspective. In: Hunter M, ed. *Prevalence, Impact, and Treatment.* Lexington, MA: Lexington Books; 1990:227-240. *The Sexually Abused Male;* vol 1.

26. Lodico MA, Gruber E, DiClemente RJ. Childhood sexual abuse and coercive sex among school-based adolescents in a Midwestern state. *J Adolesc Health.* 1996;18(3):211-217.

27. Lund EM, Vaughn-Jensen JE. Victimisation of children with disabilities. *Lancet.* 2012;380(9845):867-869.

28. MacMillan HL, Fleming JE, Trocmé N, et al. Prevalence of child physical and sexual abuse in the community. results from the Ontario Health Supplement. *JAMA.* 1997;278(2):131-135.

29. McEvoy AW, Rollo D, Brookings JB. *If He Is Raped: A Guidebook for Parents, Partners, Spouses, and Friends.* Holmes Beach, FL: Learning Publications, Inc; 1999.

30. Nagy S, Adcock AG, Nagy MC. A comparison of risky health behaviors of sexually active, sexually abused, and abstaining adolescents. *Pediatrics.* 1994;93(4):570-575.

31. Nelson DE, Higginson GK, Grant-Worley JA. Using the youth risk behavior survey to estimate prevalence of sexual abuse among Oregon high school students. *J School Health.* 1994;64(10):413-416.

32. Nyirjesy P. Vaginitis in the adolescent patient. *Pediatr Clin North Am.* 1999;46(4):733-745, xi.

33. Papp JR, Schachter J, Gaydos CA, Van Der Pol B. Recommendations for the laboratory-based detection of *Chlamydia trachomatis* and *Neisseria gonorrhoeae* – 2014. *MMWR Recomm Rep.* 2014;63(RR02):1-19.

34. Payne B, Cikovic R. An empirical examination of the characteristics, consequences, and causes of elder abuse in nursing homes. *J Elder Abuse Negl.* 1995;7(4):61-74.

35. Pearsall C. Forensic biomarkers of elder abuse: what clinicians need to know. *J Forensic Nurs.* 2005;1(4):182-186.

36. Ramsey-Klawsnik H, Teaster PB, Mendiondo MS, Marcum JL, Abner EL. Sexual predators who target elders: findings from the first national study of sexual abuse in care facilities. *J Elder Abuse Negl.* 2008;20(4):353-376.

37. Risin LI, Koss MP. The sexual abuse of boys: prevalence and descriptive characteristics of childhood victimizations. *J Interpers Violence.* 1987;2(3):309-323.

38. Schwarcz SK, Whittington WL. Sexual assault and sexually transmitted diseases: detection and management in adults and children. *Rev Infect Dis.* 1990;12(suppl 6):S682-S690.

39. Shapiro RA, Schubert CJ, Myers PA. Vaginal discharge as an indicator of gonorrhea and Chlamydia infection in girls under 12 years old. *Pediatr Emerg Care.* 1993;9(6):341-345.

40. Siegel JM, Sorenson SB, Golding JM, Burnam MA, Stein JA. The prevalence of childhood sexual assault. The Los Angeles Epidemiologic Catchment Area Project. *Am J Epidemiol.* 1987;126(6):1141-1153.

41. Siegel RM, Schubert CJ, Myers PA, Shapiro RA. The prevalence of sexually transmitted diseases in children and adolescents evaluated for sexual abuse in Cincinnati: rationale for limited STD testing in prepubertal girls. *Pediatrics.* 1995;96(6):1090-1094.

42. Sirotnak AP. Testing sexually abused children for sexually transmitted diseases: who to test, when to test, and why. *Pediatr Ann.* 1994;23(7):370-374.

43. Sorenson DD. The invisible victims. *Impact.* Minneapolis, MN: University of Minnesota, Institute on Community Integration (UAP)/Research and Training Center on Community Living; 1997.

44. Speck PM, Hartig MT, Likes W, et al. Case series of sexual assault in older persons. *Clin Geriatr Med.* 2014;30(4):779-806.

45. Starling SP. Syphilis in infants and young children. *Pediatr Ann.* 1994;23(7):334-340.

46. Tharinger D, Horton B, Millea S. Sexual abuse and exploitation of children and adults with mental retardation and other handicaps. *Child Abuse Negl.* 1990;14(3):301-312.

Chapter 7

MULTIDISCIPLINARY TEAMWORK ISSUES

Eileen Allen, MSN, RN, FN-CSA, SANE-A, SANE-P*
Angelo P. Giardino, MD, PhD
Eileen R. Giardino, PhD, RN, CRNP

For victims of sexual assault or abuse, the event often triggers the need for a wide range of services. Since the late 1980s those who provide care and services to sexual assault patients have attempted to coordinate their response, in part, to decrease the initial repetition of questions, explanations, and interactions between the patient and strangers. This coordination process has evolved into the multidisciplinary team (MDT) model for interactions with children and the sexual assault response team (SART) model for interactions with adolescent and adult patients.

In cases of suspected child sexual abuse, the health care provider who conducts the evaluation is responsible for identifying and reporting the suspected abuse and completing an accurate medical evaluation, including history, physical examination, and collection of laboratory specimens. A multidisciplinary team is involved, with collaboration required to provide medical treatment and make appropriate referrals for the child and family for services such as mental health counseling and social services. In addition, medical, mental health and social services professionals are often required to interact with Child Protective Services (CPS) agencies and law enforcement personnel. The roles, goals, and perspectives of each professional are unique, and yet to effectively benefit the patient, collaborative communication and interactions are essential.

Revised Chapter 7 for the second edition.

In cases of sexual assault of adolescents, adults, and elders, many communities have adopted a SART model. Nurses and physicians with specialized education in the forensic aspects of health care for sexual assault patients are recognized as sexual assault forensic examiners (SAFEs). They are responsible for documenting the medical history and history of the incident, developing a plan of care, performing forensic medical evaluations, documenting findings, providing treatment, and referring patients to follow-up care, as needed. SAFEs also collaborate with sexual violence advocates and law enforcement personnel to form SARTs, which operate using a victim-centered approach to coordinated care and service. It is essential that SART members understand and respect the goals and role boundaries of each team member, in order to meet the needs of the patient while accomplishing the objectives of their individual roles.

— Benefits of teamwork:

1. Improved information sharing among clinicians and other professionals

2. Joint decision making and planning

3. Collaborative educational approaches

4. Mutual support

— Interdisciplinary teams share responsibility for collecting and processing components of patient and family evaluations. Formal protocols at the state, local, or organizational level are helpful in addressing specific details of these shared responsibilities. Important aspects include:

1. Clarity in the roles and responsibilities of each agency

2. Delineation of steps that must be accomplished at each stage of the process

3. Explicit declaration of time frames essential for completing each stage

4. Assignment of responsibility for each step

5. Practical advice for handling both routine and special circumstances

— When handling conflict among individuals and agencies:

1. Be aware that team success is measured by the effectiveness with which conflict is resolved rather than the amount of conflict produced.

2. Quickly address less important, peripheral issues and focus attention on more important, central issues that require discussion and resolution.

3. Deal with conflict constructively, keeping the focus on the purpose outlined in the group's mission statement (**Table 7-1**).

Table 7-1. Dealing With Team Conflict

— Be respectful and consider all points of view. Listen to one another and make sure each position is understood. Restate each position in your own words.

— Avoid personalizing your position and stay focused on the issue.

— Offer suggestions rather than mere criticism of other points of view.

— Remember that conflict within a team is natural and work toward mutually agreeable resolutions.

— Stay focused on the team's agreed-upon purpose, and refer to your protocol for guidance.

Reporting Sexual Assault and Abuse

Health care providers are responsible for reporting all cases of suspected sexual abuse of children. State laws have been passed to remove the barriers that keep people from reporting, as follows:

— Immunity for good faith reporting (a person can still be sued in civil court but can claim immunity under this statute)

— Standards to guide reasonable suspicion (concern over possible maltreatment need not be absolutely diagnosed before reporting)

— Rules regarding anonymity of the reporter

— Relaxation of privileged communication rights, such as provider-patient privilege, that would apply in settings other than child maltreatment

— Procedures for reporting and how the information is processed

— Guidelines regarding protective custody for the child, if deemed necessary

— Penalties for failure to report

State statutes may employ various wordings to describe the level of suspicion that requires reporting, eg, cause to believe, reasonable cause to believe, known or suspected abuse, reason to suspect, and observation or examination that discloses evidence of abuse. The overarching intent remains to ensure that health care professionals report suspicions of possible maltreatment when clinical interactions would lead a competent professional to consider child abuse or neglect as a reasonably likely diagnosis or cause to explain the case before them. The primary motivation is to stop further maltreatment and obtain help for the family.

In many jurisdictions, similar reporting responsibilities exist for cases of sexual assault involving vulnerable adults. Depending on local or state statutes, this population may include certain elders, developmentally delayed persons, those residing in institutions, and others.

In recent years federal regulations such as the Violence Against Women Act have protected the rights of most individuals seeking services related to sexual assault victimization. Specifically victims must be afforded the opportunity to receive health care and social services assistance without mandating police notification. In fact notifying police of a sexual assault disclosed by an adult patient without the patient's consent may be a violation of confidentiality. It is important that health care providers and health care facilities be familiar with local and state laws and regulations related to reporting sexual assault and abuse cases.

COLLABORATIVE INVESTIGATION AND INTERVENTION
CPS
— At state or county level, is usually designated as the responsible governmental entity because of legal mandate; central to reporting, investigation, and treatment related to alleged child sexual abuse

— Lead agency in assessing child and family social service needs, developing intervention strategies that include treatment for child and family, and ongoing follow-up and monitoring of child maltreatment cases until they are closed

— Works with law enforcement to investigate (**Figure 7-1**)

— Works with the courts to determine issues involving custody and parental rights

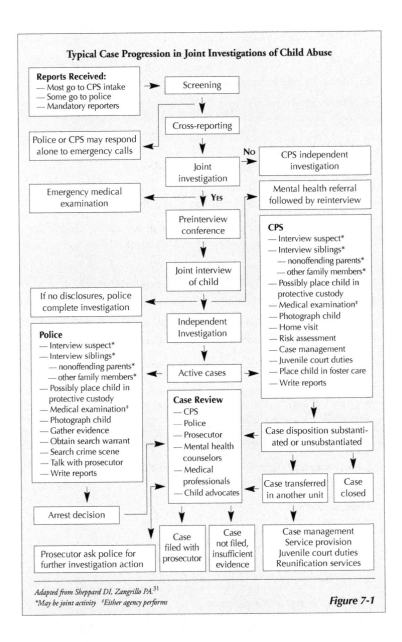

Typical Case Progression in Joint Investigations of Child Abuse

Reports Received:
— Most go to CPS intake
— Some go to police
— Mandatory reporters

Screening

Cross-reporting

Police or CPS may respond alone to emergency calls

Joint investigation — **No** → CPS independent investigation

Yes → Mental health referral followed by reinterview

Emergency medical examination

Preinterview conference

CPS
— Interview suspect*
— Interview siblings*
 — nonoffending parents*
 — other family members*
— Possibly place child in protective custody
— Medical examination‡
— Photograph child
— Home visit
— Risk assessment
— Case management
— Juvenile court duties
— Place child in foster care
— Write reports

Joint interview of child

If no disclosures, police complete investigation

Independent Investigation

Police
— Interview suspect*
— Interview siblings*
 — nonoffending parents*
 — other family members*
— Possibly place child in protective custody
— Medical examination‡
— Photograph child
— Gather evidence
— Obtain search warrant
— Search crime scene
— Talk with prosecutor
— Write reports

Active cases

Case Review
— CPS
— Police
— Prosecutor
— Mental health counselors
— Medical professionals
— Child advocates

Case disposition substantiated or unsubstantiated

Case transferred in another unit

Case closed

Arrest decision

Case filed with prosecutor

Case not filed, insufficient evidence

Case management
Service provision
Juvenile court duties
Reunification services

Prosecutor ask police for further investigation action

Adapted from Sheppard DI, Zangrillo PA.[31]
**May be joint activity ‡Either agency performs*

Figure 7-1

— CPS Process Stages (**Table 7-2**):

1. Intake
2. Initial assessment/investigation
3. Family assessment
4. Case planning
5. Service provision
6. Evaluation of family progress and case closure

LAW ENFORCEMENT AGENCIES

— Become involved because sexual assault and abuse are criminal acts

— Responsible for criminal investigation and are specially trained in conducting interviews, collecting crime scene evidence, and interrogating suspects

— Work with health care providers to interpret information uncovered during investigations

— Conduct a series of interviews with multiple people who may be able to shed light on details related to the abuse situation

— Gather physical evidence and search the crime scene when indicated

— Support CPS in child abuse cases, accompanying them to isolated, potentially dangerous locations

— Provide immediate response to emergency situations

— Enforce standing court orders and may assist in removing children from the home when danger is imminent

— Arrest suspects

SEXUAL VIOLENCE ADVOCATES

— Provide information about choices and options for reporting and seeking medical attention

— Work with other team members to ensure patient is fully informed about her/his rights as a victim of crime

PHASE	DESCRIPTION
Intake	— Receive reports of suspected child sexual abuse — Evaluate reports against statutory and agency guidelines — Determine urgency of response — Educate reporters on state laws, agency guidelines, and CPS functions
Initial assessment/ investigation	Gather sufficient evidence to decide: — If child sexual abuse has occurred — Level of risk for future maltreatment — If child is safe at home — Types of services needed to reduce risk
Family assessment	— Obtain information about nature, extent, and causes of risk — Gain deeper understanding of how abuse occurred — Analyze personal and environmental factors that contributed to abuse
Case planning	— Determine strategies to change conditions and behaviors that resulted in child sexual abuse — Collaborative planning is best when possible — Court often involved
Service provision	— Care plans implemented — CPS arranges, provides, and/or coordinates the delivery of services to child and family
Evaluation of family progress and case closure	Ongoing assessment directed at: — Child's safety — Achievement of treatment goals — Risk reduction

Table 7-2. CPS Process

Adapted from DePanfilis D, Salus MK.[8]

— Accompany patients while at exam location, police station, and to court proceedings

— Offer emotional support in a nonjudgmental manner throughout the exam and interview processes

— Educate patients about psychological impact of sexual assault and availability of crisis intervention and counseling services

MENTAL HEALTH PROFESSIONALS

— Help the patient deal with the short- and long-term impact of sexual abuse

— Assist in the initial evaluation and provide treatment after the assessment

— Provide services in the immediate aftermath of victimization; may also treat patients who delay disclosure for months or years after the incident

— May provide services in the home for children and their families

— Develop a treatment plan to outline supports beneficial to long-term outcomes of sexual assault and abuse

COURT AND JUDICIAL PROCEEDINGS

For many victims, reporting the incident may be their first direct interaction with law enforcement or the legal system. Some adults may have familiarity with parts of the investigative or judicial processes through personal experience with traffic violations, municipal court issues, divorce or custody hearings, etc. For most, knowledge of the actual workings of the criminal court system is limited to the inaccurate depictions on television.

Children become involved with the court system through possible maltreatment; contested custody arrangements within divorce proceedings; adoption issues; suspected offenses, ie, delinquency offenses; or traffic offenses. Rarely is a child called as a witness in a nonabuse-related criminal or civil case. Children require handling that differs from that accorded adults, possibly involving a modification of the court environment to make it more child sensitive, eg, using less complex language, downsizing furniture, or talking directly to the judge.

JUVENILE COURTS

— Exercise power over minors brought into the system because of all forms of child abuse; neglect; abandonment; unwillingness to submit to parental control, ie, incorrigibility; and delinquency

— May ask a child witness to provide factual information that may result in taking the child into state custody

— Two legal doctrines underlie the role of the juvenile court:

1. Parens patriae: government has the authority to step in and limit the parents' authority over their children when the court perceives a danger to the children's physical or mental health.

2. Best interests of the child: government must consider what is reasonably in the child's best interest when deciding if the child should be removed from the care of the parents or be allowed to remain in their care.

— Purposes of the juvenile court with respect to child maltreatment are as follows:

1. Protect the child from further maltreatment and harm

2. Provide services and treatment to the child and family

3. Terminate parental rights

4. Provide permanent placement for the maltreated child

5. Order mental health evaluation of children and parents when needed

— Has broad discretion in addressing issues and invokes judicial authority to facilitate the social welfare system's goal of rehabilitating and treating the abusive family when possible

— Guiding principles are as follows:

1. Children are presumed to lack the mental competency and maturity possessed by adults.

2. The child's caregivers must be shown to be unfit, unable, unwilling, or unavailable to care adequately for the child before the court intervenes.

3. Court intervention may be taken to promote the best interests of the child.

— Judges in juvenile court usually welcome information from CPS caseworkers, psychiatrists, private agency social workers, physiologists, and physicians because their decisions can only be as good as the information at their disposal.

— The 2 roles that the health professional may be asked to assume in the court process are as follows:

1. Provide direct knowledge of information pertinent to the specific case at hand

2. Provide the court with an interpretation of the information that has been offered (expert witness)

CRIMINAL COURT

— Although sexual assault and abuse are crimes in all states, full criminal prosecution may not be possible for various reasons:

1. Juvenile courts were viewed traditionally as the ideal place for handling child abuse and neglect cases because they focus on family needs and the provision of services to the child and family.

2. It is sometimes difficult to prove sexual assault in the criminal court because of constitutional rights regarding evidence afforded defendants.

3. Criminal court is seen as especially threatening and potentially damaging to victims, specifically due to multiple required interviews, inevitable delays that can extend for years, insensitive questioning, and the defendant's right to face-to-face confrontation with the accuser in court.

— The court's proceedings may lead to consequences affecting the victim and the victim's family and community, including the following:

1. Loss of employment

2. Loss of income

3. Disruption or dissolution of the family

4. Incarceration of the accused and potential feeling of guilt on the victim's part

5. If there is an acquittal, designation of the victim by family, friends, and community as a liar

— Reasons for carrying out prosecution include the following:

1. Clearly establishes the perpetrator as solely responsible for the maltreatment

2. Helps to vindicate the victim and establish a sense of fairness while recognizing the innocence of the victim

3. Reduces the risk of further episodes of sexual assault or abuse if the perpetrator is found guilty

4. Establishes a criminal record for the offender

— Health care providers may be asked to participate in 2 ways:

1. Provide direct knowledge of information surrounding the specific case at hand (a fact witness)

2. Provide the court with an interpretation of the information being discussed (an expert witness); this is permitted when the expert is felt to have a broad base of knowledge and expertise in the details concerning sexual assault or abuse situations

— Testifying requires that the health care provider become familiar with the facts of the case as documented in medical records and meet with the attorneys involved to understand the types of questions that may be posed.

— Support for the victim in judicial proceedings include the following:

1. Advocacy centers: help the victim work through what to expect in court and how to deal with the questioning process

2. Provision of a supportive person to accompany the victim to the court and explain what is happening in the proceedings

3. Clarifies that the victim is not judged by his or her performance in the courtroom

IMPACT ON THE VICTIM
— No universal set of responses or uniform impact

— Mental and physical health issues are generally found in long-term assessments of adults with a history of sexual assault.

— Physical health effects:

1. Generally limited impact and treated with standard medical therapies

2. Gastrointestinal disorders, usually functional, include irritable bowel syndrome, nonulcer dyspepsia, and chronic abdominal pain

3. Gynecologic and urologic disorders include chronic pelvic pain, dysmenorrhea, and menstrual irregularities

4. Somatization

— Mental health effects:

1. Symptoms range in severity from mild to severe

2. Course ranges from relatively short-term effects to those which are long-term or even lifelong

3. Internalization versus externalization: some respond by internalizing and suffer depression and withdrawal, while other respond by externalizing and manifest addictions, aggression, and disruptive behaviors

4. Possible impacts include behavioral problems, posttraumatic stress disorder (PTSD), interpersonal difficulties, and cognitive and emotional distortions

5. Adult survivors often have difficulties related to early damaging sexual experiences, including depression, low self-esteem, suicide attempts, multiple personality disorder, school failure, regressive behavior, PTSD, drug and alcohol abuse, running away, sexual promiscuity, prostitution, and delinquent behavior

REFERENCES

1. Baglow LJ. A multidimensional model for treatment of child abuse: a framework for cooperation. *Child Abuse Negl.* 1990;14(3):387-395.

2. Barry DM, Cell PM. *Campus Sexual Assault Response Teams: Program Development and Operational Management.* Kingston, NJ: Civic Research Institute; 2009.

3. Berkowitz CD. Medical consequences of child sexual abuse. *Child Abuse Negl.* 1998;22(6):541-550.

4. Berliner L, Elliott DM. Sexual abuse of children. In: Myers JEB, Berliner L, Briere J, Hendrix CT, Jenny C, Reid TA, eds. *The APSAC Handbook on Child Maltreatment*. 2nd ed. Thousand Oaks, CA: Sage Publications; 2002:55-78.

5. Bulkley JA, Feller JN, Stern P, Roe F. Child abuse and neglect: laws and legal proceedings. In: Briere J, Berliner L, Bulkley JA, Jenny C, Reid T, eds. *APSAC Handbook on Child Maltreatment*. Thousand Oaks, CA: Sage Publications; 1996;271-296.

6. Cage RL, Pence DM. Criminal investigation of child sexual abuse. *Portable Guide to Investigating Child Abuse*. Washington, DC: US Department of Justice; 1997.

7. Crowley SR. *Sexual Assault: The Medical-Legal Examination*. Stamford, CT: McGraw-Hill/Appleton & Lange; 1999.

8. DePanfilis D, Salus MK. *Child Protective Services: A Guide for Caseworkers*. Washington, DC: US Department of Health and Human Services, National Center on Child Abuse and Neglect; 1997.

9. Dubowitz H, DePanfilis D, eds. Handbook for Child Protection Practice. Thousand Oaks, CA: Sage Publications; 2000.

10. Ells M. *Forming a Multidisciplinary Team to Investigate Child Abuse: Portable Guide to Investigating Child Abuse*. Washington, DC: US Department of Justice; 1998.

11. Fargason CA, Barnes D, Schneider D, Galloway BW. Enhancing multi-agency collaboration in the management of child sexual abuse. *Child Abuse Negl*. 1994;18(10):859-869.

12. Finkel MA, Ricci LR. Documentation and preservation of visual evidence in child abuse. *Child Maltreat*. 1997;2(4):322-330.

13. Girardin BW, Faugno DK, Seneski PC, Slaughter L, Whelan M. *Color Atlas of Sexual Assault*. Saint Louis, MO: Mosby; 1997.

14. Golding J. Long-term physical health problems associated with sexual assault history. *The APSAC Advisor*. 2000;13:16-20.

15. Goldner JA, Dolgin CK, Manske SH. Legal issues. In: Monteleone J, ed. *Recognition of Child Abuse for the Mandated Reporter*. 2nd ed. Saint Louis, MO: GW Medical, Inc; 1996:191-210.

16. International Association of Forensic Nurses. *Atlas of Sexual Violence*. Henry T, volume ed. Saint Louis, MO: Elsevier; 2013.

17. Jenny C. *Medical Evaluation of Physically and Sexually Abused Children: The APSAC Study Guide 3*. Thousand Oaks, CA: Sage Publications; 1996.

18. Jenny C. Medical issues in sexual abuse. In: Briere J, Berliner L, Bulkley JA, Jenny C, Reid T, eds. *The APSAC Handbook on Child Maltreatment*. Thousand Oaks, CA: Sage Publications; 1996:195-226.

19. Jenny C. Medical issues in sexual abuse. In: Myers JEB, Berliner L, Briere J, Hendrix CT, Jenny C, Reid TA, eds. *The APSAC Handbook on Child Maltreatment*. 2nd ed. Thousand Oaks, CA: Sage Publications; 2002:235-247.

20. Jenny C, Sutherland SE, Sandahl BB. Developmental approach to preventing the sexual abuse of children. *Pediatrics*. 1986;78(6):1034-1038.

21. Kaplan R, Adams JA, Starling SP, Giardino AP. *Medical Response to Child Sexual Abuse: A Resource for Professionals Working With Children and Families*. Saint Louis, MO: STM Learning, Inc; 2011.

22. Katner D, Plum HJ. Legal issues. In: Giardino AP, ed. *Recognition of Child Abuse for the Mandated Reporter*. 3rd ed. Saint Louis, MO: GW Medical, Inc; 2002:309-350.

23. Kempe CH. Sexual abuse, another hidden pediatric problem: the 1977 C. Anderson Aldrich lecture. *Pediatrics*. 1978;62(3):382-389.

24. Lanning KV. Criminal investigation of sexual victimization of children. In: Myers JEB, Berliner L, Briere J, Hendrix CT, Jenny C, Reid TA, eds. *The APSAC Handbook on Child Maltreatment*. 2nd ed. Thousand Oaks, CA: Sage Publications: 2002:329-347.

25. Lanning KV, Walsh B. Criminal investigation of suspected child abuse. In: Briere J, Berliner L, Bulkley JA, Jenny C, Reid T, eds. *The APSAC Handbook on Child Maltreatment*. Thousand Oaks, CA: Sage Publications; 1996:246-270.

26. Ledrey LE, Burgess AW, Giardino AP. *Medical Response to Adult Sexual Assault: A Resource Guide for Clinicians and Related Professionals*. Saint Louis, MO: STM Learning, Inc; 2011.

27. Myers JEB. Expert testimony. In: Briere J, Berliner L, Bulkley JA, Jenny C, Reid T, eds. *The APSAC Handbook on Child Maltreatment.* Thousand Oaks, CA: Sage Publications; 1996.

28. Pence D, Wilson C. *Team Investigation of Child Sexual Abuse: The Uneasy Alliance.* Thousand Oaks, CA: Sage Publications; 1994.

29. Sgroi SM, ed. *Handbook of Clinical Intervention in Child Sexual Abuse.* Lexington, MA: Lexington; 1982.

30. Sgroi SM, Bunk BS. A clinical approach to adult survivors of child sexual abuse. In: Sgroi SM, ed. *Evaluation and Treatment of Sexually Abused Children and Adult Survivors.* Lexington, MA: Lexington; 1988:137-186. Vulnerable Populations; vol 1.

31. US Department of Justice, Office on Violence Against Women. *A National Protocol for Sexual Assault Medical Forensic Examinations: Adults/Adolescents.* 2nd ed. Washington, DC: US Department of Justice, Office of Violence Against Women; 2013. NCJ 228119. National Criminal Justice Reference Service Web site. https://www.ncjrs.gov/pdffiles1/ovw/241903.pdf. Accessed April 15, 2015.

32. Sheppard DI, Zangrillo PA. Coordinating investigations of child abuse. *Public Welf.* 1996;54:21-31.

33. Wolraich ML, Aceves J, Feldman HM, et al. American Academy of Pediatrics. Committee on Psychosocial Aspects of Child and Family Health. The child in court. *Pediatrics.* 1999;104(5 pt 1):1145-1148.

34. Zellman GL, Faller KC. Reporting of child maltreatment. In: Briere J, Berliner L, Bulkley JA, Jenny C, Reid T, eds. *The APSAC Handbook on Child Maltreatment.* Thousand Oaks, CA: Sage Publications; 1996.

DOCUMENTATION AND REPORTING

Mary J. Spencer, MD, FAAP*
Martin A. Finkel, DO, FACOP, FAAP
Randell Alexander, MD, PhD
J.M. Whitworth, MD

CHILDREN

A standardized forensic medical record is used to record relevant data related to sexual abuse concerns. The format is similar to the medical record used at either office-based or hospital-based practices. Acceptable medical practice dictates that clinicians follow the standard set of assessment parameters used in evaluating any medical condition. In suspected Child Abuse Examinations, the examiner should assume that child protective services (CPS), law enforcement, and defense counsel will review the record; therefore, it must be constructed with exacting attention to detail in anticipation of legal scrutiny. It must:

— Be legible

— Be well constructed

— Be educational

— Contain exact quotations by the child or parent/caretaker

— Contain carefully documented medical history and visual findings

— Construct an accurate diagnosis and treatment recommendations

— Contain defensible conclusions

Revised Chapter 8 for the second edition.

Principles for Documenting the Forensic Interview

— Records of the forensic interview should include questions asked by the interviewer and responses provided by the parent/caretaker and the child, who should be interviewed independently. Questions and answers should be quoted verbatim.

— Questions should be developmentally appropriate, not leading or suggestive, but rather open-ended.

— In many centers, a complete, comprehensive forensic interview is conducted by a licensed, trained forensic interviewer.

— Many centers record the interview on tape, with the child's permission, for later evaluation. The advantage of a taped interview is that it can be played at trial, in addition to the child's testimony.

— Interviews can be observed by investigating law enforcement, child protective services, and at times, district attorneys, in order to conduct one comprehensive interview.

— The child's behavior may be observed during the interview. If any drawings are made during the interview, they should be documented with the date, time, and any relevant description by the child.

The Medical Record

— Serves as the vehicle to formalize a diagnostic assessment for the clinician

— Serves as a tool to inform caseworkers, law enforcement, and the courts

— Generally reviewed in the context of case management discussions in a multidisciplinary team review

Purpose of the Medical Examination

Although the examination and medical report may have investigative value, the purpose of examining a child suspected of being abused is to diagnose and treat any residual consequences of the alleged sexual contact. The medical professional's primary concern is the patient's well-being.

Establishing the Diagnosing and Treating Physician Relationship

— Explain in a developmentally appropriate way that the examination is designed to diagnose and treat the patient.

1. Enhances potential admissibility of the child's medical history under the diagnosing and treating physician's exception to hearsay

2. Allows the clinician to fully explain the basis on which the diagnostic assessment was made

— Allow the child to express any special concerns, and encourage the child to tell the truth.

— Educate parents, colleagues in child protection, mental health professionals, and law enforcement personnel as to the potential medical consequences of sexual abuse and the need to make referrals to diagnostic and treatment services for children suspected of having been sexually abused.

Medical History Documentation

— The medical record must accurately reflect the medical evaluation and stand on its own.

— Diagnosis rests on the interpretation and integration of the following:

1. The medical history

2. Physical examination findings

3. Laboratory test results

— Record all information verbatim.

— The treatment exception for hearsay allows for admissibility of the child's description of symptoms, sensations, or pain associated with the presenting concern.

— The child's description of the cause of the injury or "illness" often provides precise details that would be difficult to explain if the child had not experienced a particular causal event.

— If the child states that the injury or contact was at the hands of a certain individual, explain why the identity of that individual would be important to the diagnosis at hand.

— If the child is too young to verbalize the abuse, or emotionally unavailable to do so, observe and record behavioral changes and emotional state.

— Do not rely on information provided by CPS, law enforcement, or a nonoffending parent as the sole data when formulating a diagnosis.

— Clinicians have been discouraged from speaking to the child on the presumption that the telling will be traumatic for the child or that there may be discrepancies between new information and the initial disclosure, thereby presenting difficulties in prosecution. If discrepancies arise they should be addressed.

— The medical history can often explain or suggest resultant physical findings.

Components of the Medical Record

Historical information in the medical record is usually provided by the parent or caretaker and includes:

— Birth history

— Family history

— Social history

— Parent-child comments and interactions

— Developmental history

— Hospitalizations/emergency room visits

— Surgery

— Medications/allergies

— Review of body systems, with particular attention to genitourinary and gastrointestinal systems

— History obtained from the caretaker regarding the presenting concern

Review of the Genitourinary System

In reviewing the genitourinary (GU) system, include questions concerning the following:

— History of urinary tract infections, vaginal discharges, vaginal odor, vaginal bleeding, diaper dermatitis, or urinary incontinence

— Use of bubble baths

— Treatment for any sexually transmitted infections (STIs)

— Menstrual history

— Use of tampons

— Abortions

— Accidental genital injuries

— Vaginal foreign bodies

— Prior examination of the genitalia for any reason other than routine health care

— Self-exploratory activities/masturbation

Review of the Gastrointestinal System
Review of the gastrointestinal (GI) system should cover the following concerns:

— Age of toilet training and whether there were any difficulties

— Use of rectal suppositories, enemas, or medications for inducing bowel movements

— History of constipation or painful bowel movements

— Frequency and character of stools

— History of recurrent vomiting, diarrhea, blood stools, hemorrhoids, fecal incontinence, rectal itching, or pinworm infestation

Medical History Provided by the Child
Key steps in compiling a legally defensible medical record are as follows:

— Document the child's age at the time of the statements.

— Note the duration of elapsed time between the suspected abuse and the child's statements.

— Specify who was present when the child made the statement, where the statement was made, and to whom it was made.

— Document whether specific statements were made in response to questions or were spontaneous.

— Note whether the child's responses were made to leading or nonleading questions.

— Note if the child's statement was made at the first opportunity that the child felt safe to talk. The child's interview is best undertaken without the presence of the parent/caretaker so the child feels free to talk and often during the physical examination as that system is being examined.

— Document the child's emotional state. Note if the child was excited or distressed when the statement was made and, if so, what signs or symptoms of excitement or distress were observed. It is important to note the child's cooperation, agitation, and behavior during the physical examination.

— Document whether the child was calm, placid, or sleeping before making the statement or soon thereafter.

— Use the exact words that the child used to describe the characteristics of the event.

— Document the child's physical condition at the time of the statement.

— Note any suspected incentives for the child to fabricate or distort the truth.

Recording Physical Examination Findings

— The record should include introductory statements to reflect the purpose for which the examination was undertaken and background information regarding how the child came for an examination.

— Describe the physical appearance of the child, behavior and cooperation, demeanor, and relevant statements made during the examination of the child.

— Include the overall medical condition of the child, general physical examination findings, and describe in meticulous detail the appearance of all genital and anal structures and injuries, including collection of any foreign debris and documentation of bleeding.

— Describe and photograph, with a measuring device, the type, size, color, and shape of each extragenital injury with the child's explanation for the injury.

— Include photographic, colposcopic, or videocolposcopy methods of visual documentation in presenting the case. The use of toluidine blue dye is used an adjuvant in acute cases of sexual contact to detect more obscure injuries.

— Make accurate conclusions when you integrate physical examination findings, laboratory results, and medical history into a diagnostic assessment.

FORMULATING A DIAGNOSIS

— Consider and incorporate the salient aspects of each of the following when formulating a diagnosis:

1. Historical details and behavioral indicators reflective of the contact

2. Symptoms that can be directly associated with the contact

3. Acute and healed genital/anal injuries

4. Extragenital trauma

5. Forensic evidence

6. STIs

— Throughout the diagnostic and treatment process and report writing, remain objective, know the limitations of clinical observation, incorporate differential diagnostic considerations, and formulate a diagnosis in an unbiased manner.

NETWORKS

Formal networks link child abuse physicians to other advanced medical providers and accomplish the following functions, among others:

— Enhance the education of practitioners regarding child abuse and process issues, such as reporting, investigation, and court procedures

— Create peer review mechanisms, which allow:

1. Improved accuracy and increasing uniformity of conclusions

2. Quality assurance

3. Additional weight to the solidity of conclusions as they are perceived by others

— Incorporate interdisciplinary decision making more frequently

— Provide greater consultation opportunities between members of the network and professionals in the community

— Improve the opportunities for research by creating a larger database than individual practitioners or clinics could maintain alone

— Establish a larger, more organized coalition for child abuse advocacy

— Allow an opportunity for reduction of professional stress by providing professional and personal support for clinicians

Telemedicine

— In general, pediatricians have been slow to embrace virtual assessment because of the importance of the interaction between the physician and the parent-child dyad.

— A successful telemedicine program begins with a detailed needs assessment that focuses early on profiling the target consumer of the program. If the people are unwilling or unable to use the electronic equipment or service, it will languish.

— Use of telemedicine technology for real-time evaluations, is new and offers challenges as well as significant rewards for clinicians and children:

1. It is an effective tool to extend expertise to rural communities.

2. It can increase the accuracy of diagnosis.

3. Unnecessary investigations can be reduced.

4. The range of multidisciplinary teams can be increased.

5. Careful preplanning is required.

— In deploying a new telemedicine program the following 2 elements
   are critical:

   1. The community must know about the program in detail, and key
      players in abuse evaluations must have a sense of participation or
      partial ownership.

   2. All users must receive detailed training and support from the center
      to develop and maintain a sense of partnership in doing good
      things for abused children.

— Distance learning: refers to teaching beyond the range of one's
   voice; has come to infer the use of television and/or computers
   as a means of education

— Systems specific to child abuse education are generally part of larger
   telemedicine networks and use "store and forward" technology:

   1. An image is posted to other members of the network, perhaps
      asking an opinion or functioning as a test.

   2. Users log onto a secure Web site or respond to an email at their
      own convenience.

   3. If using the Internet, additional encryption is desirable for the
      highly sensitive photographs that are part of sexual abuse cases.

   4. Images sent digitally can be altered by each party to add arrows,
      question marks, and other notations to aid in the learning process.

— Videoconferencing allows users to connect over the Internet with
   a video camera, monitor, computer, and sound system.

— The equipment used for effective electronic communications
   depends on the needs of the group and the funding provided.
   The recruitment of partners for the project is essential.

Technologies
— The most important component in any technologic apparatus is
   the expertise of the examiner. Without using a visual aid, there
   is no ability to provide visual documentation for later review or
   a second opinion. Visual documentation is helpful for teaching
   purposes, peer review, and courtroom testimony.

— Colposcopy:

1. Uses a low-power microscope with a light source and camera and was designed for gynecologists to evaluate and document lesions of the cervix in adult patients

2. Offers the ability to standardize documentation, preserve evidence of what the examiner sees, and provides magnification of small lesions

3. If colposcopy is not available macrophotography can be substituted.

— Store and forward examinations are performed by an independent examiner in one location capturing images and a medical record and transmitting them electronically or physically to another independent examiner for consultation, interpretation, or review.

— The limitations of store and forward communications are as follows:

1. Focus and clarity of the photographs

2. Selection of photographs for transmission

3. Sometimes incomplete historical information

4. Timeliness of feedback

— Standard photographs are hampered by delays in store and forward formats due to the need to have them processed, printed, and then scanned into a format suitable for transmission.

— Digital imaging can be stored on a computer and printed whenever needed, maintain original quality over time, and can be transmitted electronically as often as required. The digital equipment now used produces images equal to analog images.

— The concern that these digital images may be altered can be addressed by the use of software that ensures the integrity of the image.

— Synchronous or real-time evaluation of children with allegations of abuse may also be available.

THE ELECTRONIC RECORD

— Records of sexual abuse examinations can be kept in the following formats:

1. Paper hardcopy: traditional medical record. Paper hardcopy is easy to read but its storage requirements are considerable and copying records is labor-intensive. The medical examination record and digital DVD or other photographic evidence must be kept in a confidential storage area and are subject to subpoena by the courts.

2. Conventional 35-mm photographs or slides: kept as part of the medical record or separately. Photographs and slides may be dislodged from the rest of the written record and have the same disadvantages listed above.

3. Videotape of the forensic genital examination: provides more perceptual information than a photograph alone but requires storage space.

4. Digital photographs or short digital video clips: quality comparable to standard photographs. Newer digital cameras are superior to standard cameras, and their photographs can be copied to a DVD and stored with the confidential medical record. They may require considerable memory for storage, with video clips taking large amounts of space. Several 10- to 15-second clips are required to capture the examination without exhausting the computer's memory capacity.

— The entire medical record may be electronic, which has the following advantages:

1. Reduces or eliminates storage problems

2. Allows easy access

3. Has the ability to combine text and photographs in a seamless record

4. Allows tailoring specific formats for dissemination to others

— All electronic records should be backed up, with consideration given to using a separate location so that a disaster in one location will not wipe out the child's record.

ADOLESCENTS AND ADULTS

The purpose of the adolescent/adult medical examination is to provide good medical care and evaluation of the victim and to collect forensic evidence to assist in the identification of the perpetrator and, later, for court evidence. A patient advocate often accompanies the victim in the examination room unless the victim objects. The process of the examination is explained to the patient who must consent to the performance of the medical examination, collection of forensic evidence, and photography.

THE MEDICAL RECORD

— Must be legible and contain carefully documented medical and assault histories

— Serves as a tool to provide information to law enforcement and the courts

— Serves to record the collection of forensic evidence for law enforcement

— Documents extragenital and anogenital injury associated with the sexual assault

History

Pertinent medical history includes preexisting injuries; menstrual history; recent voluntary use of drugs or alcohol; other sexual contact 5 days prior to the sexual assault; social history; and assault-related history in specific detail, including acts described by the victim.

The Medical Examination

— Vital signs and general demeanor of the victim

— Thorough examination of the skin of the victim for assault-related physical injury

— Head, neck, and oral examination with labeled diagrams of injury

— Male or female genital and anal examinations by direct observation with the use of camera documentation and magnification and toluidine blue dye for better visualization of microscopic injury

— Listing of evidence submitted to the crime lab

— Oral/genital/anal/rectal swabs and/or slides for forensic investigation with the time collected and the name of collector

— Toxicology samples when appropriate

— Reference samples of blood, urine, hair, and saliva

— Examination methods including use of a Wood's light or equivalent light source, colposcopy, toluidine blue, anoscopy, and others

— Chain of evidence must be a priority at all times; evidence must be dated, timed, labeled with the name of the victim and examiner, stored properly, and signed out by law enforcement

Nonforensic Examination Aspects

— Prophylaxis for STIs in the victim of sexual assault

— Prophylaxis against pregnancy

— Treatment of physical injury or hospital referral, when appropriate

— Follow-up with patient's physician, when necessary

— Postexam shower, change of clothes, and teeth brushing

— Postassault counseling and crisis intervention

REFERENCES

1. Centers for Disease Control and Prevention. Sexually transmitted diseases treatment guidelines, 2015. *MMWR Recomm Rep.* 2015;64(3):1-137.

2. Christian CW, Lavelle JM, De Jong AR, Loiselle J, Brenner L, Joffe M. Forensic evidence findings in prepubertal victims of sexual assault. *Pediatrics.* 2000;106(1):100-104.

3. Ernst AA, Green E, Ferguson MT, Weiss SJ, Green WM. The utility of anoscopy and colposcopy in the evaluation of male sexual assault victims. *Ann Emerg Med.* 2000;36(5):432-437.

4. Finkel MA, Ricci LR. Documentation and preservation of visual evidence in child abuse. *Child Maltreat.* 1997;2(4):322-330.

5. Giardino AP, Giardino ER, Pierce-Weeks J. Documenting the evaluation of suspected child maltreatment cases. In: Clements PT, Burgess AW, Fay-Hillier TM, Giardino ER, Giardino AP, eds. *Nursing Approach to the Evaluation of Child Maltreatment.* Saint Louis, MO: STM Learning, Inc; 2015:285-302

6. Jones JS, Dunnick C, Rossman L, Wynn BN, Nelson-Horan C. Significance of toluidine blue positive findings after speculum examination for sexual assault. *Am J Emerg Med.* 2004;22(3):201-203.

7. Ledray LE, Faugno D, Speck P. SANE: advocate, forensic technician, nurse? *J Emerg Nurs*. 2001;27(1):91-93.

8. Ledray LE, O'Brien C. The sexual assault exam components and documentation. *Medical Response to Adult Sexual Assault: A Resource for Clinician and Related Professionals*. Saint Louis, MO: STM Learning, Inc; 2011:89-106.

9. Myers JEB. *Evidence in Child Abuse and Neglect Cases*. 3rd ed. New York, NY: John Wiley; 1997.

10. Myers JEB. *Legal Issues in Child Abuse and Neglect Practice*. 2nd ed. Thousand Oaks, CA: Sage Publications; 1998.

11. Santucci KA, Nelson DG, McQuillen KK, Duffy SJ, Linakis JG. Wood's lamp utility in the identification of semen. *Pediatrics*. 1999;104(6):1342-1344.

12. Teixeira WR. Hymenal colposcopic examination in sexual offenses. *Am J Forensic Med Pathol*. 1981;2(3):209-215.

13. Whitworth JM, Wood B, Morse K, Rogers H, Haney M. The Florida Child Protection Team Telemedicine Program. In: Wootton R, Oakley AMM, eds. *Teledermatology*. London, UK: Royal Society of Medicine Press, Ltd; 2002:135-149.

14. Woodling BA, Heger A. The use of the colposcope in the diagnosis of sexual abuse in the pediatric age group. *Child Abuse Negl*. 1986;10(1):111-114.

Chapter 9

PHYSICAL EVALUATION OF ADOLESCENTS AND ADULTS

Diana Faugno, MSN, RN, CPN, SANE-A, SANE-P, FAAFS, DF-IAFN*
Donna Gaffney, RN, DNSc, FAAN
Iris Reyes, MD, FACEP
Elizabeth M. Datner, MD

The following review of sexual assault victims focuses primarily on female victims. Refer to *Chapter 6* for information specific to male sexual assault and to *Chapter 14* for specifics regarding sexual assault of the elderly. Ideally the sexual assault evaluation is done at a rape crisis center, where the focus is on providing a compassionate setting for the victim and skilled medical and forensic evidence collection.

OBTAINING THE HISTORY OF A SEXUAL ASSAULT
ROLE OF THE HEALTH CARE PROVIDER

— Pay close attention to detail.

— Maintain a caring, nonjudgmental approach.

— Clearly convey to each patient the following points:

1. No one ever deserves to be raped.

2. The perpetrator is responsible for the assault ("This is not your fault.")

3. The patient made the best choices possible for survival under the circumstances.

— With adolescent patients, make efforts to establish a trusting relationship and to make them aware that regardless of their activity, they are not at fault and no one had the right to force them to participate in sexual activity against their will.

Revised Chapter 9 for the second edition.

— Make patients aware of clinician mandatory reporting requirements before they disclose information.

— Encourage patients to report the assault to police.

— Make the patient aware that physical evidence can be recovered through first menses or 28 days after an incident in reproductive-aged menstruating females; therefore, attempts should be made to collect physical evidence early regardless of whether or not the patient has decided to pursue the case.*

— Most states have crime-victim compensation programs that cover the financial costs of the evaluation and evidence collection.

— Responsibilities of the health care provider include:

1. Treat physical injuries.

2. Perform a careful physical examination. Rule out any life-threatening conditions, with assessment of the victim's airway, breathing, and circulation (ABCs) as a priority. Treating these vital functions supersedes any data collection or gathering of forensic evidence.

3. Collect evidence.

4. Document all pertinent aspects of the history.

5. Provide treatment and care in terms of pregnancy and sexually transmitted infection (STI) prophylaxis and psychologic support.

6. Arrange for follow-up care and counseling for the victim.

7. Inform patients that refusal/declining any or all procedures, services, or questions is up to them and that refusal/declining will not affect care.

— Provide a private, quiet environment so that the patient feels safe and in control of what is happening to him or her.

— If the person accompanying the patient is suspected of being the perpetrator, notify law enforcement/security and provide a safe place for the patient.

Refer to Publisher's Note on page xliv.

— Limit repetitive questioning if possible.

— Inform the patient before beginning the physical examination that it will take about 30 to 60 minutes, but paper work may take longer.

— During the examination, be sure to listen carefully, speak quietly, and perform the evaluation in an unhurried manner.

HISTORY OF THE ADULT VICTIM

— The purpose is to record the events that occurred and guide the clinician in collecting evidence, caring for injuries, and developing a treatment plan.

— Elements of a general history include:

1. Past history of medical illness

2. Recent surgery

3. Medications

4. Allergies

5. Tetanus immunization and other immunizations as appropriate

6. History of STIs

7. Contraception use

8. Last consensual sexual contact

9. Any drug use

10. Last menstrual period, use of pads or tampons

11. Obstetric history

— For elements of a forensic interview see *Chapter 10.*

THE PHYSICAL EXAMINATION

— The purpose of the physical examination is to identify any injuries requiring medical attention and to collect forensic evidence.

1. Be prepared to perform the physical examination, but be aware that you will need to collect forensic evidence as well. Be prepared to use an evidence collection kit and have one available (**Table 9-1**).

Table 9-1. Evidence Collection Kit

RECOMMENDED CONTENTS

---

1. Instructions

2. Checklist

3. History and physical documentation forms

4. Equipment for specimen collection:

    — Paper bags (plastic may produce mildew which contaminates evidence)

    — Large paper

    — 6" cotton-tipped swabs and packaging containers/envelopes

    — Comb

    — Envelopes

    — Patient discharge information (May substitute with individualized institution discharge instruction)

    — Tubes for blood sampling or blood card

    — Buccal swab

    — Bindle paper

    — Cardboard box and cardboard continuers or paper envelopes for specimen placement

    — The last 3 items are supplies that will be needed for the examination and provided most often by the hospital or clinic.

    — Forceps

    — Scissors

    — Labels for clinical samples

2. Law enforcement, emergency medical services/transport, or private vehicles are the most common modes of transportation for sexual assault patients presenting to centers/institutions. Transport should be done in a timely fashion and with notification to the center/institution that a sexual assault patient will be arriving.

3. If no SANE nurse/staff is available, emergency room staff (MD or RN) will perform the examination. The evidence needs to be collected in a timely fashion.

— The patient will determine who he/she would like present during his/her examination.

— Perform a thorough physical examination, including evidence and documentation of nongenital physical trauma.

— Patients should remove all clothing, as outlined in *Chapters 3* and *4.*

— The examination should move from head to foot, paying particular attention to signs of injury (**Figure 9-1, Figure 9-2, Table 9-2**).

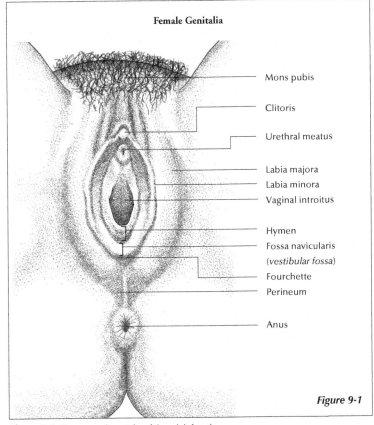

Figure 9-1. *The external genitalia of the adult female.*

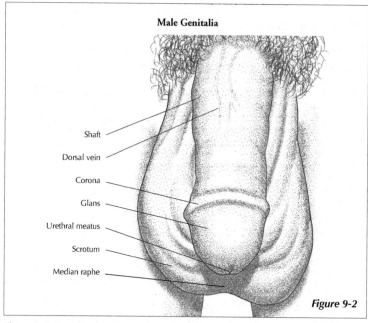

Male Genitalia

Shaft
Dorsal vein
Corona
Glans
Urethral meatus
Scrotum
Median raphe

Figure 9-2

Figure 9-2. Frontal view of the external male genitalia.

Table 9-2. Female and Male Genital Structures and Characteristics

FEMALE

— *Anus:* The terminal opening of the digestive tract, which serves as the opening of the rectum. This area has a concentration of nerve endings. Anal folds, or wrinkles of perianal skin radiating from the anus, are caused by the closure of the external anal sphincter.

— *Cervix:* The lower portion of the uterus that protrudes into the vagina.

— *Clitoris:* A small cylindrical body of erectile tissue situated at the most anterior portion of the vulva. A fold of tissue, called the "hood" or prepuce, covers the clitoris. During arousal, the clitoris enlarges and protrudes from the hood. The clitoris is the most sensitive part of the female anatomy.

(continued)

Table 9-2. Female and Male Genital Structures and Characteristics *(continued)*

FEMALE (CONTINUED)

— *Fossa Navicularis:* The area of the vaginal vestibule located between the posterior attachment of the hymen and the posterior fourchette. It presents as a shallow depression at the base of the vulva. This is created by labial traction. There is no line of demarcation.

— *Hymen:* The circular band of tissue that surrounds (completely or partially) the opening of the vagina. The physical appearance and elasticity of the hymen change over a woman's life span because of hormonal fluctuation (primarily estrogen).

— *Hymen Morphology*

— *Annular:* Circumferential hymen tissue presents 360 degrees around vaginal opening.

— *Bump:* Solid elevation of hymenal tissue.

— *Crescentic:* Posterior rim of hymen, with attachments at the 10 to 1 o'clock and 1 to 2 o'clock positions.

— *Cribriform:* Hymen with multiple small hymenal openings.

— *External ridge:* Longitudinal ridge (raised area) on the external surface of the hymen from the rim to the fossa navicularis or urethra.

— *Fimbriated:* A hymen with a ruffled, and/or fringed edge.

— *Hymenal cleft:* Division or split in the rim of the hymen that does not cross the base of the hymen.

— *Longitudinal vaginal ridge:* A longitudinal ridge extending from the hymenal rim into the vagina, usually on the posterior or posterolateral walls, and parallel to the vaginal axis.

— *Redundant:* Hyman of any type that is folded on itself and does not "open" to reveal the orifice, even when multiple positions and methods are used.

— *Septate hymen:* Two hymenal openings with a band of hymenal tissue in between.

— *Imperforate:* No hymenal opening. This is a rare condition.

(continued)

Table 9-2. Female and Male Genital Structures and Characteristics *(continued)*

FEMALE (CONTINUED)

— *Labia majora:* Latin for "larger lips." These are rounded folds of skin forming the lateral boundaries of the vulva. These outer folds of skin protect the more delicate structures underneath. The lips have hair at time of puberty.

— *Labia minora:* Latin for "smaller lips." The longitudinal folds of tissue enclosed within the labia majora that are located on either side of the vaginal orifice. These folds of tissue cover the vaginal orifice and urethral meatus.

— *Mons pubis:* The rounded eminence in front of the pubic symphysis formed by a collection of fatty tissue beneath the integument. It becomes covered with hair at the time of puberty.

— *Os:* The opening located at the center of the cervix, leading to the uterus.

— *Perineum:* The area between the vaginal introitus and anus.

— *Posterior fourchette:* A fold of mucous membrane that connects the labia minora at the base of the vulva.

— *Rectum:* Terminal portion of the lower intestine.

— *Uterus:* A hollow muscular organ, pear shaped, with a small internal cavity. It is where the fetus grows before birth.

— *Urethral meatus:* The opening to the urethra. Its major purpose is the release of urine from the bladder.

— *Vagina:* The structure that opens to the outside of the body at the vaginal introitus and extends 3 to 5 inches inside the body, ending at the cervix.

— *Vaginal introitus:* Located below the urethral meatus and situated behind the labia minora; the entrance to the vagina.

— *Vaginal Vestibule:* The space posterior to the clitoris, between the labia minora.

— *Vulva:* The external genitalia of the female, or pudendum. Includes the clitoris, labia majora, labia minora, vaginal vestibule, urethral orifice, vaginal orifice, hymen, fourchette, and posterior commissure.

(continued)

Table 9-2. Female and Male Genital Structures and Characteristics *(continued)*

MALE

— *Coronal ridge:* The widest portion around the glans.

— *Ejaculation:* The release of reproductive fluid via the male urethra. The ejaculate may or may not contain spermatozoa.

— *Foreskin (prepuce):* The movable hood of skin covering the glans of the penis. During erection, the foreskin rolls back just below the coronal ridge. In circumcised men, the foreskin has been removed.

— *Frenulum:* On the underside of the penis, with a different texture to its skin, this area is often highly responsive to stimulation.

— *Glans:* The cone-shaped head of the penis. This fleshy "head" of the penis is most sensitive to stimulation. Usually larger in diameter than the shaft, the glans is responsible for the greatest sensation during intercourse.

— *Penis:* The male organ of reproduction and urination.

— *Perineum:* The area between the base of the scrotum and the anus. Beneath the skin are more chambers that fill with blood during arousal, just as the penis does.

— *Scrotum:* The sac encasing the testicles just below the penis.

— *Semen:* A thick fluid released by the male during ejaculation. It consists of fluids from various glands plus the spermatozoa.

— *Shaft:* The cylindrical part of the penis located between the glans and the body, which is filled with vascular chambers. During arousal these chambers fill with blood, causing the shaft to stiffen and producing and erection. Unlike many other animals, the human has no bone or gristle to ensure stiffness.

— *Testicles:* Two spherical glands within the scrotum that produce sperm. The sperm are carried through spermatic cords, joining fluids produced by the prostate gland and seminal vesicles to produce semen, which is then ejaculated. One of the cords is called the epididymis and the difference in the length of the 2 epididymides is responsible for one testicle being slightly lower than the other.

— *Urethral opening:* At the end of the penis, this opening serves as the duct through which both urine and ejaculate (semen) flow.

1. TEARS is an acronym for remembering types of injuries:

   T: Tear (laceration) or tenderness
   E: Ecchymosis (bruising)
   A: Abrasion
   R: Redness (erythema)
   S: Swelling (edema)

2. Tears or lacerations: occur when the continuity of the skin is broken and disrupted by blunt force, usually applied in a vertical manner, perpendicular to the plane of the skin. Tearing, ripping, crushing, overly stretching, or pulling apart result in tearing, often over a bony surface that contributes to the severity of the injury. The laceration's edges are irregular and can be aligned to fit together. This is not the same as a cut, which is made with a sharp instrument. The margins of the laceration may be bruised or crushed and connective tissue strands may bridge across the interior of the wound. Lacerations often contain foreign material, including trace evidence.

3. Ecchymosis (bruising) and contusions: bruises lie below the intact epidermis and consist of an extravascular collection of blood that has leaked from ruptured capillaries or blood vessels. It is not possible to specifically identify the exact "age" of a bruise using color as a guideline because other factors, such as impaired blood clotting, compromised immune status, certain malignant diseases, diabetes, alcoholism, malnutrition, and age, influence the color changes that a bruise undergoes. Contusions may cause far more serious injuries and can occur anywhere in the body. Both result from blood vessel leakage when blunt force is applied to a tissue. Petechiae are tiny red or purple spots on the skin or other tissue. Petechiae less than 3 mm in diameter are pinpoint-sized hemorrhages of small capillaries in the skin or mucous membranes. Bruises, contusions, and petechiae do not blanch when pressure is applied.

4. Abrasions: superficial injuries to the skin, limited to the epidermis and superficial dermis, are normally caused by rubbing, sliding, or compressive forces against the skin in a parallel manner rather than vertical force.

5. Redness or erythema: should not be mistaken for bleeding under the skin. Erythema blanches under gentle pressure and is usually diffuse and does not exhibit a pattern. The cause can be a forceful slap or increased pressure to the skin, momentarily forcing blood out of the capillaries in the area of contact and then, when pressure is withdrawn, to return to the capillaries, which may dilate. The result is redness or flushing of the skin.

— Use diagrams and photographs to document identified injuries.

— Collect forensic evidence as the examination progresses. (See *Chapter 10.*)

LABORATORY TESTS

— Perform laboratory studies as needed for the medical treatment of the victim in addition to what is forwarded to law enforcement under the guidelines of the evidence collection kit.

— Use water, saline solution, or standard lubricants during the speculum and rectal examinations. This will not interfere with forensic testing but should be discussed with the local crime lab; document the variance on the report.

— Recommended laboratory evaluations are as follows:

1. Pregnancy testing (either urine or serum testing)

2. Rapid plasma reagin (RPR) or VDRL (test for syphilis at initial visit and again at 3 months)

3. Hepatitis serology (test for hepatitis B recommended; hepatitis C testing not generally required)

4. Gonorrhea/Chlamydia testing (Urine NAATs are accurate and convenient, replacing the need for intrusive culturing in many situations. Follow the procedure at your local institutions.)

5. Human immunodeficiency virus (HIV) testing (at initial visit with locally mandated counseling and again at 3, 5, and 12 months; the site best suited to perform appropriate posttest counseling should perform these studies)

6. Blood sample for typing to differentiate victim from perpetrator (goes with the evidence collection kit)

INTERPRETING INJURIES

The clinician must recognize that visible physical findings in the anogenital area can be caused by consenting or nonconsenting sex. The injury may also be caused by infection, friable tissue, medical conditions, etc. Whether an injury or no visible injury is present, the SANE will document it, but the injury itself cannot tell its cause; therefore, history given by the patient is important, as is understanding that sometimes there will be no given history, due to drug and/or alcohol ingestion. During history taking, the clinician will note what the patient might recall about the sexual acts, bearing in mind that sexual assault patients may not be able to recall specific actions of the assailant due to the neurobiology of trauma.

A complex relationship exists among the variables that can influence injury type and location. A comprehensive history is critical to understanding the presence or absence of injury. The variables influencing injury can be grouped as factors related to the victim, the perpetrator, the circumstances, or the environment (**Table 9-3**).

Table 9-3. Variables Influencing Injury Type and Location

FACTORS RELATED TO THE VICTIM

— Anatomy and physiology of the reproductive structures
— Health and developmental status
— Condition of the genital structures
— Previous sexual experience
— Lubrication of the vaginal vault (natural or artificial)
— Partner participation
— Positioning and pelvic tilt
— Psychologic response

FACTORS RELATED TO THE ASSAILANT

— Object of penetration
— Lubrication
— Male sexual dysfunction
— Force of penetration

(continued)

Table 9-3. Variables Influencing Injury Type and Location *(continued)*

FACTORS RELATED TO CIRCUMSTANCES

— Previous history with assailant
— Lack of communication

FACTORS RELATED TO THE ENVIRONMENT

— Location of the assault
— Materials and surfaces in surrounding area

FOLLOW-UP CARE

— Refer or arrange for follow-up medical care for the victim at 1 to 2 weeks and at 2 to 4 months after the initial evaluation.

— The most significant sequelae after sexual assault are, typically, the psychological reactions of patients and their families.

— All patients should receive counseling and referral for ongoing follow-up during their initial evaluation or within the next 1 to 2 days. Utilize rape crisis centers for assistance.

REFERENCES

1. Anglin D, Mitchell C. Intimate partner violence. In: Marx JA, Hockberger RS, Walls RM, et al, eds. *Rosen's Emergency Medicine: Concepts and Clinical Practice*. 7th ed. Philadelphia, PA: Mosby; 2010:815-829.

2. Anglin D, Schneider DC. Elder abuse and neglect. In: JA Marx, RS Hockberger, Walls RM, et al, eds. *Emergency Medicine: Concepts and Clinical Practice*. 7th ed. Philadelphia, PA: Mosby; 2010:830-837.

3. American College of Emergency Physicians. *Evaluation and Management of the Sexually Assaulted or Sexually Abused Patient*. 2nd ed. Dallas, TX: American College of Emergency Physicians; 2013.

4. American College of Obstetricians and Gynecologists. *Guidelines for Women's Health Care: A Resource Manual*. 3rd ed. Washington, DC: American College of Obstetricians and Gynecologists; 2007.

5. American College of Obstetricians and Gynecologists. Committee opinion no. 547: health care for women in the military and women veterans. *Obstet Gynecol.* 2012;120(6):1538-1542.

6. Basson R, Baram DA. Sexuality, sexual dysfunction, and sexual assault. In: Berek JS, ed. *Berek & Novak's Gynecology.* 15th ed. Philadelphia, PA: Lippincott Williams & Wilkins; 2012:270-304.

7. US Department of Justice, Office on Violence Against Women. *A National Protocol for Sexual Assault Medical Forensic Examinations: Adults/ Adolescents.* 2nd ed. Washington, DC: US Department of Justice; 2013. National Criminal Justice Reference Service Web site. https:// www.ncjrs.gov/pdffiles1/ovw/241903.pdf. Accessed March 18, 2015.

8. Ernst A, Green E, Ferguson M, Weiss S, Green W. The Utility of anoscopy and colposcopy in the evaluation of male sexual assault victims. *Ann Emerg Med.* 2000;36(5):432-436.

9. Girardin BW, Faugno DK, Seneski PC, Slaughter L, Whelan M. Findings in sexual assault and consensual intercourse. In: Girardin BW, Faugno DK, Seneski PC, Slaughter L, Whelan M, eds. *Color Atlas of Sexual Assault.* Saint Louis, MO: Mosby; 1997:19-65.

10. Ingemann-Hansen O, Charles AV. Forensic medical examination of adolescent and adult victims of sexual violence. *Best Pract Res Clin Obstet Gynaecol.* 2013;27(1):91-102. doi: 10.1016/j.bpobgyn.2012.08.014.

11. Larkin H, Paolinetti L. Pattern of anal/rectal injury in sexual assault victims who complain of rectal penetration. Paper presented at: International Association of Forensic Nurses 6th Annual Scientific Assembly; October 1-5, 1998; Pittsburgh, PA.

12. Ledray L, Barry L. SANE expert and factual testimony. *J Emerg Nurs.* 1998;24(3):284-287.

13. Ledray LE, Netzel L. DNA evidence collection. *J Emerg Nurs.* 1997;23(2):156-158.

14. Ledray LE, Simmelink K. Efficacy of SANE evidence collection: a Minnesota study. *J Emerg Nurs.* 1997;23(2):182-186.

15. Lowe SM, Rahman N, Forster G. Chain of evidence in sexual assault cases. *Int J STD AIDS*. 2009;20(11):799-800. doi: 10.1258/ijsa.2009.009001.

16. Negrusz A, Moore CM, Stockham TL, et al. Elimination of 7-aminoflunitrazepam and flunitrazepam in urine after a single dose of Rohypnol. *J Forensic Sci*. 2000;45(5):1013-1022.

17. Riggs N, Houry D, Long G, Markovchick V, Feldhaus KM. Analysis of 1076 cases of sexual assault. *Ann Emerg Med*. 2000;35(4):358-362.

18. Rambow B, Adkinson C, Frost TH, Peterson GF. Female sexual assault: medical and legal implications. *Ann Emerg Med*. 1992;21(6):717-731.

19. Ramin SM, Saron AJ, Stone IC Jr, Wendel GD Jr. Sexual assault in postmenopausal women. *Obstet Gynecol*. 1992;80(5):860-864.

20. Sachs C, Wheeler M. Examination of the sexual assault victim. In: Roberts JR, Hedges JR, eds. *Clinical Procedures in Emergency Medicine*. 5th ed. Philadelphia, PA: Saunders; 2010:1069-1083.

21. Sandrick KM. Medicine & law. tightening the chain of evidence. *Hosp Health Netw*. 1996;70(11):64, 66.

22. Slaughter L, Brown CR. Cervical findings in rape victims. *J Obstet Gynecol*. 1991;164(2):528-529.

23. Slaughter L, Brown CR. Colposcopy to establish physical findings in rape victims. *Am J Obstet Gynecol*. 1992;166(1 pt 1):83-86.

24. Slaughter L, Brown CR, Crowley S, Peck R. Patterns of genital injury in female sexual assault victims. *Am J Obstet Gynecol*. 1997;176(3):609-616.

25. Speck P, Ballantyne J. *Post-Coital DNA Recovery Study*. Washington, DC: National Criminal Justice Reference Service; 2015.

26. Tucker S, Claire E, Ledray LE, Werner JS, Claire E. Sexual assault evidence collection. *Wis Med J*. 1990;89(7):407-411.

27. Tjaden P, Thoennes N. *Full Report of the Prevalence, Incidence, and Consequences of Violence Against Women: Findings From the National Violence Against Women Survey*. Washington, DC: US Department of Justice, Office of Justice Programs, National Institute of Justice; 2000. National Criminal Justice Reference Service Web site. https://www.ncjrs.gov/pdffiles1/nij/183781.pdf. Accessed March 18, 2015.

28. Turner B. Management of retained foreign bodies and rectal sexual trauma. *Nurs Times*. 2004;100(38):30-32. Nursing Times Web site. http://www.nursingtimes.net/nursing-practice-clinical-research/management-of-retained-foreign-bodies-and-rectal-sexual-trauma/204150.article. Published September 21, 2004. Accessed March 18, 2015.

29. US Department of Homeland Security, US Immigration and Customs Enforcement. Human trafficking. US Immigration and Customs Enforcement Web site. http://www.ice.gov/human-trafficking. Updated October 19, 2012. Accessed March 5, 2015.

30. Yorker B. Nurses in Georgia care for survivors of sexual assault. *Georgia Nurs*. 1996;56(1):5-6.

Chapter 10

FORENSIC EVALUATION OF ADOLESCENTS AND ADULTS

Diana K. Faugno, MSN, RN, CPN, SANE-A, SANE-P, FAAFS, DF-IAFN*
Holly M. Harner, CRNP, PhD, MPH, SANE
Patrick O'Donnell, PhD
Joanne Archambault
Kathy Bell, RN
Kathryn M. Turman
Patricia M. Speck, DNSc, APN, FNP-BC, DF-IAFN, FAAFS, FAAN*

The immediate medical needs after sexual assault, including care for acutely critical physical needs, are similar to those of victims of any trauma. However, when patients are victims of a violent crime such as rape or domestic violence, and when the victim may know the accused, the clinician must determine the safety needs of the victim.

— If the person who committed the crime is known to the victim, the victim may fear retaliation for seeking medical care.

— It is necessary to seek available hospital or clinic security measures as indicated.

— If the patient who was the victim wishes to return to the perpetrator, as is common in cases of intimate partner and marital rape, the health care provider should review a safety plan with the victim before discharge.

FORENSIC MEDICAL HISTORY

It is important for health care providers to maintain a trauma-informed, professional, sensitive, and nonjudgmental manner throughout the history

Revised Chapter 10 for the second edition.

of the event. If possible, the victim need only give enough information to law enforcement to begin an investigation. If not, someone from the police department and a local victim advocacy organization should be present during the forensic medical history immediately following the assault. If the treating clinician is a male and the victim is a female, it is recommended a female chaperone be present.

HEALTH HISTORY

— Conduct an abbreviated health history of acute and chronic illnesses; current medications, including nonprescription, herbal, and/or illegal; and anaphylactic histamine–mediated allergies to medications and foods.

— Include a gynecologic history to document the victim's first day of her last menstrual period, contraceptive method, current pregnancy status, and last consensual coitus through her first menses or 28 days.

— Ask the victim about any transient and chronic psychiatric conditions, including major depression, anxiety disorders, and schizophrenia.

ASSAULT HISTORY

— The elements of a forensic medical interview focused on the assault include the following:

1. Brief description of the incident

2. Number and identity of the attacker(s), if known

3. Time of the attack

4. Location where the assault took place

5. Type of sexual acts that occurred, ie, kissing or fondling of breasts or anogenital areas, vaginal and/or anal penetration, oral penetration with a penis (see **Table 10-1**)

6. Contact with ejaculate, urine, or vaginal secretions

7. Use of physical force, eg, strangulation, weapons, restraints, contraceptives, or condoms by the perpetrator

8. Use of objects to penetrate or coerce the victim

Table 10-1. Definitions of Sexual Conduct

— *Fellatio:* any mouth-to-penis contact

— *Frottage:* rubbing for the purpose of sexual gratification

— *Cunnilingus:* mouth-to-vulva

— *Sexual intercourse:* contact of the penis to the vagina

— *Anal intercourse or anal sodomy:* contact of penis to the anus

— *Anilingus:* mouth-to-anus contact

— *Oral sodomy:* mouth-to-vagina, -anus, or -penis

— For forensic medical purposes, document whether the patient changed clothing, bathed, urinated, defecated, or douched since the assault. While not a determinant in DNA recovery from the vaginal vault or cervix, the clothing and soiled objects may contain evidence.

— Document all direct quotes made by the patient with quotation marks.

— Document victim use of alcohol or drugs, including prescription medications written for others.

1. Incapacitation from drugs, either given unwittingly or voluntarily ingested by a person, creates vulnerability; when given to the potential victim, the drugs are most often gamma hydroxybutyrate (GHB) or flunitrazepam (Rohypnol). Alcohol is often involved, as well.

2. If the victim's recollection of the event is poor or if the substance found is not remembered, consider intentional or unintentional incapacitation for the purposes of altering the victim's capacity to consent and their working memory.

ACUTE CARE OF THE SEXUAL ASSAULT VICTIM

1. Obtain written consent to perform a forensic medical examination. Be sure to obtain the victim's verbal consent and prepare them for each phase of the examination. If the provider perceives patient resistance, stop and explain the process again. Regain their consent and build trust for each step, empowering the patient.

— The purpose of the forensic medical examination is to identify, evaluate, document, and treat injuries, while collecting samples with potential evidentiary value useful in adjudication processes, ie, family or criminal courts. (See *Chapter 9* for details.)

2. Examine the oral cavity carefully, looking for fellatio syndrome (**Figure 10-1**). Use cotton swabs to obtain a sample of fluid between the gums, lips, and teeth. Air-dry the swabs before packaging as evidence. Document any findings on the chart.

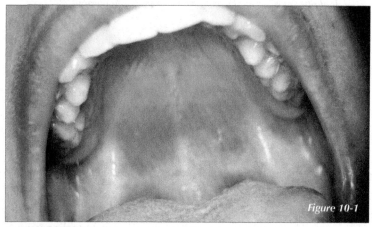

Figure 10-1

Figure 10-1. Focal submucosal hemorrhages at the junction of hard and soft palates, termed fellatio syndrome.

3. Swab stains or areas on skin identified by the patient with swabs moistened with sterile water. Use a woods lamp/ALS light to illuminate any findings followed by swabbing. If there is no positive Woods lamp/ALS light, swab areas based on history or lack of history. Closely inspect fingernails for evidence of foreign material or dirt, and swab fingernails using one cotton-tipped applicator for each hand.

4. Comb hair over clean paper, eg, 8.5" x 11" printing paper, to collect debris and loose hair. This applies to pubic hair as well. Bindle fold and seal the trace elements. At minimum, initial and date the seal, document the location of the collection and describe the material collected, eg, dark substance or hair-like material.

5. When found, remove foreign bodies, ie, sand, dirt, or other debris; place them in a clean envelope; and seal the envelope. At minimum, initial and date the seal; document the location of the foreign body; and describe the material collected, eg, dark substance, sand-like material, or hair-like material. The laboratory will definitively identify the material.

6. Nongynecologic injuries commonly include trauma from kicking, strangulation, and restraints, as well as human bites. Injuries found in vulnerable "sexual" body regions include the breast and anogenital areas.

7. When providers find injury, describe the location, size, color, and pattern of injury. Recommendations include photodocumentation using the rule of thirds, fourths, or fifths in taking pictures to identify the patient and the patient's injuries, beginning with the gross anatomy and ending with the close-up of each injury, with and without a standardized reference, eg, a ruler or coin, to indicate size.

8. Speculum examination follows the complete external examination of the external genital area, including the posterior fourchette, fossa navicularis, peri-urethral area, hymen, clitoral hood and clitoris, labia majora and minora, and perineum. With speculum inserted, look for evidence of trauma to the cervix and cul-de-sac. Take samples from the posterior fornix and the cervical os. These swabs will be analyzed by the crime lab for antigen determination, seminal factors, and DNA testing.

9. Begin by visually inspecting the external genitalia and other surrounding areas, including the inner thighs. Use a handheld magnifying lens if needed, and document injuries with photographs. After swabbing for DNA or trace evidence, palpate to determine and document pain levels. Encourage the patient to assist by pointing to painful areas without obvious bruising or redness.

10. Gynecologic injuries include those to the vulvar, labial, introitus, urethral, vaginal, perianal, and cervix areas, with characteristics of petechial, abrasions, cuts, lacerations, contusions, and hematomas.

11. Thoroughly inspect the vaginal introitus, photographing introitus and hymeneal injury, including petechia, cuts, lacerations, abrasions, swelling, hematomas, or contusions.

12. Insert the speculum to avoid contamination of the fields where evidence exists. Examine and photograph the vagina and cervix. Evidence demonstrates increased DNA recovery by swabbing the cervix first, followed by a sweep of the posterior fornix with a cotton swab dried and placed in the evidence kit.

13. Carefully examine the buttocks and anus for evidence of trauma, including fissures, small lacerations, and bruises. Collect swabs based on history and your community protocol.

— Be aware that while samples from the vagina are best collected sooner rather than later, recent research expands timing in DNA recovery in extended postcoital intervals through the first period following the assault.*

— Even if the patient has no complaints of pelvic trauma or discomfort, proceed with a pelvic examination, since most patients will not have visible physical injury. Indicate the beginning time of the examination and document all findings.

— Be aware that genital trauma increases in postmenopausal female victims due to decreased estrogen levels. Toluidine blue dye identifies microlacerations not apparent initially and increases the number of visible findings.

CHAIN OF EVIDENCE

Chain of evidence, or *chain of custody*, refers to the direct line of custody of evidence from time of collection until presentation at court. Establishing chain of custody between the clinician and the court renders the evidence admissible. Failure to maintain the chain of custody renders the evidence inadmissible.

— Place all evidence gathered in separate envelopes or containers, seal them, and initial (**Figure 10-2** and **Table 10-2**).

— Once all collected specimens and other evidence is separately packaged, package them together, seal, and label them. Turn the completed package over to the police or place it in a secured space, eg, a locked cabinet, closet, or room, for later disposition. Maintain the chain of custody.

— Obtain a receipt for the evidence. Have both the person handing over the evidence and the person receiving it sign and date the receipt. If the persons are not known, copy identification and place with the records.

— (For further documentation principles, see *Chapter 8*.)

*Refer to Publisher's Note on page xliv.

Figure 10-2

Figure 10-2. *Improperly sealed evidence envelope; seal does not wrap around the edges of the envelope for a proper seal. Date and examiner's name are indicated. Signature crosses envelope and seal.*

Table 10-2. Guidelines for Evidence Collection Following Sexual Assault*

CLOTHING COLLECTION

Materials Needed: 2 paper sheets, 5-10 paper bags, labels, pieces of paper

Instructions: Collect all clothing worn at the time of the attack, including shoes. Use critical thinking skills with clothing collection based on the history given.* Patients should undress over 2 sheets placed on the floor, handing each item of clothing to the nurse. Each piece of clothing should be placed in a separately labeled paper bag and sealed. Do not shake out clothing or cut through preexisting rips or tears. If any stains are present on the clothing, place a piece of paper over the stain prior to folding. If clothing is wet/damp, allow it to air-dry before placing in labeled paper bags. After collecting the clothing, the top paper sheet should be carefully folded, placed in a labeled paper bag, and sealed.

Case*: A sexual assault occurred in the patient's bedroom 2 days ago. Critical thinking skill: Assuming the patient is not wearing the same clothes worn 2 days ago, there is no need for paper to step on. After 2 days, it is more important to get the patient's bedding than the clothes she put on after the assault.

(continued)

Table 10-2. Guidelines for Evidence Collection Following Sexual Assault*
(continued)

PHYSICAL EXAMINATION AND EVIDENCE COLLECTION

Skin

Materials Needed: Woods lamp/ALS light, cotton-tipped swabs, normal sterile saline (NSS), labels, sterile water, paper or cardboard containers per evidence collection kit

Instructions: Scan the skin with the Woods lamp/ALS light. Areas that react to ultraviolet light may provide biological evidence. Swab these areas with 2 moistened cotton swabs, air-dry, and place in a labeled paper or cardboard container. Collect debris from skin and put in labeled container or bindle. Follow your crime lab procedure for moistened swabs.

Fingernails

Materials Needed: 2 plastic fingernail scrapers or 2 moistened swabs, paper towels, labels, envelopes

Instructions: Obtain trace evidence from fingernails by scraping nails over a paper towel or swabbing the fingernail. Fold evidence in paper towel if collected. Place in a labeled envelope and seal. Evidence from each hand should be gathered and stored in separate envelopes labeled "right hand" or "left hand." Research suggests that swabbing the fingernails is best for evidence collection.

Oropharynx

Materials Needed: Cotton-tipped swabs, labels, paper or cardboard containers per evidence collection kit

Instructions: Swab oral mucosa and along the gingiva and teeth with cotton swab, air-dry, and place in a labeled cardboard or paper container. Oropharyngeal evidence may be collected if oral-genital contact occurred. Buccal swabs are for DNA. These should be collected separately and not placed with the other swabs for drying. Keep separate at all times.

Head Hair

Materials Needed: Paper towels, envelope, labels

Instructions: Cut or pull 15 full-length head hairs—as permitted by patient and by jurisdiction—from back, center, and right and left sides of the head, catching the loose hairs in a paper towel. Place paper towel in labeled envelope and seal. **Most programs no longer do this.** *(continued)*

Table 10-2. Guidelines for Evidence Collection Following Sexual Assault*
(continued)

PHYSICAL EXAMINATION AND EVIDENCE COLLECTION *(CONTINUED)*

Genitalia

Materials Needed: 6 cotton swabs, 3 4x4 gauze pads, 2 envelopes, comb, scissors, labels, sterile water, paper towels, containers per evidence collection kit

Instructions: Place paper towel under victim's buttocks. Comb through pubic hair in downward motion, catching loose hairs in paper towel. Fold paper towel, place in labeled envelope, and seal.

Swab external genitalia area with 2 swabs. Allow to air-dry and place in labeled container.

Swab the vaginal walls and vault with 2 cotton swabs, allow to air-dry, and place in a labeled container. Cervical os swabbing comprises (1) leaving 1-2 cotton swabs in the cervix to absorb fluid for 10-15 seconds and (2) sweeping the posterior fornix with the same swabs, capturing as much material as possible. Air-dry swabs and place them in a labeled container. External anal swabs should also be obtained, based on history. Follow your community protocol.

BLOOD SAMPLE COLLECTION

Genitalia

Materials Needed: 1 purple-topped tube, 3 red-topped tubes, labels

Instructions: Collect 3 mL of blood in labeled purple-topped tube, for reference DNA. Blood work for sexually transmitted infection (STI) testing—for HIV, rapid plasma reagin [RPR], and hepatitis B—may be collected in labeled red-topped tubes if indicated. Some states use buccal swabs rather than blood for reference DNA. Patient needs to consent to this procedure.

---

*Follow your crime lab's suggestions and your community protocol for evidence collection.

PHARMACOLOGIC NEEDS*
PREVENTION OF SEXUALLY TRANSMITTED INFECTIONS (STIs)
(See *Chapter 11.*)

FORENSIC EVIDENCE COLLECTION
Table 10-2 offers general guidelines for collecting evidence. Only trained health care professionals should undertake evidence collection after sexual assault. Improperly collected and poorly handled evidence damages the victim's criminal case and influences the victim's mental health.

DNA EVIDENCE COLLECTION IN SEXUAL ASSAULT
IMPORTANCE OF DNA EVIDENCE
DNA evidence is valuable to the prosecution when recovered from sexual assault victims and crime scenes and in the conviction of the accused. The Combined DNA Index System (CODIS) and other DNA databases containing convicted offender profiles obtained from biological evidence recovered from victims, offenders, and crime scenes give new value to the thousands of unanalyzed rape kits sitting in evidence storage facilities nationally.

— Newer DNA methods improve sexual assault victims' credibility, historically challenged in court.

— Backlogs, now tested with newer DNA detection methods both exonerate and convict the accused.

— Experiencing a biological response after rape causes severe stress and fragmented memory.

— Reassure the patient that memory will return if not incapacitated, and it will be associated with the 5 senses, ie, sight, smell, taste, hearing, and touch.

— Even fragmented memory returns, and as memory returns, so does order.

— Encourage victims to journal their recollections. Advise victims to avoid assignment of certain words, ie, shame, self-blame, my fault, to the emotional reaction.

Follow CDC guidelines[5] and your local protocol for treatment.

— Tell the victim that they were a target for the purposes of the assailant and not complicit in the crime against them.

— Advise the victim that their reactions are normal reactions to stress.

— Explain biological processes if questioned.

— Anticipate recovery experiences and timing and advise the victim accordingly.

— The emphasis on victim identification of the accused is less important today, given DNA advances.

— Victim services providers and criminal justice officials help victims understand and cope, regardless of the outcome of DNA testing.

— Provide victims with simple but thorough explanations of DNA testing methods, which will vary with elements of their case, including the timing of sample collection, the investigation process, and judicial procedures.

— In victim-centered care, providing materials that match the capacity of the individual, eg, the individual's first language or health disparities, is the overarching goal of all sexual assault response team (SART) members.

Forensic DNA Testing

Serologic Tests

Before the late 1980s and the introduction of DNA testing, forensic examination of biological crime scene evidence involved 2 broad categories of serologic tests:

1. Tests used to identify specific body fluids

2. Tests to individualize (human or nonhuman) or type (blood, semen, saliva) biological evidence

Identifying a body fluid involves first determining whether a substance is blood or semen or something else, for example. Then a second serologic test demonstrates that the fluid is of human origin. The methods changed little over the past 30 years; laboratories used serologic tests to type and individualize biological fluids and, when tested, discarded them. At the time, only a few useful serologic markers existed and the elements expressed in various body fluids were exclusive, ie, excluded suspects without the marker.

Drawbacks to typing body fluids include the following:

— Markers expressed in components of bodily fluids cannot be separated, creating complications when analyzing mixtures from 2 or more individuals.

— Some individuals (nonsecretors) do not express their ABO blood type in their semen or saliva.

— Two individuals often share the same patterns or types for serologic markers; therefore, it is difficult to identify the actual source for the markers. Illustrated by the ABO system, individuals are grouped into 4 broad categories (A, B, O, and AB), with type A, for example, found in 25% to 40% of individuals of Caucasian, African American, and Hispanic populations.

— Thus, the use of serologic markers proved inconclusive because of the low discrimination power of serologic testing.

— When no suspect existed, forensic testing of evidence collected following complaints of sexual assault did not occur and the evidence kits were returned to storage in property rooms. Today, these evidence kits comprise the *rape kit backlog.*

DNA Testing

Two tragic sexual assault–homicides in a small village in England led to a revolution in forensic DNA evaluation. The raped and strangled bodies were found within a short distance of each other, albeit 3 years apart, and forced testing of the biological evidence from the scene using newer DNA methods. Dr. Alec Jeffreys, an academic scientist working at nearby Leicester University, studied a repetitive DNA sequence of the human gene found in myoglobin. He discovered that an amazing level of variability and individuality revealed uniqueness in the probed repetitive sequence in human DNA analysis. Termed the *multi-locus probe,* its potential uses in the analysis of human pedigrees were quickly recognized; however, there was a remote chance that 2 individuals shared the same multi-locus DNA pattern. The incorporation of the repetitive sequence into a technique known as *restriction fragment length polymorphism (RFLP)* resulted in the first generation of forensic DNA tests. Analyzing sperm evidence from the 2 homicide cases with RFLP found a single male responsible for both crimes, who was eventually tried and convicted for both murders.

Restriction Fragment Length Polymorphism Analysis

— First, a calculation of the common RFLP patterns identifies the major differences among racial groups.

— Purified DNA is then specifically dissected using restriction enzymes, which recognize a specific sequence in the DNA molecule and cleave (snip) the molecule with the specific sequence. When cleaved, the DNA molecules of a forensic sample become a collection of fragments of many different sizes. The fragments are separated by size, subjected to electrophoresis, and transferred to a nylon membrane.

— DNA fixes to the membrane by heating, and after subjection to a panel of single-locus probes, sequentially recognizes a unique site in the human genome.

— An image developed on x-ray film has a series of bands, which differs in position because each represents a different DNA fragment size.

— RFLP testing makes it unlikely that DNA samples collected from 2 different individuals will exhibit the same DNA banding pattern (except for identical twins).

— RFLP testing rapidly replaced serologic testing, but 2 problems remain:

  1. RFLP requires a large sample to obtain DNA testing results not usually present in rape cases.

  2. RFLP requires that a biological sample be fresh for obtaining DNA results, also not guaranteed following rape.

Polymerase Chain Reaction (PCR) Analysis

— The PCR process, invented by Dr. Kary Mullis et al in the 1980s, revolutionized the analysis of small quantities of DNA. Molecular biology, medical diagnostics, and forensic science changed in kind. Before PCR, scientists needed to clone a piece of DNA in a labor-intensive process. PCR allows a scientist to create millions of copies of a specific DNA sequence in hours, where isolation and analysis is rapid, accurate, and identical to the original.

— First, a primer, ie, a short, chemically synthesized segment of DNA, typically 15 to 40 nucleotides long, is created. Primers correspond to unique DNA sequences in the human genome, and a pair of primers flank the designated region of interest.

— An enzyme involved in replicating DNA from bacteria found in thermal hot springs is then used along with a thermocycler, ie, an instrument capable of cyclically altering the temperature of a DNA reaction mix, creating denaturation, annealing, and elongation phases for PCR, to replicate the specific DNA sequence.

— Copies multiplied exponentially in the process make extremely small quantities of DNA, useful in future analysis.

— PCR testing consumes DNA from the sample after duplication. PCR is typically 50 to 100 times more sensitive than traditional RFLP testing.

— Segments of analyzed DNA tend to be relatively short, so the technique works well even with degraded DNA.

— The PCR process analyzes DNA from nonbiological evidence, eg, cigarette butts and drinking glasses, and biological evidence, eg, single hairs; minute amounts of sperm; and biological human remains from landslides, mass graves, fire scenes, and plane crashes.

CONVICTED OFFENDER DATABASES

— As of 1998, all 50 states have authorized legislation requiring certain convicted offenders to provide biological samples for analysis and entry into the Combined DNA Index System (CODIS) database.

— Legislation in the states varies widely concerning collection, analysis, sample storage, and maintenance of the databases.

Combined DNA Index System (CODIS)

— The DNA Identification Act of 1994 formalized the authority of the Federal Bureau of Investigation (FBI) to establish a national DNA index system for law enforcement purposes. This index (CODIS) consists of three hierarchic levels, as follows:

1. All DNA profiles originate at the local level (local DNA index system [LDIS]).

2. They then flow to the state level (state DNA index system [SDIS]). SDIS allows laboratories within a state to exchange DNA profiles.

3. They finally reach the national level (national DNA index system [NDIS]). NDIS is the highest level and allows participating laboratories to exchange and compare DNA profiles between states.

4. The tiered approach allows state and local laboratories to operate their databases in accordance with specific legislative and legal requirements.

— The 2 parts of the CODIS system are as follows:

1. *The forensic index**: contains DNA profiles from crime scene evidence, often referred to as forensic unknowns.

2. *The offender index*: contains DNA profiles of individuals convicted of crimes that require a biological sample provided from the offender to law enforcement for DNA profiling.

IMPORTANT BIOLOGICAL EVIDENCE IN SEXUAL ASSAULTS
(**Table 10-3**)

Table 10-3. Guidelines for Collecting Samples From the Human Body
— Patients have the right to request sample collection in extended postcoital interval timing following rape and with delayed reporting, including collection through the first menses or 28 days.
— Patients have the right to decline sample collection and to return at a later date, including collection through the first menses or 28 days.
— Use only one drop of water to moisten swabs.
— Use only paper to package evidence. Freeze-dry all other evidence, including throughout the freeze-dry transport.
— Evidence dictates one swabbing for the cervix followed by the posterior fornix.
— Use only cotton-tipped swabs. Follow your community standards.
— Do not lick sticky seals on evidence envelopes.
— Maintain chain of custody at all times. Follow your community standards for sample collection and packaging.

Follow CDC guidelines[5] and your local protocol for treatment.

— Investigators working sexual assault cases must examine the entire range and locations of possible biological evidence that is potentially probative in solving a particular case.

1. Following sexual assault, make certain that a complete evidence kit is collected from the victim, even in extended postcoital intervals up to and through menses.

2. Swabbings that concentrate samples, eg, fewer swabs, rather than dilute available DNA, eg, more than 2, increase the amount of detectible DNA.

3. Collect swabbings from possible bite marks; breast swabs and/or body swabs when there is a history of kissing, licking, or sucking; fingernail swabbings; clothing worn immediately after the assault; and clothing worn to the hospital, including undergarments.

4. Combined cervical (first) and posterior fornix (after the cervix) swabbings from reproductive-aged victims yield more DNA detection than separate swabbings.

5. Collect any loose hairs from the victim or the victim's clothing.

— Collecting biological evidence from the suspect

1. If in custody, collect penile swabs from male suspects, including the glans, shaft, and scrotum areas.

2. Routinely collect fingernail swabbings during a suspect examination because they often prove probative in cases with digital penetration.

3. Collect clothing from the suspect because body fluids from the victim may be transferred to the suspect's clothing.

4. If the suspect is not wearing the same clothing believed to have been worn during the assault, obtain a warrant or consent to search any premises where investigators believe the clothing may be found.

5. Document genital abnormalities, tattoos, and venereal warts, which may help corroborate the identity of the suspect.

6. Note evidence of scratches, bites, and abrasions, which may corroborate the use of force by the suspect and/or resistance by the victim.

7. Be aware that some jurisdictions require a search warrant or court order before authorizing a suspect examination to obtain forensic biological evidence. A standard operating procedure to facilitate this step of the sexual assault investigation is invaluable.

— Close examination of the environment where the assault took place

1. Examine vehicles, apartments, and houses under appropriate conditions with an alternate light source to detect the presence of possible biological fluids.

2. Look for condoms, tissues, and hairs at the scene.

— Collecting reference samples

— Follow your local practice. Reference sample collection from the victim, suspect, and all consensual partners is no longer the standard because DNA identifies with minute amounts.

COLLECTION PROCEDURES: FOLLOW YOUR
COMMUNITY STANDARDS FOR EVIDENCE COLLECTION

Unknown Specimens

— DNA on clothing: Remove clothing one item at a time and place in separate paper sacks. Take care not to fold through an observed stain, use clean paper as a separator, and fold the item. Photograph stains before packaging. Examine clothing for signs of force and relay information to police officers. Ask whether clothing from the assault is available at another site and relay this information to police officers. Document using documentation form.

— Oral swabs in cases of oral copulation: Take 2 cotton swabs and carefully swab between the cheek and gums, upper and lower lip and gums, where the gum meets the palate, and behind the incisors. Label and package swabs.

— Biological material in hair: Comb the area onto a paper used to catch material. If sticky or dried, moisten with sterile water and absorb the fluid with one cotton-tipped applicator. If material is resistant to collection, cut the suspected area as a last resort. Place any collected trace materials in a paper bindle. Be sensitive to how the collection process will affect the victim's appearance.

— Biological material on skin. Follow your community protocol:

1. Semen: Use a double swab technique. Moisten a cotton swab with one drop of sterile water and roll over the area; set this swab aside in a protected area to dry. Roll another unmoistened swab over the same area, taking the same care to protect and dry the material. Label and package both swabs. Avoid rubbing the area because additional cells dilute samples.

2. Saliva and bite marks: Use a double swab technique. Moisten a cotton swab with one drop of sterile water and roll over the area; set this swab aside in a protected area to dry. Roll another unmoistened swab over the same area, taking the same care to protect and dry the material. Label and package both swabs. Avoid rubbing the area because additional cells dilute samples.

— DNA on miscellaneous items and surfaces:

1. Condoms: When performing a pelvic examination, condoms may be found in the vagina. When found, photograph and carefully remove them. Follow local practices determined by the resource team in your area. Some will instruct to place the condom in multiple paper bags and include them in the evidence collection kit. Other communities will freeze-dry the condom in the envelope to prevent DNA degradation on the internal surfaces of the condom and transfer the evidence with the kit. Either way, the crime laboratory will later collect swabs from both the inside and outside surfaces of the condom in preparation for DNA analysis.

2. Shoes: Photograph any stained areas with the shoes on the person, then remove the shoes and photograph again from different angles. Collect the shoes in a paper bag.

3. DNA from an unknown hair: If a loose hair is observed on the examined person, photograph and collect it using clean-gloved fingers. Sticky-surfaced, clear tape on waxed notepaper works well to pick it up, depending on the type of surface location. Never use forceps or tweezers to collect unknown hair evidence because you may pluck the victim's or suspect's own hair.

Known Reference Specimens

— Collect oral swabs by rolling a cotton swab on the inside of the buccal areas of the cheeks, drying and packaging the samples in a labeled carton.

— Blood specimens from the victim are rarely collected because a buccal swab is adequate for DNA identity and less invasive.

— Follow the community standard for DNA references from the victim.

SUMMARY

— Meticulous and thorough sample collection is important because collected evidence may be probative, not only to implicate the guilty but also to exonerate the innocent.

— Always follow your community standards for evidence collection.

— Recognize that advances in DNA analysis supersede directives in the Quick Reference.

REFERENCE

1. American College of Emergency Physicians. *Evaluation and Management of the Sexually Assaulted or Sexually Abused Patient.* Washington, DC: US Department of Health and Human Services, Health Resources and Services Administration, Maternal and Child Health Bureau; 1999.

2. Bechtel K, Podrazik M. Evaluation of the adolescent rape victim. *Pediatr Clin North Am.* 1999;46(4):809-823, xii.

3. Budowle B, Chakraborty R, Giusti AM, Eisenberg AJ, Allen RC. Analysis of the VNR locus (D1S80) by the PCR followed by high-resolution PAGE. *Am J Hum Genet.* 1991;48(1):137-144.

4. Centers for Disease Control and Prevention. Public health service guidelines for the management of health-care worker exposures to HIV and recommendations for postexposure prophylaxis. *MMWR Recomm Rep.* 1998;47(RR-7):1-28. Centers for Disease Control and Prevention Web site. http://www.cdc.gov/mmwr/preview/mmwrhtml/00052722.htm. Accessed June 2, 2015.

5. Centers for Disease Control and Prevention. Sexually transmitted diseases treatment guidelines, 2015. *MMWR Recomm Rep*. 2015;64(3):1-137.

6. Federal Bureau of Investigation. *The FBI's Combined DNA Index System (CODIS) Program Brochure*. Washington, DC: US Department of Justice; 2000.

7. Frégeau CJ, Fourney RM. DNA typing with fluorescently tagged short tandem repeats: a sensitive and accurate approach to human identification. *Biotechniques*. 1993;15(1):100-119.

8. Gaensslen RE. *Sourcebook in Forensic Serology, Immunology, and Biochemistry*. Washington, DC: National Institute of Justice; 1983.

9. Hampton HL. Care of the woman who has been raped. *N Engl J Med*. 1995;332(4):234-237.

10. Inman K, Rudin N. *An Introduction to Forensic DNA Analysis*. New York, NY: CRC Press; 1997.

11. Jeffreys AJ, Wilson V, Thein SL. Individual specific 'fingerprints' of human DNA. *Nature*. 1985;316(6023):76-79.

12. Lenahan LC, Ernst A, Johnson B. Colposcopy in evaluation of the adult sexual assault victim. *Am J Emerg Med*. 1998;16(2):183-184.

13. Linden JA. Sexual assault. *Emerg Med Clin North Am*. 1999;17(3):685-697, vii.

14. Mayntz-Press KA, Sims LM, Hall A, Ballantyne J. Y-STR profiling in extended interval (> or = 3 days) postcoital cervicovaginal samples. *J Forensic Sci*. 2008;53(2):342-348.

15. Mullis K, Faloona F, Scharf S, Saiki R, Horn G, Erlich H. Specific enzymatic amplification of DNA in vitro: the polymerase chain reaction. *Cold Spring Harb Symp Quant Biol*. 1986;51(pt 1):263-273.

16. National Research Council. *DNA Technology in Forensic Science*. Washington, DC: National Academy Press; 1992.

17. National Research Council. *The Evaluation of Forensic DNA Evidence*. Washington, DC: National Academy Press; 1996.

18. Reynolds R, Sensabaugh G, Blake E. Analysis of genetic markers in forensic DNA samples using the polymerase chain reaction. *Anal Chem.* 1991;63(1):2-15.

19. Saferstein R, ed. *Forensic Science Handbook.* Vol 1. Englewood Cliffs, NJ: Prentice Hall, Inc; 1982.

20. Saferstein R, ed. *Forensic Science Handbook.* Vol 2. Englewood Cliffs, NJ: Prentice Hall, Inc; 1988.

21. Schwarcz SK, Whittington WL. Sexual assault and sexually transmitted diseases: detection and management in adults and children. *Rev Infect Dis.* 1990;12(suppl 6):S682-S690.

22. Speck PM, Ballantyne J. *Post-Coital DNA Recovery Study.* Washington, DC: National Institute of Justice; 2015.

23. Stewart FH, Trussell J. Prevention of pregnancy resulting from rape: a neglected preventive health measure. *Am J Prev Med.* 2000;19(4):228-229.

24. Sweet D, Lorente M, Lorente JA, Valenzuela A, Villanueva E. An improved method to recover saliva from human skin: the double swab technique. *J Forensic Sci.* 1997;42(2):320-322.

25. Trussell J, Koenig J, Ellertson C, Stewart F. Preventing unintended pregnancy: the cost-effectiveness of three methods of emergency contraception. *Am J Public Health.* 1997;87(6):932-937.

26. Wambaugh J. *The Blooding.* New York, NY: Bantam Doubleday Dell Publishing Group; 1989.

Chapter 11

SEXUALLY TRANSMITTED INFECTIONS

Aimee Chism Holland, DNP, WHNP-BC, FNP-C*
Kelley Catron, DNP, WHNP-BC*
Natalie Baker, DNP, ANP-BC, GNP-BC*
Ashton Tureaud, DNP, MSN, CRNP, FNP-C, SANE*
Margot Schwartz, MD
Jeanne Marrazzo, MD, MPH
Patricia M. Speck, DNSc, APN, FNP-BC, DF-IAFN, FAAFS, FAAN*

Male and female victims of sexual assault often fear acquiring sexually transmitted infections (STIs). In addition, women who are sexually assaulted may fear becoming pregnant as a result.

SEXUALLY TRANSMITTED INFECTIONS

— If the sexual assault patient comes for medical care within 72 hours of the assault, many STIs will not have had sufficient time to incubate and thus will not be detected.

— If *Chlamydia trachomatis* is present in the semen of the assailant, it may be detected in a female assault victim immediately after assault.

— It is rarely possible to determine whether an STI was present prior to assault. Proving that an STI was acquired as the result of an assault may carry important legal or emotional ramifications.

— Factors that predict risk for acquiring an STI include the following:

1. Whether or not penile penetration and ejaculation occurred

2. The type of sexual assault that occurred, ie, vaginal, anal, or oral

3. The number of assailants

Revised Chapter 11 for the second edition.

4. The patient's susceptibility to infection

5. The size of the inoculum for a given pathogen

6. The organism's infectivity

— If recognized at the postassault examination, gonorrhea, *Chlamydia*, and trichomoniasis can be treated.

— Vaccination for preventable STIs such as hepatitis B and human papillomavirus (HPV) should be considered.

— HIV postexposure prophylaxis (PEP) should also be considered.

RECOGNITION AND TREATMENT OF COMMON SEXUALLY TRANSMITTED INFECTIONS AND ASSOCIATED SYNDROMES
Sexually transmitted infections can be caused by bacteria, viruses, protozoa, or treponemes. In addition, ectoparasites such as lice or scabies are parasites that live on skin or hair and may be transmitted during an assault. **Table 11-1** summarizes the treatment options for STIs commonly diagnosed after sexual assault.

Table 11-1. Antibiotic Regimens Recommended by the Centers for Disease Control and Prevention (CDC) to Treat STIs

GONORRHEA* (UNCOMPLICATED URETHRITIS, CERVICITIS, OR PROCTITIS)

Antibiotic	Dose and Route	Duration
First Line:		
Combo Ceftriaxone	250 mg IM‡	Single dose
and Azithromycin	1 g PO	Single dose
or		
If Ceftriaxone is not available, prescribe:		
Cefixime	400 mg PO	Single dose

(continued)

Table 11-1. Antibiotic Regimens Recommended by the Centers for Disease Control and Prevention (CDC) to Treat STIs *(continued)*

CHLAMYDIA (UNCOMPLICATED CERVICITIS OR PROCTITIS)

Antibiotic	Dose and Route	Duration
First Line:		
Azithromycin	1 g PO	Single dose
or		
Doxycycline	100 mg PO bid[§]	7 days
Alternatives:		
Levofloxacin	500 mg qd PO	7 days
Ofloxacin	300 mg bid PO	7 days
Erythromycin base	500 mg qid PO	7 days
Erythromycin		
ethylsuccinate	800 mg qid PO	7 days

TRICHOMONIASIS

Antibiotic	Dose and Route	Duration
First Line:		
Metronidazole	2 g PO	Single dose
or		
Tinidazole	2 g PO	Single dose
Alternative Regimen:		
Metronidazole	500 mg bid PO	7 days

PRIMARY HERPES SIMPLEX VIRUS INFECTION (FIRST CLINICAL EPISODE)

Antibiotic	Dose and Route	Duration
Acyclovir	400 mg PO tid	7-10 days
Acyclovir	200 mg PO 5 times daily	7-10 days
Famciclovir	250 mg PO tid	7-10 days
Valacyclovir	1 g PO bid	7-10 days

(continued)

> **Table 11-1. Antibiotic Regimens Recommended by the Centers for Disease Control and Prevention (CDC) to Treat STIs** *(continued)*
>
> BACTERIAL VAGINOSIS
>
> | Antibiotic | Dose and Route | Duration |
> | --- | --- | --- |
> | *First Line:* | | |
> | Metronidazole | 500 mg PO bid | 7 days |
> | Metronidazole gel (0.75%) | 5 g intravaginally qd | 5 days |
> | Clindamycin cream (2%) | 5 g intravaginally qhs | 7 days |
> | | | |
> | *Alternative Regime:* | | |
> | Clindamycin | 300 mg PO bid | 7 days |
> | Clindamycin ovules | 100 mg intravaginally qhs | 3 days |
> | Tinidazole | 2 g PO | 2 days |
> | Tinidazole | 1 g PO | 5 days |
>
> *When treating for gonorrhea, also treat empirically for Chlamydia
> ‡IM=intramuscularly, PO=orally, mg=milligrams, g=gram.
> §qd=once daily, bid=twice daily, tid=3 times daily, qid=4 times daily, qhs=at night
> Adapted from Centers for Disease Control and Prevention.[6]

Chancroid

— Caused by the bacteria *Haemophilus ducreyi*

— An uncommon cause of genital ulcer in most areas of the United States

— Signs/symptoms: ulcers that are often painful (differentiating them from ulcers of syphilis); tender regional lymphadenopathy

— Diagnosed only by culture; if suspected, consult an expert

— Probable diagnosis can be made if all of the following criteria met:

    — One or more genital ulcers present

    — No evidence of *T. pallidum* infection in ulcer exudate or by serologic test for syphilis performed at least 7 days after onset of ulcer

    — Clinical presentation, genital ulcer appearance, and lymphadenopathy present

    — HSV test on ulcer is negative

Mucopurulent Cervicitis

— Characterized by the presence of mucopurulent endocervical exudate, with easily induced cervical bleeding and edematous cervical ectopy possible

— Over half of all cases have no known etiology.

— Controversial criteria for diagnosis; in women under age 25 years, presence of at least 30 polymorphonuclear lymphocytes per 1000 hpf on examination of endocervical exudate suggests but does not offer definitive evidence of infection; many experts recommend that this test not be performed.

— If mucopurulent cervicitis is noted, woman should be tested for gonorrhea and *Chlamydia*.

Pelvic Inflammatory Disease (PID)

— Refers to any combination of endometritis, salpingitis, tubo-ovarian abscess, and pelvic peritonitis

— Associated with sexually transmitted pathogens as well as bacteria that normally colonize the vagina

— Must recognize and treat early to avoid sequelae such as infertility, chronic pelvic pain, and ectopic pregnancy. (See **Table 11-2** for recommended treatments.)

— Signs/symptoms: lower abdominal pain, nausea and/or vomiting, fever >38.3°C (>101° F), abnormal mucopurulent discharge, sometimes a change in menstrual pattern, abdominal tenderness, adnexal tenderness, cervical motion tenderness, abundance of white blood cells visualized on wet prep of vaginal discharge, elevated erythrocyte sedimentation rate, elevated C-reactive protein

— Empiric treatment should be initiated if the patient is experiencing pelvic or lower abdominal pain and at least one of the following are present upon examination: cervical motion tenderness (CMT), uterine tenderness, or adnexal tenderness.

— Hospitalization may be needed for patients who are pregnant; unable to take oral therapy; with suspected tubo-ovarian abscess; or who have severe illness with nausea, vomiting, a higher fever, or another surgical diagnosis

Table 11-2. Recommended Treatment for Pelvic Inflammatory Disease

OUTPATIENT

Recommended:

— Ceftriaxone 250 mg IM (single dose)
   plus
   Doxycycline 100 mg PO bid for 14 days, with or without
      metronidazole 500 mg PO twice daily for 14 days
      or

— Cefoxitin 2 g IM and Probenecid, 1 g PO concurrently (single dose)
   plus
   Doxycycline 100 mg PO bid for 14 days, with or without
      metronidazole 500 mg PO twice daily for 14 days
      or

— Another third generation cephalosporin, eg, ceftizoxime or cefotaxime
   plus
   Doxycycline 100 mg PO bid for 14 days, with or without
      metronidazole 500 mg PO twice daily for 14 days

INPATIENT

Recommended:

— Intravenous Cefotetan 2 g IV every 12 hours *or* Cefoxitin 2 g IV
      every 6 hours
   plus
   Doxycycline 100 mg IV *or* PO every 12 hours (for 24 hours if IV *or*
      for 14 days if PO)
      or
— Clindamycin 900 mg IV every 8 hours
   plus
   Gentamicin loading dose IV or IM (2 mg/kg of body weight),
      followed by a maintenance dose (1.5 mg/kg) every 8 hours.
      Single daily dosing (3-5 mg/kg) can be substituted

(continued)

Table 11-2. Recommended Treatment for Pelvic Inflammatory Disease *(continued)*

ALTERNATIVE

— Ampicillin/Sulbactam 3 g IV every 6 hours
   __plus__
   Doxycycline 100 mg PO *__or__* IV every 12 hours

Adapted from Centers for Disease Control and Prevention.[6]

Proctitis and Proctocolitis

— Proctitis is inflammation of mucosal lining of distal 10-12 cm of rectum; it is transmitted through anal intercourse.

— Signs/symptoms of proctitis: inflammation of the rectum with anorectal pain or itching, tenesmus (a sensation that one must defecate when colon is empty), or rectal discharge; caused by *Neisseria gonorrhoeae, C. trachomatis, Treponema pallidum*, herpes simplex virus, human papillomavirus, and human immunodeficiency virus (HIV).

— Proctocolitis is inflammation of the mucosal lining of the colon and rectum that extends to 12 cm above the anus. It is considered a more severe form of proctitis. Depending on the pathogen, it can be transmitted orally or through anal intercourse or oral-anal contact.

— Signs/symptoms of proctocolitis: those listed for proctitis plus diarrhea and/or abdominal cramping. In addition to pathogens that cause proctitis, proctocolitis may also be caused by *Campylobacter* sp., *Shigella* sp., *Entamoeba histolytica*, or *Chlamydia trachomatis* (lymphogranuloma venereum serotype).

— Diagnosed on anoscopy or sigmoidoscopy, abdominal and perianal examination, Gram stain of exudate or mucus obtained from the anus, rectal cultures and cultures for herpes simplex virus, darkfield examination, and RPR; obtain stool samples for evaluation of enteric pathogens.

— Treatment varies depending on clinical findings. (See **Table 11-3** for more information on recommended treatments.)

Table 11-3. Recommended Treatment for Proctitis and Proctocolitis

CLINICAL FINDING	TREATMENT
Presence of anorectal exudate or polymorphonuclear leukocytes on Gram stain of anorectal secretions	Ceftriaxone 250 mg IM ***plus*** Doxycycline 100 mg PO bid for 7 days
Herpes simplex virus (suspected or documented)	Acyclovir 400 mg PO tid for 7-10 days* *or* Acyclovir 200 mg PO 5 times daily for 7-10 days* *or* Famciclovir 250 mg PO tid for 7-10 days* *or* Valacyclovir 1 g PO bid for 7-10 days*
Lymphogranuloma venereum	Doxycycline 100 mg PO bid for 21 days

Extend duration if complete healing is not achieved.
Adapted from Centers for Disease Control and Prevention.[4,6]

Pediculus Pubis (Pubic Lice)
— Caused by *Phthirus pubis*

— Signs/symptoms: itching and/or visible lice or nits in the pubic hair; may also affect other areas of the body with hair, including the thighs, eyelashes, eyebrows, and trunk

— Treatments*:

1. Permethrin 1% cream rinse (Nix) recommended; important to follow package instructions for length of time medicine is left on skin before washing

None of these should be used around the eyes.

2. Lindane 1% shampoo (Kwell, Scabene); not first line treatment unless other treatments contraindicated; should not be used in pregnant or lactating women, young children, elderly people, individuals with severe dermatitis or open skin lesions, or those with seizure disorders

3. Malathion lotion 0.5% (Ovide) and oral ivermectin have not been approved by FDA for treatment of pediculis pubis.

4. All clothing and bedding must be washed and dried at high temperatures to prevent reinfection.

Scabies
— Caused by *Sarcoptes scabiei*

— Signs/symptoms: severe itching and papular erythematous rash, often with linear burrows, vesicles, and pustules; commonly affects the finger webs and arms, trunk, inguinal area, labia majora, penis, scrotum, or buttocks

— Diagnosis confirmed by microscopic examination of a scraping from a fresh papule under oil may reveal the mite, eggs, or feces of *S. scabiei.*

— Treatments:

1. Permethrin 5% cream (Elimite) recommended; important to follow package instructions for length of time medicine is left on skin before washing.*

2. Lindane 1% lotion or cream can be used as an alternative; observe the precautions listed above.

3. All clothing and bedding must be washed and dried at high temperatures to prevent reinfection.

Viral Hepatitis
Hepatitis A, hepatitis B, and hepatitis C viruses can be transmitted by sexual contact.

Over-the-counter permethrin is not effective in eliminating scabies.

— Hepatitis A:

1. Shed in the feces; transmission is fecal-oral which can be transmitted through sexual activity.

2. Men who have sex with men (MSM), illicit drug users, and persons with chronic liver failure are at increased risk of sexually acquired hepatitis A.

3. Flu-like symptoms generally occur 2-4 weeks after exposure and can include low-grade fever, nausea, vomiting, anorexia, malaise, myalgia, arthralgia, easy fatigability, upper respiratory symptoms, and anorexia.

4. Disease is self-limited; treatment is supportive; anti-HAV IgM diagnostic

5. For persons who have not previously received Hepatitis A vaccine, postexposure prophylaxis is recommended; single dose Hepatitis A vaccine or immune globulin should be given.

— Hepatitis B:

1. Transmitted through blood or body fluids containing blood

2. Symptoms present 6 weeks to 6 months after exposure; highly variable, ranging from low-grade fever, jaundice, dark urine, pruritus, nausea, vomiting, and anorexia to death. Small subset of patients will develop chronic disease.

3. Acute illness confirmed with positive HbsAg.

4. Serological testing should be done in sexual assault victims who have previously been vaccinated to determine adequate immunity. Start Hepatitis B series if previously unvaccinated; give hepatitis B immune globulin if inadequate immunity.

— Hepatitis C

1. Can be transmitted from sexual contact, but transmission risks are low

2. Symptoms present 6-7 weeks after exposure. Most individuals with hepatitis C do not have symptoms.

3. Acute illness confirmed with positive antibody test

HISTORY AND PHYSICAL EXAMINATION

— **Table 11-4** lists important information to obtain from the sexual assault patient regarding the sexual history. In 2013, the United States Department of Justice's Office of Violence Against Women published a national protocol to be used for sexual assault medical forensic evaluations performed for adults and adolescents.*

Table 11-4. Important Information to Assess STI Risk for Survivors of Sexual Assault

1. Date and time of assault

2. Interval between the assault and the initial medical evaluation

3. Number of assailants

4. Description and identification, if possible, of the assailant(s)

5. If the assailant is known, is his/her HIV status known?

6. Are the assailant's histories of STI and risk behaviors, such as intravenous drug use, known?

7. Description of the assault, including type of sexual contact, ie, vaginal, anal, and oral; penetration by a body part or other object; ejaculation; condom use; extragenital contact, ie, vaginal, anal, and oral; trauma or threats that occurred; use of weapons by the assailant. Include a description of any contact with the assailant's blood or bodily fluid, especially on mucosal surfaces or breaks in the skin.

8. History of consensual sexual intercourse (ever, most recent, including any voluntary sexual intercourse that occurred between the assault and the initial evaluation, or between the initial evaluation and follow-up examination)

9. Last menstrual period and pregnancy status (for female patients)

10. Use of contraception (for female patients)

11. History of bathing, urinating, defecating, douching, changing clothes, or brushing teeth between the assault and the initial examination

12. History of STI in patient

(continued)

This protocol can be found at https://www.ncjrs.gov/pdffiles1/ovw/241903.pdf and contains a section focused on STI evaluation and care.

> **Table 11-4. Important Information to Assess STI Risk for Patients of Sexual Assault** *(continued)*
>
> 13. History of previous sexual assault
> 14. Any symptoms including vaginal or rectal discharge; pelvic or rectal pain; genital, perianal, or oral lesions
> 15. History of prior or chronic medical conditions, including thrombosis, liver disease, or hypertension, which are theoretical contraindications to pregnancy prophylaxis
> 16. Medication allergy

— Perform a targeted examination for STIs along with collection of specimens for STI testing. Use the acronym **TEARS** (**T**ears, ie, breaks in skin; **E**cchymosis; **A**brasions; **R**edness; **S**welling) to help describe exam findings.

1. Examine the genitals, mouth, throat, and anus.

2. Inspect the lower abdomen, inguinal areas, thighs, hands, palms, and soles for rashes or lesions.

3. Examine the inguinal and femoral areas for lymphadenopathy.

4. In women, perform a speculum examination of the vagina and cervix and a bimanual pelvic examination; perform a colposcopy to evaluate internal genital trauma.

5. In men and women, evaluate the anus for seminal fluid and signs of trauma, eg, relaxed external sphincter, fissures, and hemorrhoids.

6. If anorectal injury is suspected perform proctoscopy or anoscopy.

7. In men, inspect the penis, including retraction of the foreskin and visualization of the urethral meatus; examine the prostate gland during a digital rectal examination.

Diagnostic Evaluation
(See **Table 11-5** for STI evaluations in adult and adolescent men and women.)

Table 11-5. Recommended Evaluation for STIs in Adult and Adolescent Victims of Sexual Assault

WOMEN

— Saline preparation of vaginal fluid to examine for motile trichomonads, clue cells, yeast, and white blood cells
— Culture of vaginal fluid for *T. vaginalis*
— Culture or nucleic acid amplification (NAA) tests for *N. gonorrhoeae* and *C. trachomatis*
— Serum testing for HIV antibody, HIV viral load, HIV resistance testing, CD4 T lymphocyte count, hepatitis B (surface antigen and antibody), hepatitis C antibody, and syphilis
— Culture of suspicious lesions for herpes simplex virus if diagnosis was not established
— Based on routine cervical cancer screening guidelines, screen for HPV in women ≥30 years old

MEN

— Culture or NAA tests for *N. gonorrhoeae* and *C. trachomatis* from any site of penetration or attempted penetration
— Gram stain of any rectal or urethral discharge for evidence of gram-negative intracellular diplococci and PMNs
— Serum testing for HIV antibody, HIV viral load, HIV resistance testing, CD4 T lymphocyte count, hepatitis B (surface antigen and antibody), hepatitis C antibody, and syphilis

FOLLOW-UP EXAMINATIONS

— Two weeks after the assault or sooner (1 week) if no prophylactic therapy was provided
— Repeat tests as above, unless prophylactic treatment was provided or if symptoms are reported
— Follow-up serologic testing for HIV, hepatitis B (surface antigen and antibody), hepatitis C antibody, and syphilis at 4-6, 12, and 24 weeks after exposure if initial results were negative

— NAA tests are sensitive in detecting *C. trachomatis* and *N. gonorrhoeae*. While false positive results occur rarely, in a sexual assault evaluation, it may be necessary to confirm nonculture tests by a second FDA-approved NAA test that targets a different molecule from the initial test. Ligase chain reaction (LCR) and polymerase chain reaction (PCR) tests are approved using specimens only from the cervix, urethra, and urine. Other nonculture tests for *C. trachomatis* are the DNA probe, fluorescent antibody, and enzyme immunoassay (EIA) tests. Culture for gonorrhea and *Chlamydia* are the gold standard for legal evidence.

— If prophylactic treatment was used after nonculture techniques during the initial evaluation, retesting for legal evidence is problematic.

— Male sexual assault patients are at a higher risk for syphilis, HIV, and enteropathogens; they should be tested and treated for these illnesses if symptomatic.

— Perform baseline serologic tests for hepatitis B (in a victim not previously vaccinated) and syphilis; offer serologic testing for HIV; perform serum or urine pregnancy tests for women.

— Perform a follow-up examination in 1-2 weeks to detect newly acquired infections and continue efforts to counsel and treat victims of sexual assault.

  1. Include repeat testing for gonorrhea and *Chlamydia*.

  2. Include saline microscopy of vaginal fluid in women if they did not receive prophylactic therapy against specific STIs or if they have new symptoms of STIs.

— Perform follow-up serologic testing for syphilis, HIV, hepatitis B, and hepatitis C at 4-6, 12, and 24 weeks after the assault if the test results were negative at the initial examination. Also, offer follow-up pregnancy tests to women of childbearing age.

TREATMENT AND PROPHYLAXIS OF STIs

— Offer treatment for any STIs diagnosed at the initial follow-up examination; be aware that follow-up rates for victims of sexual assault are poor and encourage the patient to come for care.

— Offer routine prophylaxis at the initial examination (see **Table 11-6**).

Table 11-6. STI Prophylaxis in the Adult Patient of Sexual Assault

— Ceftriaxone 250 mg IM once
   plus
   Azithromycin 1 g PO once
   plus
   Metronidazole 2 g PO once (for women or men who were assaulted by women)
— Hepatitis B vaccine if no prior history of vaccination or natural immunity; first dose at initial examination, second dose at 1 month after first dose, and third dose at 6 months after the initial dose
— HPV vaccine if no prior history of vaccination; first dose at initial examination, second dose at 2 months after first dose, and third dose at 6 months after the initial dose
— HIV postexposure prophylaxis: see **Table 11-7.**

Table 11-7. Recommended Regimens for HIV Postexposure Prophylaxis to be Initiated Within 72 Hours of Sexual Exposure to HIV

Treatment Regimens (4 Weeks)

Preferred Regimen
— Truvada (Tenofovir and Emtricitabine) *plus* Isentress (Raltegravir)

Alternate Regimen
— Truvada (Tenofovir and Emtricitabine) *plus* Reyataz
   (Ritonavir-boosted Atazanavir)
— Truvada (Tenofovir and Emtricitabine) *plus* Prezista
   (Ritonavir-boosted Darunavir)

Adapted from US Department of Health and Human Services, Panel on Antiretroviral Guidelines for Adults and Adolescents.[12]

HIV Postexposure Prophylaxis
— Postexposure prophylaxis (PEP) is most effective when taken within 72 hours of exposure.

— The risk of acquiring HIV infection through sexual assault is low, but HIV seroconversion has occurred after sexual assault. The highest rates of HIV acquisition are with receptive anal intercourse among MSM and with receptive vaginal intercourse.

— Individuals with high viral loads of HIV in the blood are more likely to transmit HIV through sexual intercourse than are those with low viral loads.

— Serum levels are generally highest immediately after seroconversion during the acute or primary HIV illness or in the late stages of acquired immunodeficiency syndrome (AIDS).

— If the HIV status of the assailant is not known, determine if the assailant has any known risk factors for HIV, eg, intravenous drug use or being an MSM, and note the type of contact that occurred during the assault and to which body fluids the victim may have been exposed; the number of assailants may also be a factor, as may the type and severity of physical trauma.

— Be aware that STIs are cofactors for HIV transmission, so the presence of an STI, especially a genital ulcer, may increase the likelihood that HIV transmission will occur.

— If the patient did not know the assailant, so that risk cannot be established, consider the length of time since the exposure, the health and reproductive status of the patient, the local epidemiology of HIV, and the patient's attitude toward postexposure prophylaxis. Clearly discuss the risks versus benefits of postexposure prophylaxis before it is given.

— The choice of antiretroviral agents used for postexposure prophylaxis is based on guidelines for occupationally exposed individuals and for treating patients with known HIV infection.

— Each facility should consult with an infectious disease specialist to determine and maintain the HIV postexposure prophylaxis drug regimen prescribed to patients.

— Sexual assault patients should be informed that the efficacy of HIV postexposure prophylaxis is unknown and is not a cure for HIV. After the patient starts this regimen, management should be continued under the care of a HIV specialist that includes regular laboratory evaluation and follow-up visits.

— Three to 5 days of this prophylaxis regimen should be prescribed for the patient to cover the time needed until the HIV specialist appointment.

— Once antiretroviral agents are initiated, encourage the patient to continue uninterrupted treatment for 4 weeks, unless the assailant was confirmed to be HIV negative and is not likely to be in the process of seroconversion or a prohibitive side effect develops.

— Side effects of antiretroviral agents are common; counsel the patient about what to expect; encourage the patient to call if side effects develop. Common side effects of antiretroviral therapy include gastrointestinal symptoms, fatigue, myalgia, headache, insomnia, rash, hepatotoxicity, nephrolithiasis, and bone marrow suppression.

— Baseline laboratory testing that includes screening for HIV, hepatitis B, hepatitis C, a complete metabolic profile (CMP), and a complete blood count (CBC) should be performed within 3 days of receiving the regimen. If a protease inhibitor is used, assess serum glucose levels; if indinavir is used, do an amylase evaluation and urinalysis; if didanosine is used, perform an amylase test. Obtain a baseline HIV test in 6 weeks, 3 months, and 6 months after exposure.

— Most individuals will seroconvert within the first 3 months after exposure.

— Educate the patient regarding the symptoms of primary HIV infection: prolonged febrile or flu-like illness, fatigue, lymphadenopathy, rash, and pharyngitis.

— For high-risk exposures, postexposure prophylaxis should be offered regardless of cost. The approximate cost of the postexposure prophylaxis medication regimen is between $800 and $1200.

— **Table 11-7** lists the suggested regimens for HIV postexposure prophylaxis.

Emergency Oral Contraception

— Immediate access to emergency contraception should be made available to all female sexual assault patients who seek medical care and should be utilized within 120 hours after unprotected sex.

— The copper intrauterine device (IUD) is considered the most effective emergency contraception method available. Placement by a health care practitioner is required. This method should be avoided in women known to have a gonorrhea or *Chlamydia* infection due to the increased risk of pelvic inflammatory disease (PID).

— Ulipristal is considered the most effective oral method of emergency contraception. Ulipristal requires a prescription.

— Levonorgestrel is less effective than Ulipristal but more effective than the traditional Yuzpe regimen. Levonorgestrel does not require a prescription.

— Other products available for oral emergency contraception use with a prescription include: My Way, Next Choice One Dose, Plan B One-Step, and Take Action. These products require the patient to take 1 pill within 120 hours of having unprotected sex.

— **Table 11-8** lists recommended regimens available for emergency contraception use.

Table 11-8. Recommended Regimens for Emergency Oral Contraception

COPPER IUD (PARAGARD)(99% EFFECTIVE)

— Insert within 120 hours after unprotected sex

ULIPRISTAL (ELLA)(98%-99% EFFECTIVE)

— 30 mg tablet PO single dose
— 98%-99% effective

LEVONORGESTREL REGIMEN (59%-94% EFFECTIVE)

— Levonorgestrel 0.75 mg PO now and repeated 12 hours later
　　or
— Levonorgestrel 1.5 mg PO single dose   *(continued)*

Table 11-8. Recommended Regimens for Emergency Oral Contraception (*continued*)

YUZPE REGIMEN (47%-89% EFFECTIVE)

— 100-120 micrograms of ethinyl estradiol and 500-600 micrograms of levonorgestrel in each dose now and repeated 12 hours later

Adapted from Zieman M.[14]

— The most common side effects of emergency oral contraception are nausea and vomiting. Other effects include irregular bleeding, delayed return of menses, fatigue, headaches, breast tenderness, and abdominal pain.

— Counsel all women who receive emergency oral contraception regarding predicted efficacy and potential side effects, and remind them that oral contraception or hormonal contraceptives do not prevent STIs.

— Instruct the patient to seek pregnancy testing if menses does not resume within a week of the expected date.

REFERENCES

1. Aberg JA, Daskalakis DC. Nonoccupational exposure to HIV in adults. UpToDate Web site. http://www.uptodate.com/contents/nonoccupational-exposure-to-hiv-in-adults. Updated July 24, 2014. Accessed April 29, 2015.

2. Centers for Disease Control and Prevention. Hepatitis C information for health professionals. Centers for Disease Control and Prevention Web site. http://www.cdc.gov/hepatitis/HCV/index.htm. Updated July 17, 2014. Accessed April 29, 2015.

3. Centers for Disease Control and Prevention. Parasites - lice - pubic "crab" lice. Centers for Disease Control and Prevention Web site. http://www.cdc.gov/parasites/lice/pubic/index.html. Updated September 24, 2013. Accessed April 29, 2015.

4. Centers for Disease Control and Prevention. Proctitis, proctocolitis, and enteritis. Centers for Disease Control and Prevention Web site. http://www.cdc.gov/std/treatment/2010/proctitis.htm. Updated August 18, 2014. Accessed April 29, 2015.

5. Centers for Disease Control and Prevention. Sexually transmitted disease treatment guidelines, 2010. *MMWR Morb Mortal Wkly Rep.* 2010;59(RR-12):1-116.

6. Centers for Disease Control and Prevention. Sexually transmitted diseases treatment guidelines, 2015. *MMWR Morb Mortal Wkly Rep.* 2015;64(RR3):1-137.

7. Kiefer MM, Chong CR. *Pocket Primary Care.* Philadelphia, PA: Wolters Kluwer Health; 2014.

8. Klausner JD, Hook EW. *Current Diagnosis & Treatment of Sexually Transmitted Diseases.* New York, NY: McGraw Hill; 2007.

9. Papadakis MA, McPhee SJ. *Current Medical Diagnosis and Treatment 2015.* New York, NY: McGraw Hill, 2014.

10. Sexual Assault Forensic Examiner Program, Office of the Maine Attorney General. Sexual assault forensic examiner program guidelines for the care of the sexual assault patient. Office of the Maine Attorney General Web site. https://www1.maine.gov/ag/crime/victims_compensation/Guidelines%20for%20the%20Care%20of%20the%20Sexual%20Assault%20Patient.pdf. Published January 2011. Accessed April 29, 2015.

11. Smith DK, Grohskopf LA, Black RJ, et al. Antiretroviral postexposure prophylaxis after sexual, injection-drug use, or other nonoccupational exposure to HIV in the United States: recommendations from the U.S. Department of Health and Human Services. *MMWR Recomm Rep.* 2005;54(RR02):1-20.

12. US Department of Health and Human Services, Panel on Antiretroviral Guidelines for Adults and Adolescents. Guidelines for the use of antiretroviral agents in HIV-1-infected adults and adolescents. National Institutes of Health Web site. http://aidsinfo.nih.gov/contentfiles/lvguidelines/adultandadolescentgl.pdf. Updated April 28, 2015. Accessed April 29, 2015.

13. White C. Genital injuries in adults. *Best Pract Res Clin Obstet Gynaecol.* 2013;27(1):113-130.

14. Zieman M. Emergency contraception. UpToDate Web site. http://www.uptodate.com/contents/emergency-contraception. Updated March 30, 2015. Accessed April 29, 2015.

Chapter 12

PREGNANCY

Donna Campbell Dunn, PhD, CNM, FNP-BC*
Annie McCartney, MSN, WHNP-BC*
Mary Katherine Dunne Atkins, BSN, RN*
Janice B. Asher, MD
Elizabeth M. Datner, MD
Patricia M. Speck, DNSc, APN, FNP-BC, DF-IAFN, FAAFS, FAAN*

Violence in pregnancy is a challenging situation because there are 2 victims involved: mother and fetus. Multiple scenarios may occur in regard to sexual assault and pregnancy. For example, sexual assault can be domestic violence, can be committed against a woman who is already pregnant, or result in the victim becoming pregnant.

SEXUAL ASSAULT AND PREGNANCY
DOMESTIC VIOLENCE DURING PREGNANCY
— Abusers commonly employ physical violence, emotional abuse, intimidation, isolation, and sexual assault to gain control or power over a partner.

— The most common mental health consequence of intimate partner violence (IPV) is depression. Signs and symptoms of depression are reported by approximately 40% of abused women.

— Posttraumatic stress disorder (PTSD) is another commonly reported health condition in women experiencing IPV and it is reported to affect 19%-84% of victims.

— IPV should be screened at least once per trimester but preferably every visit. Unfortunately, the first prenatal appointment is often the first and only time screening for IPV occurs.

*Revised Chapter 12 for the second edition.

— A causative factor for IPV in pregnancy and postpartum is a history of violence by the victim's partner, especially within the last 12 months before pregnancy.

— Escalation of IPV in frequency and intensity during pregnancy can arise from:

1. New opportunities for continuation of power and control

2. Jealousy toward the baby

3. Anger because the pregnancy was unplanned and undesired but not aborted

4. Obstetric complications and financial concerns induce stress which in return precipitates the escalation of IPV.

— Research has shown that women abused during pregnancy often delay initiation of their prenatal care until the third trimester. They are also twice as likely to miss routine prenatal visits throughout the pregnancy.

— Unplanned pregnancy can result from IPV because the abuser uses power and coercion to force sexual activity and deny use of contraception.

— Barriers to identifying and preventing IPV in pregnancy include the following:

1. Pregnancy may cause women to feel more emotionally and financially vulnerable, especially if they are dependent on a partner's health insurance and income.

2. Anxiety may arise in attempts to keep the family together and prevent raising a child in a broken home.

3. False hope that the IPV is situational and will disappear in the postpartum period when baby is finally home

Pregnancy as a Window of Opportunity for Intervention

— The numerous visits with clinicians that pregnancy affords and the common goal of delivering a healthy baby provide the opportunity for a trusting relationship to develop between patient and provider.

— During pregnancy, an abused woman may do on behalf of her baby what she would not otherwise do for herself.

— Social, economic, and community support systems are more easily accessed during pregnancy education, and referrals should be provided appropriately by clinicians.

Domestic Violence and Child Abuse

— Child abuse and maternal abuse are inextricably linked. Nearly 60% of abused children have mothers who are also abused.

— Women who were abused as children have earlier first pregnancies than women without a history of childhood abuse.

— Women who were sexually abused as children are almost 5 times as likely to be sexually abused as adults.

— Unintended pregnancy is a common outcome in abusive relationships because abused women may not be able to negotiate sexual activity or contraceptive use.

— Barriers to addressing domestic violence in pregnancy are as follows:

1. Pregnant women may feel more vulnerable emotionally and financially, including being dependent on a partner's health insurance.

2. Women may also be particularly anxious to keep their families together.

3. A woman may hope that the situation will improve after the baby is born and that her most intense fears are groundless.

SEXUAL ASSAULT AND ABUSE OF PREGNANT WOMEN

— Pregnant women who are abused may be at increased risk for various obstetric, medical, and psychosocial complications.

1. Late onset of prenatal care or inconsistent prenatal care has been shown to increase the negative impact to mother and fetus.

2. During an attack, much of the harm is often the result of the attacker focusing on the breast, abdomen, and genitals.

— Because of the increased vascularity of the vulva and external structures, blunt trauma to the external genitals in the second and third trimester may be much more severe for the pregnant women than in a nonpregnant woman. Hematomas are commonly seen in labia of a pregnant woman following blunt trauma.

— Vulvar, hymenal, and vaginal tearing are rarely seen due to increased estrogen levels throughout pregnancy. When injury is seen, especially in the second and third trimester, suspect instrumentation.

— Cervical bruising is common due to the increased vascularity during pregnancy.

1. Sexual assault of the pregnant woman who has a placenta previa places the pregnant woman and the fetus at risk for potentially fatal hemorrhage.

2. Sexual assault carries an overall increased risk of miscarriage, rupture of membranes, fetal injury, and fetal death.

— Clinical manifestations include inadequate prenatal care; abdominal and genital trauma; signs of physical trauma such as bruising, lacerations, etc; adverse outcome for the pregnancy; unintended pregnancy and sexually transmitted infections (STIs); depression; drug and alcohol abuse; and pregnancy termination.

— Red flags in identifying abuse and assault are as follows:

1. History of abuse in 12 months prior to pregnancy

2. Unintended pregnancy

3. Adolescent or childhood pregnancy

4. Late entry into prenatal care

5. Poor compliance with appointments, medical recommendations

6. Maternal trauma, particularly of the breast, abdomen, or genitals

7. Fetal trauma, particularly fractures

8. Poor weight gain

9. STIs, eg, syphilis, human papillomavirus (HPV), human immunodeficiency virus (HIV), trichomoniasis, gonorrhea, *Chlamydia*, particularly when present in a child

10. Depression

11. Chronic pelvic pain, dysmenorrhea, sexual dysfunction

12. Generalized pain, eating/sleeping disturbances, strong emotional reactions such as anxiety, fear, guilt, anger

13. Substance abuse

14. Partner refuses to leave or answers questions for woman

Clinician Response to Abuse During Pregnancy

— First, identify the abuse through your assessment; this is a powerful form of intervention.

— Every patient should be screened for sexual abuse periodically during prenatal care. As an example, the American Congress of Obstetricians and Gynecologists (ACOG) suggests that screening should occur at the initial prenatal visit, once per trimester thereafter, and at the postpartum visit. It is important to understand that this is the recommended minimum for screening, and that if at any time abuse is suspected, screening should occur.

— If abuse is suspected, ACOG recommends taking a history of the nature and severity of the abuse to adequately assess danger and potential lethality.

— If a patient calls or presents to the office after an attack, she should be encouraged to go to a local medical facility immediately and to forgo bathing, douching, urinating/defecating, brushing teeth, cleaning under fingernails, smoking, eating, or drinking.

— Ideally, the patient should be taken immediately to a medical facility for assessment by a SANE-certified nurse. In areas in which this is not possible, the health care provider can perform the interview and assessment but must be sure to remain sensitive to the patient's emotional status and must document findings in detail without assigning incriminating language such as "rape" or "sexual abuse." In other words, stick to medical language only.

— Evidence can be recovered through first menses or 28 days after the incident in reproductive-aged menstruating females.*

— Be aware that the pelvic examination and the experience of labor may be particularly traumatic for women who have been sexually abused or assaulted. In many cases, victims of male perpetrators are more comfortable with female examiners.

— When a woman seems especially frightened while being examined, make the examination as patient-driven as possible.

— As with all victims of abuse, it is vital to assist the pregnant patient to take necessary steps to ensure her own safety as well as the safety of her baby.

1. Offer assistance at each prenatal appointment.

2. Make safety assessment and safety planning a part of every prenatal visit for all women, not just those who are being abused.

3. Provide safety information and lists of local resources, hotlines, and shelters. Because women may not feel safe taking such information or may deny needing it, place it in all restrooms and exam rooms, where it can be read in private.

4. Document the patient's statements concerning abuse, including the perpetrator's name and weapons used, and if patient consents, notify the police.

5. Document the physical findings associated with battering and sexual assault, ideally using photographs.

ROLE OF PEDIATRICIANS IN PREVENTING BOTH CHILD ABUSE AND DOMESTIC VIOLENCE

— Perform a domestic violence assessment.

— Ask questions about domestic violence in the child's presence, as long as the child is young enough that he or she will not report the content of the discussion back to the abusive parent.

— Incorporate the topics of child and domestic abuse in the context of discussions about discipline or into general home safety questioning.

*Refer to Publisher's Note on page xliv.

— When both maternal and child abuse are suspected, the pediatric practitioner is legally obligated to report the abuse and take steps to ensure the safety of mother and child. In many states, this involved filing a child abuse and neglect (CAN) report to the local DHR agency. Interdisciplinary, collaborative approaches are important in this regard.

ABUSE AND ASSAULT IN ADOLESCENT PREGNANCY

— Women aged 16-24 years experience the highest per-capita rate of IPV.

— Adolescents are overrepresented among abused pregnant women, with as many as 29% of pregnant adolescents experiencing abuse, including sexual abuse and assault.

— Pregnant teens, compared to those who are not pregnant, are much more likely to have a history of childhood sexual abuse.

— Teen parenthood is associated with particularly painful outcomes for both mothers and their babies:

1. Teen mothers display more aggressive, inappropriate, and abusive behavior toward their babies.

2. Two major risk factors for infanticide are maternal age under 15 years and short inter-pregnancy intervals among cases where the maternal age is under 17 years.

3. School-aged children of adolescent mothers have more cognitive and behavioral problems than children of adult mothers.

— Abused teens are more likely to smoke cigarettes and abuse drugs and alcohol during pregnancy.

— Their school drop-out rate is twice that of nonabused teens.

— They have a much higher rate of STIs.

— They enter into prenatal care much later than nonabused mothers.

— They are less likely than adult women to have long-term emotional, financial, and familial attachments to their partners.

— They may feel less compelled or threatened to remain in abusive relationships.

— If they are in school, systems and social supports are in place to assist them and their children.

SEXUAL ASSAULT RESULTING IN PREGNANCY

Most women who have been raped do not seek medical care and, therefore, do not have access to emergency contraception or STI prophylaxis. An estimated 22 000 pregnancies in the United States could be prevented if all women who had been raped had emergency contraception available to them within 72 hours of assault.

PROPHYLAXIS AND TREATMENT OF STIS IN PREGNANCY

Because of the effects of certain antibiotics and other medications on the fetus, the treatment of pregnant women with STIs may differ from that of nonpregnant women:

— Genital herpes (herpes simplex virus [HSV] type II): acyclovir may be used for a primary outbreak, for any outbreak at term or for recurrent herpes. Herpes prophylaxis should begin at 36 weeks in pregnancy.

— HPV, condyloma acuminata, or genital warts: podophyllin is contraindicated in pregnancy, but cryotherapy and acid preparations can be safely used.

— *Trichomonas*: pregnant women may be treated with a 2g single-dose regimen of metronidazole.

— *Chlamydia*: Azithromycin 1g single dose oral regimen is safe and linked with markedly improved compliance. Amoxicillin 500mg orally 3 times a day for 7 days is also a recommended regimen if azithromycin is unavailable. Erythromycin 500mg orally 4 times a day for 7 days is an alternative treatment option. Doxycycline and all other tetracyclines are contraindicated in pregnancy because they damage fetal bones and teeth.

— Gonorrhea: treat with ceftriaxone 250mg IM* unless the woman cannot take cephalosporins. Azithromycin 2g orally should be used if unable to take cephalosporins. Quinolones are contraindicated.

*Intramuscularly

— Syphilis: penicillin is the drug of choice, but pregnant women who are allergic to penicillin cannot take tetracycline (the alternative given to nonpregnant women who are allergic to penicillin). Erythromycin cannot be used because it does not adequately treat fetal syphilis, which can cause fetal and neonatal death along with other potentially devastating complications. Penicillin-allergic pregnant women should undergo penicillin desensitization in a hospital setting and receive a therapeutic course of penicillin. Jarisch-Herxheimer reaction occurs rarely in pregnant women, causing uterine contractions. Thus patients receiving penicillin should remain in the clinic or physician's office when they receive their first dose of penicillin.

— Hepatitis B: use of hepatitis B and hepatitis B immunoglobulin vaccines is not contraindicated in pregnancy.

— HIV infection: HIV-positive women should be offered treatment to reduce the risk of HIV transmission to the fetus. HIV-positive mothers should not breastfeed because HIV crosses into breast milk.

REFERENCES

1. Alhusen JL, Ray E, Sharps P, Bullock L. Intimate partner violence during pregnancy: maternal and neonatal outcomes. *J Womens Health (Larchmt)*. 2015;24(1):100-106. doi: 10.1089/jwh.2014.4872.

2. American Academy of Pediatrics, Committee on Child Abuse and Neglect. The role of the pediatrician in recognizing and intervening on behalf of abused women. *Pediatrics*. 1998;101(6):1091-1092.

3. American College of Obstetricians and Gynecologists. ACOG committee opinion no. 518: intimate partner violence. *Obstet Gynecol*. 2012;119(2 pt 1):412-417.

4. American College of Obstetricians and Gynecologists, Committee on Health Care for Underserved Women. ACOG committee opinion no. 592: sexual assault. *Obstet Gynecol*. 2014;123(4):905-909.

5. Asher J, Berlin M, Petty V. Abuse of pregnant adolescents: what have we learned? *Obstet Gynecol*. 2000;95(4 suppl 1):41S.

6. Berenson A, San Miguel VV, Wilkinson GS. Prevalence of physical and sexual assault in pregnant adolescents. *J Adolesc Health*. 1992;13(6):466-469.

7. Boyer D, Fine D. Sexual abuse as a factor in adolescent pregnancy and child maltreatment. *Fam Plann Perspect*. 1992;24(1):4-11, 19.

8. Campbell JC, Alford P. The dark consequences of marital rape. *Am J Nurs*. 1989;89(7):946-949.

9. Campbell JC, Oliver C, Bullock L. Why battering during pregnancy? *AWHONNS Clin Issues Perinat Womens Health Nurs*. 1993;4(3):343-349.

10. Centers for Disease Control and Prevention. Sexually transmitted diseases treatment guidelines, 2015. *MMWR Recomm Rep*. 2015;64(3):1-137.

11. Dietz PM, Spitz AM, Anda RF, et al. Unintended pregnancy among adult women exposed to abuse or household dysfunction during their childhood. *JAMA*. 1999;282(14):1359-1364.

12. Duffy SJ, McGrath ME, Becker BM, Linakis JG. Mothers with histories of domestic violence in a pediatric emergency department. *Pediatrics*. 1999;103(5 pt 1):1007-1013.

13. Dunn D, McCartney A. Asking the tough questions: obstetrical screening for depression and intimate partner violence. *J Health Care Poor Underserved*. 2014;25(4):1496-1506.

14. Elster AB, Ketterlinus R, Lamb ME. Association between parenthood and problem behavior in a national sample of adolescents. *Pediatrics*. 1990;85(6):1044-1050.

15. Fildes J, Reed L, Jones N, Martin M, Barrett J. Trauma: the leading cause of maternal death. *J Trauma*. 1992;32(5):643-645.

16. Fiscella K, Kitzman HJ, Cole RE, Sidora KJ, Olds D. Does child abuse predict adolescent pregnancy? *Pediatrics*. 1998;101(4 pt 1):620-624.

17. Flanagan P, Coll CG, Adreozzi L, Riggs S. Predicting maltreatment of children of teenage mothers. *Arch Pediatr Adolesc Med*. 1995;149(4):451-455.

18. Gazmararian JA, Adams MM, Saltzman LE, et al. The relationship between pregnancy intendedness and physical violence in mothers of newborns. the PRAMS Working Group. *Obstet Gynecol*. 1995;85(6):1031-1038.

19. Gazmararian JA, Lazorick S, Spitz AM, Ballard TJ, Saltzman LE, Marks JS. Prevalence of violence against pregnant women. *JAMA*. 1996;275(24):1915-1920.

20. Grant LJ. Effects of childhood sexual abuse: issues for obstetric caregivers. *Birth*. 1992;19(4):220-221.

21. Holmes MM, Resnick HS, Kilpatrick DG, Best CL. Rape-related pregnancy: estimates and descriptive characteristics from a national sample of women. *Am J Obstet Gynecol*. 1996;175(2):320-324; discussion 324-325.

22. Horon IL, Cheng D. Enhanced surveillance for pregnancy-associated mortality--Maryland, 1993-1998. *JAMA*. 2001;285(11):1455-1459.

23. Martin SL, Mackie L, Kupper LL, Buescher PA, Moracco KE. Physical abuse of women before, during, and after pregnancy. *JAMA*. 2001;285(12):1581-1584.

24. Mayer L. The severely abused women in obstetric and gynecologic care. guidelines for recognition and management. *J Reprod Med*. 1995;40(1):13-18.

25. Mayer L, Liebschutz J. Domestic violence in the pregnant patient: obstetric and behavioral interventions. *Obstet Gynecol Surv*. 1998;53(10):627-635.

26. McCauley J, Kern DE, Kolodner K, et al. Clinical characteristics of women with a history of childhood abuse: unhealed wounds. *JAMA*. 1997;277(17):1362-1368.

27. McFarlane J. Abuse during pregnancy: the horror and the hope. *AWHONNS Clin Issues Perinat Womens Health Nurs*. 1993;4(3):350-362.

28. McFarlane J, Parker B. Preventing abuse during pregnancy: an assessment and intervention protocol. *MCN Am J Matern Child Nurs*. 1994;19(4):321-324.

29. McKibben L, De Vos E, Newberger EH. Victimization of mothers of abused children: a controlled study. *Pediatrics*. 1989;84(3):531-535.

30. Overpeck MD, Brenner RA, Trumble AC, Trifiletti LB, Berendes HW. Risk factors for infant homicide in the United States. *N Engl J Med*. 1998;339(17):1211-1216.

31. Raj A, Silverman JG, Amaro H. The relationship between sexual abuse and sexual risk among high school students: findings from the 1997 Massachusetts Youth Risk Behavior Survey. *Matern Child Health J*. 2000;4(2):125-134.

32. Rhodes H, Hutchinson S. Labor experiences of childhood sexual abuse survivors. *Birth*. 1994;21(4):213-220.

33. Schechter S, Gary LT. *Health Care Services for Battered Women and Their Abused Children: A Manual About Advocacy for Women and Kids in Emergencies (AWAKE)*. Boston, MA: Children's Hospital; 1992.

34. Sinozich S, Langton L. *Rape and Sexual Assault Victimization Among College-Age Females, 1995-2013*. Washington, DC: US Department of Justice, Office of Justice Programs, Bureau of Justice Statistics; 2014. NCJ 248471. Bureau of Justice Statistics Web site. http://www.bjs.gov/index.cfm?ty=pbdetail&iid=5176. Accessed May 4, 2015.

35. Speck P, Ballantyne J. *Post-Coital DNA Recovery Study*. Washington, DC: National Criminal Justice Reference Service; 2015.

36. Stevens-Simon C, McAnarney ER. Childhood victimization: relationship to adolescent pregnancy outcome. *Child Abuse Negl*. 1994:18(7):569-575.

37. Stewart DE. Incidence of postpartum abuse in women with a history of abuse during pregnancy. *Can Med Assoc J*. 1994;151(11):1601-1604.

38. Stier DM, Leventhal JM, Berg AT, Johnson L, Mezger J. Are children born to young mothers at increased risk of maltreatment? *Pediatrics*. 1993;91(3):642-648.

39. Thompson RS, Krugman R. Screening mothers for intimate partner abuse at well-baby care visits: the right thing to do. *JAMA*. 2001;285(12):1628-1630.

40. Wright RJ. Identification of domestic violence in the community pediatric setting: need to protect mothers and children. *Arch Pediatr Adolesc Med*. 2000;154(5):431-433.

41. Wright RJ, Wright RO, Isaac NE. Response to battered mothers in the pediatric emergency department: a call for an interdisciplinary approach to family violence. *Pediatrics*. 1997;99(2):186-192.

Chapter 13

ACQUAINTANCE AND INTIMATE PARTNER RAPE

Olivia S. Ashley, DrPH*
Janice B. Asher, MD
Christine M. Peterson, MD
Elizabeth M. Datner, MD
Bruce D. Rubin, MD

ACQUAINTANCE RAPE AND DATE RAPE

Acquaintance rape and date rape are unusual among crimes in that they may not be recognized as crimes by the perpetrator, the criminal justice system, society, and sometimes, even the victim. Nonetheless, acquaintance rape and date rape *are* crimes and they are more common than stranger rape. For perpetrators, the legal consequences of acquaintance rape and stranger rape are the same, and for victims, the psychological consequences may be devastating.

EPIDEMIOLOGY

— It is estimated that about 52 200 rapes and/or sexual assaults involving victims aged 12 or older take place each year in the United States, two thirds of which are not reported to the police.

— From 1995 to 2010, about 9% of rape and sexual assault victims were male.

— More than half of female victims of rape report being raped by an intimate partner and 41% by an acquaintance.

— More than half of male victims report being raped by an acquaintance.

*Revised Chapter 13 for the second edition.

— Adolescents and young adults are 2 to 3 times more likely than adults aged 25 or older to be raped or sexually assaulted, with the majority experiencing date rape, not stranger rape.

— Although prevalence estimates vary (ranging from approximately 3% to 9% per year), most studies have found that approximately 5% of college women each year experience attempted or completed rape. Approximately 0.6% to 3% of college men each year experience attempted or completed sexual assault.

RISK FACTORS

— Risk factors for sexual violence perpetration include (**Table 13-1**):

Table 13-1. Sexual Violence Perpetration: Risk Factors	
— Childhood abuse	— Sexual violence victimization during adolescence or adulthood
— Exposure to parental violence/family conflict	— Past sexual violence perpetration
— Peer attitudes and behaviors	— Victim blaming
— Hypermasculine/all male peers	— Empathic deficits
— Gang membership	— Cue misinterpretation
— Conflict with partner/partner violence	— Rape myth acceptance
— Early sexual activity and having multiple sexual partners	— Hostility toward women/adversarial sexual beliefs
— Impersonal sex	— Traditional gender role adherence
— Exposure to sexually explicit media	— Belief that violence is acceptable
	— Increased suicidality
	— Increased high-risk sexual behavior

ROLE OF ALCOHOL AND OTHER DRUGS IN ACQUAINTANCE RAPE

— About 54% of victims presenting to the emergency department for evaluation after sexual assault report involvement of alcohol or other drugs during the event.

— Alcohol is a disinhibitor and increases acceptance of sexual aggression.

— Other drugs used in sexual assaults include*:

1. Flunitrazepam (Rohypnol), a fast-acting benzodiazepine

2. Ketamine

3. Gamma-hydroxybutyrate (GHB) and its congeners

VICTIMS' RESPONSE TO DATING VIOLENCE AND ACQUAINTANCE RAPE

— Victims who have been raped by a known perpetrator may be less likely to report the rape than those raped by a stranger because victims may blame themselves and not want to get their acquaintance in trouble.

— Victims may not want to go through the difficult and sometimes humiliating ordeal of a trial.

Psychologic Consequences

— Psychologic sequelae of date rape include:

1. Depression

2. Anxiety

3. Posttraumatic stress disorder (PTSD)

4. Self-blame, which is linked to greater PTSD symptom severity

5. Suicide attempts

— Characteristics of PTSD include:

1. Involuntary reexperiencing of the traumatic event through thoughts, nightmares, and/or flashbacks

2. Avoidance of activities, including those that were previously pleasurable

3. Avoidance of circumstances in which the rape occurred

4. A state of increased psychomotor arousal, which may be associated with sleep disturbances and panic attacks

5. Depression

6. Decreased appetite

These drugs cause disinhibition and anterograde amnesia, so that the victim does not clearly remember the incident.

EFFECTIVE CLINICIAN RESPONSES

— Because the victim of acquaintance rape may never seek medical or forensic evaluation, clinicians must routinely raise the subject of healthy relationships and acquaintance rape with patients.

— Included should be information about sexually transmitted infections (STIs) and emergency contraception.

— Once an assault has occurred, the clinician's responsibility is as follows*:

1. Offer first-line support to survivors of sexual assault by any perpetrator: be nonjudgmental, provide care and support, ask about history of violence, help access information about resources, assist to increase safety, provide or mobilize social support

2. Take a complete history, recording events to determine what interventions are appropriate, and conduct a complete physical examination (head-to-toe, including genitalia)

3. Identify and treat injuries

4. Prevent STIs and pregnancy

5. Conduct psychologic assessment with appropriate referral for counseling

6. Collect forensic evidence

PREVENTING DATING VIOLENCE AND ACQUAINTANCE RAPE

— School and college-based programs endeavor to educate males about their ethical and legal responsibility to be certain they have their sex partner's consent before engaging in intimate activity.

— Effective perpetration prevention also focuses on:

1. Increasing legal knowledge about sexual assault

2. Improving date rape attitudes

3. Decreasing beliefs in rape myths

4. Reducing hostility toward women

Chapters 9 through 12 outline the specifics of these steps.

5. Increasing intentions to intervene to confront inappropriate behaviors of other men

6. Decreasing hyper-gender ideology

7. Decreasing positive outcome expectancies for nonconsensual sex

8. Increasing positive outcome expectancies for intervening

9. Decreasing comfort with other men's inappropriate behaviors

10. Increasing awareness of services for victims and perpetrators

— The message must be conveyed that rape is always unacceptable.

— Young women are being taught about sexual assault risk factors and dating behaviors that put individuals at risk.

— Effective prevention for young women who have been previously victimized focuses on increasing self-efficacy related to handling sexual situations and improving psychological adjustment to reduce sexual assault survivors' risk of revictimization.

DOMESTIC VIOLENCE AND PARTNER RAPE

Domestic violence is a major public health and human rights concern, with intimate partner violence and sexual violence being among the most pervasive forms of violence against women. Individuals who disclose any form of violence by an intimate partner, or another family member, or sexual assault by any perpetrator should be offered immediate support, including asking about history of violence and listening carefully, but not pressuring the individual to talk. Clinicians must help victims to increase safety for themselves and their children where needed.

DOMESTIC VIOLENCE OVERVIEW

Domestic violence is a pattern of abusive behavior in any relationship that is used by one partner to gain or maintain power and control over another intimate partner.

— At the outset, episodes of domestic violence may occur infrequently, but subsequently, they are likely to occur with greater regularity and intensity.

— Domestic violence occurs on a continuum, ranging from one hit that may or may not impact the victim to chronic, severe battering.

— Physical abuse includes threat of harm or any forceful physical behavior that intentionally or accidentally causes bodily harm or property destruction (**Table 13-2**).

Table 13-2. Physically Abusive Behaviors

— Hitting	— Biting	— Holding down or preventing from leaving
— Beating	— Punching	
— Choking	— Backhanding	— Throwing and/or threatening with objects
— Pushing	— Arm twisting	
— Slapping	— Shoving	— Locking out of the home
— Kicking	— Kicking	— Refusing to get a partner help or medical attention
— Hair pulling	— Burning	
		— Forced use of alcohol or other drugs

— Although death is the most serious sequela of domestic violence, many forms of domestic abuse result in significant short- and long-term physical and mental health problems.

— Risk factors include:

1. Low income, although marital rape is not limited to any specific socio-economic group

2. Young age

3. Heavy alcohol or other drug use

4. Depression

5. Belief in strict gender roles

6. Experiencing early childhood abuse, witnessing parental intimate partner violence, and experiencing parental boundary violations

Sexual Abuse
— Sexual abuse includes, but is not limited to:

1. Forcing an unwanted sexual act

2. Marital rape

3. Attacks on sexual parts of the body

4. Forcing sex after physical violence has occurred

5. Treating one in a sexually demeaning manner

6. Forcing one to strip or forcefully stripping

7. Sadistic sexual acts

8. Making sex conditional on one's behavior or agreement to include unwanted practices, eg, pornography or sex toys

9. Using coercion to force sex

10. Taking unwanted sexual photographs

11. Sharing such photographs with other people or the Internet without consent

12. Forcing one into prostitution

— Rape within a relationship can have the same components of forcible sex that occur in acquaintance rape, eg, coercion, physical force, physical and trauma to the victim.

— Marital rape is rarely an isolated incident, but instead a repeated if not frequent occurrence.

Role of Coercion
— Sexual coercion is the act of using pressure, alcohol or other drugs, or force to have sexual contact with someone against his or her will and includes persistent attempts to have sexual contact with someone who has already refused.

— Individuals acquiesce to unwanted sexual activity in an effort to maintain relationships and partner satisfaction as well as to avoid negative outcomes.

— They use submission to avoid further harassment or aggression, which could end in death or injury.

CLINICAL PRESENTATION AND SEQUELAE

Physical Injuries and Symptoms

— Victims may have obvious physical signs of traumatic injury, but they may also complain of noninjury signs and symptoms, such as chronic abdominal pain, that may seem unrelated to an abusive relationship (**Table 13-3**).

Table 13-3. Domestic Violence and Partner Rape: Typical Medical Complaints

— Headache	— Heart beating too fast
— Shortness of breath	— Choking sensations
— Feeling tired/low energy	— Numbness and tingling
— Constipation/loose bowels/diarrhea	— Painful sexual intercourse
— Trouble sleeping	— Pelvic pain
— Neck pain	— Urinary tract infection
— Chest pain	— Vaginal pain

— Injury types seen more commonly in domestic violence injuries than in injuries caused by other means include:

1. Tympanic membrane (eardrum) rupture

2. Rectal or genital injury

3. Facial scrapes, bruises, cuts, or fractures

4. Neck scrapes or bruises

5. Abdominal cuts or bruises

6. Tooth loose or broken

7. Head scrapes or bruises

8. Body scrapes or bruises

9. Arm scrapes or bruises

— Bladder and kidney infections are associated with intimate partner violence.

— Female victims of marital rape experience significant levels of gynecological problems.

— In one study, 15% of women who had experienced more than one sexual assault by an intimate partner reported the development of one or more STIs after a rape or sexual assault by their intimate partner.

Psychologic Effects
— Persons being abused may show outward signs of depression such as crying and poor eye contact.

— Other psychological signs of domestic violence range from anxiety and chronic fatigue to suicidal tendencies and the battered woman syndrome.

— Batterers sometimes use child custody proceedings as a way to continue exerting control.

Intersection With HIV
— In one nationally representative study, almost 12% of HIV infection among women were due to intimate partner violence. Compared to women who have not experienced violence, women with a history of intimate partner violence are more likely to report HIV risk factors, including unprotected sex, injection drug use, and alcohol abuse.

IDENTIFICATION OF ABUSE
— Health care providers frequently, and often unknowingly, come into contact with individuals affected by violence, since abuse victims make extensive use of health care resources.

— It is important for providers to be familiar with and able to recognize symptoms that may be indicative of spousal rape.

— There is disagreement about whether "universal screening" or "routine inquiry," ie, asking women in all health care encounters, should be implemented. The World Health Organization recommends that health care providers should ask about exposure to intimate partner violence when assessing conditions that may be caused or complicated by intimate partner violence. The American Congress of Obstetricians and Gynecologists recommends that physicians screen all patients for intimate partner violence.

— While computerized screening is felt by patients to be nonjudgmental and more anonymous, in person screening allows for tailored questioning and more emotional connection with the provider.

— Domestic violence screening can be conducted by making the following statement and asking 3 simple questions (**Table 13-4**):

Table 13-4. Domestic Violence Screening

"Because violence is so common in many women's lives, and because there is help available for women being abused, I now ask every patient about domestic violence."

QUESTIONS

1. Within the past year, or since you have been pregnant, have you been hit, slapped, kicked or otherwise physically hurt by someone?

2. Are you in a relationship with a person who threatens or physically hurts you?

3. Has anyone forced you to have sexual activities that made you feel uncomfortable?

— Providers should ensure that the consultation is conducted in private. Strategies to separate patient and partner are as follows:

1. Posting a sign stating a policy of having partners leave during the physical examination.

2. Ordering tests and accompanying the patient to the test site while the partner is asked to wait.

3. Having a staff member ask the partner to come outside of the examining room to provide additional insurance information.

— If the patient denies abuse but you strongly suspect abuse has occurred, document it, and let her or him know there are resources available. Make sure the patient knows that she or he is not alone. It may be helpful to return to questions about abuse with the following introductory statement: "An injury like yours often occurs because of being punched. Is that what happened?"

— When there is physical abuse, it is not uncommon to find out that sexual abuse has also occurred. It is vital to ask about the possibility.

— Written information on intimate partner violence should be available in health care settings in the form of posters and pamphlets or leaflets made available in private areas such as women's washrooms.*

The Clinician's Response to Domestic Violence

— Communicate to the patient a concern for safety and an appreciation of the complex dynamics of an abusive relationship.

— Recognize that a hallmark of abuse is that the victim, rather than the perpetrator, feels embarrassed, ashamed, and blameworthy for the abuse.

— Support and validate the patient who discloses abuse. Particularly effective statements include the following:

1. I'm glad you told me about this.

2. I believe what you've told me.

3. The abuse is not your fault.

4. No one deserves to be assaulted.

5. The situation is likely to become worse, not better.

6. If you are not safe, your child cannot be safe.

7. Help is available.

Documentation

— Documentation is critical because it may eventually be useful in a court of law, including if custody issues arise.

— Document the patient's statements regarding abuse as well as the physical findings.

---

*With appropriate warnings about taking them home if an abusive partner is there

— Use the patient's own words.

— Include the following information: name of the perpetrator; nature of the weapon used; dated photographs of the injuries, body maps, or written descriptions; and whether injuries appeared recent or old.

INTERVENTION

— A useful clinical tool for domestic violence assessment is the RADAR model:

R = Routine screening

A = Ask direct questions

D = Document findings

A = Assess safety

R = Review options and refer

— Once a victim of domestic violence is identified, refer the patient to a domestic violence expert; this individual may be a hospital-based or community-based social worker, a colleague who is knowledgeable about domestic violence, a local domestic violence advocacy organization, or the national domestic violence hotline (**1-800-799-SAFE**).

— Offer emergency contraception to female survivors of sexual assault presenting within 5 days of sexual assault, ideally as soon as possible after the assault, to maximize effectiveness.

— Offer STI screening and sexual assault forensic examinations.

— Consider offering HIV postexposure prophylaxis (PEP) for women presenting within 72 hours of a sexual assault. Women survivors of sexual assault should be offered prophylaxis for *Chlamydia*, gonorrhea, *Trichomonas*, and syphilis, depending on prevalence. Hepatitis B vaccination without hepatitis B immune globulin should be offered.

— Injectable contraception that can be used surreptitiously may protect women by eliminating the need for their partner's consent or cooperation.

— Use caution in prescribing any sedatives to a domestic abuse victim. These medications can impair the patient's ability to adequately defend, escape, or seek immediate help if needed.

— Remember that safety is the paramount goal in abuse intervention.

1. Insisting that abuse victims leave their partner is neither the responsibility nor the right of the clinician.

2. Assist the victim to take the necessary steps to ensure personal safety and that of the children.

— Safety assessment includes immediate and long-term aspects.

1. Immediate safety: Indicators that it may not be safe to return home that day are finding out that the partner has recently obtained a gun; that the frequency and/or severity of attacks has escalated; and that the partner has made suicidal and/or homicidal threats, threatened the children, displayed violence toward a pet, or escalated alcohol and/or other drug abuse.

2. Long-term safety: While the clinician must respect the patient's autonomy if the patient decides it is safe to go home, you should ask, "What will you do if this happens again?" thus assisting the patient in planning safety and/or exit strategies. It is also helpful to review safety measures or give out printed material.

— In-house social workers and advocacy groups in the community can assist in obtaining referral information. Note that routine referral for couples counseling is not recommended.

— For patients who wish to maintain confidentiality regarding abuse, take the same precautions as for other similarly sensitive health care issues, such as HIV status.

SOCIETAL REACTION TO MARITAL RAPE

— It was not until the late 1970s that laws reflected an understanding of marital rape as a crime.

— Social awareness of the prevalence of marital rape has been accompanied by corresponding legal aid to its victims.

SPECIAL POPULATIONS

Immigrants

— Immigrants may be particularly vulnerable to abusive relationships, possibly as a result of the following:

1. They may be completely dependent economically on their partner.

2. They may be particularly isolated because of an inability to speak English comfortably.

3. There may be disincentives for an abuse victim who is unfamiliar with the local language, culture, and laws to disclose abuse, such as economic dependence on the partner, little means of supporting one's self or one's children, lack of opportunity to disclose abuse if the partner is the translator, and/or fewer options for escape from the situation.

4. Victims may have come from a culture in which the subordination of women is the norm.

— Be aware of the importance of cultural sensitivity and knowledge of the culture.

— Become familiar with local resources for individuals from other countries and cultures.

Women With Disabilities

— Women with disabilities are at increased risk for physical and sexual abuse and assault for the following reasons:

1. Physical vulnerability

2. Dependence on caregivers, including family members, health care workers, and attendants

3. Difficulty making and carrying out a safety or escape plan

4. Lack of accessibility to services

— In one study, a history of sexual abuse was reported among 7% of 13 to 18 year olds with mobility impairment.

Lesbian, Gay, Bisexual, Transgender, and Queer (LGBTQ) Relationships
— LGBTQ physically and/or sexually abusive relationships are filled with the same problems as heterosexual relationships, but additional issues may make terminating a violent LGBTQ relationship more difficult or dangerous:

1. The abusive partner may threaten to "out" the victim, ie, disclose his or her LGBTQ status. This threat may have tremendous real or perceived implications for employment and family relationships.

2. LGBTQ individuals may live within small social frameworks. Leaving an abusive partner may mean leaving an entire social network, increasing the sense of isolation.

3. Abusers may threaten to out their partners' HIV status or addiction to authorities and employers.

4. The abusive partner may claim to be the victim. Particularly in relationships in which one member of the couple is larger or appears physically stronger or more "masculine," outsiders may draw erroneous conclusions as to who is the batterer.

5. There is a perceived and real lack of resources for abused partners in LGBTQ relationships, especially for males and transgender individuals.

— Lesbian women and gay men report levels of intimate partner violence and sexual violence equal to or higher than those of heterosexuals.

REFERENCES

1. American College Health Association. *American College Health Association National College Health Assessment II: Spring 2010 Reference Group Executive Summary*. Linthicum, MD: American College Health Association; 2010.

2. American Congress of Obstetricians and Gynecologists. Screening tools - domestic violence. American Congress of Obstetricians and Gynecologists Web site. http://www.acog.org/About-ACOG/ACOG-Departments/Violence-Against-Women/Screening-Tools--Domestic-Violence. Accessed May 21, 2015.

3. An Abuse, Rape, and Domestic Violence Aid and Resource Collection. Stages of healing. An Abuse Rape, and Domestic Violence Aid and Resource Collection Web site. http://www.aardvarc.org/rape/about/healing.shtml. Updated March 16, 2011. Accessed May 21, 2015.

4. Anderson IB, Kim SY, Dyer JE, et al. Trends in gamma-hydroxybutyrate (GHB) and related drug intoxication: 1999 to 2003. *Ann Emerg Med.* 2006;47(2):177-183.

5. Avegno J, Mills TJ, Mills LD. Sexual assault victims in the emergency department: analysis by demographic and event characteristics. *J Emerg Med.* 2009;37(3):328-334.

6. Beebe R, Myers J. *Medical Emergencies, Maternal Health & Pediatrics.* Clifton Park, NY: Delmar Cengage Learning; 2011. *Professional Paramedic;* vol 2.

7. Black MC. Intimate partner violence and adverse health consequences: implications for clinicians. *Am J Lifestyle Med.* 2011;5(5):428-439.

8. Black MC, Basile KC, Breiding MJ, et al. *The National Intimate Partner and Sexual Violence Survey: 2010 Summary Report: Executive Summary.* Atlanta, GA: Centers for Disease Control and Prevention, National Center for Injury Prevention and Control; 2011.

9. Centers for Disease Control and Prevention. Adverse health conditions and health risk behaviors associated with intimate partner violence—United States, 2005. *MMWR Morb Mortal Wkly Rep.* 2008:57(5):113-117. Centers for Disease Control and Prevention Web site. http://www.cdc.gov/mmwr/preview/mmwrhtml/mm5705a1.htm. Accessed May 21, 2015.

10. Centers for Disease Control and Prevention. Intimate partner violence: consequences. Centers for Disease Control and Prevention Web site. http://www.cdc.gov/violenceprevention/intimatepartnerviolence/consequences.html. Updated March 3, 2015. Accessed May 21, 2015.

11. Centers for Disease Control and Prevention. Intimate partner violence: risk and protective factors. Centers for Disease Control and Prevention Web site. http://www.cdc.gov/violenceprevention/intimatepartnerviolence/riskprotectivefactors.html. Updated February 11, 2015. Accessed May 21, 2015.

12. Chang JC, Dado D, Schussler S, et al. In person versus computer screening for intimate partner violence among pregnant patients. *Patient Educ Couns.* 2012;88(3):443-448.

13. Conroy NE, Krishnakumar A, Leone JM. Reexamining issues of conceptualization and willing consent: the hidden role of coercion in experiences of sexual acquiescence [published online ahead of print September 22, 2014]. *J Interpers Violence.* pii: 0886260514549050.

14. Darden SK, James R, Ramnarine IW, Croft DP. Social implications of the battle of the sexes: sexual harassment disrupts female sociality and social recognition. *Proc Biol Sci.* 2009;276(1667):2651-2656.

15. Eberhard-Gran M, Schei B, Eskild A. Somatic symptoms and diseases are more common in women exposed to violence. *J Gen Intern Med.* 2007;22(12):1668-1673.

16. emedicinehealth. Domestic violence signs and symptoms. emedicinehealth Web site. http://www.emedicinehealth.com/domestic_violence/page4_em.htm. Reviewed June 20, 2014. Accessed May 21, 2015.

17. Foshee VA, Bauman KE, Arriga XB, Helms RW, Koch GG, Linder GF. An evaluation of Safe Dates, an adolescent dating violence prevention program. *Am J Public Health.* 1998;88(1):45-50.

18. Foshee VA, Bauman KE, Ennett ST, Suchindran C, Benefield T, Linder GF. Assessing the effects of the dating violence prevention program "Safe Dates" using random coefficient regression modeling. *Prev Sci.* 2005;6(3):245-258.

19. Gay Men's Domestic Violence Project. Types of domestic abuse. Gay Men's Domestic Violence Project Web site. http://gmdvp.org/domestic-violence/types-domestic-abuse/. Accessed May 21, 2015.

20. Gentleman A. Prosecuting sexual assault: 'raped all over again'. *The Guardian.* April 13, 2013. The Guardian Web site. http://www.theguardian.com/society/2013/apr/13/rape-sexual-assault-frances-andrade-court. Accessed May 21, 2015.

21. Gerber GL, Cherneski L. Sexual aggression toward women: reducing the prevalence. *Ann N Y Acad Sci.* 2006;1087:35-46.

22. Hamby S, Finkelhor D, Turner H. Teen dating violence: co-occurrence with other victimizations in the National Survey of Children's Exposure to Violence (NatSCEV). *Psychol Violence.* 2012;2(2):111-124.

23. Hanson KA, Gidycz CA. Evaluation of a sexual assault prevention program. *J Consult Clin Psychol.* 1993;61(6):1046-1052.

24. Hidden Hurt: Domestic Abuse Information. Marital rape. Hidden Hurt: Domestic Abuse Information Web site. http://www.hiddenhurt. co.uk/marital_rape.html. Accessed May 21, 2015.

25. Hidden Hurt: Domestic Abuse Information. Sexual abuse, domestic violence and marital rape. Hidden Hurt: Domestic Abuse Information Web site. http://www.hiddenhurt.co.uk/sexual_abuse.html. Accessed May 21, 2015.

26. Internet Mental Health. Posttraumatic stress disorder. Internet Mental Health Web site. http://www.mentalhealth.com/home/dx/ posttraumaticstress.html. Accessed May 21, 2015.

27. Jemtå L, Fugl-Meyer KS, Oberg K. On intimacy, sexual activities and exposure to sexual abuse among children and adolescents with mobility impairment. *Acta Paediatr.* 2008;97(5):641-646.

28. Kilpatrick DG, Resnick HS, Ruggiero KJ, Conoscenti LM, McCauley J. *Drug-Facilitated, Incapacitated, and Forcible Rape: A National Study.* Charleston, SC: Medical University of South Carolina, National Crime Victims Research and Treatment Center; 2007.

29. Krebs CP, Lindquist CH, Warner TD, Fisher BS, Martin SL. *The Campus Sexual Assault (CSA) Study: Final Report Prepared for the National Institute of Justice.* Research Triangle Park, NC: RTI International; 2007.

30. Linder JR, Collins WA. Parent and peer predictors of physical aggression and conflict management in romantic relationships in early adulthood. *J Fam Psychol.* 2005;19(2):252-262.

31. Love Is Respect. What is sexual coercion? Love Is Respect Web site. http://www.loveisrespect.org/content/what-sexual-coercion/. Published April 28, 2014. Accessed May 21, 2015.

32. Main Line Health. Behavioral Health: Domestic Violence Tips for Health Care Professionals. Main Line Health Web site. http://www.mainline-health.org/oth/Page.asp?PageID=OTH000387. Accessed May 21, 2015.

33. Martin EK, Taft CT, Resick PA. A review of marital rape. *Aggress Violent Behav.* 2007;12(3):329–347.

34. Marx BP, Calhoun KS, Wilson AE, Meyerson LA. Sexual revictimization prevention: an outcome evaluation. *J Consult Clin Psychol.* 2001;69(1):25-32.

35. McFarlane J, Malecha A, Watson K, et al. Intimate partner sexual assault against women: frequency, health consequences, and treatment outcomes. *Obstet Gynecol.* 2005;105(1):99-108.

36. National Association of Social Workers. Domestic violence assessment and intervention provided by the Family Violence Prevention Fund. National Association of Social Workers Web site. https://www.socialworkers.org/pressroom/events/domestic_violence/assessment.asp. Accessed May 21, 2015.

37. National Domestic Violence Hotline. National Domestic Violence Hotline homepage. National Domestic Violence Hotline Web site. http://www.thehotline.org/. Accessed May 21, 2015.

38. National Institute on Drug Abuse. DrugFacts: club drugs (GHB, ketamine, and rohypnol). National Institute on Drug Abuse Web site. http://www.drugabuse.gov/publications/drugfacts/club-drugs-ghb-ketamine-rohypnol. Updated December 2014. Accessed May 21, 2015.

39. National Sound Mental Health Administration. *North Sound Mental Health Administration Regional Training Committee Training Module: Post-Traumatic Stress Disorder.* National Sound Mental Health Administration Web site. http://www.nsmha.org/PDFs/RTC/Modules/PTSD_Training_Module.pdf. Published August 9, 2007. Accessed May 21, 2015.

40. Okeson S. Many abusers use custody battles as way to seek control. News-Leader. January 14, 2012. News-Leader Web site. http://archive.news-leader.com/article/20120115/NEWS01/201150333/custody-battles-abusers. Accessed May 21, 2015.

41. Planty M, Langton L, Krebs C, Berzofsky M, Smiley-McDonald H. *Female Victims of Sexual Violence, 1994-2010*. Washington, DC: US Department of Justice, Office of Justice Programs, Bureau of Justice Statistics; 2013. NCJ 240655.

42. Plummer SB, Findley PA. Women with disabilities' experience with physical and sexual abuse: a review of the literature and implications for the field. *Trauma Violence Abuse*. 2012;13(1):15-29.

43. Rape, Abuse & Incest National Network. Drug-facilitated sexual assault. Rape, Abuse & Incest National Network Web site. https://rainn.org/get-information/types-of-sexual-assault/drug-facilitated-assault. Accessed May 21, 2015.

44. Rape, Abuse & Incest National Network. Post-traumatic stress disorder (PTSD). Rape, Abuse & Incest National Network. https://www.rainn.org/effects-of-sexual-assault/post-traumatic-stress-disorder. Accessed May 21, 2015.

45. Reich CM, Jones JM, Woodward MJ, Blackwell N, Lindsey LD, Beck JG. Does self-blame moderate psychological adjustment following intimate partner violence? *J Interpers Violence*. 2015;30(9):1493-1510. doi: 10.1177/0886260514540800.

46. Reina AS, Lohman BJ, Maldonado MM. "He said they'd deport me": factors influencing domestic violence help-seeking practices among Latina immigrants. *J Interpers Violence*. 2014;29(4):593-615.

47. Salazar LF, Vivolo-Kantor A, Hardin J, Berkowitz A. A web-based sexual violence bystander intervention for male college students: randomized controlled trial. *J Med Internet Res*. 2014;16(9):e203. doi: 10.2196/jmir.3426.

48. San Diego LGBT Community Center. Challenges specific to LGBT relationship violence. San Diego LGBT Community Center Web site. http://www.thecentersd.org/programs/behavioral-health-services/special-concerns.html. Accessed June 2, 2015.

49. Sareen J, Pagura J, Grant B. Is intimate partner violence associated with HIV infection among women in the United States? *Gen Hosp Psychiatry*. 2009;31(3):274-278.

50. Stiles-Shields C, Carroll RA. Same-sex domestic violence: prevalence, unique aspects, and clinical implications [published online ahead of print September 4, 2014]. *J Sex Marital Ther.* doi: 10.1080/0092623X.2014.958792.

51. Tharp AT, DeGue S, Valle LA, Brookmeyer KA, Massetti GM, Matjasko JL. A systematic qualitative review of risk and protective factors for sexual violence perpetration. *Trauma Violence Abuse.* 2013;14(2):133-167

52. Truman JL, Langton L. *Criminal Victimization, 2013.* Washington, DC: US Department of Justice, Office of Justice Programs, Bureau of Justice Statistics; 2014. NCJ 247648.

53. Ullman SE, Filipas HH, Townsend SM, Starzynski LL. Psychosocial correlates of PTSD symptom severity in sexual assault survivors. *J Trauma Stress.* 2007;20(5):821-831.

54. US Department of Justice. Domestic violence. US Department of Justice Web site. http://www.justice.gov/ovw/domestic-violence. Updated July 23, 2014. Accessed May 21, 2015.

55. US Department of Justice, Office of Justice Programs, Bureau of Justice Statistics. NCVS Victimization Analysis Tool (NVAT). Washington, DC: Bureau of Justice Statistics; 2012. Bureau of Justice Statistics Web site. http://bjs.ojp.usdoj.gov/index.cfm?ty=nvat. Accessed May 21, 2015.

56. Vagi KJ, Rothman EF, Latzman NE, Teten Tharp AT, Hall DM, Breiding MJ. Beyond correlates: a review of risk and protective factors for adolescent dating violence perpetration. *J Youth Adolesc.* 2013;42(4):633-649.

57. Vantage Professional Education. Domestic violence and intimate partner violence response guidelines. Vantage Professional Education Web site. http://www.vantageproed.com/viol/violdiet.htm. Published 2009. Accessed May 21, 2015.

58. Varcarolis EM. Substance-related and addictive disorders. In: Varcarolis EM, ed. *Essentials of Psychiatric Mental Health Nursing: A Communication Approach to Evidence-Based Care.* 2nd ed. Saint Louis, MO: Elsevier; 2013:362-396.

59. Walters ML, Chen J, Breiding MJ. *The National Intimate Partner and Sexual Violence Survey (NISVS): 2010 Findings on Victimization by Sexual Orientation.* Atlanta, GA: Centers for Disease Control and Prevention, National Center for Injury Prevention and Control; 2013.

60. What you should know about rape and sexual assault. DateHookup Web site. http://www.datehookup.com/content-what-you-should-know-about-rape-and-sexual-assault.htm. Accessed May 21, 2015.

61. World Health Organization. *Global and Regional Estimates of Violence Against Women: Prevalence and Health Effects of Intimate Partner Violence and Non-Partner Sexual Violence.* Geneva, Switzerland: World Health Organization; 2013. World Health Organization Web site. http://apps.who.int/iris/bitstream/10665/85239/1/9789241564625_eng.pdf?ua=1. Accessed May 21, 2015.

62. World Health Organization. *Psychological First Aid: Guide for Field Workers.* Geneva, Switzerland: World Health Organization; 2011. World Health Organization Web site. http://whqlibdoc.who.int/publications/2011/9789241548205_eng.pdf. Accessed May 21, 2015.

63. World Health Organization. *Responding to Intimate Partner Violence and Sexual Violence Against Women: WHO Clinical and Policy Guidelines.* Geneva, Switzerland: World Health Organization; 2013.

Chapter 14

SPECIAL SETTINGS

Patricia M. Speck, DNSc, APN, FNP-BC, DF-IAFN, FAAFS, FAAN*
Michael Clark, MSN, CRNP
Hannah Ufberg Rabinowitz, MSN, CRNP
Thomas Ervin, RNC, FN, BSc
Sharon W. Cooper, MD, FAAP

RAPE AND SEXUAL ABUSE IN OLDER ADULTS

The true prevalence of rape committed against older adults can only be inferred from the existing literature. Existing social services for sexual assault victims are generally not designed to address the normal sexual needs or sexual abuses and assaults presented by older adults, especially considering their vulnerabilities, exposure patterns, and physical and emotional responses.

INCIDENCE OF SEXUAL ABUSE AMONG OLDER ADULTS

— Older adults are less likely to experience violent crime than younger individuals.

— The overall incidence of elder abuse is thought to be significant, with estimates of 10 cases per 100 000 population per year. Thus those over age 50 years would represent about 3% of sexual assault victims.

— Many incidents of abuse remain undetected or undisclosed, either by the victim, those intimately involved in the care of older adults in homes or institutions, or to state investigative agencies.

DEFINING RAPE AND SEXUAL ASSAULT OF OLDER ADULTS

— In the past the definition of rape focused exclusively on forced vaginal intercourse by a male with a female who was not his wife.

Revised Chapter 14 for the second edition.

— Currently the definitions of the terms rape, sexual assault, and sexual abuse include victims and perpetrators of both genders, and the definition of the nature of the sexual contact includes both oral and anal penetration.

— Sexual abuse of older adults is defined as nonconsensual sexual activity that occurs when a person over age 60 years is forced, tricked, coerced, or manipulated into unwanted sexual contact. It also includes situations in which the older adult is incapable of giving consent because of severe cognitive impairments and other impairments, which require court intervention, including impairments associated with aging. Marriage of the accused and the victim creates a complexity not consistently addressed by institutions or criminal justice systems.

— This definition is not limited to rape but can include other forms of unwanted sexual contact, eg, fondling, etc.

— Older adults participate in sexual activity and seeing older adults as asexual may inhibit the ability to recognize and respond to patterns of sexual victimization, eg, force, tricks, coercion, or manipulation.

EXPOSURE TO SEXUAL ABUSE

— Older adults differ significantly from younger victims in characteristics that leave them vulnerable and exposed to the threat of sexual assault.

— Sexual abuse in the older adult often implies a violation of a relationship between caregiver and dependent. Older adults usually rely on the perpetrator because of physical or cognitive limitations or impairments.

— Older adults may also differ from younger victims in their ability to report and respond to assaults based on their relative degree of isolation and physical or cognitive impairments.

— Many older adults do not know their assailants. Attacks by strangers are frequently accompanied by higher levels of violence. Generally, assaults on older women are more violent, brutal, and sadistic.

SEXUAL ABUSE OF OLDER ADULTS WHO RESIDE IN INSTITUTIONAL SETTINGS

— Those residing in nursing homes fall into 2 subpopulations:

1. Those admitted for short stays from hospitals to undergo rehabilitation associated with acute illness

2. Those staying much longer because of disabilities that cannot be managed in the community; these individual may be more vulnerable to sexual assault

— Sexual abuse and physical abuse allegations of institutionalized persons are, in general, not reported promptly, and law enforcement personnel are rarely summoned by institutions, eg, due to liability, to investigate. Even when allegations are substantiated, minimal disciplinary action occurs, with extremely rare cases leading to criminal prosecution despite severe abuse.

— Often the incidents are witnessed, but not reported, or residents inform a family member who does not follow through.

— Indicators of sexual abuse include psychologic manifestations, eg, sleep disorders, irritability, mood swings, or depression, that may also accompany aging changes or other psychosocial problems in men and women and are, thus, nonspecific.

— Signs of abuse in older patients (rule out medical causes of the following):

1. Bedsores, bruises

2. Falls, broken bones

3. Agitation, withdrawal, fear

4. Frequent crying, strained relationships

5. Uncleanliness, poor hygiene of patient

6. Complaints of poor treatment

7. Overdose, head injury

8. Weight loss

— Psychologic warning signs that may alert health care providers that the patient may be a past victim of a sexual assault are as follows:

1. Aggressive/regressive behavior

2. Mistrust in others

3. Disturbed peer interactions

4. Nightmares

— Physical warning signs that may alert health care providers that the patient may be a present victim of sexual abuse are as follows:

1. Trouble walking or standing, not present before

2. Bleeding, infection, and irritation in the genital areas

3. Bruising on arms, inner thighs, and/or breast tissue

4. Contracting an STI

5. Unusual fear and anxiety

6. Withdrawing from activities and socialization

7. Acting stressed and/or fearful around others, especially the abuser/assailant

8. Sudden onset of fraility

— Some incidents are discovered accidentally during perineal care, with physical findings such as signs of trauma to anogenital or surrounding tissue.

— Some cases have been detected through signs and diagnostic findings that confirmed the presence of sexually transmitted infections (STIs).

— Nursing home residents are often immunocompromised and may have had minimal sexual experiences in older age. The onset of symptoms, eg, fever, malaise, changes in blood pressure, or skin rashes, in a patient suspected to have been abused or assaulted requires a thorough medical assessment.

— Rape of older persons is associated with increased morbidity and mortality in the first year following the assault.

Perpetrators in Nursing Homes
— Three approaches are used by perpetrators in assaulting frail older adults:

1. The *confidence* approach is used with mobile, more highly functional victims and involves gaining the victim's confidence through verbal manipulation or coercion.

2. A *blitz* approach involves overtaking the victim through injurious force.

3. A *surprise* approach employs the use of threats but no force when the victim is either unsuspecting or incapacitated.

Reporting and Investigating Suspected Abuse

— Nursing homes are obligated to investigate suspected abuse within 5 days of a report to the nursing home administration.

— If sexual abuse is suspected, it is important for the nursing home staff and administration to apply trauma-informed care principles to avoid subjecting the victim to unnecessary further trauma during the investigation process.

— Carefully consider the location of the interview, taking special care to establish that the interview process is as safe as possible for the resident.

— Be aware that it may be problematic to perform a thorough physical assessment for the following reasons:

1. Joint contractures

2. Victim resistance because of the pain of the assault

3. Difficulty communicating with a patient who has dementia and cognitive impairment

— Forensic evidence may be difficult to obtain if the incident is discovered in a delayed manner*; however, recent studies support collection of evidence and use of second generation Y-STR if Y-STR and PCR are negative.

— It should be clear that the nursing home can be held liable when foreseeable risks may have contributed to a sexual assault, eg, failure to check backgrounds of employees or residents.

Refer to Publisher's Note on page xliv.

SEXUAL ASSAULT OF OLDER ADULTS
RESIDING IN NONINSTITUTIONAL SETTINGS

— Family members perpetrate the majority of abuse and violence inflicted on older adults outside of an institutional setting.

— Physical abuse of an older person reflects familial culture and tolerance for violence.

— Five types of offenders commit violence against family members, with sexual abuse rarely occurring among the first 2 types:

1. The competent caregiver with a pattern of violent reactions for the purpose of controlling behavior of the older person

2. The willing but physically or cognitively impaired caregiver

3. The caregiver with a "user mentality" who expects to gain something from the caregiving relationship

4. The unstable, angry, and volatile caregiver who lashes out toward less powerful individuals

5. The sadistic caregiver who gains pleasure by harming or intimidating others

— The 2 distinct phases of sexual abuse are covert sexual abuse and overt sexual abuse.

1. Covert sexual abuse: sexual interest may be expressed or sexual activity discussed. The perpetrator treats the victim as a sex object or potential sexual partner.

2. Overt abuse: activities such as voyeurism and inflicting pornography on the victim may escalate to various degrees of sexual contact, ranging from kissing and fondling to oral-genital contact to various forms of oral, vaginal, or anal penetration.

IMMEDIATE AND LONG-TERM RESPONSES
OF OLDER SEXUAL ASSAULT VICTIMS

— Rape trauma syndrome

1. Acute phase: marked by disorganization and fear; somatic symptoms may be seen in all survivors of sexual abuse and include tension headaches, fatigue, sleep disturbances, and gastrointestinal irritability.

2. Reorganization phase: involves the process of stabilization and begins 4 to 8 weeks after the assault; symptoms are often consistent with those of posttraumatic stress disorder (PTSD). Criteria include a stressor of significant magnitude such that it would likely evoke distinguishable symptoms in most individuals, the victim reexperiencing the trauma through recurrent and sometimes intrusive recollection of the event, and the victim developing a constricted view of and reduced involvement with the environment.

— Other symptoms of rape trauma syndrome include exaggerated startle response or hyperarousal state, guilt, impaired memory surrounding the event, and problems with concentration and attention not associated with medical conditions.

FRAMEWORK FOR WORKING WITH OLDER SEXUAL ASSAULT VICTIMS
— As mentioned, existing services for those experiencing sexual victimization are generally not designed to meet the needs of older adults.

— The concepts, theories, and practices characteristic of victimology and those related to gerontology must be integrated to address the needs of older victims of sexual assault.

1. *Victimology* addresses selected aspects of sexual victimization, including the vulnerability patterns of the victim, the exposure patterns of the incident, and factors that influence the degree of adaptation on the victim's part after the traumatic event.

2. *Gerontology* addresses selected aspects of the aging process, defining age in terms of the ability of an individual to respond to stressors and looking at the older adult more holistically. The focus is on the quality of life of the individual as measured by how well day-to-day functioning is in accord with the values and expectations of the older adult. It also takes into account the coping strategies and supports that help the older adult maintain optimal functioning.

— Older adults differ in their ability to adapt successfully to stress, which is termed allostatic loading. Failure to return to homeostasis results in death.

— Gerontologists attempt to view aspects of successful aging, specifically selective optimization with compensation. The individual optimizes the adaptation process by employing successful chosen and practiced behaviors to respond to stressors and accommodates by modifying conditions to meet ability level.

— Health care providers often frame their interactions with older adult patients using a problem-oriented perspective. The common endpoint in considering the adaptive capabilities of an older adult revolves around an assessment of the overall frailty of the individual.

— Appreciation of the altered responses to stress and the allostatic load from stress and the need to look at contextual factors in supporting the quality of life for older adults are central to providing effective care for the older victim of sexual assault.

EFFECTIVE CLINICAL RESPONSE TO ELDER SEXUAL ABUSE
Effective clinical care responses include the following:

— Prompt detection of sexual abuse

— An understanding of the cognitive, physical, and emotional issues unique to elder victims of sexual abuse

— A nonjudgmental, developmentally appropriate, and trauma-informed philosophy that contributes to a caring approach to interviews, examinations, and other caregiving activities

— Support for the adaptation and optimal return of functioning

Screening
— The initial evaluation of geriatric patients should include a social history and assessment, screening for indicators of all types of abuse, even in the absence of any suspicion of abuse.

— Because many older adults come to the emergency department for evaluation through an emergency medical system, EMTs, paramedics, and other transport personnel should be trained in the needs of older adult victims of sexual abuse or assault.

1. Be aware that older patients will deteriorate under allostatic loads and changes in physical environment.

2. Be alert to and make note of residential conditions, physical signs, and verbal or other behaviors indicative of sexual assault or abuse.

3. Be aware of the need to preserve evidence that may be important to a forensic investigation.

4. Generally, do not wash the patient or change her or his clothing.

5. If clothing is removed, keep it in a paper bag to prevent bacterial overgrowth.

6. See *Chapter 10* for the details of forensic evidence collection.

Interview
— Before conducting the interview of a sexual assault patient, consider the following details:

1. Who should conduct the interview? The literature is mixed about the interviewer being the same gender as the victim, but if possible, victim choice creates safety and caring, which is a common attribute among specially trained providers.

2. Where should the interview take place? Usually holding the interview away from the site of the suspected assault is preferable. Interviews may be conducted in the victim's residence as long as the interviewer provides a sense of safety and privacy. The victim should be assured that the assailant will not overhear the interview or be privy to what was said.

3. How should the interview be conducted?

— Build rapport with the victim.

— Address the victim by her or his last name unless otherwise directed by the patient.

— Avoid caretaker speech, in which the patient is addressed in familiar terms.

— Have a family member or other trusted individual present.

— Allow the older adult as much control as possible.

— Make sure the interviewee knows that he or she has the right to terminate the interview at any point.

— Initiate questions in an open-ended manner and provide sufficient time for the older adult to answer.

— Be alert to any subtle sensory impairment in the victim, but also ask directly if he or she has any difficulty seeing or hearing.

— Perform a brief mini-mental status examination if there is any question regarding cognitive impairment that could hinder the interview. Consider a different time of day to enhance cognition. Provide time and space, and anticipate additional interviews for details, not usually available immediately following a sexual trauma.

— Speak in a well-modulated, slower-paced, and lower-pitched voice to counter the effects of age-related hearing loss. You may also place earpieces of a stethoscope in the ears of the older patient and speak through the diaphragm or employ a small portable amplifying device.

— Ask one question at a time.

— Be alert to indirect verbal references to sexual assault or cues that indicate fear, guilt, shame, or inappropriate sexual references. While they may be associated with the current assault, it may also resurrect feelings from previous sexual assaults.

4. What actions need to be taken as a result of information gathered during the interview? If action must be taken, provide emotional support to the victim as the top priority.

5. What information should the interviewer share and with whom?

Examination

— Only providers with training and expertise in geriatric sexual assault care, along with compassion and exceptional communication skills, should examine the older sexual assault victim.

— Older adult female sexual assault victims have an increased incidence and degree of genital trauma, mostly because of normal postmenopausal changes, as follows:

1. Menopause generally occurs between ages 45 and 55 years.

2. Structural changes result from a decline in the hormone levels after ovulation ceases.

3. Estrogen levels fall, resulting in smaller, smoother labia and clitoris, ie, atrophy.

4. The uterus and ovaries diminish in size and breast tissue diminishes and fat deposits increase, and there is a loss of subcutaneous support, ie, elasticity.

5. There is loss of adipose tissue, and elasticity of tissue of the labia majora diminishes.

6. Pubic hair thins.

7. Bartholin's glands and vaginal tissue produces lesser amounts of vaginal secretions, causing a decrease in lubrication during intercourse and resulting dyspareunia, ie, painful intercourse.

8. Vaginal walls may be light pink or pale and appear tissue paper thin and dry, ie, atrophy. They also lose some capacity for expansion and, without routine stretching, eventually collapse and adhese.

9. Some older women also develop urinary frequency or urgency or stress incontinence.

— Be aware that less serious injuries have more serious consequences, eg, increased morbidity and mortality among older adult patients, so that seemingly minor injuries may require greater attention and the person may require more frequent monitoring for sepsis and persistent allostatic loading, increasing activity from all bodily systems.

— When sexual assault is a possibility, evidence of bruising to the perineum, pain with micturition, vaginal bleeding, and discharge are all ominous signs.

— Proceed carefully and slowly with the pelvic and rectal examination, reassuring the patient and realizing that it may take longer than with a younger woman.

— Be alert to difficulty walking or sitting and torn, stained, or bloody clothing.

— Red flags for suspecting sexual assault are as follows:

1. Pain or itching of the genital area

2. Recurrent vaginal infections

3. Bruising or bleeding of the external genitalia, vaginal, or anal area

4. Unexpected or unreported reluctance to cooperate with toileting, bathing, or the physical examination of the genitalia

Provision of Care and Resources

— Offer explanations and instructions that are clear and unambiguous.

— Provide written instructions using large bold lettering.

— Take the time to thoroughly discuss everything and pause to encourage thought and eventual questions.

— Relate new information and tasks to previous experiences.

— Use language that is familiar to the patient.

— Make a follow-up phone call within 24 hours.

— Plan for follow-up referrals and communicate the plans clearly to the patient.

— Include the patient's family whenever possible in any educative effort.

Reporting Requirements

— Be familiar with state elder abuse reporting laws.

— Provide training to staff regarding the detection and management of elder abuse.

SEXUAL ASSAULT IN CORRECTIONAL SETTINGS
OVERVIEW OF THE PROBLEM

— Poor systems surveillance with resultant inaccurate epidemiology reports of the incidence and prevalence of prison rape

— Inadequate laws to protect prisoners or to provide adequate reporting abilities to victims

— Indifference of correctional staff to the impact of such sexual assaults

— Insufficient facility capability to provide isolation and, therefore, protection for vulnerable inmates

— High incidence of mentally impaired victims, for whom no special provisions are made and investigation of complaints is inadequate

— Mixing of juveniles into the adult prison population, placing them at extreme risk for exploitation, victimization, and subsequent mental health injury

— Unavailability of counseling for victims of prisoner-on-prisoner sexual assault

— Inadequate medical services for the STI risk

— Inadequate training programs on male and female prisoner-on-prisoner sexual abuse for both high-level corrections officials and front-line staff

— Nonexistent standard operating procedures for response to prisoner-on-prisoner sexual assault

— Inadequate numbers of guards and monitoring systems to ensure safety of the prison population

— Need to consistently report sexual assault behind bars to local authorities and prosecutorial agencies for investigation and possible criminal prosecution

— Lack of recognition and action to address the problem of racial tensions within prisons, which also contributes to violent sexual assaults of specific minority groups

— Poor attention to the gang dynamics that exist in the prison systems and the need to prevent multiple-perpetrator sexual assaults

— Common practice of merely transferring perpetrators to different units, where further abuse of a different group of potential victims is facilitated instead of taking appropriate disciplinary action

— Practice of placing more than one prisoner per cell, ie, double celling, without consideration of whether there has been a prior report or suspicion of a sexual assault involving one or more than one of the inmates

— Poor public awareness of the serious and tragic nature of this type of crime, leading to misrepresentations of prison rape as a joke in the media

— Poor recognition that prison rape is a contributing factor to prison homicides, violence against inmates and staff, and institutional riots and insurrections

— Poor attention to the problem of custodial abuse of inmates

— Inadequate federal laws to affect prison funding for the complex problem of prisoner sexual assault

— As a result of the statistical analysis of prison rape, the Prison Rape Elimination Act (PREA) was passed in 2003 with unanimous support from both parties in Congress. The purpose of the act was to "provide for the analysis of the incidence and effects of prison rape in Federal, State, and local institutions and to provide information, resources, and recommendations and funding to protect individuals from prison rape."

— The act also created the National Prison Rape Elimination Commission and charged it with developing draft standards for the elimination of prison rape. Those standards were published in June 2009, and were turned over to the Department of Justice for review and passage as a final rule. That final rule became effective August 20, 2012.

SCOPE OF THE PROBLEM

— From 22% to 25% of prisoners are victims of sexual pressuring, attempted sexual assault, or completed rapes.

— Ten percent of prisoners are victims of a completed rape at least one time during the course of their incarceration.

— Two thirds of those reporting sexual victimization have been repeatedly victimized on an average of nine times during their incarceration, with some male prisoners experiencing up to 100 incidents of sexual assault per year.

CONSEQUENCES OF ATTACKS

— Forced sex without subsequent trauma is unlikely, and that trauma may be equally physical and emotional or mostly emotional or psychologic.

— Regardless of the type or extent of trauma sustained, there will be consequences for the individual, society, and those professionals working with these special populations and the aftermath of their experiences.

— Mental health ramifications:

1. Extreme

2. There are more mentally ill inmates in prison than in psychiatric hospitals, and most correctional facilities have minimal mental health capability.

3. Include PTSD, anxiety, depression, and the exacerbation of existing mental disorders

4. Inmates at risk for suicide become more unstable and are much more likely to attempt or succeed at committing suicide to avoid continuous trauma

5. May display anger, depression, loss of self-esteem and self-worth, alteration of self-image, and a desire for revenge

— Categories of inmates especially vulnerable to sexual assault:

1. Young and inexperienced

2. Short in stature, slightly built, and physically weak

3. Mentally ill or with developmental disabilities

4. Not streetwise or lacking in savvy

5. Not gang-affiliated

6. Homosexual, overtly effeminate, or transgendered

7. Violated the "code of silence" or seen as a "snitch"

8. Disliked by the staff or other inmates

9. Prior sexual assault victims

ROLE OF MEDICAL PROFESSIONALS

— Health care professionals are obligated to provide unbiased, professional care.

— Clinical guidelines for medical management must address the following (**Table 14-1**):

1. Viral hepatitis (A, B, C, and D)

2. Human immunodeficiency virus (HIV) infection

3. Tuberculosis (TB)

4. STIs

5. Endocarditis prophylaxis

6. Varicella

Table 14-1. Process of Identification of Infectious Diseases in the Prison Population

INFECTIOUS DISEASE	SCREEN, ASSESS, AND TEST INMATES
TB infection and possible TB disease	— On initial incarceration before being placed in general population — Annually — When clinically indicated — To find evidence of spread surrounding a case of contagious TB disease
HIV infection	— If history of risk behavior — If clinical indications — Before release — For surveillance purposes — After an exposure
Other infections transmittable by casual contact	— On intake and before being placed in the general population — Before assigned to the food service area — If clinical indications — With contact investigators

ROLE OF SOCIAL SERVICES PROFESSIONALS AND PRISON STAFF
— Cope with the reality of life behind bars.

— Exercise necessary caution without developing paranoia or disregard for the humanity of those incarcerated.

— Be aware of gang-related incidents and seek to take preventive action.

— Keep in mind that the overall control of the institution is paramount to the individual's needs.

— Adhere to a high professional and personal ethic.

SEXUAL PREDATORS AND MOVING FROM VICTIM TO PREDATOR
— Sexual predators may be used to intimidate, control, or punish other inmates for real or perceived transgressions of the prison law.

— In addition to having a very high incidence of PTSD and depression, individuals who survive a single sexual assault or multiple sexual assaults may themselves become violent both as an act of immediate self-defense and to avoid further victimization.

— The transition from victim to predator may follow the individual beyond penal confinement, contributing to the over 75% rate of return to incarceration for inmates.

REFERENCES

1. Ballantyne J. *DNA Profiling of the Semen Donor in Extended Interval Post-Coital Samples.* Washington, DC: National Center for Forensic Science; 2013. Document No 241299.

2. Bickley LS. *Bates' Guide to Physical Examination and History Taking.* 11th ed. Philadelphia, PA: JB Lippincott; 2012.

3. Burgess AW. *Rape and Sexual Assault III: A Research Handbook.* New York, NY: Garland Publishing, Inc; 1991.

4. Burgess AW, Dowdell EB, Prentky RA. Sexual abuse of nursing home residents. *J Psychosoc Nurs Ment Health Serv.* 2000;38(6):10-18.

5. Burgess AW, Holmstrom LL. Rape trauma syndrome. *Am J Psychiatry.* 1974;131(9):981-986.

6. Capezuti EA, Swedlow DJ. Sexual abuse in nursing homes. *Marquette's Elder's Advisor*. 2000;2(2):51-61.

7. Cartwright PS, Moore RA. The elderly victim of rape. *South Med J*. 1989;82(8):988-989.

8. Chelala C. More mentally ill people reported in US prisons. *BMJ*. 1999;319(7204):210.

9. Clarke ME, Pierson W. Management of elder abuse in the emergency department. *Emerg Med Clin North Am*. 1999;17(3):631-644, vi.

10. Cotton DJ, Groth AN. Inmate rape - prevention and intervention. *J Prison Jail Health*. 1982;2(1):47-57.

11. Cotton DJ, Groth AN. Sexual assault in correctional institutions: prevention and intervention. In: Stuart IR, ed. *Victims of Sexual Aggression: Treatment of Children, Women, and Men*. New York, NY: Van Nostrand Reinhold; 1984.

12. Deming JE, Mittleman RE, Wetli CV. Forensic science aspects of fatal sexual assaults on women. *J Forensic Sci*. 1983;28(3):572-576.

13. Dumond RW. Inmate sexual assault: the plague that persists. *Prison J*. 2000;80(4):407-414.

14. Dumond RW. The sexual assault of male inmates in incarcerated settings. *International Journal of the Sociology of Law*. 1992;20(2):135-157. NCJ 139657.

15. Dumond RW, Dumond DA. The treatment of sexual assault victims. In: Hensley C, ed. *Prison Sex: Practice and Policy*. Boulder, CO: Lynne Rienner Publishers; 2002:67-100.

16. Faugno DK, Speck PM. Basic anogenital and oral anatomy. In: Ledray LE, Burgess AW, Giardino AP, eds. *Medical Response to Adult Sexual Assault: A Resource for Clinicians and Related Professionals*. Saint Louis, MO: STM Medical Publishing; 2011.

17. Federal Bureau of Prisons. *Federal Bureau of Prisons Report on Infectious Disease Management*. Washington, DC: Federal Bureau of Prisons; 2001.

18. Fulmer T, Paveza G, Abraham I, Fairchild S. Elder neglect assessment in the emergency department. *J Emerg Nurs.* 2000;26(5):436-443.

19. Groth AN. The older rape victim and her assailant. *J Geriatr Psychiatry.* 1978;11(2):203-215.

20. Harrington SPM. New Bedlam: Jails--not psychiatric hospitals--now care for the indigent mentally ill. *Jail Suicide/Mental Health Update.* 1999;9(2):12-17.

21. Hazelwood RR, Burgess AW. *Practical Rape Investigation.* Boca Raton, FL: CRC Press; 1995.

22. Kane RL, Ouslander JG, Abrass IB, Resnick B. *Essentials of Clinical Geriatrics.* 7th ed. New York, NY: McGraw-Hill; 2013.

23. Knowles GJ. Male prison rape: a search for causation and prevention. *Howard Journal of Criminal Justice.* 1999;38(3):267-282.

24. Lionheart Foundation. Corrections in the US. Lionheart Foundation Web site. http://lionheart.org/prison/corrections-in-the-us/. Accessed May 29, 2015.

25. Loggins SA. Rape as an intentional tort. *Trial.* 1985:45-55.

26. Maier SL. "I have heard horrible stories…": rape victim advocates' perceptions of the revictimization of rape victims by the police and medical system. *Violence Against Women.* 2008;14(7):786-808. doi: 10.1177/1077801208320245.

27. Mariner J. *No Escape: Male Rape in US Prisons.* New York, NY: Human Rights Watch; 2001.

28. Mayntz-Press KA, Sims LM, Hall AM, Ballantyne J. Y-STR profiling in extended interval (> or = 3 days) postcoital cervicovaginal samples. *J Forensic Sci.* 2008;53(2):342-348.

29. National Center on Elder Abuse, American Public Human Services Association. *The National Elder Abuse Incidence Study.* Washington, DC: National Center on Elder Abuse, American Public Human Services Association; 1998.

30. Prison Rape Elimination Act, 42 USC §15601-15609 (2003).

31. Ramsey-Klawsnik H. Elder sexual abuse: preliminary findings. *J Elder Abuse Negl.* 1991;3(3):73-89.

32. Ramsey-Klawsnik H. Interviewing elders for suspected sexual abuse: guidelines and techniques. *J Elder Abuse Negl.* 1993;5(1):5-18.

33. Ramsey-Klawsnik H. Speaking the unspeakable: an interview about elder sexual abuse. *Nexus.* 1998;4(1):4-6.

34. Sanders AB. Care of the elderly in emergency departments: conclusions and recommendations. *Ann Emerg Med.* 1992;21(7):830-834.

35. Speck P, Ballantyne J. *Post-Coital DNA Recovery Study.* Washington DC: National Criminal Justice Reference Service; 2015. National Criminal Justice Reference Service Web site. //www.ncjrs.gov/pdffiles1/nij/grants/248682.pdf. Accessed May 29, 2015.

36. Struckman-Johnson C, Struckman-Johnson D. Sexual coercion rates in seven Midwestern prison facilities for men. *Prison J.* 2000;80(4):379-390.

37. Struckman-Johnson C, Struckman-Johnson D, Rucker L, Bumby K, Donaldson S. Sexual coercion reported by men and women in prison. *J Sex Res.* 1996;33(1):67-76.

38. Torrey EF. How did so many mentally ill persons get into America's jails and prisons? *American Jails.* 1999;13(5):9-13.

39. US Department of Justice, Office of Justice Programs, Bureau of Justice Statistics. *Criminal Victimization in the United States, 1995.* Washington, DC: US Department of Justice, Office of Justice Programs, Bureau of Justice Statistics; 2000. NCJ 171129.

40. Yurick AG, Speir BE, Robb SS, Ebert NJ. *The Aged Person and the Nursing Process.* 3rd ed. Norwalk, CT: McGraw-Hill/Appleton & Lange; 1989.

Chapter 15

PSYCHOLOGICAL AND SOCIAL SUPPORTS

Paul Thomas Clements, PhD, RN, DF-IAFN*
Sandra L. Bloom, MD
Jeffrey R. Jaeger, MD
Ann E. Gaulin, MS, MFT
Janice B. Asher, MD

REVISED TRAUMA THEORY: UNDERSTANDING THE TRAUMATIC NATURE OF SEXUAL ASSAULT

Sexual assault has immediate and long-term consequences that can be devastating for the physical, emotional, and psychosocial relational health of the victim. Exposure to the overwhelming stress of assault alters the psychobiology, personal adjustment, and systems of meaning for the victim, and the consequences of these changes influence physical health, mental health, ever-evolving social development, perceptions of and reactions to revictimization experiences, and the ability to parent. The trauma of sexual assault has an effect on every level of a person's adjustment. Trauma theory presents a comprehensive biopsychosocial and philosophic model within which one can understand these effects to enhance targeted and sensitive assessment and intervention.

TRAUMA THEORY

— Trauma theory helps to understand how victims' bodies and minds respond normally to abnormal events and then become stuck as a "state becomes a trait."

— In work with disaster victims, combat veterans, Holocaust survivors, and, more recently, those exposed to acts of terrorism, trauma is well defined, representing experiences of terror, exposure to atrocities, or the fear of imminent death.

*Revised Chapter 15 for the second edition.

— According to the DSM-5 the formal diagnosis of posttraumatic stress disorder (PTSD) mandates that the victim must experience, witness, or be confronted with an event or events that involve actual or threatened death or serious injury or threat to physical integrity of self or others.

— Child victims of sexual abuse and many victims of intimate partner rape are not in imminent fear of loss of life or even loss of physical integrity. Yet sexual abuse and nonlife-threatening rape are some of the most traumatizing of experiences.

— The discrepancy is explained by the complexity of the interaction of the victim and the offender throughout the traumatic event. Events occurring during and subsequent to the traumatic event can make a profound difference in how the victim experiences and interprets the event.

— Thus it is not only the trauma itself that does damage to the victim, it is how the individual's mind and body perceive, process, and react to the traumatic experience combined with the unique response of the individual's social group.

Heredity's Legacy: The Autonomic Nervous System

— Sexual assault can significantly impact and alter the victim's world view. The way we think, the way we learn, the way we remember things, the way we feel about ourselves, the way we feel about other people, and the way we make sense of the world are all profoundly altered by traumatic experience.

— Like all mammals, humans are equipped to respond to emergencies with a fight-or-flight reaction via the autonomic nervous system, which has 3 purposes:

1. Creates a state of extreme hyperarousal

2. Serves a protective function, preparing the individual to respond automatically and aggressively to a perceived threat

3. Preferentially steers the individual toward action and away from the time-consuming effort of thought and language

— Prolonged hyperarousal leaves people physically and emotionally exhausted, burdened with hair-trigger tempers, irritable, and tending to perpetuate violence.

— When hyperarousal stops being a state and becomes a trait, human beings lose their capacity to accurately assess and predict danger. A consequence may be avoidance; dissociation, ie, numbing or "freezing"; or reenactment instead of adaptation and survival.

— Very complex brains and powerful memories are unique to humans and indicate extreme intelligence; however, this very intelligence creates a vulnerability to the effects of trauma in the form of flashbacks, body memories, posttraumatic nightmares, and behavioral reenactments.

— Dependence on language is important, with experiences that occurred before the age language was acquired not integrated into consciousness and a coherent sense of identity. The individual becomes haunted by an unresolved, or even unknown, past and may become very frustrated without being able to remember what happened.

— Humans are particularly ill-suited to having the people to whom they are attached also be the people doing the violating. The nature and intensity of the relationship with the offender will impact the severity of the traumatic responses and recovery process.

— Trauma profoundly disrupts the ability to manage emotional experience and people tend to either overreact or underreact. An impaired ability to respond with the appropriate emotional signal impairs the capacity to create and maintain healthy relationships.

— Humans are also physiologically designed to function best as an integrated whole, from which emerges meaning, purpose, values, belief, identity, and wisdom. The fragmentation that accompanies traumatic experience degrades this integration and impedes maximum performance.

1. Humans have a need for order, safety, and adequate protection.

2. Without balance between stimulation and soothing, humans cannot reason properly or make sense out of what happened.

3. When trauma cannot be adequately processed, it often leads to placing oneself at risk for subsequent victimization.

Fight-or-Flight Response
— Changes in physiologic function occur that are so dramatic that in many ways people are not the same when they are terrified as when they are calm.

— Attention becomes riveted on the potential threat, which may be actual or perceived, so the capacity for reasoning and exercising judgment is negatively influenced by the rising anxiety and fear.

— People become less attentive to words and more focused on threat-related signals in the environment.

— As fear and anxiety rise to severe and panic levels, they may lose language functions entirely and move into a state of physical and emotional numbness, ie, dissociation.

— People can take in vital information only in nonverbal form at this stage, specifically through physical, emotional, and sensory experiences, which, due to the increased level of fear, can lead to a misinterpretation of any perceived threat.

— As the level of arousal increases, dissociation may be triggered as an adaptive response to hyperarousal, physiologically lowering heart rate and reducing anxiety and pain.

— Each episode of danger connects to every other episode in the human mind, so the greater the perception of the danger exposure, the greater the sensitivity to danger. Even minor threats can eventually trigger an involuntary sequence of physical, emotional, and cognitive responses.

Learned Helplessness
— Repetitive exposure to helplessness is so toxic to emotional and physiologic stability that, in the service of continued survival, persons are compelled to adapt to the helplessness itself, a phenomenon termed learned helplessness.

— If people are subjected to a sufficient number of experiences teaching them that nothing they do will affect the outcome, they give up trying.

— Once the mechanism of learned helplessness is in place, it does not automatically reverse when escape becomes possible.

— Adults in situations of domestic violence may be exposed repetitively to marital rape and experience the same sense of helpless adaptation. Persons exposed to other forms of sexual assault may also freeze up and be unable to protect themselves when similar triggering circumstances are presented.

Thinking Under Stress—Action, Not Thought

— The ability to think clearly is severely impaired when individuals are under extreme stress. Decisions tend to be based on impulse and an experienced need to self-protect.

— Decisions are characterized by inflexibility, oversimplification, direction toward action, and poor construction, with an intolerance of mistakes, denial of personal difficulties, and anger as a problem-solving strategy.

Remembering Under Stress

— Exposure to trauma alters people's memory, producing extremes of remembering too much and recalling too little. Unlike other memories, traumatic memories appear to become etched in the mind, unaltered by the passage of time or by subsequent experience.

— There may be 2 memory systems that normally work together but are disrupted by extreme stress:

1. One for verbal learning: the "normal" memory, based on language, which is highly vulnerable to high levels of stress.

2. The other, largely nonverbal: when a person is overwhelmed by fear, "speechless terror" and dissociation may result; the mind shifts to a mode of thinking characterized by visual, auditory, olfactory, and kinesthetic images as well as physical sensations and strong feelings.

— Processing of information is more rapid and the possibility of survival is generally greater in the face of threat.

— Problems arise because these powerful images, feelings, and sensations do not just go away once the danger has passed. They are deeply imprinted, in fact, more strongly so than normal, everyday memories. This kind of memory may be difficult or impossible to erase, although one can learn to cognitively override some responses.

— A flashback is a sudden, intrusive reexperiencing of a fragment of one of those traumatic unverbalized memories.

1. Likely to occur when people are stressed or frightened or when triggered by any association with the traumatic event, ie, "environmental cuing"

2. Minds are flooded by images, emotions, and physical sensations.

3. Feels like the traumatic experience is happening again, with difficulty separating past from present or real from perceived

4. Often individuals do not recognize that they are having a flashback but instead feel that they are "losing their mind" or having a "panic attack."

5. Flashbacks may occur in the form of physical symptoms, ie, "body memory."

6. As people try to limit situations that promote hyperarousal and flashbacks (typically limiting relationships that trigger emotions) and employ behaviors designed to control emotional responses, they may become progressively numb to all emotions and feel depressed and alienated. In this state it takes greater and greater stimulation to feel a sense of being alive. Thus they engage in risk-taking behaviors, eg, self-mutilation, because it is the only way they feel "inside" themselves again. This is one of the most devastating aspects of prolonged stress.

— The person may also develop amnesia of the traumatic event. The memory is there but no words are attached to it, so it cannot be talked about or even thought about. Trying to make a victim remember can increase the level of stress and result in additional problematic reactions.

— For healing to occur, people must put the experience into a narrative, give it words, and share it with themselves and others. Words allow one to put things into a time sequence that finally allows a flashback to become a true memory instead of a haunting presence. This also promotes a decrease in expressing the experience through maladaptive or dangerous behaviors.

Emotions and Trauma—Dissociation

— A fundamental reason that few people die from emotional upsets is the built-in "safety valve" called dissociation.

— Dissociation is defined as "a disruption in the usually integrated functions of consciousness, memory, identity, or perception of the environment." It allows one to do more than one thing at a time. Some compare it to daydreaming while still continuing the daily activities of living.

— One way to dissociate is commonly seen and involves splitting off experience from feelings about that experience.

— Cutting off all emotions, or emotional numbing, occurs only in extreme cases of repetitive and almost unendurable trauma.

1. Normal responses and emotional experiences that could lead back to the traumatic memory are increasingly shut off.

2. The person is likely to become increasingly depressed.

3. Slow self-destruction through addictions or self-mutilation or fast self-destruction through suicide are often the final outcomes of these syndromes.

4. Rage at others may also occur, and people who allow rage to become dominant can become significant threats to other people as well as to themselves.

Endorphins and Stress—Addiction to Trauma

— Endorphins are naturally released within the human body and relieve distress, calming anxiety, improving mood, and decreasing aggression.

— Endorphins are also analgesics, chemically related to morphine and heroin.

— People exposed to repeated experiences of prolonged stress experience repeatedly high levels of circulating endorphins and are likely to develop stress-induced analgesia. It is hypothesized that this represents an addiction to their own internal endorphins, so that they feel calm only when they are under stress. Relieving stress for these individuals can lead to fearfulness, irritability, hyperarousal, or even violence.

Trauma Bonding

— Trauma bonding refers to a relationship based on terror and the distortion of normal attachment behavior into something perverse and cruel.

— For victims of repetitive abuse, abusive relationships may become the normative idea of what relationships are all about. This is known as trauma learning.

Traumatic Reenactment

— People who have been traumatized develop what may begin as life-saving coping mechanisms, but these mechanisms may lead to compulsive repetition. This is an attempt to gain mastery over trauma, but it is often done in maladaptive ways.

— Through reenactment, people are trying to repeatedly "tell their story" in very overt or highly disguised ways. They may use the language of physical symptoms or deviant behavior.

— As emotional, physical, or social symptoms of distress pile up, victims try to extricate themselves by using the same protective devices that they used to cope with threat in the first place: dissociation, avoidance, aggression, destructive attachments, damaging behaviors, and substance addiction.

The Consequences of Traumatic Experience

— Adjustment problems

— Psychiatric disturbance, including posttraumatic stress disorder (PTSD), major depression, dysthymia, suicidality, self-mutilation, somatic complaints, poor self-esteem, anxiety disorders, sleep disturbances, substance abuse disorders, learning disabilities, conduct disorders, delinquency, aggression, increased health risk behaviors, and inappropriate sexual behavior

— Substance misuse, both illicit and prescription

— Comorbid problems, eg, panic disorder and social phobia, borderline personality disorder, somatoform disorders, obsessive-compulsive disorder, and anxiety disorders

— In adult survivors of child sexual abuse: poorer social and interpersonal relationship functioning, greater sexual dissatisfaction and dysfunction, and a greater tendency toward revictimization through adult sexual assault and physical partner violence

— Most common clinical presentation:

　1. Seven clusters of symptoms described as complex PTSD or disorders of extreme stress not otherwise specified (DESNOS)

　2. Includes alterations in regulating affective arousal, alterations in attention and consciousness, somatization, alterations in self-perception, alterations in perception of the perpetrator, alterations in relations to others, and alterations in systems of meaning

　3. Differentiates adult victims of childhood interpersonal violence and abuse from adult-onset trauma syndromes associated with disasters

Sexual Assault and Neurobiologic Changes

— Early adverse experiences raise the sensitivity to the effects of stress later in life and make a person more vulnerable to stress-related psychiatric disorders.

— Early abuse affects brain development; the left hemisphere appears to be more vulnerable than the right.

— Women with a history of prior physical or sexual assault show a significantly attenuated cortisol response to the acute stress of rape compared to women without such a history.

— Women who develop PTSD secondary to childhood sexual abuse show a much higher rate of neurologic "soft sign" scores, ie, subtle neurologic changes, than women who were also sexually abused as children but did not develop PTSD. These differences could not be explained by alcoholism or head injury.

HEALTH CONSEQUENCES OF TRAUMA

— Victims of trauma suffer a multitude of physical disorders not directly related to their injuries.

— PTSD has been connected to fibromyalgia, chronic pain, irritable bowel syndrome, asthma, peptic ulcer, other gastrointestinal illness, and chronic pelvic pain.

— There is evidence that the HPA Axis (hypothalamic-pituitary-adrenal axis) can become dysregulated in PTSD, which contributes to widespread impairment in functions such as memory and stress reactivity and to physical morbidity.

Stress, Moods, and Immunity

— Even mild stress has an impact on the immune system. This can be further heightened by dysregulation of the HPA Axis.

— Interpersonal stressors have a different impact than nonsocial stressors.

1. Objective stressful events are related to greater immune changes than subjective self-reports of stress.

2. Immune response varies with the duration of the stressor.

3. Interpersonal events are linked to different immune outcomes than nonsocial events.

— Factors such as stress, negative emotion, clinical depression, lack of social support, and repression or denial can negatively influence both cellular and humoral indicators of immune status and function.

— Stress and negative emotion are convincingly linked to disease onset and progression.

Chronic Violence and Health

— Women who have been sexually abused and sexually assaulted routinely come to their gynecologists with a number of complaints. Assessment for sexual abuse should be routinely conducted.

— Sexual assault and abuse can take a heavy toll on sexual adjustment.

— Associations have been found between childhood maltreatment and adverse adult health outcomes, such as perceived poor overall health, physical and emotional functional disability, distressing physical symptoms, and health risk behavior.

Sexual Assault and Revictimization

— While victims of sexual assault tend to be revictimized, this risk is especially high among child sexual abuse survivors. Victimization before age 14 years almost doubles the risk of later adolescent victimization.

— Revictimization appears to arise because the childhood and family factors associated with childhood sexual abuse are also associated with increased sexual risks during adolescence.

— Exposure to childhood sexual abuse may encourage early onset sexual activity, which places the victim at greater risk for sexual problems over the period of adolescence.

— Prostitution is a special case of revictimization, with a marked and dramatic relationship between prostitution and a previous history of sexual abuse.

— Victim-to-victimizer behavior

1. A victim is both helpless and powerless, and helplessness is a noxious human experience that people seek to avoid.

2. Once victimized, a possible outcome is to assume the power of the perpetrator by becoming someone who terrorizes and abuses others. This can include reenactment, repetition, or displacement of the trauma.

3. Such behavior can reduce anxiety and provide a certain excitement, and the combination of these 2 effects can become habit-forming.

4. These effects can be culturally influenced; for example, boys may accommodate more easily to the victimizer role and women to the victim role in traditionally focused cultures.

5. Childhood victimization is a significant predictor of the number of lifetime symptoms of antisocial personality disorder and of a diagnosis of antisocial personality disorder; however, there is no one-to-one direct relationship between being victimized and becoming a victimizer, and most sexually abused people do not go on to victimize others.

Sexual Assault and Parenting

— Violence in one generation often leads to violence in the next. Parenting behavior can be profoundly affected by the impact of trauma.

— Mothers who were abusive to their children have been found to be more dissociative about their own history, tending to idealize their own childhoods more, to avoid dealing with the implications of the past, and to be inconsistent in their childhood descriptions as compared to mothers who broke the cycle of abuse.

— Maternal sexual abuse history combined with maternal drug use places daughters at elevated risk.

— PTSD is significantly overexpressed in the children of mothers diagnosed with PTSD. The onset of maltreatment was significantly earlier among children whose mothers meet PTSD criteria than among other maltreated children.

— Prolonged hyperarousal accompanies stress in those previously exposed to trauma.

— There is a close connection between child abuse and domestic violence.

— Abused mothers who were able to break the abusive cycle:

1. Were significantly more likely to have received emotional support from a nonabusive adult during childhood

2. Were more likely to have participated in therapy during some period of their lives

3. Were more likely to have had a nonabusive and more stable, emotionally supportive, and satisfying relationship with a mate

— Abused mothers who reenacted their maltreatment with their own children:

1. Experienced significantly more life stress

2. Were more anxious, dependent, immature, and depressed

3. Identified with their abuser or with a nonprotective parent

4. Had poor attachment with their own parents

5. Used dissociation or other defensive behaviors to protect themselves from memories of their abuse

6. Had not been able to discuss their abuse with a supportive person

Responding to Sexual Assault: Creating Sanctuary
Creating sanctuary refers to the process involved in creating safe environments that promote healing and sustain human growth, learning, and health. All medical and social institutions must find ways to address the problem by creating environments that promote and sustain better physical, emotional, and relational health.

— Change the presenting question with which we verbally or implicitly confront another human being whose behavior we do not understand from "What's wrong with you?" to "What's happened to you?"

1. Shifts the perspective, moving toward a position of compassion and understanding and away from blame and criticism.

2. Using the term "survivor" instead of "victim" immediately provides an important ingredient and foundation for recovery: hope.

— Focus on the human need for safety:

1. Includes not just physical safety but psychological, social, and moral safety as well; an environment cannot truly be safe unless all of these levels of safety are addressed

2. Psychological safety: the ability to be safe with oneself

3. Social safety: the ability to be safe in groups and with other people

4. Moral safety: the maintenance of a value system that does not contradict itself and is consistent with healthy human development as well as physical, psychological, and social safety

— Because the individual has been exposed to helplessness, interventions to help overcome the traumatizing experience must focus on adaptive methods of mastery and empowerment and avoid further experiences of helplessness.

1. Must understand that prolonged hyperarousal and loss of ability to manage emotional states appropriately produce many behaviors that are socially objectionable or even destructive but represent the individual's only method of coping with overwhelming and uncontrollable emotions.

2. Offer better substitutes, ie, healthy and sustainable human relationships.

3. Reduce stress when good decisions must be made.

4. To reduce memory problems, provide opportunities for individuals to talk about their experiences, including programs that focus on nonverbal expression, eg, art, music, movement, drama, and sports, which can be vital adjuncts to healing efforts.

5. In developing techniques to help people manage their emotions more effectively, build and reinforce the acquisition of emotional intelligence.

— For individuals who are addicted to trauma, intervention strategies must focus on helping to "detoxify" them from this behavior.

1. By providing environments that insist on the establishment and maintenance of safety

2. By providing opportunities to learn how to create relationships not based on terror and the abuse of power, even though abusive power feels "normal" and "right"

3. By providing direct relationship coaching and the experience of engaging in relationships that are not abusive and that do not permit or tolerate abusive and punitive behavior

— Individuals who have been sexually assaulted or significantly traumatized must be able to grieve. Many survivors refer to such abuse as "soul murder," reflective of how traumatic the abuse was and that a part of their life was taken or destroyed.

1. Unresolved grief prevents recovery from the psychological and physical problems that result from exposure to a traumatic experience.

2. To heal, survivors must open up the old wounds, remember and reconstruct the past, resolve the accompanying painful emotions, and reconnect to their internal world and the world around them.

SOCIAL SUPPORTS

The rape trauma syndrome is comparable to what was originally described by government researchers as posttraumatic stress disorder. Interventions must take into account this syndrome and where the survivor is in his or her recovery. Disclosure of abuse is not always as easy as sometimes described. If and when the survivor chooses to reach out and tell his or her story, the nature and extent of the support provided can play a critical role in the survivor's ability to modulate symptoms and recover from the trauma. Some survivors may encounter the realities of pervasive societal stigma and stereotypes, including being blamed for the situation or feeling like they are now "damaged goods." It is important to be aware of these potential realities of disclosure to reinforce that the survivor is not responsible for any acts of violation committed against them.

NATURE OF SOCIAL SUPPORTS

Social Services

— Rape crisis centers are traditionally nonprofit, community-based organizations staffed by paid professional counselors and volunteers.

1. Services are usually free and offered to adult and child survivors of both genders.

2. They traditionally offer a 24-hour hotline, hospital and court accompaniment, short-term crisis counseling services, and a strong advocacy-based organizational system within the community.

3. State coalitions of rape crisis centers have sprung up to distribute state and federal funding, monitor quality of services, and help establish guidelines for community education and training about sexual violence.

4. Collaborative efforts have been made between rape crisis centers and domestic violence agencies.

5. Many rape crisis centers have established partnerships with district attorneys, police, hospitals, and other agencies to provide more comprehensive services to individuals and families with increasingly more complex problems.

— Domestic violence programs are often found related to services for survivors of sexual assault.

1. Counseling for survivors of domestic violence has traditionally focused on safety planning, eg, for remaining safe in the home and for the planning process for leaving the home, empowerment, and restoration of self-esteem.

2. The goals of counseling sexual assault survivors are the treatment and prevention of the debilitating effects of posttraumatic stress disorder.

— Victim assistance programs are often funded through a prosecuting attorney's office and provide services for all victims of violent interpersonal crime.

1. Their main function is to offer court accompaniment and victim compensation services to survivors who report their assaults to the police department.

2. Much of their funding comes from states' victim compensation funds collected from adjudicated offenders.

3. Assistance in filing monetary claims to the state usually depends on the survivor making a police report about his or her assault.

Health Care System
— Acute care:

1. In the postassault setting the medical provider's chief role is to assess and treat the victim's acute medical needs and collect evidence.

2. The medical provider can also play an important role as a social support for victims, both in the acute setting and throughout recovery.

3. Medical personnel can employ strategies that begin the healing process, or at least prevent repeat traumatization. This includes use of the term survivor and clarifying that the abuse was not the survivor's fault.

4. Members of the medical team must ensure a safe, private environment for history-taking and examination.

5. The responsibility for calling a friend, family member, or rape crisis counselor may also belong to the medical acute care provider.

6. The health care provider can also assist with the restoration of a sense of order and predictability.

7. The patient's safety must be emphasized.

8. Take care to inform the patient in advance what will happen during the examination and how long it might last, and ask for the patient's permission to begin the examination; this will help restore the victim's sense of control over what is happening to his or her body.

9. Health care institutions have a responsibility to their staff and to survivors to adequately train and support staff involved in the care of sexual assault victims.

10. The creation and maintenance of a caring health care environment is crucial.

— Sexual assault nurse examiner (SANE) and sexual assault response team (SART) programs:

1. SANE programs provide 24-hour availability of personnel who can offer immediate, comprehensive, and compassionate evaluation and treatment for sexual assault victims. Program goals are to lessen the traumatizing nature of the rape examination, reduce repeated questioning and examination of the victim, and increase effective collection and preservation of evidence. SANE practitioners can be nurses, nurse practitioners, physician assistants, or other health care providers. These individuals are called immediately when a sexual assault victim is identified, whether by law enforcement personnel, rescue personnel, or emergency department staff. They are responsible for completing the entire evidentiary examination, including leading the team interview; conducting assessments of sexually transmitted infection (STI) and pregnancy as well as their prevention strategies; performing the colposcopy evaluation with photographs; and ensuring appropriate referrals for support and care, which often take lower priority when the responsibility for this is left to busy emergency department personnel.

2. A SART team may include SANE staff, law enforcement personnel, and rape crisis center staff or volunteers. It is also

activated immediately upon identification of a sexual assault victim. Early involvement of law enforcement personnel reduces repeated questioning of the victim because the medical history obtained by the SANE practitioner can link with the questioning by law enforcement personnel. A rape crisis center volunteer can establish an early link with the victim should he or she wish to pursue a relationship with the agency later. Many communities have SART partner agencies located at one site, which fosters better interagency cooperation and communication and can further reduce survivor trauma.

— Postacute care medical support:

1. Nonacute care medical providers are likely to provide postassault care and support for most survivors.

2. The unique confidential relationship between a health care provider and a patient makes the patient-provider relationship a natural place for survivors to turn to for support.

3. It is also reasonable to expect all medical providers to have the basic skill set required to assess, evaluate, and treat the psychosocial complications of sexual assault.

4. Health care providers should be familiar with the phases of rape trauma syndrome; be comfortable treating depression; provide a safe, nonjudgmental setting where survivors can feel comfortable discussing their experience, their feelings, and their fears; and have access to referral information should a patient decide to pursue professional post–sexual assault counseling.

— Churches and religious groups:

1. Pastors, priests, nuns, rabbis, and other interdenominational church-community leaders are now reaching out for special training in counseling their worshippers who have disclosed sexual abuse issues. They are also learning assessment skills to refer their members to mental health care providers as they learn of the longer-term effects of severe trauma.

2. Collaboration of rape crisis centers with the community churches can be mutually beneficial, allowing rape crisis centers to access an audience that may not have heard their message and to provide workshops and training to church-sponsored groups and thereby increase awareness of sexual abuse issues and increase access to services for survivors. Posttraumatic stress disorder and its impact on victims and their families are now being taught at many seminaries and pastoral colleges.

— Other social supports:

1. Most survivors of sexual assault turn to someone in their informal support network immediately after an assault; this form of social support is very important to recovery.

2. Social support reliably moderates psychological distress after sexual assault, with the extent of informal support determined by the number of people with whom the survivor felt she could confide as a moderating factor in the severity of physical symptoms and perceived health up to 1 year after the assault.

3. The reaction of those close to the survivor can affect recovery, with sexual assault traumatizing family members and significant others in addition to the victim. How they cope with trauma influences how they interact with the victim, as follows:

   — Maladaptive responses: overprotection, encouraging the victim to keep the assault secret, focusing primarily on their own sense of victimization, blaming the victim

   — Adaptive responses: empathy and allowing the victim to express fears without fear of criticism while responding to his or her own concerns as a secondary issue

4. Girlfriends, husbands or boyfriends, and police have received the highest ratings of supportiveness; physicians were rated the lowest.

5. Victims of "attempted" rapes have just as many problems with adjustment 3 months after the assault as those who identified their assault as "completed," yet they receive much less support in that period, indicating that support is at least partially related to society's perception of the stressfulness of the assault.

PROGRAM DEVELOPMENT

The steps to establishing or improving a community's response to sexual assault vary according to size of the community, presence and organization of existing victims' rights or advocacy organizations, and level of knowledge of the health care community regarding sexual assault. Those outlined here reflect principles to be included.

— Involve the multiple agencies and disciplines necessary to develop effective services. This facilitates communication and cooperation.

1. Develop a task force with clearly defined goals.

2. Members include hospital administrators, emergency department nurses, rape crisis center leaders, law enforcement representatives, and the judiciary. Special efforts should be made to recruit representatives from underserved minority communities and sexual minorities.

3. Schedule regular meetings and ensure that all voices are heard to maintain continued engagement from all parties.

— Invite respected leaders to participate and lend support to the effort. This helps to ensure community support, with administrators more willing to promote the needs of the agency or program if their superiors have been publicly and visibly involved from the outset of a project.

— Optimize efforts by using existing personnel and resources as building blocks.

— Provide for coordination of services across multiple disciplines. This has been found to be predictive of a relatively positive victim experience with the social support system. The coordination of services should be prioritized as they unfold and are developed.

1. Look objectively at what attributes of sexual assault support systems have proved successful.

2. Provide for interagency training.

3. Keep the services victim-centered rather than agency- or service-centered.

— Provide education and risk reduction strategies.

1. Target prevention efforts at the attitudes and stereotypes of men in particular and society as a whole.

2. Target young boys at the elementary and middle school levels.

3. Develop or incorporate innovative prevention strategies for use at high schools and colleges.

4. Develop special programs to change sexual stereotypes and interpersonal violence to attract more men to serve as instructors and male role models.

5. Remember to perform outreach activities for parents to reduce the risk for sexual abuse of children. Services to families of sexual assault survivors greatly increase the chance of successful recovery.

— Address funding issues, exploring private and corporate foundations interested in funding targeted social service projects.

MOVING BEYOND A DON'T ASK–DON'T TELL APPROACH TO ABUSE AND ASSAULT
DON'T ASK
Interpersonal violence is not detected in the majority of cases because of acknowledged or unacknowledged barriers limiting the effectiveness of clinicians.

Acknowledged Barriers
Clinicians perceive many barriers to routinely screening for or asking relevant questions pertaining to violence, as follows:

— I haven't been trained to do this.

— I don't have time to do this.

— It isn't my job/it isn't a medical problem.

— I'm not a domestic violence expert.

— This doesn't happen in the patient population I see.

— This is a personal problem and isn't my business.

— If it's so bad, why doesn't she leave?

— What's the point? She'll just go back to him or find another abuser.

Unacknowledged Barriers

— The issue of relationship violence is too close for comfort with regard to clinicians' own personal histories as well as their sense of safety in their own communities.

— It may be perceived as a "private matter."

— Medical training itself may be viewed as an abusive experience.

— Victims of abuse may be difficult and unlikable patients.

— Physicians don't want to open a Pandora's box.

— A lack of awareness of available resources if the patient says yes to a screening for abuse.

DON'T TELL: BARRIERS TO DISCLOSURE BY THE VICTIM
— Fear of retaliation

— Shame

— Insensitive responses by their health care providers

TREATING VICTIMS WITHOUT FEELING HOPELESS
— Viewing chronic lifestyles and behaviors, such as smoking and unhealthy dietary habits, as acute illnesses that need to be "cured" is inappropriate and futile.

— Because a person in an abusive relationship is at greatest risk for being seriously injured or even killed when he or she tries to leave, urging the victim to leave without having a well-thought-out safety plan is irresponsible and leaves the victim who is not planning to end an abusive relationship feeling even more isolated and worthless.

Stages of Behavior Change
The Transtheoretical Model (TTM) of Change, or Stages of Behavioral Change Model, takes into account stages of attitude that precede behavioral change. By understanding these different stages, clinicians can appreciate how to help patients who are either unwilling or unable to leave

violent relationships. The clinician can help the patient and not become frustrated or angry about the patient's "noncompliance" in leaving an abusive relationship, and the patient does not feel like a "failure" for being unable to comply (**Table 15-1**).

Table 15-1. Stages of Behavior Change

STAGE 1: PRECONTEMPLATION

The patient does not perceive a problem. Her partner's violence is "no big deal" or is "no different from what happens in any other family." During this stage the clinician can provide information, eg, violence is common, it is not the victim's fault, it is dangerous for the victim and for children who witness the violence, and resources exist to help. The patient can be offered written material about violence, safety planning, and local resources. She can be offered a referral to a social worker or domestic violence counselor.

STAGE 2: CONTEMPLATION

The patient perceives a problem and is considering change; however, although she may be more open to information and offers of help, she probably feels intensely ambivalent about the risks versus the rewards of leaving the relationship. As a result many patients remain in this stage for many years. During this stage, stressing the rewards of leaving, expressing optimism about the possibility of change, and supporting safety measures while the patient is considering change may be of great benefit. Remind the patient that the abuse is not her fault and that help is available. Specifically in addition to discussing safety strategies, she should be offered referrals to social service and advocacy resources.

STAGE 3: PREPARATION

The patient is actively planning change. She has already taken some measures to prepare for ending the relationship. It is crucial to help her understand the potential danger for herself and her children when she does actually leave and even afterward. At this time, in addition to referrals to other experts, an exit strategy is essential. The patient should be urged to consider a plan that includes identifying people she can stay with, planning ways to save and hide money, making copies of all important papers and documents, etc.   *(continued)*

Table 15-1. Stages of Behavior Change *(continued)*

STAGE 4: ACTION

The patient has ended the relationship. She needs to appreciate that she is still vulnerable to violent assaults. Safety strategies must be emphasized. The clinician should support her decision while explaining that relapse is common; victims of abuse, for many reasons, often return to the abuser. However, this behavior is not "going around in circles." Instead it is a return to a prior stage of change and is much more likely to result in a more successful move forward later. This knowledge and attitude are important for the clinician as well. Without this understanding, clinicians can easily feel overwhelmed by frustration and anger, with the patient now perceived as "wasting our time."

STAGE 5: MAINTENANCE

The patient has maintained the successful behavior change for several months. Even at this time, she is not free from assaultive and abusive behavior from the partner. He may stalk her; he may engage in a prolonged custody battle to further exhaust, intimidate, and impoverish her; or he may engage the children in spying behavior against her. In addition, many emotional, financial, psychologic, cultural, and familial pressures may occur that do not support the changes she has made. For example her partner may urge her to come back, promising that he will never hurt her again. She may feel pressure from her children or other family members to keep the family together. She may feel emotionally and financially overwhelmed. The clinician must support her healthy behavioral changes while helping her avoid feeling demoralized if she returns to the relationship.

REFERENCES

1. Tufts KA, Clements PT, Wessell J. When intimate partner violence against women and HIV collide: challenges for healthcare assessment and intervention. *J Forensic Nurs*. 2010;6(2):66-73.

2. American Congress of Obstetricians and Gynecologists, Committee on Health Care for Underserved Women. *Sexual Assault*. Washington, DC:

American Congress of Obstetricians and Gynecologists; 2014. Committee Opinion 592. American Congress of Obstetricians and Gynecologists Web site. http://www.acog.org/-/media/Committee-Opinions/Committee-on-Health-Care-for-Underserved-Women/co592.pdf?dmc =1&ts=20150412T1258518647. Accessed April 17, 2015.

3.   American Psychiatric Association. *Diagnostic and Statistical Manual of Mental Disorders.* 5th ed. Washington, DC: American Medical Association; 2013.

4.   Banyard VL, Moynihan MM, Plante EG. Sexual violence prevention through bystander education: an experimental evaluation. *J Community Psychol.* 2007;35(4):463-481.

5.   Basile KC, Chen J, Black MC, Saltzman LE. Prevalence and characteristics of sexual violence victimization among U.S. adults, 2001-2003. *Violence Vict.* 2007;22(4):437-448.

6.   Benner SR. Soul murder, social death, and humiliation: consequences of state-sponsored rape. *The New York Sociologist.* 2010;4:1-10.

7.   Berliner L, Elliott DM. Sexual abuse of children. In: Briere J, Berliner L, Bulkley JA, et al, eds. *The APSAC Handbook on Child Maltreatment.* Thousand Oaks, CA: Sage Publications; 1996.

8.   Błaż-Kapusta B. Disorders of extreme stress not otherwise specified (DESNOS) – a case study. *Archives of Psychiatry and Psychotherapy.* 2008;2:5-11.

9.   Bloom SL. *Creating Sanctuary: Toward the Evolution of Sane Societies.* New York, NY: Routledge; 1997.

10. Bloom SL, Farragher B. *Destroying Sanctuary: The Crisis in Human Service Delivery Systems.* New York, NY: Oxford University Press; 2010.

11. Burgess AW, Hartman CR, Clements PT Jr. Biology of memory and childhood trauma. *J Psychosoc Nurs Ment Health Serv.* 1995;33(3):16-26.

12. Burgess AW, Holmstrom LL. Rape trauma syndrome. *Am J Psychiatry.* 1974;131(9):981-986.

13. Centers for Disease Control and Prevention. Sexual violence: prevention strategies. Centers for Disease Control and Prevention Web site. http://www.cdc.gov/violenceprevention/sexualviolence/prevention.html. Updated February 29, 2015. Accessed April 28, 2015.

14. Chivers-Wilson KA. Sexual assault and posttraumatic stress disorder: a review of the biological, psychological and sociological factors and treatments. *Mcgill J Med*. 2006;9(2):111-118.

15. Ciccone DS, Elliott DK, Chandler HK, Nayak S, Raphael KG. Sexual and physical abuse in women with fibromyalgia syndrome: a test of the trauma hypothesis. *Clin J Pain*. 2005;21(5):378-386.

16. Clay RA. Suicide and intimate partner violence: a federal initiative aims to bring experts from the two fields closer together in an effort to save lives. *Monitor on Psychology*. 2014;45(10):30.

17. Clements PT, Speck PM, Crane PA, Faulkner MJ. Issues and dynamics of sexually assaulted adolescents and their families. *Int J Ment Health Nurs*. 2004;13(4):267-274.

18. Clements PT, Pierce-Weeks J, Holt KE, Giardino AG, Seedat SA, Mortiere CM, eds. *Violence Against Women: Contemporary Examination of Intimate Partner Violence*. Saint Louis, MO: STM Learning, Inc; 2015.

19. De Bellis MD, Chrousos GP, Dorn LD, et al. Hypothalamic-pituitary-adrenal axis dysregulation in sexually abused girls. *J Clin Endocrinol Metab*. 1994;78(2):249-255.

20. DeGue S. Evidence-based strategies for the primary prevention of sexual violence perpetration. In: Centers for Disease Control and Prevention, ed. *Preventing Sexual Violence on College Campuses: Lessons from Research and Practice*. Not Alone: Together Against Sexual Violence Web site. https://www.notalone.gov/schools/. Published April 2014. Accessed April 28, 2015.

21. Dobie DJ, Maynard C, Kivlahan DR, et al. Posttraumatic stress disorder screening status is associated with increased VA medical and surgical utilization in women. *J Gen Intern Med*. 2006;21(suppl 3):S58-S64.

22. Drossman DA. Sexual and physical abuse and gastrointestinal illness. *Scand J Gastroenterol Suppl.* 1995;209:90-96.

23. Egeland B, Jacobvitz D, Sroufe LA. Breaking the cycle of abuse. *Child Dev.* 1988;59(4):1080-1088.

24. Egeland B, Susman-Stillman A. Dissociation as a mediator of child abuse across generations. *Child Abuse Negl.* 1996;20(11):1123-1132.

25. Elklit A, Hyland P, Shevlin M. Evidence of symptom profiles consistent with posttraumatic stress disorder and complex posttraumatic stress disorder in different trauma samples. *Eur J Psychotraumatol.* 2014;5. doi:10.3402/ejpt.v5.24221.

26. Famularo R, Fenton T, Kinscherff R, Ayoub C, Barnum R. Maternal and child post-traumatic stress disorder in cases of child maltreatment. *Child Abuse Negl.* 1994;18(1):27-36.

27. Fergusson DM, Horwood LJ, Lynskey MT. Childhood sexual abuse, adolescent sexual behaviors and sexual revictimization. *Child Abuse Negl.* 1997;21(8):789-803.

28. Focht-New G, Clements PT, Barol B, Faulkner MJ, Service KP. Persons with developmental disabilities exposed to interpersonal violence and crime: strategies and guidance for assessment. *Perspect Psychiatr Care.* 2008;44(1):3-13.

29. Focht-New G, Barol B, Clements PT, Milliken TF. Persons with developmental disability exposed to interpersonal violence and crime: approaches for intervention. *Perspect Psychiatr Care.* 2008;44(2)89-98.

30. Forman-Hoffman V, Knauer S, McKeeman J, et al. *Child and Adolescent Exposure to Trauma: Comparative Effectiveness of Interventions Addressing Trauma Other Than Maltreatment or Family Violence.* Rockville, MD: Agency for Healthcare Research and Quality; 2013. Comparative Effectiveness Reviews 107.

31. Geisser ME, Roth RS, Bachman JE, Echert TA. The relationship between symptoms of post-traumatic stress disorder and pain, affective disturbance and disability among patients with accident and non-accident related pain. *Pain.* 1996;66(2-3):207-214.

32. Gurvits TV, Gilbertson MV, Lasko NB, et al. Neurologic soft signs in chronic posttraumatic stress disorder. *Arch Gen Psychiatry.* 2000;57(2):181-186.

33. Hamer M, Steptoe A. Association between physical fitness, parasympathetic control, and proinflammatory responses to mental stress. *Psychosom Med.* 2007;69(7):660-666.

34. Häuser W, Kosseva M, Üceyler N, Klose P, Sommer C. Emotional, physical, and sexual abuse in fibromyalgia syndrome: a systematic review with meta-analysis. *Arthritis Care Res (Hoboken).* 2011;63(6):808-820. doi: 10.1002/acr.20328.

35. International Association of Forensic Nurses. *Sexual Assault Nurse Examiner (SANE) Education Guidelines.* Elkridge, MD: International Association of Forensic Nurses; 2013.

36. Jones T, Moller MD. Implications of hypothalamic-pituitary-adrenal axis functioning in posttraumatic stress disorder. *J Am Psychiatr Nurses Assoc.* 2011;17(6):393-403. doi: 10.1177/1078390311420564.

37. Kaess M, Parzer P, Mattern M, et al. Adverse childhood experiences and their impact on frequency, severity, and the individual function of nonsuicidal self-injury in youth. *Psychiatry Res.* 2013;206(2-3):265-272. doi:10.1016/j.psychres.2012.10.012.

38. Kendall-Tackett K. Psychological trauma and physical health: a psychoneuroimmunology approach to etiology of negative health effects and possible interventions. *Psychol Trauma.* 2009;1(1):35-48.

39. Ledray L. *SANE Development and Operation Guide.* Washington, DC: US Department of Justice Office for Victims of Crime; 1999.

40. MacNamara A, Rabinak CA, Fitzgerald DA, et al. Neural correlates of individual differences in fear learning. *Behav Brain Res.* 2015;287:34-41. doi:10.1016/j.bbr.2015.03.035.

41. Matsakis A. *I Can't Get Over It: A Handbook for Trauma Survivors.* Oakland, CA: New Harbinger Publications; 1996.

42. McLean CP, Su YJ, Foa EB. Posttraumatic stress disorder and alcohol dependence: does order of onset make a difference? *J Anxiety Disord.* 2014;28(8):894-901. doi:10.1016/j.janxdis.2014.09.023.

43. Myers JEB, ed. *The APSAC Handbook on Child Maltreatment.* 3rd ed. Thousand Oaks, CA: Sage Publications; 2010.

44. Paras ML, Murad MH, Chen LP, et al. Sexual abuse and lifetime diagnosis of somatic disorders: a systematic review and meta-analysis. *JAMA.* 2009;302(5):550-561.

45. Perry BD, Pollard RA, Blakley TL, Baker WL, Vigilante D. Childhood trauma, the neurobiology of adaptation, and "use-dependent" development of the brain: how "states" become "traits." *Infant Ment Health J.* 1995;16(4):271-291.

46. Perry BD. The neurodevelopmental impact of violence in childhood. In: Schetky D, Benedek E, eds. *Textbook of Child and Adolescent Forensic Psychiatry.* Washington, DC: American Psychiatric Press, Inc; 2002:221-238.

47. Romans S, Cohen M. Unexplained and underpowered: the relationship between psychosomatic disorders and interpersonal abuse -- a critical review. *Harv Rev Psychiatry.* 2008;16(1):35-54.

48. Selig C. Sexual assault nurse examiner and sexual assault response team (SANE/SART) program. *Nurs Clin North Am.* 2000;35(2):311-319.

49. Shengold L. *Soul Murder Revisited: Thoughts About Therapy, Hate, Love, and Memory.* New Haven, CT: Yale University Press; 2000.

50. Smith NB, Kouros CD, Meuret AE. The role of trauma symptoms in nonsuicidal self-injury. *Trauma Violence Abuse.* 2014;15(1):41-56. doi:10.1177/1524838013496332.

51. TeBockhorst SF, O'Halloran MS, Nyline BN. Tonic immobility among survivors of sexual assault. *Psychol Trauma.* 2015;7(2):171-178. doi:10.1037/a0037953.

52. Ullman SE. *Talking About Sexual Assault: Society's Response to Survivors.* Washington, DC: American Psychological Association; 2010.

53. US Department of Veterans Affairs. Effects of traumatic stress after mass violence, terror, or disaster. National Center for PTSD Web site. http://www.ptsd.va.gov/professional/trauma/disaster-terrorism/stress-mv-t-dhtml.asp. Accessed April 17, 2015.

54. van der Kolk BA. The body keeps the score: approaches to the psychobiology of post-traumatic stress disorder. In: van der Kolk BA, McFarlane C, Weisaeth L, eds. *Traumatic Stress: The Effects of Overwhelming Experience on Mind, Body and Society*. New York, NY: Guilford Press; 1996:214-241.

55. van der Kolk BA. The compulsion to repeat the trauma. re-enactment, revictimization, and masochism. *Psychiatr Clin of North Am*. 1989;12(2):389-411.

56. van der Kolk BA. Developmental trauma disorder. *Psychiatr Ann*. 2005;35(5):401-408.

57. van der Kolk BA. Trauma and memory. In: van der Kolk BA, McFarlane C, Weisaeth L, eds. *Traumatic Stress: The Effects of Overwhelming Experience on Mind, Body and Society*. New York, NY: Guilford Press; 1996:279-302.

58. Van Voorhees E, Scarpa A. The effects of child maltreatment on the hypothalamic-pituitary-adrenal axis. *Trauma Violence Abuse*. 2004;5(4):333-335.

59. Wathen CN, MacMillan HL. Interventions for violence against women: scientific review. *JAMA*. 2003;289(5):589-600.

Chapter 16

CAREGIVER ISSUES

Paul Thomas Clements, PhD, RN, DF-IAFN*
Sandra L. Bloom, MD
Linda E. Ledray, RN, PhD, SANE-A, FAAN
Rena Rovere, MS, FNP

CARING FOR THE CAREGIVER: AVOIDING AND TREATING VICARIOUS TRAUMATIZATION

DEFINITIONS

— Vicarious traumatization: cumulative transformative effect on the caregiver working with survivors of traumatic life events, both positive and negative. Symptoms resemble those of posttraumatic stress disorder (PTSD) but also indicate a disrupted frame of reference, including identity, worldview, and spirituality and impacts on psychologic need areas.

— Secondary traumatic stress: behavior and emotions that result from knowledge about a traumatizing event experienced by another and the stress resulting from helping or wanting to help a traumatized or suffering person; closely resembles PTSD; includes symptoms of hyperarousal, emotional numbing, avoidance, and intrusive experiences.

— Compassion fatigue: also called "caregiver burden"; the natural, predictable, treatable, and preventable unwanted consequence of working with suffering people.

— Burnout: a collection of symptoms associated with emotional exhaustion and generally attributed to increased work load and institutional stress, described by a process that includes

Revised Chapter 16 for the second edition.

gradual exposure to job strain, erosion of idealism, and lack of achievement; may result from repetitive or chronic exposure to vicarious traumatization that is unrecognized and unsupported by the organizational setting.

— Countertransference: a broader term that refers to all reactions to a client and the material he or she brings. Reactions are specific to the particular client and are tied to interactions with that client. Vicarious traumatization is a specific form of countertransference experience, differentiated from other countertransference reactions in that it can continue to affect lives and work long after interactions with the client have ceased.

Symptoms Specific to Vicarious Traumatization
— Disturbed frame of reference

— Disrupted beliefs about other people and the world, including beliefs about causality and higher purpose:

1. World is seen as a much more dangerous place

2. Caregiver may see other people as malevolent and evil, untrustworthy, exploitative, or alienating

3. Maintaining a sense of hope and belief in the goodness of humanity is increasingly difficult

— Psychologic areas affected are safety, trust, esteem, intimacy, and control:

1. Loss of secure sense of safety leads to increased fearfulness; heightened sense of personal vulnerability; excessive security concerns; behavior directed at increasing security; overprotection of family members, especially children; relational inflexibility; and increasing fear for the lives and safety of loved ones.

2. Capacity to trust may be so impaired that a belief develops that no one can be trusted. Trust in one's own judgment and perceptions can be negatively altered.

3. It becomes difficult to maintain a sense of self-esteem, particularly around areas of competence. It may also be difficult to maintain a sense of esteem about others, leading to a pervasive suspiciousness of other people's motivations and behavior.

4. Problems with intimacy may develop, leading to difficulties in spending time alone; self-medication with food, alcohol, or drugs (illicit and/or prescription); or engaging in compulsive behaviors, eg, shopping, gambling, exercise, sex, or online computer activities. These problems can also lead to isolation from others and withdrawal from relationships with family, friends, and professional colleagues.

5. The more control the caregiver feels has been lost, the more control he or she tries to exert over self and others. Efforts may also be made to narrow or restrict the scope of one's world in the hope of avoiding anything that may be experienced as being outside of one's control.

— Positive as well as negative impacts are noted. Choices must be made to support positive, rather than negative, transformational changes.

Who Is Affected?

— Vicarious traumatization has occurred in emergency workers, physicians, nurses, police officers, firemen, journalists, clergy, social service workers, colleagues, family members, and other witnesses and bystanders to disasters and other trauma.

— The rate of vicarious traumatization appears to be related to years of experience or exposure to trauma.

— Risk factors:

1. Having a past history of traumatic experience

2. Overwork

3. Ignoring health boundaries

4. Taking on too much/inability to say no to additional tasks

5. Lack of experience as a therapist

6. Too much experience as a therapist

7. Dealing with large numbers of traumatized children, especially sexually abused children

8. Working with large numbers of patients who suffer from dissociative disorders

9. Having too many negative clinical outcomes

— Protective factors:

1. Good social support

2. Strong ethical principles of practice

3. Knowledge of theory

4. Ongoing training

5. Development of competence in practice strategies and techniques

6. Awareness of the potential of vicarious traumatization and the need to take deliberate steps to minimize the impact

7. Spirituality

8. Established relaxation methods/self-soothing techniques

CAUSES

— Vicarious traumatization can be viewed as a normal reaction to abnormal stress or a picture of adaptive coping skills gone wrong.

— Biologic, psychologic, social, moral, spiritual, and philosophical components of the individual interact with the professional and sociopolitical context of the individual's life space to produce the final outcome.

Biologic Causality: Emotional Contagion

— Listening to victims of trauma can produce a noxious physiologic and psychologic state in the listener that is strongly defended against.

— Victims' social groups take measures to prevent the victims from sharing their experience and thereby spreading the contagion.

— Stress can lead to dysregulation of the hypothalamic-pituitary-adrenal (HPA) axis which can contribute toward ongoing patterns of physical and emotional sequelae. By activating the complex human stress response, this produces a variety of powerful neurochemicals, including cortisol, an immune system suppressor.

— Chronic inhibition of negative emotions produces increasing work for the autonomic nervous system, which functions as a chronic stressor with the result that biologic survival systems that should only be "on" under emergency conditions are reset to be on all the time. In essence the survival system becomes "stuck."

— Traumatized people are often overwhelmed by their emotions, particularly in the acutely traumatized state. Suppressing emotional states is bad for their health.

— Caregiving relationships help to surface those emotions, often long buried, and the caregiver is the one who is most likely to be exposed to the overwhelming nature of the victim's emotional state. Good caregiving requires that the caregiver respond to this state in certain limited and prescribed ways and respond by containing rather than expressing the caregiver's own physiologic states of hyperarousal, fear, anger, and grief.

Psychologic Causality: Loss of Positive Illusions

— As the reality of "it really happened" sets in, caregivers recognize that "it could happen to me" and feel all of the vulnerability that goes along with that recognition.

— The recurring sense of helplessness that victims feel may also affect caregivers, bringing with it a sense of hopelessness, expressed as "there's nothing I can do."

— Positive illusions about oneself, other people, and the world are destroyed by the constant exposure to traumatized people.

— The greatest conflict, the one most likely to produce symptoms, occurs in cases of family violence, including child abuse, spousal abuse, rape, and child sexual abuse, because it threatens the cherished cultural notion that family is a safe place.

Social Causality: Inability to Use Normal Social Obstacles

— Traumatic experiences shatter basic personal and cultural assumptions about the primary way we order reality. There is no safety, the world no longer makes sense, other people cannot be trusted, the future is no longer predictable, and the past is no longer known because of dissociation. After trauma, one of the most perplexing experiences for the individual victim is that the world goes on as before.

— The need to talk, to confess, and to release stored tension is powerful and important for health, but culture actively inhibits individual response.

— Listeners avoid having their own cognitive schemas disrupted, and they avoid the hyperarousal that is frequently an accompaniment of emotional contagion.

— Good caregivers are carefully trained to avoid using the kinds of social defenses that other people use against the impact of this recognition of the effects of violence on individuals. Clinicians and other caregivers are taught to screen for violence, listen carefully, avoid giving in to their own inclinations to distance themselves, and empathize with the experience and emotions of others. The inability to use the social barriers available to other people makes helping professionals more likely to experience vicarious traumatization.

Organization Causality: Sick Systems

— Organizational settings that refuse to accept the severity and pervasiveness of traumatic experience in the population they are serving thereby refuse to provide the social support required for caregivers if they are to do adequate work.

— Dysfunctional systems resemble dysfunctional families, having some or all of the following characteristics:

1. An ongoing culture of crisis where long-term and preventive solutions are not formulated because all time and resources are spent "putting out fires"

2. The replacement of democratic processes with authoritarian decision making and rigid hierarchies

3. A culture of shaming, blaming, and judgement

4. Maintenance of order through isolation, splitting, overcontrol, manipulation, and deceitful practices, leading to mistrust and avoidance

5. Little humor, with positive emotions discouraged and negative emotions tolerated or encouraged

6. Eventual development of a culture of toughness and meanness or actual violence

7. Denial that any real problems exist

8. A high degree of hypocrisy in daily functioning

9. Active discouragement of confronting reality

Moral, Spiritual, and Philosophical Causality: Theoretical Conflicts

— Most of these conflicts are not direct but instead comprise a
background of disorder and include the following:

1. Desacralization of healing

2. Commodification of health care

3. Shortcomings of the medical model

4. A bias toward individualism

5. The issue of individual violence embedded within a context
   of cultural violence

— The resulting environment has been described as a "pressure
cooker" where no one is served well except, perhaps, profiteers.

— It becomes increasingly difficult for caregivers to find the time
or psychic energy to provide the level of compassion that victims
of violence require if they are to take the first steps in recovery.

— Health care professionals may succumb to both physical fatigue
and compassion fatigue.

— In the traditional medical model, the patient is largely passive,
waiting for a cure or at least alleviation of symptoms to be delivered
by a medical practitioner.

— The trauma therapist knows that one of the keys to recovery for the
victim is empowerment, not passivity, and that further experiences
of helplessness are often damaging.

— The role of the caregiver is very different in sickness versus injury, so
that the caregiver must face various role strains and stresses, as follows:

1. How do I keep my patient safe when only my patient has the power
   to keep herself/himself safe?

2. What is the best way to empower people?

3. What is and is not my responsibility?

4. When do my interventions promote recovery and when do they
   inhibit or discourage recovery?

5. If this person is suffering from an injury as the result of a social, fixable problem, what is my role in preventing further injury to this person and to others?

— If they attempt to stay politically disengaged, or "scientifically neutral," caregivers may find themselves medicalizing or pathologizing disorders that are actually a result of a social, political, or economic problem. They may find themselves a part of an oppressive system rather than a counteragent against it.

— In contrast, if caregivers stand up and powerfully bear witness to the violence that they have observed, they are likely to be labeled as outcasts, troublemakers, lacking in scientific rigor, and subverters of the system.

SOLUTIONS

Caregivers must develop their own personal and professional strategies for bringing about change in key areas that will help reduce or prevent the further evolution of a process that could lead to burnout. **Table 16-1** offers some suggestions.

Table 16-1. Prevention Strategies for Caregivers

PERSONAL-PHYSICAL

— Engage in self-care behaviors, including proper diet and sleep.

— Undertake physical exercise.

PERSONAL-PSYCHOLOGICAL

— Identify triggers that may cause you to experience vicarious traumatization.

— Obtain therapy if personal issues and past traumas get in the way.

— Know your own limitations.

— Keep the boundaries set for yourself and others.

— Know your own level of tolerance.

— Engage in recreational activities, eg, listening to music, reading, and spending time in nature.

(continued)

Table 16-1. Prevention Strategies for Caregivers *(continued)*

PERSONAL-SOCIAL

— Engage in social activities outside of work.

— Garner emotional support from colleagues.

— Garner emotional support from family and friends.

PERSONAL-MORAL

— Adopt a philosophical, religious, or spiritual outlook and be reminded that you cannot take responsibility for the client's healing but rather must act as a midwife, guide, coach, or mentor.

— Clarify your own sense of meaning and purpose in life.

— Connect with the larger sociopolitical framework and develop social activism skills.

PROFESSIONAL

— Become knowledgeable about the effects of trauma on self and others.

— Attempt to monitor or diversify case load.

— Seek consultation on difficult cases.

— Get peer supervision from someone who understands the dynamics and treatment of PTSD.

— Take breaks during the workday.

— Recognize that you are not alone in facing the stress of working with traumatized clients; normalize your reactions.

— Use a team for support.

— Maintain collegial on-the-job support, thus limiting sense of isolation.

— Understand dynamics of traumatic reenactment.

(continued)

Table 16-1. Prevention Strategies for Caregivers *(continued)*

ORGANIZATIONAL/WORK SETTING

— Accept stressors as real and legitimate, impacting individuals and the group as a whole.

— Work in a team.

— Maintain transparency in communications.

— Create a culture to counteract the effects of trauma.

— Establish a clear value system within your organization.

— Develop clarity about job tasks and personnel guidelines.

— Obtain supervisory/management support.

— Maximize collegiality.

— Encourage democratic processes in decision making and conflict resolution.

— Emphasize a leveled hierarchy.

— View problems as affecting the entire group, not just an individual.

— Remember that the general approach to the problem is to seek solutions, not assign blame.

— Expect a high level of tolerance for individual disturbance.

— Expect a high degree of cohesion.

— Expect considerable flexibility of roles.

— Join with others to deal with organizational bullies.

— Eliminate any subculture of violence and abuse.

SOCIETAL

— General public and professional education

— Community involvement

— Coalition building

— Legislative reform

— Social action

SANE-SART History and Role Development

The development of sexual assault nurse examiner (SANE) programs began in the early 1970s, although different terminology was used to describe the role during the early years. Their development was facilitated by the landmark Violence Against Women Act (VAWA) of 1994.

Need for SANE Programs

— Because women are so often the victims of violence, women who come to emergency departments (EDs) for even minor trauma must be thoroughly evaluated. ED staff must be aware of the types of injuries most likely to result from violence, and the potential victim must be asked about the cause of the trauma.

— In 1992 the guidelines of the Joint Commission on the Accreditation of Healthcare Organizations (JCAHO) first required emergency and ambulatory care facilities to have protocols on rape, sexual molestation, and domestic abuse, and by 1997 these guidelines also required health care facilities to develop and train their staffs to use criteria to identify possible victims of physical assault, rape or other sexual molestation, domestic abuse, and abuse or neglect of older adults and children.

— The SANE's role continues to develop as an important component of the emergency medical response to survivors of sexual assault.

— The impetus began with nurses, other medical professionals, counselors, and advocates working with rape victims in hospitals, clinics, and other settings and was based on the fact that services to victims of sexual assault were inadequate and not equal to the same high standard of care as those provided to other ED clients.

History of SANE Program Development

— The first SANE programs were established in Memphis, Tennessee in 1976; in Minneapolis, Minnesota in 1977; and in Amarillo, Texas in 1979. Unfortunately these nurses worked in isolation until the late 1980s.

— In 1991 Gail Lenehan recognized the importance of this new role and published the first list of 20 SANE programs to facilitate communication and sharing of information among programs.

— In 1995 the American Nurses' Association officially recognized forensic nursing as a new specialty of nursing.

— By October 2001, over 600 SANE programs were registered.

DEFINITIONS

— SANE: a registered nurse who has advanced education in the forensic examination of sexual assault victims

— Sexual assault forensic examiner (SAFE) or forensic examiner (FE): physicians who conduct the evidentiary examination

SANE SCOPE OF PRACTICE

— Examine the sexual assault survivor to assess, document, and collect forensic evidence.

— Offer prophylactic treatment of sexually transmitted infection (STIs) and prevention of pregnancy under a preestablished medical protocol or as approved by a consulting physician or advanced practice nurse.

— Treat minor injuries and refer care of major physical trauma to the ED or a designated medical facility.

— Explain to the client that the SANE only performs a limited medical examination.

— Provide the rape survivor with information to ensure that the survivor can anticipate what may happen next, make choices about reporting and deciding who to tell, and obtain the support that will be needed when he or she leaves the SANE facility.

— Provide emotional support and crisis intervention, working with the rape crisis center advocate when one is available.

— Train other health care and community agency professionals to provide services to sexual assault victims.

OPERATION OF A SANE PROGRAM

Entry Into Hospital-based Programs

— The victim calls local law enforcement, who will provide transportation to the hospital ED or SANE examination clinic.

— The victim goes directly to the hospital ED or hospital clinic.

— The victim calls the designated crisis line for assistance.

Entry Into Community-based Programs

— The victim calls local law enforcement agencies, where he or she will be checked for injuries and, if only minor or no injuries are present, will be transported to the community-based SANE facility.

— The victim goes to the ED of a local hospital, where staff will check for injuries and, if only minor or no injuries are present, will arrange transportation to the community-based SANE facility.

— The victim goes directly to the community-based SANE program facility during office hours.

— The victim calls the designated crisis line for assistance and receives a referral to the community-based SANE facility.

SANE RESPONSIBILITIES

— When the victim is uncertain about reporting, the SANE will discuss any fears and concerns and provide information as needed to make an informed decision. The SANE explains available options and the limitations of making a delayed report and offers to complete an evidentiary examination that can be held in a locked refrigerator for a specified time in case the victim chooses to report later.

— The SANE follows mandatory reporting laws for felony crimes or child abuse.

— When the victim does not want to report, the SANE should still offer medications to prevent STIs, evaluate the risk of pregnancy, and offer pregnancy prevention; make referrals for follow-up medical care and counseling; and provide the victim with written follow-up information.

— When a report is made:

1. A complete evidentiary examination is conducted following the SANE agency protocol, generally within 72 hours of the assault.

2. The SANE obtains written consent, then performs a complete examination, including the collection of evidence in a rape kit.

3. The SANE assesses and documents injuries, provides prophylactic care for STIs, evaluates pregnancy risk and offers preventive care, initiates crisis intervention, and provides referrals for follow-up medical and psychologic care.

— When the victim is alone, the SANE discusses who should be called and where to go from the hospital on discharge, making every effort to find a place for the victim to go where she or he will feel safe and will not be alone, perhaps making arrangements for shelter placement or providing a place to sleep in a specified area of the hospital.

SANE Training

— Certification is being considered at the state and national levels.

— The International Association of Forensic Nurses (IAFN) adopted recommendations for SANE training curriculum, consisting of 40 or more hours of didactic instruction. Some programs also designate a number of clinical hours after completing the classroom training, generally ranging from an additional 40 to as many as 96 hours.

— Most SANE programs require specific criteria for maintaining certification.

SEXUAL ASSAULT RESPONSE TEAM (SART)

— To be optimally effective and to provide the best possible service, the SANE must function as part of a team, which may be organized formally as a sexual assault response team (SART) or informally.

— SARTs vary from a team of individuals who respond together and jointly interview the victim at the time of the sexual assault examination to individuals who work independently on a day-to-day basis but who communicate regularly, possibly daily, and meet weekly or monthly to discuss mutual cases and solve mutual problems to make the system work more smoothly.

— Team members typically include the following:

1. SANE

2. Law enforcement officer

3. Detective

4. Prosecutor

5. Rape crisis center advocate or counselor

6. ED medical personnel

7. School counselors, battered women advocates, counselors who work with prostitutes, and any combination of representatives of programs in the community who address the problems of sexual assault.

8. Membership changes with changes in needs and goals.

Types of SARTs
— Joint interview SART model:

1. Multiple members of the SART respond to the ED together to conduct the sexual assault examination interview. Members usually include law enforcement, the SANE, and a rape crisis center advocate. They are all present so that the victim only has to make a statement once.

2. Limitations: there may be additional pressure to report the assault, calls to law enforcement may be needed to authorize payment for services, and there is limited access to health care for STIs or pregnancy risk or prevention.

— Cooperative SART model:

1. Team members meet regularly and communicate routinely about cases, but they do not actually respond at the same time. When law enforcement personnel are called to the scene of the assault, they protect the client from further harm, protect the crime scene evidence, and take a limited statement from the victim; they may call the hospital or rape center responsible for paging the SANE and rape crisis advocate.

2. Limitations: the memory and completeness of the various accounts that are required may vary somewhat. Separate interviews require more effort on the part of all team members to be sure that they meet or communicate all that is required. All agencies must work together.

ADVANTAGES OF SANE PROGRAMS

Communities that have SANE programs can experience the following benefits:

1. Better collaboration with law enforcement

2. Higher reporting rates

3. Shorter examination times

4. Better forensic evidence collection

5. Improved prosecution

ROLE OF EMS PREHOSPITAL CARE PROVIDERS

Not only do prehospital providers need to assess injuries and provide appropriate treatment, they are responsible for protecting potential evidence during medical evaluations and interventions and for working closely with law enforcement personnel.

PSYCHOLOGY OF VICTIMS

— Prehospital providers should help victims maintain a sense of control and safety after an assault.

— One of the most important steps in the emotional support and healing process is to return control to the victim.

— Immediately using the term "survivor" when speaking to the victim who reports can instill a sense of regaining control, empowerment, and hope for recovery.

— Victims must not be judged, regardless of their circumstances, appearance, risky lifestyle, race, or class.

— During the interview, it is important to reinforce that a victim is never responsible for a sexual assault.

— Compassionate care begins with verbal and nonverbal communication:

1. Use the victim's name.

2. Introduce yourself and your role.

3. Sit at eye level if possible.

4. Speak with a low voice, using a calm, soothing tone.

5. Express admiration for the victim's courage in reaching out for help.

6. Remember that victims have suffered a life-threatening experience and reassure them that they are safe.

7. Ask permission to touch rape victims, even to take their blood pressure or assess injuries.

8. Make efforts to ensure privacy and maintain confidentiality regarding the victim's identity, history, and examination findings.

9. Explain various options and respect victims' decisions.

10. Provide information and resources as required.

FORENSIC EVIDENCE

— Remember that the victims themselves are a major part of the crime scene.

— Preserve possible evidence found on victims' skin, clothing, wounds, or body fluids, such as urine or blood.

— Focus your physical assessment on complaints or injuries. Gather only the information needed to provide appropriate medical care and ensure the victim's safety.

— Begin with an objective assessment and documentation of behavior. Try to document victims' actions and behaviors with words that would permit a viewer of your document to be able to visualize the victims' demeanor.

— Document what is visible on arrival, beginning with victim location, especially if that location is different from the location of the event.

— Preserve crime scene evidence on clothing, documenting any modifications to clothing that were made after an assault, such as clothing put on backwards, grooming, or debris removal:

1. Ensure that victims wear or bring to the hospital the clothing worn during the assault.

2. Instruct the victim to bring a change of clothing, including underwear to wear after the medical evaluation and forensic examination.

— Preserve crime scene evidence regarding wounds:

1. Focus the prehospital assessment on areas of discomfort, tenderness, or pain, without disturbing or removing clothing when possible.

2. According to Locard's exchange principle, when any 2 objects come into contact, there is a transfer from one object to the other, so evidence may be located within wound areas.

3. Describe the wounds objectively in terms of anatomical location and note the approximate size, amount of bleeding, deformity, swelling, and tissue color surrounding the area.

4. Limit first aid to these wounds to preserving life and limb because anything biological has potential DNA evidence. Do not clean wounds, but instead, wrap any that are bleeding and splint deformities. Postpone application of cold compresses to tissue swelling so that skin changes or soft tissue swelling is not affected by vasoconstriction until the medical facility has an opportunity to see and photodocument the wounds.

— Preserve crime scene evidence regarding body fluids:

1. If sexual assault victims need to empty their bladders before transport, instruct them not to wipe their genitals and to collect urine samples in jars or leak-proof containers.

2. These jars/leak-proof containers are handled as follows:

   — Label the containers with the victim's name, date, and time collected.

   — Place containers in biohazard bags.

   — Turn the bags over to the hospital staff.

3. Instruct victims not to change any sanitary device after an assault, until forensic evidence collection is completed at the medical facility. Discarded sanitary devices should be collected if possible.

4. Document a chain of custody for each item of clothing, body fluid, or debris collected (see *Chapter 4* and *Chapter 10*).

— Document everything legibly, clearly, and objectively:

1. Objective documentation comprises those things that one can visualize, hear, feel, or sense in terms of observation.

2. Subjective documentation comprises information related by the victim regarding history, degree of pain, or level of discomfort.

3. Document chief complaints in quotes from the victim when possible. If these data come from other persons, document that source.

4. Information about perpetrators or assailants may be documented but should not be solicited or questioned because it is not pertinent to prehospital medical assessment, treatment, or stabilization.

TRANSPORTING VICTIMS TO HOSPITALS
— Do not delay transport to a medical facility.

— Inform victims that they will have choices related to examinations, permission to photograph, collection of evidence for DNA screening, and medical treatment prophylaxis options.

— Allow victims to have control over which facility is sought for care.

— Advise victims of their options based on the following:

1. Forensic examiners (SANE programs)

2. Forensic equipment capabilities

3. SART support services, eg, rape crisis counselors, social workers, and/or law enforcement

4. Support of close friend or significant other

— Make victims aware of the forensic tools that may be employed, as follows:

1. Standardized sexual assault evidence collection kit

2. Colposcope: a binocular microscope able to magnify minor tissue trauma

3. Photographic capability to document tissue trauma

4. Rulers

5. Ultraviolet light sources, eg, Wood's lamp

6. Chemical markers, eg, toluidine blue dye

7. Body diagrams

REFERENCES

1. Ahrens CE, Abeling S, Ahmad S, Hinman J. Spirituality and well-being: the relationship between religious coping and recovery from sexual assault. *J Interpers Violence.* 2010;25(7):1242-1263. doi: 10.1177/0886260509340533.

2. Bloom SL. *Creating Sanctuary: Toward the Evolution of Sane Societies.* New York, NY: Routledge; 1997.

3. Bloom SL, Farragher B. *Destroying Sanctuary: The Crisis in Human Service Delivery Systems.* New York, NY: Oxford University Press; 2010.

4. Burgess AW. *Violence Through a Forensic Lens.* Prussia, PA: Nursing Spectrum Publishing; 2000.

5. Burgess AW, Holmstrom LL. Rape trauma syndrome. *Am J Psychiatry.* 1974;131(9):981-986.

6. Ciancone AC. Sexual assault nurse examiner programs in the United States. *Ann Emerg Med.* 2000;35(4):353-357.

7. Clements PT, Pierce-Weeks J, Holt KE, Giardino AG, Seedat S, Mortiere C. *Violence Against Women: Contemporary Examination of Intimate Partner Violence.* Saint Louis, MO: STM Learning, Inc; 2015.

8. Clements PT, Speck PM, Crane PA, Faulkner MJ. Issues and dynamics of sexually assaulted adolescents and their families. *Int J Ment Health Nurs.* 2004;13(4):267-274.

9. Clifton EG, Feeny NC. Medical examination of the rape victim. Merck Manual Web site. http://www.merckmanuals.com/professional/gynecology -and-obstetrics/domestic-violence-and-rape/medical-examination-of-the- rape-victim. Updated October 2014. Accessed April 28, 2015.

10. Douglas J, Burgess AW, Burgess AG, Ressler RK. *Crime Classification Manual: A Standard System for Investigating and Classifying Violent Crime.* Hoboken, NJ: John Wiley and Sons; 2013.

11. Fitzpatrick M, Ta A, Lenchus J, Arheart KL, Rosen LF, Birnbach DJ. Sexual assault forensic examiners' training and assessment using simulation technology. *J Emerg Nurs.* 2012;38(1):85-90. doi: 10.1016/j.jen.2010.10.002.

12. Giorgi G, Mancuso S, Fiz Perez F, et al. Bullying among nurses and its relationship with burnout and organizational climate. *Int J Nurs Pract.* doi: 10.1111/ijn.12376. Published March 30, 2015.

13. Goyal M, Singh S, Sibinga EMS. *Meditation Programs for Psychological Stress and Well-Being.* Rockville, MD: Agency for Healthcare Research and Quality; 2014. Comparative Effectiveness Reviews 124.

14. Harrison LC, Yanosy SM. Traumatic reenactment: how this triangle can sabotage intervention and treatment. *The International Society for Prevention of Child Abuse and Neglect (ISPCAN). SPECIAL REPORT. Summary of Selected Papers from ISPCAN's XVIIIth International Congress and Youth Empowerment Forum.* 2010;1:3-4.

15. Hines DA, Palm Reed KM. Predicting improvement after a bystander program for the prevention of sexual and dating violence. *Health Promot Pract.* doi: 10.1177/1524839914557031. Published November 7, 2014.

16. International Association of Forensic Nurses. *Sexual Assault Nurse Examiner (SANE) Education Guidelines.* Elkridge, MD: International Association of Forensic Nurses; 2013.

17. International Association of Forensic Nurses. SANE program listings. International Association of Forensic Nurses Web site. http://www.forensicnurses.org/?page=a5. Accessed April 28, 2015.

18. Janoff-Bulman R. *Shattered Assumptions: Towards a New Psychology of Trauma.* New York, NY: The Free Press; 1992.

19. Joint Commission on Accreditation of Health Care Organizations. *2015 Comprehensive Accreditation Manual for Hospitals (CAMH).* Oakbrook Terrace, IL: Joint Commission on Accreditation of Health Care Organizations; 2014.

20. Katz J, Moore J. Bystander education training for campus sexual assault prevention: an initial meta-analysis. *Violence Vict.* 2013;28(6):1054-1067.

21. Landis JM, Sorenson SB. Victims of violence: the role and training of EMS personnel. *Ann Emerg Med.* 1997;30(2):204-206.

22. Ledray LE. *Sexual Assault Nurse Examiner (SANE) Development and Operation Guide*. Washington, DC: Office of Victims of Crime, US Department of Justice; 1999.

23. Madsen LH, Blitz LV, McCorkle D, Panzer PG. Sanctuary in a domestic violence shelter: a team approach to healing. *Psychiatr Q.* 2003;74(2):155-171.

24. Mealer M, Jones J. Posttraumatic stress disorder in the nursing population: a concept analysis. *Nurs Forum.* 2013;48(4):279-288. doi: 10.1111/nuf.12045.

25. Milliken TF, Clements PT, Tillman HJ. The impact of stress management on nurse productivity and retention. *Nurs Econ.* 2007;25(4):203-210.

26. Moulden HM, Firestone P. Vicarious traumatization: the impact on therapists who work with sexual offenders. *Trauma Violence Abuse.* 2007;8(1):67-83.

27. O'Brien C. Sexual assault nurse examiner (SANE) program coordinator. *J Emerg Nurs.* 1996;22(6):532-533.

28. Office for Victims of Crime Training and Technical Assistance Center. Sexual assault advocate/counselor training. Office for Victims of Crime Training and Technical Assistance Center Web site. https://www.ovcttac.gov/saact/module7.cfm. Accessed April 28, 2015.

29. Panzer PG, Bloom SL. Introduction to the Special Section on Sanctuary® principles and practice in clinical settings. *Psychiatr Q.* 2003;74(2):115-117.

30. Patel A, Roston A, Tilmon S, et al. Assessing the extent of provision of comprehensive medical care management for female sexual assault patients in US hospital emergency departments. *Int J Gynaecol Obstet.* 2013;123(1):24-28. doi: 10.1016/j.ijgo.2013.04.014.

31. Pennebaker JW. *Opening Up: The Healing Power of Expressing Emotions*. New York, NY: Guilford; 1997.

32. Plichta SB, Clements PT, Houseman C. Why SANEs matter: models of care for sexual violence victims in the emergency department. *J Forensic Nurs.* 2007;3(1):15-23.

33. Rape, Abuse & Incest National Network. Self-care after trauma. Rape, Abuse & Incest National Network Web site. https://rainn.org/get-information/sexual-assault-recovery/self-care-for-survivors. Accessed April 28, 2015.

34. Relyea M, Ullman SE. Unsupported or turned against: understanding how two types of negative social reactions to sexual assault relate to postassault outcomes. *Psychol Women Q.* 2015;39(1):37-52. doi: 10.1177/0361684313512610.

35. Riggs N, Houry D, Long G, Markovchick V, Feldhaus KM. Analysis of 1,076 cases of sexual assault. *Ann Emerg Med.* 2000;35(4):358-362.

36. Saakvitne KW, Gamble S, Pearlman LA, Lev BT. *Risking Connection: A Training Curriculum for Working With Survivors of Childhood Abuse.* Lutherville, MD: Sidran Press; 2000:168.

37. Strout T, Amar AF, Astwood K. Women's center staff perceptions of the campus climate on sexual violence. *J Forensic Nurs.* 2014;10(3):135-143. doi: 10.1097/JFN.0000000000000034.

38. Tjaden P, Thoennes N. *Prevalence, Incidence, and Consequences of Violence Against Women: Findings From the National Violence Against Women Survey.* Washington, DC: National Institute for Justice; 1998. NCJ172837.

39. US Department of Justice, Office on Violence Against Women. *A National Protocol for Sexual Assault Medical Forensic Examinations: Adults/Adolescents.* 2nd ed. Washington, DC: US Department of Justice, Office on Violence Against Women; 2013. National Criminal Justice Reference Service Web site. https://www.ncjrs.gov/pdffiles1/ovw/241903.pdf. Accessed April 28, 2015.

40. Walker DF, Courtois CA, Aten JD, eds. *Spiritually Oriented Psychotherapy for Trauma.* Washington, DC: American Psychological Association; 2014.

41. Yancey Martin P. *Rape Work: Victims, Gender, and Emotions in Organization and Community Context.* New York, NY: Taylor & Francis Group; 2005.

Chapter 17

LEGAL ISSUES, INVESTIGATION, AND PROSECUTION

Victor I. Vieth, JD*
Patsy Rauton Lightle
Maureen S. Rush, MS
Jeanne L. Stanley, PhD
Mimi Rose, JD
Tracy Bahm, JD
Duncan T. Brown, JD
Mary-Ann Burkhart, JD
Caren Harp, JD
Susan Bieber Kennedy, RN, JD
Lisa Kreeger, JD
Susan Kreston, JD
Millicent Shaw Phipps, JD
Laura L. Rogers, JD
Cari Michele Steele, JD
Christina Shaw, JD
Dawn Doran Wilsey, JD

LAW ENFORCEMENT ISSUES

Law enforcement personnel must be cognizant of the indicators of sexual abuse and understand that some techniques have proved useful in these investigations. The investigator assigned to the case must be thorough and methodical, have a basic understanding of sexual offenses, and be comfortable seeking other experts' advice when needed.

Revised Chapter 17 for the second edition.

PROCESSING THE SCENE AND COLLECTING EVIDENCE

— The steps for a sexual assault investigation are often the same as would be taken in any criminal assault.

— Record exact time and location of the assault, employing 911 tapes and law enforcement dispatch tapes as needed for court purposes.

— While traveling to the scene, carefully note fleeing persons, vehicles, witnesses, etc.

— If the first notification of the assault is received in person, detain this person for investigation and written statement.

1. If unable to detain this person, obtain enough information to locate him or her at a later time.

2. If a third party reports the assault, document identification information for follow-up interview(s).

— Record exact time of the arrival and notify communications that you are on the scene. Do not use a telephone at the crime scene to report your arrival. Use your mobile radio, hand-held radio, or agency-issued mobile phone, but never a telephone at the scene because it may have the suspect's fingerprints on it.

— If the victim is injured, request emergency medical services (EMS) and provide first aid.

1. Do not move seriously injured persons unless it is to protect them from additional harm.

2. Be sure to document if the emergency medical technician (EMT) moves or touches anything within the crime scene. Document what, when, and why the alterations were made and if any medications were given to the victim.

3. The emergency medical staff or a law enforcement officer will take the victim to a licensed health care facility where a sexual assault evidence collection protocol is performed. This protocol provides a standardized and coordinated approach to the collection of information and forensic evidence, treatment of injuries, and prevention of sexually transmitted infections (STIs) or pregnancy.

4. Remind the victim to take an additional set of clothing because the clothing he or she is wearing will be collected for forensic evidence processing.

— An initial incident report detailing information to support a crime should be taken.

1. Record the names and addresses of all persons present when you arrive.

2. Record the names of all officers present with you at the time of arrival and any officers who come later to assist.

— Unless there is a concern for safety, only 1 officer should enter the scene.

— Isolate a large area around the assault scene to prevent loss of evidence. Establish a perimeter and secure it using crime scene tape, ropes, cones, barricades, etc and at least 1 officer to provide security until evidence collection and documentation by the forensic crime scene unit and lead investigator are completed.

— Consider the weather conditions for crimes occurring outside and protect the scene.

1. Document weather conditions; persons present; and any nearby vehicle information, including license number, make, model, and color.

2. Avoid discussion of the crime; the suspect may appear as a neighbor or an onlooker.

— Once the scene is secured and the victim is safe and located away from the scene, conduct a complete, thorough background investigation.

1. Keep a crime scene log-in or sign-in sheet at all crime scenes. The officer in charge of security for the crime scene can also be in charge of the sign-in sheet. It includes the name, agency, and telephone number of all individuals who enter and depart from the scene.

2. The security officer ensures that only authorized individuals enter through 1 designated entrance to the scene. Cross-contamination occurs when individuals are allowed to use more than 1 entrance into the building. In addition, it is extremely difficult to account for everyone who enters and departs from the scene when more than 1 entrance is used.

— Isolate and separate witnesses or suspect(s). Do not permit any conversation among them, and detain witnesses and suspects for investigators.

— Do not allow anyone to smoke, chew gum, or use the toilet or the sink in the crime scene area. Remember that the cigarette butt or gum they throw down or put in an ashtray will contaminate the scene, or their hands may distort fingerprints on the toilet handle or evidence on a hand towel. It will be tested for saliva, secretor status, and DNA and will add evidence that is not involved with the crime.

— Observe, photograph, and sketch the scene before conducting any search and before evidence is seized. The photographer should also document the date, time, weather and light conditions, and type of film and camera and must initial each roll of film.

— Note the surrounding area of the house and identify the point of entry of the suspect.

— Make a sketch using measurements from fixed points such as doors, walls, stairs, etc; it need not be drawn to scale.

— Photograph all physical evidence and place it in a separate paper bag sealed with evidence tape, labeled, and initialed.

— Process the crime scene for fingerprints.

1. Latent, or hidden, fingerprints should be photographed with an identifying marker and documented as to location, date, and time.

2. Patent prints are visible and usually made by the fingertips, which are impregnated with body oil, blood, or dirt, or when the surface is soft and pliable, such as putty or wax. These fingerprints are simply photographed and need nothing more to enhance their ridge detail.

3. An etched print occurs when a person handles an object, usually metal, and a chemical reaction from that person's body fluid on the fingers etches a print on the object. These prints look just like those "lifted" with powder and are easily identifiable by a fingerprint expert. These prints can then be compared with known fingerprint standards of the suspect(s).

— If applicable, a blood spatter expert must photograph and measure bloodstain patterns to reconstruct the scene before blood samples are collected.

— A good rule of thumb to remember is that, with every crime, the suspect leaves identifiable evidence behind at the scene or takes something of the victim with him. This theory justifies the need to thoroughly and methodically conduct the crime scene search.

— If the assault occurred outdoors, choose the search method.

1. The grid method and strip method are the best for outdoor searches that encompass a large area.

2. An alternate light source is used to process evidence for body fluids, hairs, fibers, and fingerprints.

3. If the assault occurred in a wooded area, the alternate light source, using a battery pack or generator, can be mobilized to locate seminal stains on objects such as leaves and grass.

— If the assault occurred in a vehicle, document the make, model, year, license number, vehicle identification number (VIN), and color.

1. If possible, move the vehicle to a forensic or law enforcement garage for processing.

2. If a vehicle is involved in another way, such as transporting the suspect and/or victim, check the engine to see if it is cold, warm, or hot to the touch to corroborate the victim's statement and help in setting the timeframe.

— Submit a copy of the photographs, crime scene sketch, inventory of evidence seized, and the logbook to the investigator for court purposes.

— The inventory of evidence seized includes a description of the evidence, the name of the officer who collected it, the location, date, and time collected, and a checkmark indicating that the evidence was photographed in its original position and location before collection.

— A good investigator collects evidence, uses forensic evidence from the medical examination, interviews all parties involved, canvasses the neighborhood, conducts background checks, locates the suspect, conducts interviews or interrogations of the suspect, makes the arrest, and is successful in bringing the suspect to court for a conviction.

THE INTERVIEW PROCESS

— The goal of the interview is to obtain information that will lead to an arrest and conviction of the assailant.

— Although it is uncommon, the suspect may be at the scene when the first officer arrives. If this occurs, the officer should take accurate notes, arrest the suspect if evidence is present to establish guilt, and determine if the suspect is armed.

1. Search for and seize any weapon and record the number, description, and location of the weapon seized.

2. Secure any evidence found on the suspect and document any spontaneous statements.

3. Tell the suspect that he or she is under arrest, use the "Miranda" warning as appropriate, and do not allow any conversation between suspect and other parties.

4. Do not interview or interrogate the suspect.

5. Isolate the suspect from other witnesses.

6. If he or she is arrested inside the crime scene, remove him or her as quickly as possible.

7. Do not allow the suspect to return to the crime scene if he or she is arrested outside of that area.

8. Do not allow the suspect to wash his or her hands, change clothes, or use the toilet because evidence will be lost.

9. Do not leave the suspect alone; observe and document his or her behavior.

10. Note the suspect's mental and physical condition, especially such signs as nervousness; potential influence of drugs; torn and/or stained clothing; glass, leaves, or fibers in his or her hair; and injuries to his or her skin.

11. Transport the suspect to a secure facility as soon as possible, where a "Suspect Evidence Collection Kit and Protocol" will be performed.

— The suspect will then be interviewed by an investigator skilled in interviewing techniques, ensuring that the interview is conducted in a way that maximizes the potential for discovering the truth.

— Obtain a criminal history or background check on the suspect.

— Build a rapport when interviewing the suspect, as detailed in *Chapter 4, Chapter 8,* and *Chapter 10.*

— Make inquiry into the suspect's employment history, education, means of transportation, past prison or jail time, relatives, leisure activities, and relatives with whom he or she associates.

— Obtain basic information, including full name; nickname(s); alias(es); gender; race; date of birth; Social Security number; height; weight; build, eg, small, medium, thin, average, stocky, or obese; hair color; hair length; facial hair; eye color; glasses; contacts; scars; tattoos; teeth; unusual physical features; detection of body odor; speech impediment; language/accent; mental or physical impairments; emotional condition; address that includes the name and number of people living there; and marital status.

— The suspect's body is inspected during the collection of the suspect evidence collection kit for injuries, bruises, wounds, scars, and bite marks. The officer will ask the suspect how he or she obtained the injuries and document and photograph all injuries and marks.

— Differentiating an interview from an interrogation:

1. Interview: a structured conversation presented in a nonaccusatory manner referencing the interviewee's involvement in the crime.

2. Interrogation: a conversation in which the person being interviewed is accused of being involved in the crime and is closely regulated legally.

— Interview strategy:

1. Acknowledge that the offender has a problem and that you are concerned with helping him or her.

2. Deemphasize the criminal nature of the perpetrator, avoiding threatening words, tone, or actions.

3. Interpret the suspect's body language, listen sympathetically, and ask open-ended questions.

4. Allow the suspect to make a full statement, then follow up with more probing questions.

5. If at all possible, audio or video record the interview.

6. If the statement is not recorded, reduce the statement to writing and ask the suspect to sign it. Even if the statement is recorded, you may want to consider this additional step.

7. Document all alibi statements and changes in the statement.

8. When handwritten notes are involved, as in stalking cases, request a handwriting exemplar from the suspect.

9. Strategies to expect of the suspect include denial, minimization of his or her behavior, justification for his or her actions, including suggestions that the actions were beneficial for the victim or that he or she was under undue stress; and fabrication of events to explain his or her behavior.

— Determining who interviews the victim:

1. The victim's age, his or her mental and/or physical impairments, and the availability of a forensic interviewer versus a specially trained investigator with good interview skills will play an important part in selecting the interviewer.

2. Sensitivity and experience on the part of the interviewer may determine the successful apprehension and conviction of the assailant.

— Ask the victim basic questions, such as the following:

1. Did you know the suspect? If not, describe his or her race, height, weight, color of hair, hair length, facial hair, glasses, body odor, scars, tattoos or other physical markings, and clothing.

2. Do you know the suspect's name, address, family, friends, daily routine, hobbies, work history, or present occupation?

3. What do you remember of the assault?

— Thank the victim for doing his or her best to help you gather information to identify the assailant.

— Remember that you are interested in the victim's recall of the type of restraint (if any) that was used, conversation that the assailant had with the victim, instruments used to draw or write on the victim's body, any physical or mental torture, photographs or videos taken of the victim, and sexual preference or dysfunction exhibited by the assailant.

— Follow-up with the victim on a regular basis in the event that additional details of the assault are remembered and to assure the victim that law enforcement is continuing its investigation and has not forgotten about the victim or the case. Never promise the victim that you will apprehend the assailant, but provide assurance that everything will be done to obtain this end.

— Interview the victim's family and friends.

— Perform a neighborhood canvass. Most law enforcement agencies have a standard neighborhood canvass questionnaire to serve as a guide.

1. Basic questions include the neighbor's name, address, date of birth, employment, work address, and telephone number.

2. Ask whether they were aware of the crime, when they first learned of the crime, and whether they know the victim.

3. If they know the victim, ask for the date, time, and location they last saw or talked to the victim; whether they were present at the crime scene; and what they have heard about the crime.

4. Take a statement if the neighbor has any knowledge of the crime.

SEARCH WARRANTS

— Search warrants are a significantly underutilized investigative tool.

— Developing probable cause begins at the investigation's onset.

— Officers should keep a log of information obtained daily that helps to validate the charges to be filed. These should be as detailed as possible when describing a person, place, or object.

1. Person: record all the basic personal traits such as race, gender, height, weight, eye color, hair color, hair length, build, and physical marks such as tattoos and scars.

2. Place: whether it is a residence or a place of business, the address, description of the building, landmarks, neighboring houses or buildings, outbuildings on the property; maps and/or aerial photographs may be useful; the description should be detailed enough so that the officer who has never been to the particular location can locate it by following the portrait set forth in the search warrant.

3. After obtaining probable cause, a search is made of the suspect's house, car, office, storage shed, garage, lockers, etc.

— A legal search can provide material regarding additional suspects and/or victims and corroborate the victim's statements.

— Remember that physical evidence goes beyond blood, hair, semen, and saliva, including colors, wallpaper, photos, books, television shows, or a certain song. Any sights, sounds, or other details in the victim's statement that can be corroborated through 1 or more search warrants should be.

CORROBORATING EVIDENCE

— Corroborating evidence supports the victim's statement, strengthens the prosecutor's case, reduces the victim's stress by supporting testimony, and makes it difficult for the defense attorney to attack the victim's credibility.

— To aid officers in searching for corroborating evidence, a multidisciplinary team should go over the victim's statement sentence by sentence and word for word. After each sentence, ask yourself, "Is there anything that can be corroborated?"

— The suspect's statement is treated the same way.

— Always photograph the crime scene.

Bite Marks

— Bite marks are valuable evidence and have been overlooked and missed for years as an essential part of a criminal investigation. Bite marks are latent or patent images left on a victim or subject.

— Photograph all bite marks. It is possible to match the bite mark to a dental impression, and matching or not matching could prove the suspect did or did not create the bite mark.

— Bite marks can be used much like fingerprints, with their individual morphologic characteristics and relationship with each other in the dental arch leaving a distinct mark on the victim.

— Additional bite marks may be seen elsewhere on the body, particularly a child's, in various stages of healing, indicating chronic abuse.

— Bite marks are most often found on the chest, face, abdomen, and extremities. They may be covered with blood but will almost always be covered with saliva, which contains nucleated squamous epithelial cells, valuable in DNA analysis. Be sure to swab the bite mark to collect the saliva before photographs are taken.

— The odontologist or forensic dentist relies on bite mark evidence photography to serve as a permanent record of the mark. The photography should be performed as soon as possible after the assault and follow-up photos should be taken in 3 days and again at 10 days. Reflective ultraviolet photography of the bite mark may be performed at later dates to show any latent images. By using ultraviolet lighting with photography, bite marks have shown up as long as 4 months after the assault because of the collection of blood under the skin as a result of bruising.

— All photographs should be taken by a forensic odontologist or dentist trained by a forensic odontologist. When photographing the bite mark, it is advisable to indicate size by using a ruler certified and approved by the American Board of Forensic Odontology.

— Photographs and impressions should be taken from the suspect as well as the victim.

Computer-Facilitated Sexual Exploitation of Adult Victims
— Computer-facilitated sexual assault and cyberstalking have become high-profile crimes.

— The new issues relevant to gathering computer evidence must be incorporated into the interview to give law enforcement the best chance of amassing the optimal amount of digital evidence from the suspect and consequently from the computer(s).

Preparing for the Interview
— During the interview phase, investigators are pitting their knowledge of computers and the Internet against that of the offenders.

— Investigators should consider the following when determining the approach to use in interviewing a suspect in a computer-facilitated sexual exploitation case:

1. Assess their own computer knowledge to avoid trying to bluff a suspect who knows more than they do.

2. Assess the computer knowledge of the suspect from all other evidence to determine who you are up against.

3. Obtain as much information as possible concerning the hardware and software used by the subject, for example, the suspect's username or user ID, suspect's online profile, suspect's Internet service provider (ISP), suspect's account information, and the time of day or night the suspect is usually online.

— It is best to conduct the suspect interview in a private room away from the location when a search warrant is being carried out. Audio and videotaping should be carried out to protect the detective and the department and to provide important evidence for later presentation at trial.

— Any telephone call the suspect is allowed to make may result in the removal or destruction of digital evidence or other evidence. Many computers can be accessed remotely. Alternatively, the suspect may request that the person called destroy the contents of the computer either by physically removing the computer(s) involved or by accessing the suspect's computer and destroying the evidence at the source.

— Search and seizure information

1. Obtain basic information from the suspect on the computer(s) used by him or her and how they may be protected from external scrutiny.

2. Determine hardware, software, how many computers the suspect had access to, and where they are located.

— Password and encryption issues:

1. The password helps ensure that unauthorized users do not access a computer, program, or file. The investigator should ask if there is password protection, what the passwords are, and who else has knowledge of or access to those passwords.

2. Encryption is the most effective way to achieve data security. The investigator should ask if any of the computer files have been encrypted and if so what the names of the files are, what encryption software was used, and what the keys or passwords are to decrypt the files. If the encrypted files contain incriminating evidence, this will show knowledge and intent on the suspect's part to hide or conceal that information.

— Defeating the "Some Other Dude Did It" defense:

1. Investigators should ask who else uses the computer, who else goes on the Internet from this computer, and who else goes on the Internet using the suspect's username.

2. By getting the suspect to admit exclusive dominion over the computer(s) and his username, later claims that another person was the wrongdoer may be avoided.

— Amassing character evidence:

1. Information should be elicited regarding the suspect's Internet usage and habits.

2. Later defenses that focus on the concept of victim bashing may be precluded by the suspect's own statements in these areas.

— Storage location:

1. Not all images are necessarily stored on site in the suspect's computer(s). Off-site storage is entirely possible.

2. Investigators should ask where the images are stored on the computer (files, folders, and directories) and where else the suspect stores correspondence, including floppy disks, CD-ROMs, and tapes.

Forensic Evaluation

— Investigators armed with the answers to the questions from the interview can begin the forensic analysis of the computer. A single stand-alone computer will take an average of 40 hours to analyze.

— Although the crime of sexual assault does not directly involve the use of a computer, the information found on the computer can greatly aid in the prosecution of the crime.

— The search begins with remembering that a computer is like any other crime scene and should be treated as such.

— Accessing the computer's hard drive should be done only after a number of typical and procedural steps are taken.

1. First, if the computer is off, leave it off, and if it is on, leave it on and photograph the screen.

2. Photograph the back of the computer hard drive to show where all the plugs were plugged in and what ports were empty at the beginning of the investigation.

3. When the computer must be turned off, do not follow the normal shutdown procedures but simply disconnect the power cord from the back of the computer. Properly shutting down a computer creates the possibility that some information, especially that in "temporary" memory, might be lost. Some computers start the normal shut down process if the power from the wall is interrupted. By pulling the plug from the computer, the computer does not take these steps.

— Once the decision to seize the computer is made, remove the computer so that reconstructing it will be simple and exact.

1. Photograph the computer as it was found if this has not already been done.

2. Isolate the computer from any telephone or cable connections.

3. Clearly mark all plugs and ports so that they can be replaced once the machine is in custody.

— When transporting seized items, use great caution.

1. Pack and cushion the items well and treat each piece of hardware as extremely fragile.

2. Keep all items away from magnetic devices, microwaves, radio transmitters, and other sources of energy that might delete information.

3. Transport items on the floor of the back seat of a car if possible.

— During the search, be aware that several different types of files and documents can yield a great deal of useful evidence.

1. Files, images, and saved e-mails: look at the file names under which the suspect may have the account divided. A scan of the sent item folder is also recommended. A check of the delete file is needed because most programs require users to delete twice; a file is not deleted merely because it has been sent to the delete file. E-mail headers also provide a wealth of information if read properly (see **Table 17-1**).

2. Web sites: when a person logs on to the Internet, the computer begins a series of electronic transfers of information with the ISP server. The transfers are the equivalent of the 2 machines talking with each other. These transfers include information about the suspect's computer as well as information sent by the ISP about the Web sites. The Web site's computer is also accessing information about the suspect's computer, specifically the type, speed, and size of the computer, and organizing that information in a file on the suspect's hard drive, commonly called a "cookie." When the suspect's computer logs back on to the Web site, the Web site's computer simply goes to the cookie file on the computer, finds the appropriate cookie, and identifies the computer as a past user. Cookies can be opened up and the investigator can obtain the Web address of the site and possibly even what pop-up ads were displayed on the screen.

3. History directory: computers keep a list of recently visited Web sites in a directory called history.

4. Temporary Internet files file: this contains bits and pieces of downloads and Web site information from Web sites that were visited by the suspect's computer. Cookies are also deposited in these files.

Table 17-1. How to Read an E-mail Header: Message Header and Translations

1. **Return path:** jqpublic@email.com

   Translation: Informs receiving computer who sent the message and where to send error messages if the message does not go through

2. **Received:** from ruguilty@netmao.com (4.1/SMI-4.1) id BB11011: Mon, 3 Mar 14 12:34 EST

   Translation: Shows the route the message took from sending to reception. Every time a computer receives a message, it adds a "Received:" field with address and time stamp.

3. **Received:** from localhost byjqpublic.email.com (4.1/SMI-4.1) id BB10011; Mon, 3 Mar 14 12:33 EST

   Translation: Same as example 2.

4. **Message ID:** 1234567890.BB1011@ruguilty.netmail.com

   Translation: Message ID line is the only line that cannot be altered. The ID is logged by the computer and may be traced through the computers it has been sent from, if needed.

5. **Date:** Mon, 3 Mar 2014 12:35 -0800 (EST)

   Translation: Shows date, time, and time zone when the message was sent.

6. **From:** "JQ Public" <jqpublic.email.com>

   Translation: Gives e-mail address of sender.

7. **To:** Joey Bagadonuts bagadonuts@internet.org

   Translation: Shows e-mail name and address of the recipient. In this case ".org" denotes an organization, ".com" a commercial vendor, and ".edu" an educational institution.

8. **CC:** Reggie Osborn reggoz@law.fgu.edu

   Translation: Shows names and addresses of any "CCs." This can also be a "BCC," or blind CC, in which case the name and address would be hidden.

— Created/Modified/Access Dates:

1. The "Created Date" is the date that the file was created, first saved, or downloaded onto the suspect's hard drive. This date is important because it records the date when the file first appeared on the suspect's computer.

2. The "Modified Date" shows whether and when the suspect altered or changed the file. Modification can imply knowledge of the file as well as use and affirmative possession of it.

3. The "Access Date" is useful because it shows how recently the suspect opened the file. However, the Access Date only records the most recent action taken. If a forensic examiner is too hasty and opens a file before properly creating a duplicate copy of the hard drive, all the access dates will reflect the dates law enforcement accessed them, not the suspect.

— Instant messaging:

1. Instant messaging is a useful tool for investigators who are conducting online stings.

2. The difficulty with the software is that there is no automatic logging of conversations, nor are the chats saved.

— Looking for files on a hard drive or disk:

1. Check the allocated space, ie, space that has data written into it.

2. Check the unallocated space, ie, space available for writing.

3. Check the slack space, ie, space left over from allocated space.

4. Remember that information contained in RAM space can be lost if the investigator opens large files on the hard drive or reboots the computer or if programs that depend on RAM space are run before the proper software is engaged to search it. First, check all temporary files and run a thorough search of the RAM space to preserve any potentially useful information contained therein.

5. Contact the National District Attorneys Association's National Center for Prosecution of Child Abuse for technical assistance [(703) 549-9222].

OTHER CONSIDERATIONS

— Investigators must be familiar with their state laws regarding issues such as criminal sexual conduct, privacy and wiretapping, emergency protective custody, termination of parental rights, obscenity, sexual exploitation of a minor or an elder, mandated reporting statutes, and penalties for failure to report.

— Case management is vital. Investigation of criminal sexual assault generates a tremendous amount of paperwork, and the ability of the investigator to collect, document, organize, and process the information is critical. The ultimate goal of any criminal investigation is to identify the assailant, prevent him from harming any more citizens, and successfully provide information to the prosecution for conviction.

— When an investigator is preparing a case file for court, the following information must be included:

1. Cover sheet

2. Brief synopsis that includes a chronology of events

3. Offense report with all supplemental reports

4. Arrest reports

5. Follow-up reports, statements, arrest and/or search warrants

6. Forensic laboratory reports as applicable, including DNA, trace or latent prints, question documents, polygraph results, toxicology findings, evidence, evidence forms, and chain of custody

7. Background sheets

8. Criminal histories

9. Medical information

10. Victim and Suspect Sexual Assault Evidence Collection Protocols

11. Photographs

12. Sketches

13. Videotapes, audio tapes

14. List of witnesses with their addresses and telephone numbers and their involvement in the case

— Law enforcement personnel are extremely dependent on the medical professional who collects the evidence and interprets it. Thus the medical and law enforcement professionals must work closely together to build a case.

— Once the case file is complete, the investigator should set up a meeting with the appointed prosecutor to provide this information in an orderly fashion.

— The investigator is also responsible for being well prepared for giving testimony in court. Suggestions are as follows:

1. Know your case, your victim, the circumstances, and the connection of the evidence between the suspect and the victim.

2. Meet with the prosecutor in advance of trial to review your testimony and otherwise be thoroughly prepared for court. It is also appropriate to meet with a defense attorney if requested to do so. Many defense attorneys simply intend to fully assess the state's case in order to discuss plea offers and other issues with their clients. A willingness to meet with the defense attorney shows the jury that the investigator is a fair and unbiased collector of evidence.

3. Look professional, be courteous, and speak distinctly.

4. Respond to questions with brief answers, and address your answers to the jury and judge.

5. Speak in a professional but easily understandable manner, free of the language that may be in a police report. For example, say "Mr. Jones then got out of his car" rather than "the suspect exited his vehicle."

6. If you don't understand a question, be comfortable enough to politely ask the individual to repeat the question. Asking the defense or prosecution to repeat the question also allows you a bit more time to think about the question and formulate an answer.

7. Describe in detail the steps taken in the investigation.

The Role of Police as First Responders

The role of police personnel as first responders focuses on providing empathetic care and services to victims of sexual assault and ensuring the proper performance of investigative work to support the criminal prosecutions of such cases.

Preparation for First Responders

— First responders must have access to both initial and continuing education designed to address sexual assault issues, including the following:

1. The broad range of victim reactions to sexual assaults

2. The various methods of empathetic questioning

3. The most up-to-date forensic procedures

4. The many myths, stereotypes, and assumptions about victims of sexual assault

5. The various ways victims present themselves after a sexual assault

6. The importance of avoiding value judgments regarding the impact of sexual assaults on victims

7. Changes and modifications of laws

8. The roles of race, ethnic background, age, gender, religion, economic status, disabilities, and sexual identity in sexual assault cases

— First responders must understand that from a legal standpoint, stranger rape and acquaintance rape are equally important and they are given equal weight throughout the investigation and prosecution.

— First responders must also establish relationships with available community resources and social services for sexual assault victims, which will allow the first responder to make appropriate and useful recommendations focusing on the specific needs of each victim.

— It is useful to establish relationships with service providers to address the unique issues facing elderly victims; male victims; and lesbian, gay, bisexual, and transgender victims.

— Knowing which referral sites have multilingual counselors or interpreters is also helpful.

VICTIM CONTACT

— Victims' initial contact with first responders often creates an indelible perception about the entire justice system.

— Police must begin by learning what is beneficial in interactions with victims.

— Police dispatchers:

1. Begin by assessing the safety of victims, investigating whether the victim is still in immediate danger and whether immediate medical attention is required.

2. Provide important information regarding victim care to responding police personnel.

3. Collect information used in criminal prosecutions, including basic data (name, age, current location) and time-sensitive or "flash" information that relates to the time and location of the assault, descriptions of the assailant(s), vehicles, other physical identifiers, and direction of the assailant's flight.

4. Immediately broadcast this information to all available patrol and detective units in the field so that officers can survey their patrol areas for such perpetrators.

5. May ask the victim for specific locations where the assailant may be found if the victim knew the perpetrator.

6. Give specific directions to victims to preserve important prosecution evidence and assist the forensic components of investigations.

7. Instruct victims to remain at their current location until police arrive, if it is safe to do so.

8. Remain on the phone with victims until police arrive to ensure their safety and provide psychologic support.

— Police officers:

1. Provide the initial on-scene contact.

2. Maintain confidentiality, using unmarked police cars and plain clothes officers, as well as a "low-profile" approach.

3. Make efforts to be aware of other situational factors that are important to victims, eg, by arranging support services for children or childcare while victims are engaged in medical examinations and police interviews; determining if the presence of family members or friends is helpful or harmful; enlisting family or friends to assist in gathering needed information; determining whether trained interpreters would be more helpful; or, in some cases, by helping a victim find shelter or care for a pet he or she may believe is in danger of harm by a suspect.

4. Take victims to the apprehension location to identify assailants, remaining mindful of victims' vulnerabilities, informing the victim in advance of what will take place and what is expected of him or her.

5. Be mindful of factors that impact one's ability to fulfill these roles, including the psychologic and physical status of victims that may hinder an officer's ability to gather detailed and accurate information.

6. Respect victims' request to speak with a same-gender officer.

7. Interview EMS personnel who arrived before law enforcement to obtain information they may have gathered from the victim for inclusion in final police reports.

8. Understand the need for accuracy because such records will eventually affect the criminal prosecution.

9. Take copious notes about the scene, the condition of the victim, and any statements given by the victim, detailing all irregularities at the scene.

10. Maintain written resources and referral information to give to victims who do not want the services of police or who do not want to follow through with the prosecution of the case. These should include a basic description of the medical and legal issues and procedures after a sexual assault; the location and description of sexual assault and rape crisis agencies; and lists of programs that provide services for the prevention and treatment of STIs, HIV infection, and pregnancy.

MEDICAL EXAMINATIONS

— Medical evaluations may take place in designated hospital emergency centers, requiring transport of the victim to the facility. Unless victims are medically impaired, police, rather than EMS, transport victims to hospitals.

— Offer a brief explanation of the medical examination process (see *Chapter 9* and *Chapter 10*).

INVESTIGATIVE INTERVIEWS

— Investigating officers conduct a detailed interview with the victim after the medical evaluation and treatment.

— Victims may choose to postpone giving their statement so that they have some time to rest, but most researchers find that victims are more at ease discussing the details of the assault within the first 24 hours and statements should be taken as soon as possible to avoid losing memories.

— Allow victims to give their statements at their own pace and without interruption before asking additional clarification questions.

— Interview locations are important and should usually be statement rooms that are comfortable and out of the bustle of main squad rooms; sometimes it will be necessary to give victims a choice. If interviews must be taken at the medical facility, interviewers may find it helpful to use private spaces or private patient rooms instead of sterile examination rooms.

— Interviewers must be flexible, open, and aware of the victim's needs, as well as avoid subtle insinuations about the victim's veracity.

— Closed-ended questions assist in gathering specific information.

— Open-ended questions may be used to expand victims' responses.

— Other fundamental interviewing skills include active listening and attending skills.

— Even if the victim chooses not to prosecute the assailant(s), police should follow normal procedures.

CRIMINAL PROSECUTION

— First responders must be aware that every element may become part of the "discovery," or the evidence used to prosecute criminal cases.

— Defense attorneys may be entitled to review all statements, including "flash" information, given by victims to police and dispatchers; 911 radio tapes, which may have victims or friends providing descriptive information regarding attacks and perpetrators; first responders' initial reports; investigators' interviews and final investigative reports; and forensic evidence gathered at the scene and by examining medical personnel at the hospital.

— The same criminal investigative procedures must be used whether or not the perpetrator is known to the victim, even in cases of spousal assault.

VICTIM REACTIONS

— First responders require a significant level of insight into the emotional state of victims.

— Look for general overarching themes in the victim to better understand a victim's reaction to an assault.

— Be aware that reactions differ from person to person in the degree, length, and sequence of emotional, behavioral, and analytical responses shown.

1. Varying reactions may also affect the length of time taken by victims to contact police; minutes, hours, days, months, and years may pass before victims are able or willing to approach police.

2. Length of time is not an indicator of severity or "realness"; rather, it reflects different reactions of the survivor to the incident.

— Other factors that influence the range of reactions include victims' situational and emotional condition before, during, and after the assault. For example, an elderly victim assaulted by a family member or another caretaker on whom he or she depends may have myriad fears about cooperating with the authorities.

— Rape trauma syndrome:

1. First responders are likely to encounter victims in the acute phase of the syndrome, a period marked by disorganization and a broad range of emotions, from strongly expressive to subdued affect, calmness, or composure.

2. Emotional reactions are often related to the fear, anxiety, humiliation, self-blame, shame, and anger experienced by victims.

3. Physical outcomes include bruising, contusions, breaks, and bleeding as well as genital disturbances such as discharge, bleeding, cuts, and pain.

4. Immediate behavioral reactions include disturbances in the ability to concentrate, form cohesive sentences, and focus on questions and statements.

5. The long-term reorganization process occurs and survivors experience feelings of depression, restlessness, and exhaustion (similar to what is seen in posttraumatic stress disorder); nightmares, flashbacks, disturbed eating and sleeping patterns, sexual dysfunction, and difficulty in social adjustments; and finally, with time, a reorganization of the victim's understanding of the world before and after trauma, potentially leading to a degree of resolution and integration of the event into life.

Ongoing Contact and Victim Support
— Maintain ongoing contact with victims to keep victims informed and updated throughout the legal process.

— Remain in contact to ensure a successful conclusion for victims, which may or may not mean a conviction.

— Support victims as they gain the ability to move on with their lives, reassuring them that their assault was indeed significant and it was recognized by the police as such.

Legal Issues From a Prosecutor's Perspective
Personal injury is both a crime and a civil matter. Thus the victim of a sexual assault may be involved in both the criminal and the civil legal systems.

Crimes of Sexual Assault
— The criminal law is always changing to reflect shifting community values.

— Criminal laws and penalties are created by each state and reflect unique variations peculiar to that state. Therefore it is necessary to study specific crimes, laws, and penalties for the state in which you are practicing.

— Generally, sexual offenses involve 4 types of conduct, as follows:

1. Sexual intercourse

2. "Deviant" sexual intercourse (oral or anal sex)

3. Digital penetration or penetration of the genitals with an object

4. Indecent contact, which involves touching the genitals or other body parts for sexual gratification without penetration

— If such conduct occurs under any of the following conditions, it is a crime:

1. The act occurs without the complainant's consent.

2. Force or threat of force is used—this is not limited to physical force but also includes psychological, moral, or intellectual pressure of sufficient magnitude.

3. The victim is unconscious or intoxicated by drugs or alcohol, and this is known to the assailant.

4. The complainant suffers from a mental disability rendering him or her incapable of giving consent.

5. The complainant is less than age 13 years.

6. The complainant is less than age 16 years and the assailant is 4 or more years older.

STATUTE OF LIMITATIONS

— All crimes (except murder) have a statute of limitations that puts a limit on how much time a person has to report a crime to the police for purposes of arrest and prosecution.

— Generally felonies are more serious offenses and carry a longer possible sentence than misdemeanors.

— The different time requirements for children that allow a minor to reach adulthood before disclosing abuse to authorities is a change in the law that has evolved over the past 25 years. In most instances, an investigator has to determine the statute of limitations in place at the time of the offense. In some states, there is case law tolling a statute of limitations if a suspect had an ongoing threat or other pressure to keep a victim quiet.

THE CRIMINAL JUSTICE PROCESS

— Sexual assault may be reported through the 911 system, as a result of hospital protocol, a nursing home protocol, or through reports received by county child welfare agencies, among other ways.

— Police usually take the victim for a medical examination for health reasons and for possible forensic evidence collection.

— Investigators interview the victim and any eyewitnesses, go where the assault occurred, take photographs, and collect evidence from the crime scene.

— Evidence collection often requires a search warrant if evidence is believed to be within the perpetrator's control.

— If the suspect is known to police, he or she is informed of the investigation and given the opportunity to make a statement.

— Suspects in police custody cannot be questioned without being advised of their right to refuse to give a statement, their right to have a lawyer present during police questioning, and a warning that any statement could be used against them. The recitation of these rights is commonly known as Miranda warnings.

— If the assailant is a stranger to the victim but he or she had the opportunity to observe the assailant during the attack, the victim may be shown a series of photographs or a lineup of several individuals similar to the description of the assailant and be asked to identify the perpetrator.

— If the victim is unable to identify his or her assailant, circumstantial evidence or DNA obtained from forensic examination of the victim may be sufficient to prosecute.

— At the conclusion of evidence gathering and after all statements are taken, the police submit their investigation to the district attorney, also known as the prosecutor, state's attorney, or county attorney.

1. The district attorney or assistant district attorney determines if there is enough evidence to arrest the suspect and with what crimes the suspect is to be charged based on the evidence.

2. Some jurisdictions convene a grand jury comprising community members who make the determination if there is sufficient evidence to bring the accused to trial.

3. The standard used by police and prosecutors to decide whether or not a suspect should be arrested for a crime is the finding of "probable cause." Probable cause is found when a law enforcement officer believes that a crime has probably been committed and that the suspect is probably the perpetrator; however, since the case must eventually be proved "beyond a reasonable doubt," prosecutors may evaluate the evidence collected based on whether or not a conviction can be obtained.

PRELIMINARY ARRAIGNMENT

— After arrest, the preliminary arraignment begins the judicial process.

— The defendant (the term used after arrest) is fingerprinted, photographed, and computer checked to determine if he or she has ever been arrested for other crimes.

— Bail:

1. The purpose of bail and pretrial detention is not to punish the offender; all arrested persons are presumed innocent until proven guilty.

2. The monetary amount is set based on the nature of the offense; the defendant's prior criminal history; any ties to the geographic area, ie, home, job, family, etc; the risk of flight; and any prior willful failure to appear at court hearings.

3. Bail is collateral to compel the defendant to appear at court dates.

4. If the defendant fails to appear, bail is forfeited.

5. The higher the risk of flight from trial, the higher the bail imposed.

6. Community safety and victim safety are also factored into determining bail amount.

— At the preliminary arraignment, the person is given formal notice of the charges and notice of the next court hearing.

— Conditions such as prohibiting contact with the victim, abstention from drugs or alcohol, house confinement, or electronic monitoring of the defendant may also be imposed.

Appointment of Counsel

— At the preliminary arraignment, the defendant is entitled to a lawyer.

— Depending on income, a person must either hire an attorney or, if income eligible, the public defenders office is appointed to represent the accused.

THE PRELIMINARY HEARING

— The next court proceeding in a sexual assault case in many states is the preliminary hearing.

— It is usually held within a few weeks after an arrest and is designed as one of the safeguards to ensure the accused's right to fairness.

— A judge reviews the charges and the police reports or other records to support the charges and, in some jurisdictions, may hear brief testimony (sometimes from the victim) to determine if the legal requirements of the crime are met so that the case may ultimately go to trial.

— The judge reviews the police and the prosecution's decision to arrest a suspect on the charges. If a victim testifies, the credibility of the witness is not decided nor is any corroborating evidence required. The victim simply needs to give a brief account of the essential facts to determine if there is legally sufficient evidence to have the case go to trial.

— The sexual assault victim's first encounter with the judicial system may be during the preliminary hearing. If the victim testifies, this will typically be the first time he or she speaks of the assault before a judge, a defense attorney, and the defendant in a courtroom open to the public by law.

　　1. This difficult experience can be empowering or retraumatizing, depending on the sensitivity of the judge, prosecutor, and court staff.

2. Some sexual assault preliminary hearings are held in a designated courtroom with prosecutors who are victim sensitive and competently trained in both the law and the dynamics of sexual assault to handle these cases.

3. Often, when the victim must appear, advocates are present in the courtroom to offer support and social service referrals.

— The time between the preliminary hearing and the trial varies, taking weeks or months.

— Once the preliminary hearing has ended, the case is assigned to the prosecutor who will take the case to trial.

1. The prosecutor is the director of the case; the police reports, witness interviews, hospital records, etc that tell of the events leading up to the assault and its aftermath are the script.

2. The incident is recreated for the jury by testimony from the witnesses and the production of physical and/or scientific evidence.

3. Meeting with witnesses, finding additional witnesses or evidence not initially uncovered by the police, researching the law, and thinking about trial strategy occupy both the defense attorney and the prosecutor in anticipation of a trial.

— When an alleged sexual assault is committed by an unknown assailant, lack of consent by the victim is presumed, and the central issue is the identity of the assailant.

— Generally the alleged perpetrator is known to the victim, so consent is frequently raised by the defense.

— What constitutes legal consent changes with changing community attitudes about sexuality and gender-based violence.

CORROBORATION
— The law does not require corroboration to arrest or convict a person of sexual assault; the testimony of the victim, if believed, is sufficient. At the close of a case, the judge will instruct the jury that they may convict on the victim's word alone.

— The victim's account may be the only testimonial evidence available, so physical evidence collection is critical.

— It is important to document and photograph bruising and injury, torn clothing, or a room in disarray after a struggle and to collect physical evidence such as bed sheets, towels, and clothing for forensic testing to determine the presence of sexual fluids, hairs, or blood. DNA testing is conducted by obtaining blood samples from the accused.

— A sexual assault trial often occurs several months after the incident, and it may be difficult for a complainant to convey the emotional state and demeanor during a traumatic assault to the court. Medical personnel must, therefore, accurately document observable emotional states. Accurate, timely documentation of statements from a victim or witness is also important.

— Witnesses are not permitted to give opinions or impressions about what they have observed; it is the jury's function to draw opinions and conclusions about the credibility and weight of the evidence. The exception to this rule would be the expert witness.

— Physicians, sexual assault nurse examiners (SANEs) or other nurses, social workers, or other professionals can be subpoenaed by either the prosecution or the defense to testify as a fact witness or an expert witness (**Table 17-2**).

Table 17-2. The Direct Examination: Prosecutor Questions and Expert Witness Response Suggestions

— Full name and spelling

— Current occupation
    — *State full title*
    — *Duties and responsibilities in current position*

— Prior occupation (if experience enhances credibility with the jury, such as rape crisis counselor, police officer, evidence technician, etc)
    — *State full title*
    — *Duties and responsibilities in past position*
    — *Describe relevance of past position to current testimony*   *(continued)*

Table 17-2. The Direct Examination: Prosecutor Questions and Expert Witness Response Suggestions *(continued)*

— Educational background
  — *Associate degree: date, institution, and discipline*
  — *Undergraduate degree: date, institution, and discipline*
  — *Graduate degree: date, institution, and discipline*

— Medical training and experience
  — *Residency: date, institution, and specialty*
  — *Internship: date, institution, and specialty*
  — *Fellowship: date, institution, and specialty*

— Specific sexual assault training
  — *Child sexual abuse training (be specific in amount and practicality of training)*
  — *Physical abuse training (be specific in amount and practicality of training)*
  — *Sexual assault training (be specific in amount and practicality of training)*

— Peer review participation
  — *What is peer review?*
  — *How often does peer review occur?*
  — *How is peer review conducted?*
  — *What is/are the benefit(s) of peer review?*
  — *How often do you participate in peer review?*
  — *Describe your participation in peer review.*

— Teaching
  — *Do you train other professionals in the area of sexual assault examination?*
  — *What percentage of your current position involves training others in this expertise?*
  — *Does your teaching include lecturing or hands-on training?*
  — *How long have you been responsible for training others in the area of sexual assault examinations?*
  — *Approximately how many other professionals have you trained?*

(continued)

Table 17-2. The Direct Examination: Prosecutor Questions and Expert Witness Response Suggestions *(continued)*

— Continuing education
   — *Do you participate in continuing education?*
   — *Define for the jury what constitutes continuing education.*
   — *How much continuing education do you receive on an annual basis?*
   — *How is the continuing education applicable to your expertise as a sexual assault examiner?*

— Publications
   — *Have you published any scholarly articles, studies, etc in the area of sexual assault or abuse?*
   — *Have you published any scholarly articles, studies, etc in any other areas of medical research?*

— Is there anything else that you should tell the jury about your training, experience, or background that would assist the jury in making a decision?

— In the course of your professional duties, have you ever performed a sexual assault examination to determine if a person was sexually assaulted?
   — *How many sexual assault examinations have you personally performed?*
   — *How many sexual assault examinations have you observed being performed?*

— Have you ever supervised the performance of a sexual assault examination?

— You stated earlier that you are involved in training other professionals in the performance of sexual assault examinations.
   — *Who do you train to perform sexual assault examinations?*
   — *How do you perform this training?*

— Have you previously qualified as an expert in the area of sexual assault forensic examinations?
   — *Which courts?*
   — *How many times have you qualified?*
   — *In what areas of expertise have you qualified as an expert?*

— Is the manner in which a sexual assault examination is conducted regulated by a protocol?
   — *What is a protocol for purposes of a sexual assault examination?*

(continued)

Table 17-2. The Direct Examination: Prosecutor Questions and Expert Witness Response Suggestions *(continued)*

— Is there a protocol in place in your jurisdiction for sexual assault examination?
  — *When was the protocol for sexual assault examination established?*
  — *Is the protocol ever evaluated and revised?*
  — *History of protocol being reevaluated and revised.*

— Please explain the procedure required in the protocol for sexual assault examination. This should include a short generalized answer, including information such as:
  — *Obtain a verbal history of the sexual assault.*
  — *Conduct an external physical examination.*
  — *Conduct a genital examination.*

—What is a history?
  — *Why do you obtain a history?*
  — *From whom do you obtain the history?*
  — *Why is a history obtained at the beginning of the examination?*
  — *Does a history assist you in forming your ultimate medical opinion or diagnosis?*
  — *How does the history assist you in forming a medical opinion?*

—Do you document the history that you receive?
  — *On what form do you document your findings?*

—Does the protocol require this form to be completed?
  — *Have you received training on how to correctly complete the form?*
  — *Approximately how many times have you completed this form?*

—When do you document the information that you receive while obtaining the history?
  — *Why do you document the information at this time?*

— After obtaining and documenting the history received, what do you do next?

—What is involved in performing the external examination? This should outline the items to note during the examination, such as:
  — *Temperature, blood pressure, weight, age, etc*
  — *Demeanor and attitude of patient*
  — *Bruising, scratches, etc*   *(continued)*

Table 17-2. The Direct Examination: Prosecutor Questions and Expert Witness Response Suggestions *(continued)*

— Do you document the information and findings that you obtained during the external examination?
  — *How?*
  — *When?*
  — *Where?*

— After completing the external examination, what do you do next?

— Please explain how the genital examination is conducted.
  Examination of external genitalia:
  — *Where is the **labia majora** and what is the purpose of it?*
  — *Where is the **labia minora** and what is the purpose of it?*
  — *Continue through all parts of external genitalia.*

— I would assume that your next step is to conduct an examination of the internal genital area. Are there various positions used when conducting this part of the examination?
  — *What are the different position(s) used to complete the examination?*
  — *Please describe the various positions used.*
  — *Why are multiple positions used to complete the examination?*

—What are the names of the body parts that are examined?
  — *Vagina*
  — *Hymen*

—What do you look for when examining the hymen?
  — *Are all hymens shaped the same?*
  — *What are the different shapes possible?*
  — *What is the significance of the shape of a hymen?*
  — *Does the shape of the hymen affect your examination?*
  — *Does the shape of the hymen affect whether it can be injured?*
  — *Is the hymen located on the interior or exterior of the female body?*
  — *How far inside the female body is the hymen located?*

— Continue with other significant body parts.

(continued)

Table 17-2. The Direct Examination: Prosecutor Questions and Expert Witness Response Suggestions *(continued)*

— Does the protocol require that you document these findings in a certain manner?
  — *How?*
  — *When?*
  — *Where?*

— How long does a typical sexual assault examination last?
  — *Waiting time*
  — *History*
  — *Physical examination*

— On _____, did you conduct a sexual assault examination on _____?

— In conducting this examination, was the protocol followed?

— In following the protocol, you obtained a history from the victim prior to conducting the examination. What is the history that you received?

— Did you receive additional historic information from any other source(s)?
  — *Family members*
  — *Detectives, beat officers, social workers, etc*
  — *Hearsay problems*

— In accordance with the protocol, did you record the information that you received?

— While you were taking the history, did you have an opportunity to observe the victim's demeanor and attitude?

— What was her demeanor and attitude?
  — *Based on your training and experience, was her demeanor and attitude consistent with a person who has suffered a traumatic event?*
  — *Why?*

— Did you record her demeanor on the required form?
  — *When did you do this?*

(continued)

Table 17-2. The Direct Examination: Prosecutor Questions and Expert Witness Response Suggestions *(continued)*

— Does the victim's demeanor affect your ultimate medical opinion?
  — *How?*
  — *Why?*

— After obtaining the history, your protocol requires an external examination to be conducted. Did you do this?

— Describe the examination that you conducted.

— What were your findings?
  — *Were your findings consistent with a person who has suffered a traumatic event?*
  — *Why?*
  — *How so?*

— Did you document your findings from the external examination as required by protocol?
  — *When?*
  — *How?*

— What specifically did you document on the form?

— Did you do anything to document your findings visually from the external examination?
  — *Hand-drawing on the required form*
  — *Photographs*
    — *Make sure photographs have perspective.*
    — *Use a ruler.*
    — *Use a color scale.*
    — *How do you identify the photographs as being of this victim if no face can be seen?*
    — *Did you do this in this case?*

— Is there anything else regarding the external examination that we have not discussed?

—According to protocol, did you next conduct the genital examination?

(continued)

Table 17-2. The Direct Examination: Prosecutor Questions and Expert Witness Response Suggestions *(continued)*

— Did you follow the procedures as required by the protocol?

— How did you perform the examination?

— Please describe how the examination began.
  — *External genitalia*
  — *Internal genital area*
  — *Position(s) used to complete examination*
    — *Use diagram/board to demonstrate to jury.*
    — *Define the different parts of genital area.*
    — *Explain in plain English.*

— What were your findings with respect to the examination of the external genitalia?
  — *Labia majora*
  — *Labia minora*

— Did you document your findings in accordance with protocol?

— Did you next conduct an examination of the internal genital area?

— Did you examine the part(s) of the body that you earlier described to us:
  — *Vagina?*
  — *Hymen?*
  — *Etc*

— What tools did you use to complete the examination?
  — *Swabs (size?)*
  — *Speculum*
  — *Colposcope*
    — *What is a speculum?*
    — *What is the purpose of a speculum?*

— What did you discover during the internal genital examination?
  — *Vagina*
  — *Hymen*
  — *Injuries found:*
    — *Type of injury*
    — *Location of injury*   *(continued)*

Table 17-2. The Direct Examination: Prosecutor Questions and Expert Witness Response Suggestions *(continued)*

—I am showing you what have been marked as _____. What is it?

—Please explain this diagram to the jury.

—Please explain the significance of the numbers.

—Please mark on the diagram the injuries that you found.

—You've placed a mark on the _____. What does that mark represent?

—Is the placement of an injury significant?
 — *Why?*
 — *Explain in detail.*

— Were your findings different depending on the position of the victim?
 — *Why is this significant?*

— You stated earlier that you also used a colposcope during the examination. What is a colposcope?
 — *Please explain what the function of a colposcope camera is during a sexual assault examination.*
 — *How is it used?*
 — *Does it actually touch the victim?*
 — *What is the benefit of using a colposcope rather than a traditional camera?*
 — *The subject matter is magnified by the colposcope.*
 — *Why are colposcopic photographs taken during the sexual assault examination?*

— I am showing you what have been marked as _____. What is it?

— How do you recognize this as being a photograph of _____?

— Please identify the injuries that you described finding on the victim.

— You earlier stated that the placement of the injury is significant. Using the photograph, demonstrate and explain why placement is significant.

(continued)

Table 17-2. The Direct Examination: Prosecutor Questions and Expert Witness Response Suggestions *(continued)*

— Were you able to determine the age of the injuries?
    — *How is it possible to determine the age of an injury?*
    — *Do you have an opinion regarding the age of the injury?*
    — *What is your opinion?*
    — *What do you base your opinion on?*

— Did you form an expert opinion regarding the cause of the genital injury?

— What is your expert opinion?

— What did you base your opinion on?
    — *Examination, history by victim and others, experience, continuing education, etc*

— Based on your examination, do you have an opinion as to whether your findings are consistent with the victim's history of sexual assault?

— What is your opinion?

— What do you base your opinion on?

---

1. Fact witness: a person who has seen or heard or otherwise experienced something that either the prosecution or the defense believes supports their theory of the case. Fact witnesses are asked to testify about their observations. Because the accuracy of memory can diminish over time, these observations should be documented close in time to their occurrence. If required to testify, the health care provider is usually allowed to bring any records to court and to refer to them during testimony.

2. Expert witness: if the subject matter is ruled by the judge to be beyond what a jury member would be expected to understand and if it is determined to be generally accepted in the scientific, medical, or other professional community to which the witness belongs that the witness has the requisite education and experience concerning the subject matter at issue, then that witness may be qualified as an

expert in a given field and permitted to give an opinion about the evidence. Expert testimony in sexual assault cases is often given by physicians or SANEs concerning the significance of physical findings or lack of physical findings from a forensic examination performed on an alleged sexual assault victim. The physician's or nurse's ability to educate the jury may make all the difference between a just and an unjust verdict.

— To be a successful expert witness, the following 10 factors are extremely helpful:

1. Make careful pretrial preparation: the medical witness must read and digest the entire medical record, including the laboratory reports on all of the samples taken and have an overview of all of the information pertinent to the patient. Medical witnesses must prepare a curriculum vitae or résumé before testifying, including education, training, and experience.

2. Attend a pretrial meeting with the prosecutor: the prosecutor will outline the topics that will be discussed at trial and the medical witness should educate the prosecutor regarding significant medical facts that will be of assistance. The medical expert may be able to direct the prosecutor in forming questions that will provide the expert with the right opportunity to testify regarding pertinent information. Possible topics of cross-examination should also be discussed, and the witness should ask if there is any information or report available regarding the case to help him or her better prepare for giving testimony.

3. Practice professionalism and promptness: develop a good working relationship with the prosecutor and call the day before the date of the subpoenaed appearance to determine if attendance is required. Prosecutors should inform witnesses if they are not needed. If they are needed, medical professionals should be on time to avoid problems with the judge. Plan for problems with traffic, parking, and getting lost when going to court. Dress appropriately because jurors often make preliminary decisions on credibility based on the witness' appearance. Scrubs or traditional medical attire is not appropriate for the courtroom environment.

4. Make it simple: because the average educational level of a jury panel is eighth grade, remember to structure answers in a simple and nontechnical manner. Before testifying, take a moment and consider all the words used in daily conversation that can be considered technical language and avoid them.

5. Incorporate demonstrative aids: because we are a visual society, some jurors may lose interest if no photographs or other physical evidence is presented. In addition, jurors are more likely to remember evidence if it is communicated 3 times; demonstrative aids will allow for a repeated presentation of important facts. If you are using demonstrative aids, it is important to practice and to consider how to incorporate the exhibit into the testimony. If you must leave the witness chair and approach an exhibit, ask the questioning attorney or judge if this is possible; permission will always be granted. Face the jury or have your side toward the jury; remember that your audience is the jury, not the judge or the prosecutor. Do not stand where you obscure the exhibit from the jury's sight. If you are using a felt-tipped marker, bring one to court with you and ensure that it works. Consider what color will be most visible. Be aware that it may be difficult to talk, mark, stand correctly, and make sure that every member of the jury can see the exhibit during the testimony and practice.

6. Be polite to the defense attorney: it is important to remain calm and polite even if the cross-examination is being conducted in a rude, condescending, or arrogant manner. Trust the jury to acknowledge the attitude of the defense attorney.

7. Be aware of your body language: recognize the existence of bad habits and nervous reactions and suppress them so that they are not a distraction to the jurors, perhaps undercutting the impact of your testimony.

8. Be assertive on cross-examination: questions are often couched to allow for a "yes" or "no" response, yet you may have a great deal of information to provide that would be helpful to the jury. It is extremely helpful to the prosecutor if the medical witness simply states, "I would like to explain, but my answer will be (yes or no)."

This statement notifies the prosecutor that a follow-up question should be asked on redirect examination and notifies the jury that there is additional relevant information that needs to be elicited.

9. Don't become a target: do not testify to expert information for which you are not qualified. During the pretrial meeting, you should explore all of the areas of information so that you know if you are qualified to render testimony. Extending beyond your expertise allows questions that can destroy your credibility in the present case as well as in future cases.

10. Debrief with the prosecutor: a follow-up meeting with the prosecutor is beneficial to both parties and should focus on each party providing constructive criticism or feedback to the other.

DNA Evidence

— Forensic DNA typing has become an integral part of the criminal justice system used by prosecutors to prove identity.

— DNA is used in many applications other than forensics, such as paternity determinations; identification of remains in mass tragedies and war; determination of plant, animal, and microorganism origins; and in pharmaceutical, wildlife, and diagnostic laboratories. The use of DNA in other fields assists the prosecutor's use of such evidence by demonstrating acceptance and reliance on DNA in scientific areas.

— The biologic materials collected by police officers and analyzed by forensic laboratories most commonly are blood and seminal fluid. These materials are the most likely to be left at the scene of a murder or sexual assault and are also replete with genetic material.

— Defense attorneys faced with DNA evidence linking their clients to the crimes charged may attack the validity of the evidence in an effort to prevent the jurors from ever seeing it. The appropriate time for such an attack is pretrial in an admissibility hearing.

— The Supreme Court provided a nonexclusive and nonexhaustive list of factors that judges should consider when determining reliability, as follows:

1. The testability of the theory or technique

2. Publication and peer review

3. Known or potential error rate

4. The existence of standards or protocols

5. General acceptance

— The prosecutor should avoid giving the fact finder a molecular biology lesson, offering detailed explanations of testing techniques, using technical and confusing demonstrative exhibits, and expecting the judge or jury to be fluent in the many scientific terms and acronyms associated with DNA (see *Chapter 10*).

— When presenting any DNA evidence, a qualified and competent expert is the witness who will be called to offer a brief, basic explanation of DNA. This person may be the scientist who performed laboratory testing of samples with DNA evidence or the director or supervisor of the laboratory.

— This witness will also define essential terms and present the test results. Visual displays may be helpful in demonstrating the profile rarity to the fact finder. How the statistical analysis was undertaken should also be discussed.

— The witness' education and training, forensic experience, nonforensic experience, publications, familiarity with professional literature, memberships and associations, and previous qualification as an expert are all elucidated for the jury or judge.

— The prosecutor can build trust in the witness' laboratory by questioning the expert about issues such as the laboratory following national forensic standards, quality assurance and control, internal validation of testing procedures, proficiency testing, laboratory and personnel accreditation, and peer review of the laboratory's work.

— The prosecutor can support the technology used and the results obtained by the testing laboratory by using the expert presented by the defense. The prosecutor must be prepared to question that expert on issues of bias, lack of forensic DNA typing experience, and amount of income derived from expert testimony.

— DNA database:

1. Rather than linking only a known suspect to a known crime scene sample, databases facilitate breakthroughs without traditional investigation, called "cold hits." Crime scene samples can immediately match suspects to cases, revealing serial crimes and prompting coordinated investigations.

2. While the statutes that create these databases vary widely, most detail the convictions that require sample submission and the procedure employed to limit access and ensure privacy.

— DNA has taken a prominent role in "post-conviction" proceedings such as habeas corpus and new trial petitions, pardons and clemency hearings, and parole and probation hearings.

THE TRIAL

— A criminal trial puts the burden on the state (or the commonwealth) to prove the legal elements of a crime beyond a reasonable doubt. There is no burden on the accused to prove anything.

— The accused need not testify or offer any witnesses, although he or she may elect to offer defense witnesses. From the time of the arrest, the accused is cloaked with the presumption of innocence that is removed only if there is a conviction.

— The role of the defense is to attack the state's evidence. This may be accomplished by offering evidence, defense witnesses, or the defendant's testimony.

Jury Selection

— Sexual assault trials may be decided by a jury or a judge.

1. In some states only the defense may choose between having a case heard before a judge or jury.

2. In other states, the prosecution may demand a jury trial even if the defense wants to waive the right to trial by jury and have a judge determine the verdict.

— The jury selection process is designed to create a forum of 12 persons who can listen to a case in a fair, impartial, and unbiased manner.

— The 12 jury members must agree to apply the judge's instructions about the law to the evidence as it is presented.

— Because sexual attitudes, including gender, sexual orientation, and morality, are usually deeply ingrained opinions determined by personal experience, education, and social class, jury selection becomes critically important.

Admissibility of Evidence

— For evidence to be considered admissible in a criminal trial, it must be relevant, reliable, and material to the issues at hand.

— The probative value must outweigh the prejudicial impact of the evidence.

— Preparation is key in establishing relevance and admissibility of evidence. The 5 general guidelines to preparation are as follows:

1. Know everything about the rule of evidence to be argued.

2. Know every detail about the testimony or physical evidence to be offered under the proposed rule and the purpose for its introduction.

3. Know how the evidence and current facts relate to existing case law.

4. Lay a solid foundation for the evidence at the pretrial hearing.

5. File all motions and briefs of record.

— Legislatures have passed rape shield laws to prevent the introduction of a victim's sexual life if it has no relevancy but to put the victim on trial.

— Evidence of other crimes is only admissible in narrowly drawn exceptions to the general rule of inadmissibility for evidence of previous bad acts.

— The jury must decide that the defendant committed the crime based on proof, not prejudice created by prior criminal convictions.

— However, prior convictions for crimes that support the defendant's commission of the crime on trial may be admissible if there is a common pattern that serves to prove intent or identity.

Defenses

— The most common defenses in adult sexual assault cases:

1. Consent, if the parties know each other and if there is corroboration of sexual contact

2. Misidentification, if the assailant is a stranger

3. Fabrication, if there is no corroboration of sexual contact

— The most common defenses with very young child victims:

1. Suggestibility of the child to adult questioning

2. Allegations that the child is fantasizing

3. Developmental immaturity leading to unreliable testimony

4. In divorce/custody situations, defense attorneys will sometimes contend one parent pressured a child into making a false accusation.

— The most common defenses in latency-age children and adolescents:

1. The child's retaliation for strict parenting and discipline

2. If the alleged offender is a stepparent or the companion of a parent, the child is accused of falsely disclosing abuse to get the defendant out of the house.

3. Consent is not usually raised with young victims because it is generally not a legal defense to child sexual abuse.

Outcomes

— In our criminal justice system the law enforcement officers and prosecutors must investigate sexual assault cases with great sensitivity and skill before arrest or trial. The prosecutor's job is not to seek convictions but to obtain justice.

— At the conclusion of a trial, the fact finder (whether a jury or a judge) reviews the evidence and arrives at a verdict. There is usually more than one criminal charge for the fact finder to consider.

— The defendant may be acquitted or convicted of all charges, or convicted of some and acquitted of others.

— If a jury cannot reach a unanimous verdict after a long period of deliberation, the jury is declared deadlocked and a mistrial (often referred to as a hung jury) is declared by the judge. A mistrial necessitates the case being tried again before another fact finder.

— If the defendant is convicted of a sex crime, the penalty is determined by state law. Most states have sentencing guidelines that give a suggested sentence for the crime in mitigated, standard, and aggravated ranges.

1. The mitigating or aggravating factors are decided by the sentencing judge.

2. Although a judge may deviate from the guideline recommendations, the reasons must be substantial.

3. In some states, certain sex crimes carry mandatory lengthy prison sentences. While treatment for sex offenders is available in prison facilities and outpatient clinics, the outcome of any treatment depends on many factors. Compulsive sexual behavior carries a great risk of recidivism.

REFERENCES

1. Avner JI; New York Governor's Task Force on Rape and Sexual Assault. *Rape, Sexual Assault, and Child Sexual Abuse: Working Towards a More Responsive Society.* Albany, NY: New York State Division for Women; 1990.

2. Brown ML. Dilemmas facing nurses who care for Munchausen syndrome by proxy patients. *Pediatr Nurs.* 1997;23(4):416-418.

3. Bulkley JA, Feller JN, Stern P, Roe R. Child abuse and neglect laws and legal proceedings. In: Briere J, Berliner L, Bulkley JA, Jenny C, Reid T, eds. *The APSAC Handbook on Child Maltreatment.* Thousand Oaks, CA: Sage Publications; 1996:271-296.

4. Burgess A, Holmstrom L. Rape trauma syndrome. *Am J Psychiatry.* 1974;131:981-986.

5. Canaff R. SANE testimony in child sex abuse cases: shedding light, dispelling myths for justice. *Center Piece.* 2010;2(3):1-7.

6. Ells M. Forming a multidisciplinary team to investigate child abuse. *Portable Guide to Investigating Child Abuse*. Washington, DC: US Department of Justice; 1998.

7. Fellmeth R. Legal issues. In: Chadwick DL, Alexander R, Giardino AP, Esernio-Jenssen D, Thackeray JD, eds. *Cultures at Risk and Role of Professionals*. Saint Louis, MO: STM Learning, Inc; 2014:261-286. *Chadwick's Child Maltreatment*; vol 3; 4th ed.

8. Fisher AJ, Svensson A, Wendel O. *Techniques of Crime Scene Investigation*. New York, NY: Elsevier; 1987.

9. Frioux SM, Lavelle JM. Forensic evidence collection. In: Chadwick DL, Alexander R, Giardino AP, Esernio-Jenssen D, Thackeray JD, eds. *Cultures at Risk and Role of Professionals*. Saint Louis, MO: STM Learning, Inc; 2014:371-380. *Chadwick's Child Maltreatment*; vol 3; 4th ed.

10. Fuller VM, Bell K. DNA evidence. In: Chadwick DL, Alexander R, Giardino AP, Esernio-Jenssen D, Thackeray JD, eds. *Cultures at Risk and Role of Professionals*. Saint Louis, MO: STM Learning, Inc; 2014:381-418. *Chadwick's Child Maltreatment*; vol 3; 4th ed.

11. Goldner JA, Dolgin CK, Manske SH. Legal issues. In: Monteleone J, ed. *Recognition of Child Abuse for the Mandated Reporter*. Saint Louis, MO: GW Medical Publishing; 1995:171-210.

12. Hazelwood RR, Lanning KV. Collateral materials in sexual crimes. In: Hazelwood RR, Burgess AW, eds. *Practical Aspects of Rape Investigation: A Multidisciplinary Approach*. 3rd ed. Boca Raton, FL: CRC Press; 2001:221-232.

13. Heiman W, Ponterio A, Fairman G. Prosecuting rape cases: trial preparation and trial tactic issues. In: Hazelwood RR, Burgess AW, eds. *Practical Aspects of Rape Investigation: A Multidisciplinary Approach*. 3rd ed. Boca Raton, FL: CRC Press; 2001:347-364.

14. Henry JB. *Clinical Diagnosis and Management*. Philadelphia, PA: WB Saunders Co; 1979.

15. Holmes WC, Slap GB. Sexual abuse of boys: definition, prevalence, correlates, sequelae, and management. *JAMA*. 1998;280(21):1855-1862.

16. Kinnee KR. *Practical Investigation Techniques.* Boca Raton, FL: CRC Press; 1995.

17. Kirkpatrick DG, Edmunds CN, Seymour AK. *Rape in America: A Report to the Nation.* Arlington, VA: National Victim Center; 1992.

18. Leo R. Interrogations and false confessions in rape cases. In: Hazelwood RR, Burgess AW, eds. *Practical Aspects of Rape Investigation: A Multidisciplinary Approach.* 3rd ed. Boca Raton, FL: CRC Press; 2001:234-242.

19. MacDonald JM. *Police Response to Rape.* Springfield, IL: Charles C Thomas; 1995:140.

20. Myers JEB. *Legal Issues in Child Abuse and Neglect Practice.* 2nd ed. Thousand Oaks, CA: Sage Publications; 1998.

21. Myers JEB. *Myers on Evidence of Interpersonal Violence: Child Maltreatment, Intimate Partner Violence, Rape, Stalking, and Elder Abuses.* 5th ed. New York, NY: Wolters Kluwer; 2011.

22. Myers JEB. Expert testimony. In: JEB Myers, ed. *Legal Issues in Child Abuse and Neglect Practice.* Thousand Oaks, CA: Sage Publications; 1998:221-281.

23. National Cybercrime Training Partnership. *Cyber Crime Fighting: The Law Enforcement Officer's Guide to Online Crime.* Washington, DC: Computer Crimes and Intellectual Property Section, US Department of Justice; 1999.

24. National Institute of Justice. *Electronic Crime Scene Investigation: A Guide for First Responders.* Washington, DC: National Institute of Justice, US Department of Justice; 2001.

25. Panichas GE. Rape, autonomy, and consent. *Law & Society Review.* 2001;35(1):231-270.

26. Parrish RN, Letson RA. Preparing a case for court. In: Chadwick DL, Alexander R, Giardino AP, Esernio-Jenssen D, Thackeray JD, eds. *Cultures at Risk and Role of Professionals.* Saint Louis, MO: STM Learning, Inc; 2014:223-260. *Chadwick's Child Maltreatment*; vol 3; 4th ed.

27. Ricci LR, Wientzen J. Preparing to give expert testimony. In: Chadwick DL, Alexander R, Giardino AP, Esernio-Jenssen D, Thackeray JD, eds. *Cultures at Risk and Role of Professionals*. Saint Louis, MO: STM Learning, Inc; 2014:287-298. *Chadwick's Child Maltreatment*; vol 3; 4th ed.

28. Rich J, Michaels J. The role of law enforcement in child abuse cases. In: Chadwick DL, Alexander R, Giardino AP, Esernio-Jenssen D, Thackeray JD, eds. *Cultures at Risk and Role of Professionals*. Saint Louis, MO: STM Learning, Inc; 2014:161-178. *Chadwick's Child Maltreatment*; vol 3; 4th ed.

29. Schulhofer SJ. *Unwanted Sex: The Culture of Intimidation and the Failure of Law*. Cambridge, MA: Harvard University Press; 1998.

30. Smith C. Police investigations atlas. In: Chadwick DL, Alexander R, Giardino AP, Esernio-Jenssen D, Thackeray JD, eds. *Cultures at Risk and Role of Professionals*. Saint Louis, MO: STM Learning, Inc; 2014:673-694. *Chadwick's Child Maltreatment*; vol 3; 4th ed.

31. Spaulding RP, Bigbee PD. Physical evidence in sexual assault investigations. In: Hazelwood RR, Burgess AW, eds. *Practical Aspects of Rape Investigation: A Multidisciplinary Approach*. 3rd ed. Boca Raton, FL: CRC Press; 2001:261-298.

32. *State v. Love*, 936 SW2d 236 (Mo Ct App 1997).

33. US Secret Service, International Association of Chiefs of Police, National Institute of Justice. *Best Practices for Seizing Electronic Evidence*. Washington, DC: US Secret Service, International Association of Chiefs of Police, National Institute of Justice; 2002.

34. Vieth VI. The forensic interviewer at trial: guidelines for the admission and scope of expert witness testimony concerning an investigative interview in a case of child abuse. *William Mitchell Law Review*. 2009;36(1):186-219.

35. Vieth VI. Investigating and prosecuting cases of child abuse. In: Chadwick DL, Alexander R, Giardino AP, Esernio-Jenssen D, Thackeray JD, eds. *Cultures at Risk and Role of Professionals*. Saint Louis, MO: STM Learning, Inc; 2014:179-222. *Chadwick's Child Maltreatment*; vol 3; 4th ed.

36. Vieth VI. When the child has spoken: corroborating the forensic interview. *Center Piece*. 2010;2(5):1-6.

37. Wicklander DE, Zulawski DE. *Practical Aspects of Interview and Interrogation*. Boca Raton, FL: CRC Press; 1993.

Chapter 18

SEXUAL ASSAULT RESPONSE IN THE UNITED STATES MILITARY

CDR Barbara Mullen (FNP), NC, USN*
Tawnne O'Connor, RN, BSN

OVERVIEW OF THE UNITED STATES MILITARY

To understand sexual assault and official military policy, one must understand the overall organization of the US Military. The military falls under the Department of Defense (DoD) and is directed by the Secretary of Defense, a Cabinet member who reports to the President.

BRANCHES OF THE DOD

— The DoD comprises 3 main branches: the Army, the Navy and Marine Corps, and the Air Force.

— Each branch has a unique mission and guiding principles, ie, core values.

— Each branch comprises 2 components: active and reserve.

US Army

— Consists of active duty component, Army Reserves, and the National Guard

---

*This contributor would like to note the following disclaimer: "The views expressed in this article are those of the author and do not necessarily reflect the official policy or position of the Department of the Navy, Department of Defense, nor the US Government. I am a military service member. This work was prepared as part of my official duties. Title 17, USC, §105 provides that 'Copyright protection under this title is not available for any work of the United States Government.' Title 17, USC, §101 defines a US Government work as a work prepared by a military service member or employee of the US Government as part of that person's official duties."

— 7 core values of the US Army:

1. *Loyalty:* Bear true faith and allegiance to the US Constitution, the Army, and all soldiers.

2. *Duty:* To fulfill one's obligations

3. *Respect:* Treating people as they should be treated

4. *Selfless Service:* Put the needs of others, including the nation and the Army, first.

5. *Honor:* Living up to all the Army values

6. *Integrity:* Do what is right, legally and morally.

7. *Personal Courage:* Face fear, danger, or adversity.

US Navy

Both the Navy and the Marine Corps have an active duty and reserve component and they share the same set of core values:

1. *Honor:* Maintain professionalism at all times.

2. *Courage:* The strength, both mentally and morally, to do what is right.

3. *Commitment:* Work as a team to achieve the mission.

US Air Force

— Composed of active duty components, reserve components, and the Air National Guard

— There are 3 core values of the US Air Force:

1. *Integrity First:* Do what is right.

2. *Service Before Self:* Professional duty comes before personal desires.

3. *Excellence In All We Do:* Continuously improve performance.

LEGAL SYSTEM

— All military service members are subject to the Uniform Code of Military Justice (UCMJ),* a codified statute enacted to ensure good order and discipline and to deal with service members who violate the law.

---

*Falls under Title 10, Subtitle A, Part II, Chapter 47 of US Code

— The UCMJ defines criminal acts, including minor violations, military-specific offenses, and serious common law offenses, and sets forth the methods through which commanding officers can legally manage such violations.

COURTS-MARTIAL AND OTHER MILITARY DISCIPLINE

— When an individual violates the UCMJ, options range from hearing the case before the commanding officer to a court-martial.

— A court-martial is a military trial heard in a military courtroom setting.

— There are 3 types of courts-martial, and each varies with respect to who convenes the court-martial.

General Court-Martial

— Can only be convened by flag officers, general officers, or commanding officers at an overseas command

— Reserved for the most serious offenses

— The accused may choose who hears the case: either a judge or a judge *and* a panel of at least 5 military members.

— Maximum punishments vary by offense and include:

1. Fines

2. Loss of all pay and allowances

3. Loss of rank (for enlisted members)

4. Dishonorable or bad-conduct discharge (for enlisted members)

5. Dismissal (for officers)

6. Confinement in military prison (up to life)

7. Death penalty

Special Court-Martial

— Can be convened by any commanding officer or authorized individual, regardless of command location

— Used for lesser offenses

— The accused may choose who hears the case: a judge or a judge *and* at least 3 military members.

— Maximum punishments include:

1. One year's hard labor confinement

2. Forfeiture of two-thirds of one month's pay for one year

3. Loss of all rank (for enlisted members)

4. Bad-conduct discharge

Summary Court-Martial

— Can be convened by an individual authorized to convene a special court-martial, an officer-in-charge, and all other active duty commanding officers

— Reserved for minor offenses by enlisted members

— One commissioned officer presides

— Maximum punishments include:

1. Reduction in grade

2. One month's hard labor confinement

3. 45 days' hard labor without confinement

4. Forfeiture of two-thirds of one month's pay

5. Two months' restriction

Other Military Discipline

— Nonjudicial punishment (authorized under Article 15) permits commanding officers to hear a case and determine punishment, including restriction, pay or grade reduction, or extra duty.

— Administrative action holds military members accountable for problematic action, and punishments may include administrative separation, reassignment, and career field reclassification.

DEFINITIONS OF RAPE AND SEXUAL ASSAULT IN THE MILITARY
OFFENSES CHARGEABLE UNDER ARTICLE 120
Article 120 of the UCMJ covers rape and sexual assault (**Table 18-1**).

Table 18-1. Offenses Chargeable Under Article 120	
— Aggravated sexual assault	— Indecent liberty with a child
— Aggravated sexual assault of a child	— Indecent acts
— Aggravated sexual contact	— Forcible pandering
— Aggravated sexual abuse of a child	— Wrongful sexual contact
— Aggravated sexual contact with a child	— Indecent exposure
— Abusive sexual contact	— Rape
— Abusive sexual contact with a child	— Rape of a child

Definitions of Rape and Sexual Assault

— *Rape:* occurs when there is sexual penetration with grievous bodily harm/threats of grievous bodily harm, ie, force resulting in serious bodily injury; when a perpetrator uses force, including display of a weapon, that prevents a victim from avoiding sexual contact; when a perpetrator renders a victim unconscious; or when an administered intoxicant leaves a victim unable to consent to a sexual act.

  — If the victim is younger than 12 years old, any sexual act is rape.

  — If the victim is 12 years old, criteria for rape of an adult must be met to be charged as rape of a child.

  — Intercourse with a child between 12 and 15 years old, absent any definitions for adult rape, will be charged as aggravated sexual assault of a child.

— *Sexual assault:* occurs when there is sexual penetration with nongrievous bodily harm/threats that do not constitute bodily harm, eg, a threat by a supervisor to ruin a victim's career, or when the victim is unable to appraise/consent to the sexual act, eg, when asleep or intoxicated.

— *Aggravated sexual contact:* occurs when there is no sexual penetration but, had there been penetration, the surrounding circumstances would have met one of the definitions of rape.

— *Abusive sexual contact:* occurs when there is no sexual penetration and the surrounding circumstances would have met one of the definitions of aggravated sexual assault.

— **Wrongful sexual contact**: any sexual contact without consent

— **Sodomy***: oral or anal sexual assault/rape of a male or female victim

—**Table 18-2** lists maximum punishments under Article 120.

Table 18-2. Article 120 Maximum Punishments	
USMC Violation (Article 120)	Punishment
Rape/rape of child	Death/life
Aggravated sexual assault	30 years
Aggravated sexual assault of child	20 years
Aggravated sexual abuse of child	20 years
Aggravated sexual contact (adult or child)	20 years
Abusive sexual contact with child	15 years
Indecent liberty with child	15 years
Abusive sex contact	7 years
Indecent act/forcible pandering	5 years
Wrongful sex contact	1 year
Indecent exposure	1 year

SEXUAL ASSAULT PREVENTION AND RESPONSE

The DoD established the Sexual Assault Prevention and Response (SAPR) program in 2005 with the objective of establishing a standardized system for training, prevention, and responding to and reporting sexual assault.

SEXUAL ASSAULT RESPONSE COORDINATOR (SARC)

— Serves as installation and regional coordinator for sexual assault response

— Primary responsibilities include:

1. Managing sexual assault response teams (SARTs): (See *Chapter 16* for more information.)

Falls under Title 10, Subtitle A, Part II, Chapter 47 of US Code

2. Coordinating care for victims: The SARC ensures that appropriate care is coordinated and provided from initial report through final disposition and resolution. Care occurs either within a military treatment facility or a civilian facility with a memorandum of understanding (MOU).

3. Overseeing sexual assault training for the region: For military members, awareness and prevention training is provided upon entry into the military and on an annual basis. Training for victim advocates, health care providers, chaplains, and those involved in legal and investigate processes is extensive and specific to each individual's role in the process of caring for sexual assault victims.

— The SARC is also responsible for the victim advocate (VA) program. VAs are volunteers specially trained in sexual assault advocacy who provide support and education on reporting options to victims from the time of medical treatment until the case is resolved.

RESTRICTED AND UNRESTRICTED REPORTING

To encourage active duty members to report sexual assault, the DoD established 2 types of reporting under DoD Directive (DODD) 6495.01: unrestricted and restricted (**Tables 18-3** and **18-4**). Both allow victims to receive medical care, evidence collection, follow-up care, and counseling.

Table 18-3. Unrestricted Reporting

— Initiates a full investigation involving legal, security, and investigative services

— The victim's commander is notified and provided with the victim's name.

— A case management team reviews each case on a monthly basis.

— The case management team consists of:

1. The SARC	5. A health care provider
2. The VA	6. A chaplain
3. A military criminal investigator	7. A command legal representative
4. A member of military law enforcement	8. A clinic counselor
	9. The victim's commander (possibly)

Table 18-4. Restricted Reporting

— Does not involve legal, security, or investigative service notification

— The victim's commander is notified of the sexual assault but *not* provided with any identifying information, eg, the victim's name.

— The SARC and the VA ensure the victim's access to an advocate, counseling services, and follow-up care and maintain the victim's confidentiality.

— The victim has up to one year to change the report to unrestricted.

REFERENCES

1. Department of Defense. Sexual Assault Prevention and Response (SAPR) Program. October, 6, 2005. DODD 6495.01.

2. Department of Defense. Sexual Assault Prevention and Response (SAPR) Program Procedures. June 23, 2006. DODI 6495.02.

3. Dewey E. Sexual assault nurse examiners and the courtroom. Paper presented at: Sexual Assault Nurse Examiner Training Course; October 28, 2008; Yokosuka, Japan.

4. Joint Service Committee on Military Justice. *Manual for Courts-Martial United States (2012 Edition)*. Washington, DC: US Department of Defense; 2012.

5. Naval Justice School. *Note Taking Guide for Legal Officers*. San Diego, CA: Naval Justice School—Detachment San Diego; 2006.

6. Task Force on Care for Victims of Sexual Assault. Task force report on care for victims on sexual assault. US Department of Defense Web site. http://www.defense.gov/news/May2004/d20040513SATFReport.pdf. Published April 2004. Accessed June 10, 2015.

7. Uniform Code of Military Justice. Uniform Code of Military Justice Web site. http://www.ucmj.us. Accessed June 9, 2015.

8. US Air Force. Homepage. US Air Force Web site. http://www.airforce.com. Accessed June 9, 2015.

9. US Army. Homepage. US Army Web site. http://www.goarmy.com. Accessed June 9, 2015.

10. US Department of Defense Sexual Assault Prevention and Response. Homepage. US Department of Defense Sexual Assault Prevention and Response Web site. http://www.sapr.mil. Accessed June 10, 2015.

11. US Navy. Homepage. US Navy Web site. http://www.navy.mil. Accessed June 9, 2015.

Chapter 19

Human Trafficking

Imelda Buncab, BA
Annie Heirendt, LCSW

Trafficked persons include forced or voluntary foreign migrants motivated by a desire to escape poverty, improve their economic situation, leave behind abusive relationships, flee war torn countries, escape gender discrimination, evade religious persecution, or simply seek opportunities for a better life. They can be born into exploitation through a practice known as inherited-debt bonded labor, perpetuated by widely tolerated cultural beliefs. Once trafficked, they are subjected to physical, sexual, and psychological abuse through forced labor, commercial sex, and slavery-like practices.

Overview of Human Trafficking

— Human trafficking nets tens of billions of dollars annually and is one of the top illegal activities conducted by organized criminal syndicates.

— Sex trafficking alone nets $7 billion to $19 billion annually.

— Worldwide, there are, at any one time:

— 27 million enslaved people

— 12.3 million people subjected to forced labor

— 2.5 million people victimized by human trafficking

— The United States receives 14 500 to 17 500 trafficked persons annually.

Characteristics of Traffickers and Trafficked Persons

— Traffickers are often of the same ethnicity as their victims, may come from the same communities, and may know their victims through friends or relatives.

— Traffickers may belong to privileged groups, eg, religious leaders, business owners, community leaders, or diplomats.

— Traffickers can be individual males or females, small operations of friends, family members or acquaintances, owners of small to medium-sized businesses, or brokers.

— Likelihood of becoming trafficked increases with certain vulnerabilities, including:

1. Poverty

2. Civil strife

3. Natural disaster

4. Political instability

5. Religious persecution

6. Family violence

7. Marginalization for:

   — Ethnic minority status

   — Sexual orientation

   — Gender

   — Disability

TRAFFICKER-VICTIM DYNAMICS
METHODS OF CONTROL: COERCION AND FEAR

— Traffickers utilize psychological coercion to prevent dissension and escape.

— Traffickers may threaten trafficked persons and their families with torture and death. Such threats cause psychological turmoil and internalized hopelessness in trafficked persons.

— Traffickers may withhold legal documents, eg, passports and ID cards, from trafficked persons or threaten foreign nationals with deportation.

— Traffickers may tell trafficked persons that they must repay debts for transport, room, and boarding and either pay their victims in a manner adverse to savings or withhold payment altogether.

— Traffickers may utilize drugs and alcohol to subdue and manipulate trafficked persons, lower their inhibitions, and foster dependence on the traffickers themselves.

— Traffickers may isolate trafficked persons to maintain their dependence.

— Trafficked persons may have some freedom of movement but still experience control by timed/monitored trips outside the trafficking environment or warnings against interacting with others while in public.

— Trafficked persons may be geographically isolated to remote, rural locations.

— Traffickers may convince trafficked persons that they deserve subjugation for karma, past sins, or other spiritual convictions.

— Trafficked persons who are sexually assaulted may experience paralyzing shame, and they may fear marginalization in their home communities. Traffickers may threaten to disclose sexual assault to the families of these trafficked persons.

IDENTIFYING TRAFFICKED PERSONS
OBSTACLES
— Obstacles to victim identification include:

1. Lack of awareness among practitioners

2. Language barriers

3. Trafficker accompaniment

4. Distrust of authorities among trafficked persons

5. Fear of retaliation

— Trafficked individuals may not self-perceive as victims; blame themselves for their situation; or form attachments to their traffickers, exacerbated by long-term effects of psychological coercion.

PRACTITIONER ASSESSMENT AND RESPONSE

— Practitioners should be aware of the indicators of trafficking*
highlighted in **Table 19-1**.

— In cases of suspected human trafficking, practitioners should refer
to the assessment questions in **Table 19-2**.

Table 19-1. Observational and Verbal Cues That Possible Trafficked Persons/Trafficking Survivors May Exhibit
OBSERVATIONAL AND VERBAL CUES
— Patient presents to the practitioner accompanied by an escort posing as a family member, acquaintance, or friend
— Escort talks on behalf of the patient
— Patient is overly complicit to practitioner's and/or escort's suggestions
— Patient defers to the escort to answer basic questions
— Patient does not know basic personal information, such as where he or she lives or his or her phone number
— Patient provides vague background information
— Patient does not have identification available
— Patient is disoriented as to location
— Patient either seems hesitant to leave with escort or uncomfortable with practitioner and clingy to escort
— Patient presents with symptoms of self-neglect
— Signs of physical abuse are present
— Possible language barrier
— Patient seems concerned about time spent alone with medical professional
— Patient seems hypervigilant
— Patient discloses suicidality or homicidality

Practitioners should be careful not to confuse indicators of sexual assault or domestic violence for indicators of trafficking (see Chapter 13).

Table 19-2. Human Trafficking Identification Questions

QUESTIONS

— Can you leave your job or situation if you want?

— Can you come and go as you please?

— Have you been threatened if you try to leave?

— Have you been physically harmed in any way?

— What are your working or living conditions like?

— Where do you sleep and eat?

— Do you sleep in a bed, on a cot, or on the floor?

— Have you ever been deprived of food, water, sleep, or medical care?

— Do you have to ask permission to eat, sleep, or go to the bathroom?

— Are there locks on your doors and windows so you cannot get out?

— Has anyone threatened your family?

— Has your identification or documentation been taken from you?

— Is anyone forcing you to do anything that you do not want to do?

— Because trafficked persons are often accompanied by traffickers, practitioners should speak with potential trafficked persons in a safe, private setting.

— Unless an individual's life is in imminent danger, practitioners should not act on behalf of trafficked persons or seek to remove them from their situation unless a patient requests such assistance.

— Practitioners should report suspected human trafficking to the US Department of Justice and US Department of Labor Trafficking in Persons and Worker Exploitation Task Force toll-free complaint line (1-888-428-7581).*

*Operators have access to interpreters.

Mental Health Impacts of Trafficking

— Trafficked persons experience high levels of trauma and may present with depression, anxiety, PTSD, and cooccurring disorders.

— One specific event does not cause trauma; rather, the traumatic reaction is a culmination of personal and environmental factors that either contribute to or defuse an individual's trauma reaction. On one end of the spectrum would be a single traumatic incident in which the individual experiences a threat to the physical integrity of self or others; normal childhood development and no preexisting mental health impairments would defuse the effects of the traumatic event. On the other end of the spectrum are individuals who experience pervasive, invasive trauma with environmental and personal stressors. A typical trafficked person rests at this end of the spectrum (see **Figure 19-1**).

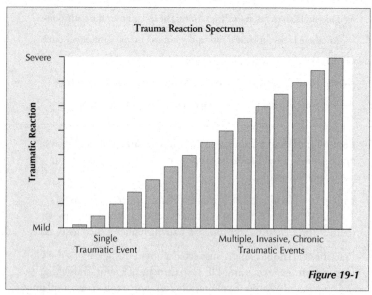

Figure 19-1. A typical trafficked person rests at the end of the spectrum and is at risk for suffering severe trauma reactions due to personal, interpersonal, and environmental contributors inherent to human trafficking.

— Trafficking survivors may experience a variety of factors that increase trauma reactions with few buffers to minimize traumatic reactions (see **Table 19-3**).

— Trafficked persons frequently experience panic attacks, which may culminate in agoraphobia. They may limit public activities or restrict movement to specific safe locations in order to feel safe in a world perceived as unsafe or hostile.

— Trafficked persons may present with symptoms congruent with PTSD, ie, increased arousal, avoidance of trauma-related stimuli, and reexperiencing.

— PTSD or acute stress disorder may not be the most appropriate diagnosis for trafficked persons experiencing severe distress. Literature shows that PTSD symptomatology is not pervasive enough in its scope to account for the experiences of chronic trauma victims.

— Trafficked persons may experience chronic PTSD or disorders of extreme stress not otherwise specified (DESNOS), characterized by interpersonal trauma, multiple traumatic events, or prolonged trauma. DESNOS includes alterations in self-regulation and interpersonal functioning in 7 key areas, as detailed in **Table 19-4**.

Table 19-3. Factors That Increase Traumatic Reaction	
PERSONAL	ENVIRONMENTAL
— Childhood trauma	— Inadequate legal support and complicity
— Mental health disorder	— Marginalization
— Genetic predisposition	— Environmental deprivation
— Low education level	— Low socioeconomic status
— Personality	— Community violence
— Drug/alcohol use	— National disaster
— Gender status	— Inadequate social support
— Cognitive deficits	— Family violence
	— Cultural stigma regarding traumatic incident

Table 19-4. DESNOS Characteristics

SELF-PERCEPTION

— Trafficked person may view self as damaged, ie, as "damaged goods"

— Trafficked person may feel sense of guilt or responsibility, eg, "I must have done something to deserve this." or "I trusted that person, so I am to blame."

— Trafficked person may feel a profound sense of shame

DISSOCIATION

— Trafficked person may experience derealization, ie, experience as the unreality of surroundings

— Trafficked person may experience depersonalization, which is experienced as the unreality of self, eg, "I feel like I am in a dream."

EMOTIONAL SELF-REGULATION

— Trafficked person may experience reduction in the ability to control impulses, ie, anger, management, eating disorders

— Trafficked person may report feelings of persistent distress

— Trafficked person may engage in self-harm behaviors, eg, cutting

— Trafficked person may engage in risky behaviors, eg, drug use

— Trafficked person may experience strong suicidal and/or homicidal urges

SOMATIZATION

— Trafficked person may experience chronic pain in addition to symptoms that may affect or be observed to affect sexual, digestive, and cardiopulmonary domains

UNSTABLE RELATIONSHIP PATTERNS

— Trafficked person may experience distrust of others

— Trafficked person may recreate trauma by victimizing others

— Trafficked person may make self vulnerable to revictimization, eg, by accepting jobs with unsafe work conditions, engaging in high-risk sexual behaviors, and placing self in environments that have a high risk for abuse *(continued)*

Table 19-4. DESNOS Characteristics *(continued)*

PERCEPTION OF PERPETRATOR(S)

— Trafficked person may adopt distorted beliefs toward the perpetrator(s)

— Trafficked person may idealize the perpetrator(s)

— Trafficked person may have revenge fantasies and a sense of wanting to get even with perpetrator(s)

SHIFT IN SYSTEMS OF MEANING

— Trafficked person may experience loss of faith in previous belief, eg, "How can I believe that God is good if this happened to me?" or "What did I do in a past life to deserve this?"

— Trafficked person may experience sense of hopelessness and despair for the future resulting from traumatization

Adapted from van der Kolk B, Roth S, Pelcovitz D, Sunday S, Spinazzola J.[27]

— Trafficked persons may present with a higher incidence of borderline personality traits than the general population.*

— Trafficked persons are at risk for revictimization through engagement in unhealthy and abusive relationships.

— Sex trafficking victims may engage in independent sexual solicitation or avoid sexual expression altogether.

— Trafficked persons may resort to impulsive self-injurious behaviors, eg, cutting, repetitive pinching, burning, scraping, or hair pulling, as a means to cope with the numbness of dissociation or the painful feelings that overwhelm their coping capacities.

— Trafficked persons may engage in substance abuse to overcome the numbing associated with traumatic responses, allowing physical and emotional feeling (**Figure 19-2**).

Borderline personality disorder criteria overlap with DESNOS symptomatology, making differential diagnosis a challenge.

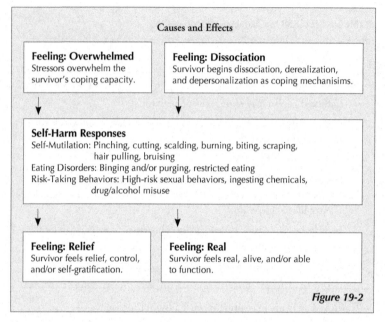

Figure 19-2. This figure displays the different types of self-harm that a survivor may carry out and the emotions felt upon inflicting that self-harm.

GENDER DIFFERENCES AND TRAUMA REACTION

— Culturally bound gender roles may deter trafficked males from disclosing mental health consequences of their trafficking experience.

— Preconceptions of masculinity may deter reporting of sexual assault in trafficked males.

— Males tend to utilize avoidance as a coping mechanism and develop lower levels of PTSD than women.

PHYSICAL HEALTH IMPACTS OF TRAFFICKING

PHYSICAL INJURIES

— Traffickers frequently use violence as a means of control, causing trafficked persons to present with signs of physical abuse.

— Sex trafficking victims may show signs of physical assault in areas of their body that do not alter their physical appearance (**Figure 19-3**).

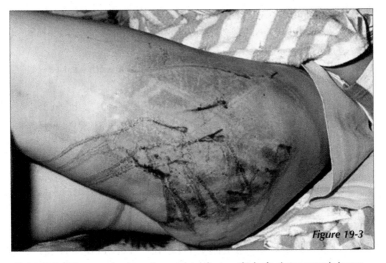

Figure 19-3. *This woman has lacerations on her left upper thigh after being severely beaten with a wire coat hanger as punishment for her disobedience to the trafficker. (Provided with permission by Detective Rick Castro.)*

— Signs of physical abuse may include cigarette burns, chemical burns, or heated liquid burns.

— Trafficked persons may present with head trauma resulting from bashing, falls from shoving, and beatings with household appliances; therefore, diagnosing possible untreated internal injuries is an important intervention for health care practitioners.

— Labor trafficking victims may present with muscle and joint pain in addition to severe injuries.

— Unregulated work environments, eg, sweatshops and trafficked construction work, expose individuals to:

1. Unsafe chemicals
2. Broken bones
3. Heat stroke
4. Skin damage
5. Stab wounds
6. Oral injuries
7. Skin infections
8. Respiratory disease

— In the agricultural sector, trafficked persons are exposed to pesticides and chemicals linked to depression, headaches, and neurological disorders.

— Trafficked persons may be subjected to inadequate living conditions for prolonged periods and may present with a variety of physical symptoms of neglect.

— Trafficked persons may have food withheld, may be subjected to inadequate diets, experience sleep deprivation, or experience overcrowding and improper sanitation, increasing trafficked persons' vulnerability to illness.

— Due to a lack of access to medical care and treatment, trafficked persons may present with a variety of chronic care needs.

— Trafficked persons may not have access to immunizations, increasing disease prevalence.

— Trafficked persons may have a higher prevalence of tuberculosis, malaria, hepatitis, and other infectious diseases.

SEXUAL HEALTH

— In general, trafficked persons have little to no education in safe sex practices, and STIs are overwhelmingly common among trafficked populations.

— The United Nations and World Health Organization have identified trafficked persons as a population at increased risk for HIV infection.

— Trafficked persons may be at increased risk for HIV and other STIs because of sexual abuse and the psychological conditions resulting from that abuse.*

— Trafficked persons who are HIV-positive may struggle with the stigma of that diagnosis, which may be exacerbated by socialization within communities of origin.

— Trafficked persons may feel that they have been given a death sentence due to observations of those with HIV in their home communities and lack of access to treatment.

Individuals with a history of trauma are at an increased risk for HIV transmission due to their likely engagement in higher-risk behavior.

— Trafficked persons may have a variety of misconceptions regarding HIV and may benefit from bolstered support, education, and assistance in accessing resources, including treatment options.

— Trafficked persons may resist STI testing due to potential marginalization within their respective communities, or they may negatively associate gynecological care with incurred abuses, eg, unwanted pregnancy, forced abortion, repeated sexual assault, or unsanitary health care.

— When testing trafficked persons, practitioners should do their best to return as much control as possible to their patients, eg, by agreeing on a signal to end the test when the patient feels overwhelmed and/ or by talking the patient through tests as they occur.

— Forensic examinations establish a criminal case against abusers, forensically confirm and document that a sexual encounter has occurred, and examine physical abuse; however, trafficked persons who experience multiple sexual encounters over a prolonged period do not typically benefit from such examinations because their abuse is not due to one particular incident.

— Because examinations are intrusive and can be overwhelming, trafficked persons should be informed that examinations are optional.

— Language and cultural barriers can hinder the ability of trafficked persons to fully participate in sexual assault examinations; therefore, practitioners caring for individuals whose English is limited or nonexistent should consider including a properly vetted translator before, during, and after the exam.

HEALTH CONSEQUENCES OF TRAFFICKING

Injuries suffered by trafficked persons, and the resulting physical and mental health consequences, are pervasive, ranging in severity from chronic symptomatologies to death (**Table 19-5**).

TRAUMA-INFORMED PRACTICE

— Operating from a trauma-informed model of care is imperative, as survivors often experience multiple forms of abuse with physiological ramifications. For example, arthritis and diabetes are associated with trauma in men, and among women, both cancer and digestive diseases are linked to trauma.

Table 19-5. Trafficking in Women: Health Consequences and Forms of Risk and Abuse

FORMS OF RISK AND ABUSE	POTENTIAL HEALTH CONSEQUENCES
Physical Abuse	**Physical Health**
— Murder	— Death
— Physical attacks (beating with or without an object, kicking, knifing, whipping, and gunshots)	— Acute and chronic physical injuries (contusions, lacerations, head trauma, concussion, scarring)
— Physical deprivation (sleep, food, light, basic necessities)	— Acute and chronic physical disabilities (nerve, muscle, or bone damage; sensory damage; dental problems)
— Physical restraint (ropes, cuffs)	— Fatigue exhaustion
— Withholding medical or other essential care	— Poor nutrition, malnutrition, starvation
	— Deterioration of preexisting conditions leading to disability or death
Sexual Abuse	**Sexual and Reproductive Health**
— Forced vaginal, oral, or anal sex; gang rape; degrading sexual acts	— HIV/AIDS
— Forced prostitution, inability to control number or acceptance of clients	— Sexually transmitted infections (STIs) and related complications, including pelvic inflammatory disease (PID), urinary tract infections (UTIs), cystitis, cervical cancer, and infertility
— Forced unprotected sex and sex without lubricants	— Amenorrhea and dysmenorrhea
— Unwanted pregnancy, forced abortion, unsafe abortion	— Acute or chronic pain during sex; tearing and other damage to vaginal tract
— Sexual humiliation, forced nakedness	— Negative outcomes of unsafe abortion, including cervical incontinence, septic shock, unwanted birth
— Coerced misuse of oral contraceptives or other contraceptive methods	— Irritable bowel syndrome, stress-related syndromes
	— Inability to negotiate sexual encounters *(continued)*

Table 19-5. Trafficking in Women: Health Consequences and Forms of Risk and Abuse *(continued)*

FORMS OF RISK AND ABUSE	POTENTIAL HEALTH CONSEQUENCES
Psychological Abuse	**Mental Health**
— Intimidation of and threats to women and their loved ones — Lies, deception, and blackmail to coerce women, to discourage women from seeking help from authorities or others; lies about authorities, local situation, legal status, family members — Emotional manipulation by boyfriend-perpetrator — Unpredictable and uncontrolled events and environment — Isolation and forced dependency (see "social restrictions and manipulation")	— Suicidal thoughts, self-harm, suicide — Chronic anxiety, sleep disturbances, frequent nightmares, chronic fatigue, diminished coping capacity — Memory loss, memory defects, dissociation — Somatic complaints, eg, chronic headache, stomach pain, trembling; immune suppression — Depression, frequent crying, withdrawal, difficulty concentrating — Aggressiveness, violent outbursts, violence against others — Substance misuse, addiction — Loss of trust in others or self, problems with or changes in identity and self-esteem, guilt, shame, difficulty developing and maintaining intimate relationships
Forced and Coerced Use of Drugs and Alcohol	**Substance Abuse and Misuse**
Nonconsensual administration and use of alcohol or drugs in order to: — Abduct, rape, prostitute women — Control activities, coerce compliance, impose long work hours, coerce women to engage in degrading or dangerous acts — Decrease self-protective defenses, increase compliance — Prevent women from leaving or escaping	— Overdose, self-harm, death, suicide — Participation in unwanted sexual acts, unprotected and high-risk sexual acts, high-risk activities, violence, crime — Addiction — Brain or liver damage, including precancerous conditions — Needle-introduced infection, including HIV and hepatitis C — Dependence on drugs, alcohol, or cigarettes to cope with abuse, stress, anxiety, fear, work, long hours, pain, personal disgust, cold, physical deprivation, insomnia, fatigue

(continued)

Table 19-5. Trafficking in Women: Health Consequences and Forms of Risk and Abuse *(continued)*

FORMS OF RISK AND ABUSE	POTENTIAL HEALTH CONSEQUENCES
Social Restrictions and Manipulation	**Social Well-being**
— Restrictions on movement, time, and activities; confinement; surveillance; manipulative scheduling in order to restrict contact with others and formation of helping relationships	— Feelings of isolation, loneliness, exclusion
— Frequent relocation	— Inability to establish and maintain helping or supportive relationships, mistrust of others, social withdrawal, personal insecurity
— Absence of social support, denial or loss of contact with family, friends, ethnic and local communities	— Poor overall health from lack of exercise, healthy socializing, health-promoting activities
— Emotional manipulation by boyfriends-perpetrators	— Vulnerability to infection from lack of information, deteriorating conditions from restricted health screening, lack of treatment
— Favoritism or perquisites with the goal of causing divisiveness between coworkers and discouraging formation of friendships	— Difficulty with (re)integration, difficulty developing healthy relationships, feelings of loneliness, alienations, helplessness, aggressiveness
— Denial of or control over access to health and other services	— Shunned, rejected by family, community, society, boyfriends
— Denial of privacy or control over privacy	— Retrafficked, reentry into high-risk labor and relationships

(continued)

Table 19-5. Trafficking in Women: Health Consequences and Forms of Risk and Abuse *(continued)*

FORMS OF RISK AND ABUSE	POTENTIAL HEALTH CONSEQUENCES
Economic Exploitation and Debt Bondage	**Economic-Related Well-being**
— Indentured servitude resulting from inflated debt	Inability to afford:
— Usurious charges for travel documents, housing, food, clothing, condoms, health care, other basic necessities	— Basic hygiene, nutrition, safe housing
	— Condoms, contraception, lubricants
	— Gloves, protective gear for factory work or domestic service
— Usurious and deceptive accounting practices, control over and confiscation of earnings	— General health care, reproductive health care, prenatal care, safe termination of pregnancy (TOP)
— Resale of women and renewal of debts	— Heightened vulnerability to STIs, infections, work-related injuries from high-risk work practices
— Turning women over to immigration or police to prevent them from collecting wages	— Potentially dangerous self-medication or foregoing medication
— Forced or coerced acceptance of long hours, large numbers of clients, and sexual risks in order to meet financial demands	— Punishment, eg, physical abuse, financial penalties, for not earning enough or for withholding tips or earnings
	— Physical or economic retribution for trying to escape, eg, abduction of other female family members to pay off debts
	— Rejection by family for not sending money or returning home without money

(continued)

Table 19-5. Trafficking in Women: Health Consequences and Forms of Risk and Abuse *(continued)*

FORMS OF RISK AND ABUSE	POTENTIAL HEALTH CONSEQUENCES
Legal Insecurity	**Legal Security**
— Restrictive laws limiting routes of legal migration and independent employment	— Acceptance of dangerous travel conditions, dependency on traffickers and employers during travel and work
— Confiscation by traffickers or employers of travel documents, passports, tickets, other vital documents	— Arrest, detention, long periods in immigration detention centers or prisons; unhygienic, unsafe detention conditions
— Threats by traffickers or employers to expose women to authorities in order to coerce women to perform dangerous or high-risk activities	— Inability or difficulty obtaining treatment from public clinics and other medical services
— Concealment of women's legal status from the women themselves	— Anxiety or trauma as a result of interrogation, cross-examination, or participation in a criminal investigation or trial
— Health providers requiring identity documents	— Deportation to unsafe, insecure locations; risk of retrafficking and retribution
	— Ill-health or deterioration of health problems as a result of reluctance to use health and other support services

(continued)

Table 19-5. Trafficking in Women: Health Consequences and Forms of Risk and Abuse *(continued)*

FORMS OF RISK AND ABUSE	POTENTIAL HEALTH CONSEQUENCES
High-risk, Abusive Working and Living Conditions	**Occupational and Environmental Health**
— Abusive work hours, practices	— Vulnerability to infection; parasites, eg, lice, scabies; communicable diseases
— Dangerous work and living conditions, including unsafe, unhygienic, overcrowded, or poorly ventilated spaces	— Exhaustion and poor nutrition
— Work-related penalties and punishment	— Injuries and anxiety as a result of exploitation by employers, risky and dangerous work conditions
— Abusive employer-employee relationships, lack of personal safety	— Injuries and anxiety as a result of domestic or boyfriend-pimp abuse
— Abusive interpersonal social and coworker relationships	
— Nonconsensual marketing, sale, and exploitation of women	

Reprinted with permission from Zimmerman C, Yun K, Watts C, et al.[29]

— Posttraumatic stress disorder is associated with an increased health risk for cardiac, respiratory, nervous, and digestive diseases, as well as arthritis. Additionally, PTSD has a high rate of comorbidity with somatization and substance abuse.

— Substance abuse before, during, and after trafficking should be assessed. In extreme cases, drug or alcohol detoxification may be necessary.

CULTURAL COMPETENCY

Trafficked persons may not perceive Western health practice as what they need for their ailment(s) and may feel more comfortable engaging in non-Western techniques. Awareness of how such techniques can complement mainstream medical care can help the provider facilitate the trafficked person's access to holistic health, thus establishing trust between patient and care provider.

SELF-CARE

Practitioners engaging with trafficked persons should be aware of the effects of vicarious trauma. (See *Chapter 16* for more information on vicarious trauma.)

REFERENCES

1. Aghatise E. Trafficking for prostitution in Italy: possible effects of government proposals for legalization of brothels. *Violence Against Women*. 2004;10(10):1126-1155.

2. American Psychiatric Association. *Diagnostic and Statistical Manual of Mental Disorders*. 5th ed. Arlington, VA: American Psychiatric Association; 2013.

3. Bales K. *Disposable People*. Berkeley, CA: University of California Press; 2004.

4. Bales K. The social psychology of modern slavery. *Sci Am*. 2002;286(4):80-88.

5. Bales K, Fletcher L, Stover E. *Hidden Slaves: Forced Labor in the United States*. Washington, DC: University of California, Berkeley; 2004.

6. Biderman's Chart of Coercion. http://www.nwrain.net/~refocus/coerchrt.html. Accessed July 7, 2015.

7. Briere J, Spinazzola J. Phenomenology and psychological assessment of complex posttraumatic states. *J Trauma Stress*. 2005;18(5):401-412.

8. Cameron S, Newman E. Introduction: understanding human trafficking. In: Cameron S, Newman E, eds. *Trafficking in Human$: Social Cultural and Political Dimensions*. Tokyo, Japan: United Nations University Press; 2008.

9. Clawson HJ, Salomon A, Goldblatt Grace L. Treating the hidden wounds: trauma treatment and mental health recovery for victims of human trafficking. US Department of Health and Human Services Web site. http://aspe.hhs.gov/hsp/07/HumanTrafficking/Treating/ib.htm. Published March 2008. Accessed July 7, 2015.

10. Davis RE. Refugee experiences and Southeast Asian women's mental health. *West J Nurs Res*. 2000;22(2):144-162; discussion 162-168.

11. Family Violence Prevention Fund. *Turning Pain into Power: Trafficking Survivors' Perspectives on Early Intervention Strategies*. San Francisco, CA: Family Violence Prevention Fund; 2005.

12. Gajic-Veljanoski O, Stewart DE. Women trafficked into prostitution: determinants, human rights and health needs. *Transcult Psychiatry*. 2007;44(3):338-358.

13. Haley J, Stein W, Kittleson M, eds. *The Truth About Abuse*. New York, NY: Book Builders LLC; 2005.

14. Herman JL. Recovery from psychological trauma. *Psychiatry Clin Neurosci*. 1998;52(S1):S98-S103.

15. Hughes DM. Hiding in plain sight: a practical guide to identifying victims of trafficking in the US: with particular emphasis on victims of sexual trafficking as defined by the trafficking victims protection act 2000. http://www.uri.edu/artsci/wms/hughes/hiding_in_plain_sight. pdf. Published October 2003. Accessed July 7, 2015.

16. International Labor Organization. *A Global Alliance Against Forced Labor*. Geneva, Switzerland: International Labor Office; 2005.

17. Luxenburg T, Spinazzola J, van der Kolk B. Complex trauma and disorders of extreme stress (DESNOS) diagnosis, part one: assessment. *Directions in Psychiatry*. 2001;21(25):373-394. Trauma Center at Justice Resource Institute Web site. http://www.traumacenter.org/ products/pdf_files/DESNOS.pdf. Accessed July 7, 2015.

18. Norman SB, Means-Christensen AJ, Craske MG, Sherbourne CD, Roy-Byrne PP, Stein MB. Associations between psychological trauma and physical illness in primary care. *J Trauma Stress*. 2006;19(4):461-470.

19. Sbordone R. Post-traumatic stress disorder: an overview and its relationship to closed head injuries. *NeuroRehabilitation*. 1999;13:69-78.

20. Skolnik L, Boontinand J. Traffic in women in Asia. *Pacific Forum Appl Res Public Policy*. 1999;14:76-81.

21. Surtees R. *Trafficking of Men—A Trend Less Considered: The Case of Belarus and Ukraine*. Geneva, Switzerland: International Organization for Migration; 2008.

22. Tudorache D. General considerations on the psychological aspects of the trafficking phenomenon. In: Schinina G, Guthmiller A, Nikolovska M, O'Flaherty L, Janskijevic I, eds. *Psychosocial Support to Groups of Victims of Human Trafficking in Transit Situations.* Geneva, Switzerland: International Organization for Migration; 2004.

23. Ugarte M, Zarate L, Farley M. Prostitution and trafficking of women and children from Mexico to the United States. In: Farley M, ed. *Prostitution, Trafficking and Traumatic Stress.* Binghamton, NY: Hawthorne Maltreatment & Trauma Press; 2003.

24. United Nations Office on Drugs and Crime. Human trafficking FAQs. United Nations Office on Drugs and Crime Web site. http://www.unodc. org/undoc/en/human-trafficking/faqs.html. Accessed July 7, 2015.

25. US Department of Health and Human Services. Screening Tool for Victims of Human Trafficking. Washington, DC: US Dept of Health and Human Services. US Department of Justice Web site. http:// www.justice.gov/sites/default/files/usao-ndia/legacy/2011/10/14/ health_screen_questions.pdf. Accessed July 7, 2015.

26. US Department of State. *Trafficking in Persons Report.* Washington, DC: US Department of State; 2014.

27. van der Kolk BA, Roth S, Pelcovitz D, Sunday S, Spinazzola J. Disorders of extreme stress: the empirical foundation of a complex adaptation to trauma. *J Trauma Stress.* 2005;18(5):389-399.

28. World Health Organization. *Guidelines for Surveillance of Sexually Transmitted Diseases.* New Delhi, India: Regional Office for Southeast Asia; 2000.

29. Zimmerman C, Yun K, Shvab I, et al. *The Health Risks and Consequences of Trafficking in Women and Adolescents: Findings from a European Study.* London, England: London School of Hygiene and Tropical Medicine; 2003.

30. 22 USC § 7102, 7105.

31. 22 USC § 7105 (c) (3), 1595.

Chapter 20

Strangulation in Living Patients

Jennifer Pierce-Weeks, RN, SANE-P, SANE-A
Megan Lechner, MSN, RN, CNS, SANE-P, SANE-A

Introduction

— *Strangulation*: asphyxiation characterized by closure of the blood vessels or air passages of the neck as a result of external pressure

— Divided into 4 categories: hanging, ligature, manual, positional

— Considered a blunt force trauma, regardless of category

— Warrants thorough medical evaluation because of immediate risk of death and potential delayed lethality

— Life-threatening medical emergencies and death following manual strangulation have been reported hours to weeks following the event.

Assessment

— Physical signs and symptoms may or may not be present and differ depending on many variables, including type of strangulation, force used, duration of strangulation, and multiple strangulation attempts during assault.

— (**Table 20-1** lists signs and symptoms of strangulation.)

— Obtain vital signs and oxygenation saturation (SaO2) levels upon arrival and at intervals throughout the patient's stay.

— Ask for a description of the event and document that description using the patient's own words.*

Patients may refer to strangulation as being "choked," but except when quoting a patient, "strangulation" or "blunt traumatic injury to the neck" should be used throughout the medical record.

Table 20-1. Signs and Symptoms of Strangulation

— Loss of consciousness	— Lightheadedness
— Bleeding	— Voice changes
— Coughing	— Memory loss
— Dyspnea	— Incontinence of bladder or bowel
— Headache	— Numbness or tingling of extremities
— Otorrhagia	— Odynophagia or dysphagia
— Neck tenderness	— Crepitus
— Vision changes	— Nausea or vomiting
— Throat pain	— Irritability

— Consider risks commonly associated with hanging when patients report use of a ligature or indicate that they were lifted partially or completely off the ground during strangulation (**Figure 20-1**).

— Inquire after and document the patient's thought process during the attack.* (**Table 20-2** details a consistent, 4-step victim thought process from beginning of strangulation to loss of consciousness.)

— Avoid assumptions regarding patient behavior and fully evaluate for the possibility that such behavior is the result of strangulation or other trauma.

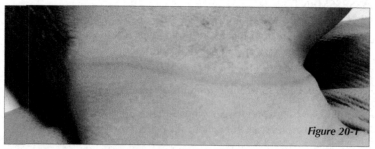

Figure 20-1

Figure 20-1. *When hanging or ligature use is present, it is not uncommon to find obvious ligature marks on the patient's neck.*

*Provides context for presenting symptoms such as acute stress reactions or self-inflicted injuries to the face and neck that may occur during a patient's struggle to stay alive

---

Table 20-2. Subjective Process of Strangulation in Victims

1. Denial: not believing that this is happening

2. Realization: suddenly understanding what is happening

3. Primal: fighting for life

4. Resignation: understanding that the perpetrator is going to kill you

---

Adapted from McClane GE, Strack GB, Hawley D.[13]

— Carefully assess the heads and necks of strangulation patients, looking closely for signs and symptoms previously described.

— Neck injuries commonly include abrasion (**Figure 20-2**), mild to extreme bruising (**Figures 20-3** through **20-5**), hematomas (**Figure 20-6**), and petechiae (**Figure 20-7**).

— Palpate the patient's neck, shoulders, and upper chest for crepitus or subcutaneous emphysema to identify tracheal and thorax injuries and to recognize soft tissue injuries when palpated.

— Assess the patient's tympanic membranes, oral cavity, skin, and scalp for petechiae, a common finding resulting from venous congestion (**Figure 20-8**).

— Carefully inspect behind the ears, as coocurring injury is frequently found in this location (**Figures 20-9** and **20-10**).

— Inspect the eyelids (outer and inner), conjunctiva, and sclera for the presence of petechiae. Subconjunctival hemorrhage or hyphema may be present (**Figure 20-11**).

— Perform cranial nerve assessment and auscultation of the heart, lungs, and carotid arteries to identify abnormalities.

— Consider collecting evidence from the patient's body that could corroborate the description of the strangulation event and prove beneficial in prosecution.

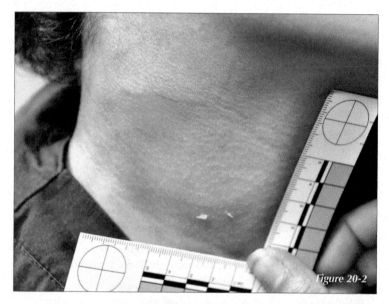

Figure 20-2.
Abrasion.

Figure 20-3.
Mild bruising.

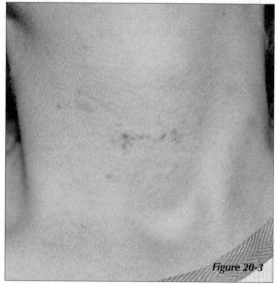

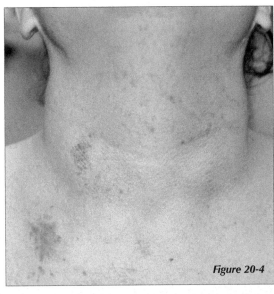

Figure 20-4

Figure 20-4.
Moderate bruising.

Figure 20-5.
Severe bruising.

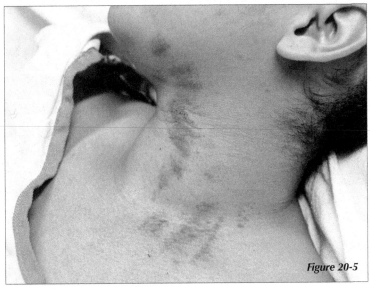

Figure 20-5

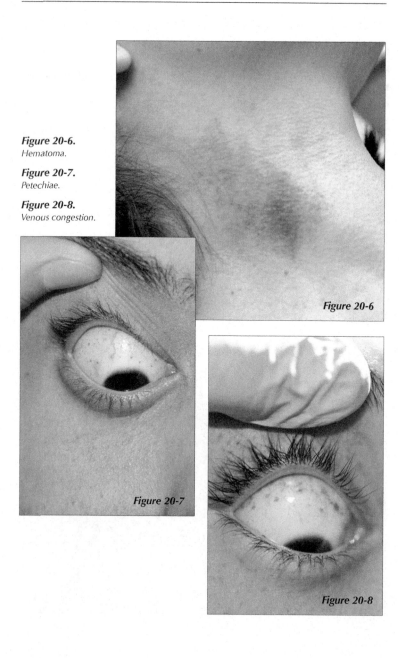

Figure 20-6.
Hematoma.

Figure 20-7.
Petechiae.

Figure 20-8.
Venous congestion.

Figure 20-6

Figure 20-7

Figure 20-8

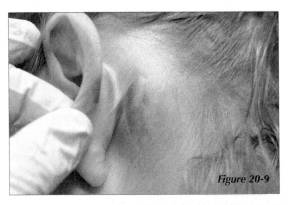

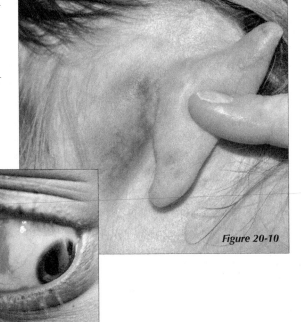

Figure 20-9.
Coocurring injury related to strangulation found behind the ear.

Figure 20-10.
Coocurring injury related to strangulation found behind the ear.

Figure 20-11.
Subconjunctival hemorrhage.

Assessment Tools

— Assessment tools or forms typically include sections to document the following:

1. A history of the strangulation event

2. The method or manner of strangulation

3. Whether there were multiple strangulation attempts

4. Signs and symptoms present during and after the assault

5. The amount of pressure or pain the assailant inflicted during the strangulation

— Tools should allow documentation of the physical assessment, including:

1. Glasgow Coma Scale

2. Documentation of heart and lung sounds

3. Initial and follow-up SaO2 levels

4. Head and neck diagrams to document physical findings

— Diagrams should include magnified body maps for the eyes, eyelids, ears, and mouth.

— Findings should be described, measured, and photographed when possible.

Photography

— Obtain informed consent* prior to photographing injuries so copies can be released to investigating agencies or used for educational purposes.

— First, photograph identifying information, including the patient's name, date of birth, age, sex, medical record number, and date of service.

— Start the photo series with a full-length orientation photo of the patient.

— Photograph each injury a minimum of 3 times,‡ including:

1. A middistance photograph for orientation

2. A close-up of the injury

3. A close-up of the injury with a standard (**Figure 20-12**)

---

*Informed consent may be waived if the person is unable to provide it, eg, in cases of trauma or if the patient is a minor.

‡ Take all photographs at a 90-degree angle to the injury.

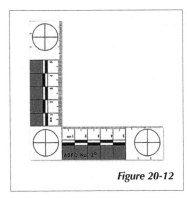

DIAGNOSTIC TESTING
(See **Table 20-3** for typical and recommended testing following blunt carotid injury.)

DISPOSITION
If the patient is discharged within the first 48-72 hours of strangulation, give the patient detailed instructions of symptoms that warrant returning to the emergency room (**Tables 20-4** and **20-5**).

Figure 20-12

Figure 20-12. *American Board of Forensic Odontology No. 2 reference scale.*

Table 20-3. Strangulation-Related Uses of Various Assessment Tools and Tests	
TEST	RATIONALE
Pulse oximetry	Evaluation of oxygen status
Soft tissue of the neck X-ray	Evaluation of subcutaneous emphysema Identification of tracheal deviation, edema, hematoma
Cervical spine X-ray	Identification of a fractured hyoid bone
Computed axial tomography (CT) scan	Detailed evaluation of neck structures
Carotid Doppler ultrasound	Identification of carotid artery dissection
CT scan with angiogram	Detailed evaluations of neck structures including the vessels
Chest X-ray	Identification of pulmonary edema, aspiration, or pneumonia

(continued)

429

Table 20-3. Strangulation-Related Uses of Various Assessment Tools and Tests *(continued)*

TEST	RATIONALE
Magnetic resonance imaging	Comprehensive evaluation of the neck structures
Pharyngoscopy	Identification of pharyngeal petechiae, edema, and other injury
Fiber-optic laryngobronchoscopy	Evaluation of the vocal cords and trachea

Adapted from McClane GE, Strack GB, Hawley D.[13]

Table 20-4. Symptoms Warranting Return for Immediate Evaluation

— Increasing or severe headache pain

— Increasing neck pain

— Drooping eyelid

— Difficulty speaking or understanding speech

— Difficulty walking

— Difficulty breathing

— Dizziness or lightheadedness

— Numbness, paralysis, or weakness, usually on one side of the body

— Seizure

— Sudden confusion

— Sudden decrease in the level of consciousness

— Sudden loss of balance or coordination

— Sudden vision problems, eg, blurry vision, blindness in one eye

— Vomiting

— Vaginal bleeding (if pregnant)

— Thoughts of suicide

Table 20-5. Symptoms Warranting Return for Documentation

— Pinpoint red or purple dots on face or neck

— Bruises on your face, neck, or body

— Burst blood vessels in your eye

— Swelling of your face or neck

REFERENCES

1. Anscombe AM, Knight BH. Case report: delayed death after pressure on the neck: possible causal mechanisms and implications for mode of death in manual strangulation discussed. *Forensic Sci Int.* 1996;78(3):193-197.

2. Banks M. *Visual Methods in Social Research.* London, UK: Sage Publications; 2001.

3. Dayapala A, Samarasekera A, Jayasena A. An uncommon delayed sequela after pressure on the neck: an autopsy case report. *Am J Forensic Med Pathol.* 2012;33(1):80-82. doi: 10.1097/PAF.0b013e318221bab7.

4. DiMaio VJM, Dana SE. *Handbook of Forensic Pathology.* 2nd ed. Boca Raton, FL: CRC Press; 2007.

5. Funk M, Schuppel J. Strangulation injuries. *WMJ.* 2003;102(3):41-45.

6. Hawley DA, McClane GE, Strack GB. A review of 300 attempted strangulation cases part III: injuries in fatal cases. *J Emerg Med.* 2001;21(3):317-322.

7. Helwig FC. Histopathologic studies of the brain in delayed death following strangulation. *Am J Forensic Med Pathol.* 1989;10(3):266-267.

8. Iserson KV. Strangulation: a review of ligature, manual, and postural neck compression injuries. *Ann Emerg Med.* 1984;13(3):179-185.

9. Kiani SH, Simes DC. Delayed bilateral internal carotid artery thrombosis following accidental strangulation. *Br J Anaesth.* 2000;84(4):521-524.

10. Laughon K, Glass N, Worrell C. Review and analysis of laws related to strangulation in 50 states. *Eval Rev.* 2009;33(4):358-369.

11. Line WS Jr, Stanley RB Jr, Choi JH. Strangulation: a full spectrum of blunt neck trauma. *Ann Otol Rhinol Laryngol.* 1985;94(6 pt 1):542-546.

12. Lumb PD, Milroy CM, Whitwell HL. Neuropathological changes in delayed death after strangulation. *Emerg Med News.* 2002;24(5):1-42.

13. McClane GE, Strack GB, Hawley D. A review of 300 attempted strangulation cases part II: clinical evaluation of the surviving victim. *J Emerg Med.* 2001;21(3):311-315.

14. Sethi PK, Sethi NK, Torgovnick J, Arsura E. Delayed left anterior and middle cerebral artery hemorrhagic infarctions after attempted strangulation: a case report. *Am J Forensic Med Pathol.* 2012;33(1):105-106. doi: 10.1097/PAF.0b013e3182198672.

15. Shields LB, Corey TS, Weakley-Jones B, Stewart D. Living victims of strangulation: a 10-year review of cases in a metropolitan community. *Am J Forensic Med Pathol.* 2010;31(4):320-325.

Chapter 21

Risks to Children and Adolescents on the Internet

Eileen M. Alexy, PhD, RN, APN, PMHCNS-BC
Elizabeth Dowdell, PhD, MS, RN

Understanding New Media

— Computers, mobile phones, interactive gaming systems, and tablets are now all counted among Internet access devices (IADs), which allow increased access to children and adolescents and make it more difficult for caregivers to supervise online activities.

— The global nature of the Internet allows little regulation or control over available content by any single entity or government, and new software and hardware have made it easier than ever to post and retrieve content online. Picture, audio, and video files can now be uploaded to social networking sites, shared on peer-to-peer (P2P) networks, or transferred from one wireless device to another via infrared ports.

— (See **Appendix 7-1** for a glossary of terms associated with new media.)

Risks of New Media

Social Media: Prevalence and Risk[4]

— More than 60% of adolescents aged 13 to 17 years have at least one social networking profile.

— Seventy-five percent of teenagers own cell phones, and 25% of those teens use them for social media.

— Twenty-two percent of teenagers log in to their favorite social networking sites more than 10 times a day, and more than 50% log in once a day.

— Many children and adolescents are transparent and disinhibited in sharing information via social media and express disconnection from the potential consequences of their transparency, viewing such interactions as private and separate from the adult world.

SELF-EXPLOITATION BEHAVIORS AND SEXTING

— *Sexting:* self-generated, sexually explicit photos and text messages sent via electronic media.

— Legal consequences for adolescents include charges of producing, distributing, and possessing child pornography and indecent exposure.

— Social consequences can be devastating for teens if photos are viewed by classmates, teammates, or community members.

— Sexting may reflect poorly on the individuals involved and affect academic acceptance and future employment if discovered by admissions or human resources personnel.

— A recent study of youth aged 12 to 17 years reported that 4% had created and then sent nude, nearly nude, or sexually suggestive images via electronic media.[12]

— In another study of high school students, 31.3% knew someone who had engaged in sexting, and 17.6% of boys and 13.4% of girls had been sexted.[8]

ONLINE SEXUAL SOLICITATION AND EXPLOITATION

— Online sexual solicitation and exploitation may include attempts by an adult to engage a child or an adolescent in:

1. Disclosure of personal information

2. Sexual talk

3. Sexual activity

4. Sending nude or sexual photographs

5. Offline contact

— An online predator may lie about his age or gender, treat sexual activity as a game, send photographs of child pornography to portray sexual activities as normal behavior, or send tangible items such as money and gifts in order to lure victims.

— Individuals who send and request child pornography are known as *traders*.

— Individuals seeking offline contact with minors are known as *travelers*.

— Individuals who trade child pornography and attempt to meet minors in person are known as *combination trader-travelers*.

— The majority of aggressive sexual solicitations are perpetrated by males.

EXPOSURE TO INAPPROPRIATE MATERIAL

— Inappropriate material: generally defined as being sexual, violent, or hateful in nature.

— Increased exposure to inappropriate sexual content results, in part, from adoption of aggressive and unethical marketing strategies, such as:

1. Embedding *malware* in e-mails designed to take over a browser and direct the user to sexually explicit Web sites

2. Creating explicit Web sites with intentionally misspelled versions of existing domain names

PREVENTION EFFORTS
SAFETY GUIDELINES AND SUPERVISION

— Denying access to online services is not a realistic solution.

— Discussions about online behavior should be pragmatic and stress common sense strategies, ie, privacy, civility, and ethics.

— Supervision of online activity is more effective than either warnings or safety discussions.

— Trust and open communication are essential for online safety; therefore, caregivers should give adolescents a 24-hour warning before accessing their social networking profiles.

— When an adolescent discloses a disconcerting online experience, it is imperative to not overact or immediately blame the youth.

— (**Table 21-1** details safety guidelines to be made available to parents and mandated reporters.)

Table 21-1. NCMEC and WiredSafety Recommended Safety Guidelines

— Do not reveal identifying information in chat rooms or on social networking sites, and never disclose this information to unknown persons.

— Do not say or post anything online that would not be said offline.

— Do not post anything online that parents, teachers, or employers would not want to see.

— Never continue a conversation that elicits uncomfortable feelings or becomes personal, and report such conversations to an adult.

— Never send or post a self-photograph or offer a physical description of one's self or one's family members online. If photographs are posted online, make sure the images do not include personal information.

— Do not post information about anyone without permission, and know what information friends are posting.

— Never answer e-mails or instant messages that are suggestive, obscene, rude, or elicit uncomfortable feelings. Report such messages to an adult and forward the messages to the appropriate authorities for investigation.

— Never arrange a face-to-face meeting with an online acquaintance without permission from a parent or caregiver. If a meeting is arranged, it is extremely important that a parent or caregiver be present and that the meeting be arranged in a public place.

— Never reveal a password to anyone online, not even to online service staff members. Do not share passwords with friends, online or offline.

— Never allow open access to IM services or social networking profiles. Use the tools provided by the service provider to opt-out or limit access to such information, and use tools that require verification when adding someone to a friends list.

Adapted from Aftab P[1] and Surratt A.[16]

FILTERING AND BLOCKING

Filtering and blocking tools provide only minimal protection on computers, and mobile phones, interactive gaming devices, and tablets with wireless access are not usually equipped with extensive filtering and blocking tools.

THE ROLE OF HEALTH CARE PROVIDERS IN THE DIGITAL AGE

AWARENESS AND RISK ASSESSMENT

— By asking questions about Internet behaviors, health care providers can detect risky Internet behaviors or problems early and gain insight into child and adolescent online behaviors and practices (**Table 21-2**).

Table 21-2. Assessment Questions for Parents and Children

— Does the child go online daily? If so, does he or she spend more than 2 hours per day online?

— Is the computer in a public space at home?

— Is the computer a desktop or a laptop?

— Does the child have a cell phone with Internet access?

— What types of Internet services does the child use, eg, chat rooms, IM, and/or e-mail?

— Do the parents have a set of house rules regarding Internet use (see **Tables 21-1** and **21-3**)?

— Do the parents have the child's password(s) for e-mail, cell phone, social networking sites, Web sites, blogs, and other Internet-based applications?

— Does the child have an online profile? Where is this profile posted? Have the parents seen the profile?

— What has the child shared about himself or herself online? Where is he or she sharing this information?

— If the child participates in chat rooms, what type(s) of chat rooms?

— Who is the child communicating with online?

— What does the child know about the individual(s) he or she is chatting with online? How did he or she meet the individual(s)?

— What types of Web sites does the child access?

— Encourage parents to routinely surf the Web with their children, because it provides an excellent opportunity to spend quality time with them and to gain a better understanding of what they are being exposed to online.

— Encourage efforts to balance the amount of time children spend online with offline activities.

— Encourage the establishment of house Internet rules (**Table 21-3**).

Table 21-3. Internet Rules for Parents

— Talk to your child about sexual victimization and potential online danger.

— Spend time with your children online.

— Have your children teach you about their favorite online destinations.

— Keep the computer in a common room in the house, not in your child's bedroom.

— Use parental controls provided by your service provider, blocking software, or both.

— Use of chat rooms should be heavily monitored.

— Maintain access to your child's online account and randomly check his or her e-mail. Be up front with your child about your access and reasons why.

— Instruct your children:

  — to never arrange a face-to-face meeting with someone they met online

  — to never upload (post) pictures of themselves online or for people they do not personally know

  — to never give out identifying information

  — to never download pictures from an unknown source

  — to never respond to messages or bulletin board postings that are suggestive, obscene, belligerent, or harassing

  — that whatever they are told online may or may not be true

(continued)

Table 21-3. Internet Rules for Parents *(continued)*

— Find out what computer safeguards are used by your child's school, the public library, and at the homes of your child's friends.

— Encourage children not to sleep with their electronics in bed or near them. Help your child establish routine patterns of technology use during the day and at night.

— Understand that even if your child were a willing participant in any form of sexual exploitation that he or she is not at fault and that the offender always bears complete responsibility for his or her actions.

Reprinted from United States Department of Justice; Federal Bureau of Investigation.[18]

— Encourage children and adolescents to share both good and bad online experiences with their parents, educators, or clinicians.

— Encourage families and individual family members to report inappropriate, dangerous, or predatory online behaviors to their local police and the NCMEC CyberTipline® (http://www.missingkids.com/cybertipline/).

Handling the Disclosure of Online and Offline Victimization

— When a child discloses online or offline victimization, remain calm and nonjudgmental.

— Children who are sexually victimized may be embarrassed or ashamed and may recant their stories after disclosure.

— Often, children who are lured to meet in person with someone they encountered online are curious or troubled adolescents looking to have their needs for attention and affection met.

— The legalities of Internet crimes against children and criminal proceedings brought against offenders differ from state-to-state. Caregivers should be aware of local age of consent laws and definitions of sexual assault and statutory rape.

— If a health care provider suspects a child has been victimized through the Internet, it is essential that the health care provider report it.

APPENDIX 21-1

Appendix 21-1. Glossary of New Media and Information Technology Terms

— *Bluetooth:* Enables short-range wireless connection between electronic devices. Generally, allows users to synchronize and coordinate mobile and fixed computer devices.

— *Broadband:* Telecommunications with a wide band of available data transmission frequencies. Multiple frequencies send information concurrently, and more information can be transmitted in a given amount of time.

— *Browser:* Usually describes programs for Internet access. Originated as a generic term for user interfaces to navigate, read, or browse online text files.

— *Chat abbreviations:* Abbreviations or acronyms used in instant and text messaging, eg, "R yor parNts om? We shud Met IRL. U swNd hot :o)!" ("Are your parents home? We should meet in real life. You sound hot [smiley face]!)

— *Chat room:* Provides a venue for communities of users to communicate in real time. Forums and discussion groups, in comparison, allow users to post messages but not in real time.

— *Client:* The requesting program in a client-server relationship. A Web browser is an example of a client, as it requests information from a computer. The computer handling the request and sending back the information is the server.

— *Domain name:* Locates an organization or another entity on the Internet. Contains at least 2 components separated by a period, eg, *fbi. gov.* The top-level domain name (to the right of the period) reflects the organization's purpose (.gov = US government). The second-level domain name (to the left of the period) defines the organization or entity (FBI).

— *E-mail spoofing:* Forgery of an e-mail header such that the message appears to have originated from someone or somewhere other than the actual source. Perpetrators sending viruses often use e-mail spoofing.

— *Flaming:* Use of inflammatory or derogatory comments online.

(continued)

Appendix 21-1. Glossary of New Media and Information Technology Terms
(continued)

— *Graphical user interface (GUI)*: Incorporates graphics into user-computer interaction. The first computer interfaces were text-based, not graphical, and usually required users to memorize prescribed commands.

— *Instant messaging (IM)*: Real-time text message exchange via software application. Generally allows users to see if friends, or "buddies," are currently online. Contemporary mobile phones allow users to always be available on IM.

— *I seek you (ICQ)*: Downloadable chat program that allows chatting, paging, and device-to-device calling card calls.

— *Interoperability*: Ability of a system or a product to work with other systems or products without special effort on the part of the customer or user.

— *Internet protocol (IP) address*: A unique address used by electronic devices to identify and communicate with each other online. Identifies (1) a particular network and (2) a particular device, ie, a server or workstation within that network.

— *Internet relay chat (IRC)*: Chatting systems that include a set of rules and conventions and client or server software. Users can start or join chat groups, and some encourage users to register permanent nicknames and personal profiles.

— *Jump drive*: A portable flash memory storage device, aka, USB drive, flash drive, keychain drive, or disk-on-key.

— *Key logger:* Spyware that invisibly records a user's keystrokes and either transmits them on an ongoing basis or saves them for later transmission.

— *Malware*: Programming designed to infiltrate or harm a system, eg, worms, viruses, Trojan horses, spyware, and key loggers.

— *P2P network*: Allows users to connect with and access files on one another's hard drives, eg, Napster, Kazaa, Limewire, and BitTorrent.

— *Phishing*: A scam in which a perpetrator sends legitimate-looking, fraudulent e-mails in an effort to gather personal and financial information from recipients.

(continued)

Appendix 21-1. Glossary of New Media and Information Technology Terms
(continued)

— *Podcast*: Files, usually audio files, distributed to subscribers. Can also transmit images, text, and video.

— *Proxy server*: An intermediary between a Web client and a Web server that holds commonly accessed and recently used content to provide quicker downloads and increased server security. Allows direct access from behind a firewall.

— *Rich site summary (RSS)*: An XML-based vocabulary that specifies a means of describing Web content available for feeding, distribution, or syndication online.

— *Spam*: Unsolicited or unwanted e-mail.

— *Spim*: Spam delivered via instant messaging.

— *Spyware*: Secretly gathers information about a user for relay to advertisers or other interested parties.

— *Transmission control protocol/Internet protocol (TCP/IP)*: The basic communication language of the Internet as well as private networks, eg, intranets and extranets.

— *Trojan horse*: Malicious or harmful coding contained in seemingly harmless programming or data.

— *Uniform resource locator (URL)*: The Web address for a specific source of information.

— *Wireless communication*: Telecommunications in which electromagnetic waves carry a signal over the communication path.

— *Wireless application protocol (WAP)*: Communication protocols to standardize Internet access for wireless devices.

— *Wi-Fi*: Wireless local area networks using specifications in the 802.11 family. Wi-Fi-enabled devices can connect to the Internet when within range of an online wireless network.

REFERENCES

1. Aftab P. Parry Aftab's guide to keeping your kids safe online. WiredSafety Web site. http://www.wiredsafety.org/resources/pdf/socialnetworktips.pdf. Published 2006. Accessed June 15, 2015.

2. Aftab P. *The Parent's Guide to Protecting Your Children in Cyberspace.* New York, NY: McGraw-Hill; 2000.

3. Alexy EM, Burgess AW, Baker T. Internet offenders: traders, travelers, and combination trader-travelers. *J Interpers Violence.* 2005;20(7):804-812.

4. American Academy of Child & Adolescent Psychiatry. *Children and Social Networking.* Washington, DC: American Academy of Child & Adolescent Psychiatry; 2012.

5. Armagh DS. A safety net for the Internet: protecting our children. *Juvenile Justice.* 1998;5(1):9-15.

6. Crosson-Tower C. *Understanding Child Abuse and Neglect.* 6th ed. Boston, MA: Allyn & Bacon; 2013.

7. Dowdell EB, Bradley PK. Risky internet behaviors: a case study of online and offline stalking. *J Sch Nurs.* 2010;26(6):436-442. doi: 10.1177/1059840510380209.

8. Dowdell EB, Burgess AW, Flores JR. Original research: online social networking patterns among adolescents, young adults, and offenders. *Am J Nurs.* 2011;111(7):28-36; quiz 37-38. doi: 10.1097/01.NAJ.0000399310.83160.73.

9. Finkelhor D, Mitchell KJ, Wolak J. *Online Victimization: A Report on the Nation's Youth.* Durham, NH: Crimes Against Children Research Center; 2000. University of New Hampshire Web site. http://www.unh.edu/ccrc/pdf/jvq/CV38.pdf. Accessed June 15, 2015.

10. Jankowski N, Jones S, Samarajiva R, Silverstone R. Editorial. *New Media Soc.* 1999;1(1):5-9.

11. Lanning KA. Cyber pedophiles: a behavioral perspective. *APSAC Advisor.* 1998;11(4):12-18.

12. Lenhart A. *Teens and Sexting: How and Why Minor Teens Are Sending Sexually Suggestive Nude or Nearly Nude Images via Text Messaging*. Washington, DC: Pew Internet & American Life Project; 2009. Pew Research Center Web site. http://www.pewinternet.org/~/media//Files/Reports/2009/PIP_Teens_and_Sexting.pdf. Accessed June 15, 2015.

13. Lenhart A, Purcell K, Smith A, Zickuhr K. *Social Media & Mobile Internet Use Among Teens and Young Adults*. Washington, DC: Pew Internet & American Life Project; 2010. Pew Research Center Web site. http://pewinternet.org/~/media//Files/Reports/2010/PIP_Social_Media_and_Young_Adults_Report_Final_with_toplines.pdf. Accessed June 15, 2015.

14. Phipps C. Children, adults, sex and the criminal law: in search of reason. *Seton Hall Legis J*. 1997;22:1-60.

15. Summit RC. The child sexual abuse accommodation syndrome. *Child Abuse Negl*. 1983;7(2):177-193.

16. Surratt A. Cox Communications Teen Internet Safety Survey, Wave II - in partnership with the National Center for Missing & Exploited Children (NCMEC) and John Walsh. PR Newswire Web site. http://webcache.googleusercontent.com/search?q=cache:KE1y_YdiEIkJ:multivu.prnewswire.com/player/44526-cox-teen-summit-internet-safety/docs/44526-2007_Cox_Teen_Internet_Safety_Survey_Results.ppt+&cd=1&hl=en&ct=clnk&gl=us. Published March 2007. Accessed June 16, 2015.

17. Toth P, McClure K. An overview of selected legal issues involved in computer related child exploitation: many questions, few answers. *APSAC Advisor*. 1998;11(4):19-22.

18. United States Department of Justice; Federal Bureau of Investigation. A parent's guide to Internet safety. Federal Bureau of Investigation Web site. http://www.fbi.gov/stats-services/publications/parent-guide/parentsguide.pdf. Accessed June 15, 2015.

19. Wolak J, Finkelhor D. *Sexting: A Typology*. Durham, NH: Crimes Against Children Research Center; 2011. University of New Hampshire Web site. http://www.unh.edu/ccrc/pdf/CV231_Sexting%20Typology%20Bulletin_4-6-11_revised.pdf. Accessed June 15, 2015.

Photographic Appendix

Presented in order by age group of the victim, from young children to elderly persons, the photographs in this gallery are intended to supplement the information contained in the text—to reflect the findings most characteristic of the various age groups, whether normal or pathologic. While many findings are seen across the life span, generally only one example is offered, placed within the age group where it is most prevalent. For a comprehensive photographic representation of sexual assault, please consult *Sexual Assault Victimization Across the Life Span: A Color Atlas*, ISBN 1-878060-61-9.

Infant Sexual Abuse: 0-3 Years Old

History of Sexual Abuse
Normal and Nonspecific Findings

Case Study 1

This 2-year-old was brought by her mother because the mother suspected that the child's father had fondled her. Older siblings had reported this repeated occurrence over time. The most recent incident was over 72 hours before the time of the examination. Other female children in this family had also been "rubbed" by their natural father. Disclosure occurred because an older sibling saw a program at school.

Figure 1. *There is a normal color pattern throughout. The hymen is redundant. The continuity of the hymenal rim cannot be assessed in this view (supine position).*

The perpetrator pled guilty to child molestation of 2 children and was sentenced to 2 years in prison and registration as a child sex offender. The mother of the children divorced the father.

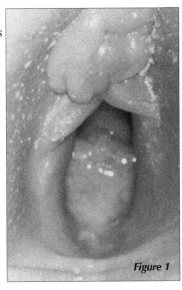

Figure 1

Special Cases
Males

Case Study 2

This 3-month-old circumcised male was brought for an examination while his parents were in a domestic violence conflict. The infant's toxicology screen was positive for amphetamines.

Figure 2-a. *Erythema at 5 o'clock on the glans penis.*

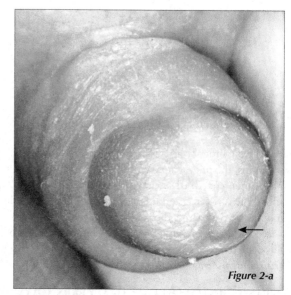

Figure 2-a

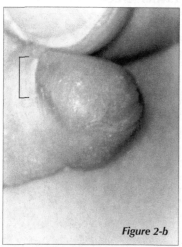

Figure 2-b

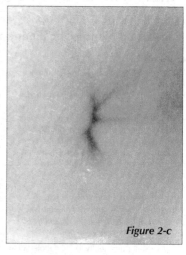

Figure 2-c

Figure 2-b. *Erythema at 8 o'clock on the undersurface of the glans penis.*

Figure 2-c. *Perianal erythema. There was no anal spasm or laxity. The perianal folds are flattened, consistent with his relaxed state.*

Disabled

Case Study 3

This 3-year-old female has Prader-Willi syndrome. Her natural father penetrated her digitally and attempted penile-vaginal penetration multiple times. He did the same with her other 3 sisters and molested her brother. The last time she was penetrated was 2 weeks before the examination. She had a history of *Candida* infections.

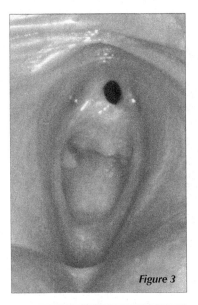

Figure 3. A crescentic hymen with a vaginal tag at 9 o'clock and a patulous urethra. Candida albicans *was present on the culture from this examination.*

The father confessed to the abuse and is serving 18 years in prison with registration as a child sex offender.

Figure 3

Nonassault Variants
Labial Adhesions

Case Study 4

This 2-year-old child had a history of blood in her diaper.

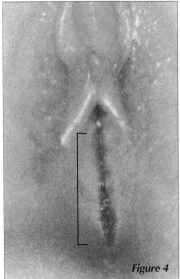

Figure 4. Labial adhesions run from midlabia posteriorly. The anterior opening is not evident in the photograph. The posterior aspect of the labial adhesion is beginning to separate, evident as the examiner gently separates.

Figure 4

Infection
Bacterial

Case Study 5

One of 2 twin 3-year-old girls was examined because of a report that the father had been molesting the girls over the last 3 days. The father was the main care provider because the mother was in an inpatient drug recovery program.

Figure 5-a. A vivid erythema around the base of the hymen from 3 to 11 o'clock. Cultures of vaginal secretions revealed Staphylococcus epidermidis.

Figure 5-b. Erythema is most distinct from 6 to 9 o'clock. The hymen is normal.

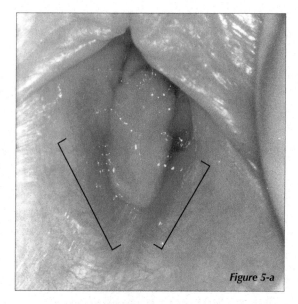

Figure 5-a

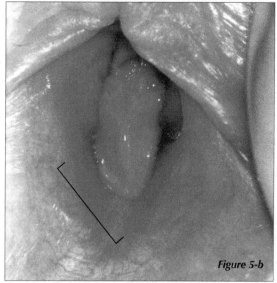

Figure 5-b

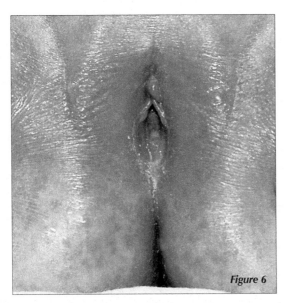

Figure 6

Fungal

Case Study 6

This 3-year-old female has diaper dermatitis.

Figure 6. Satellite lesions characteristic of diaper dermatitis associated with Candida albicans. *Cultures revealed* Candida albicans. *Parents may assist in holding the child for examination (35 mm).*

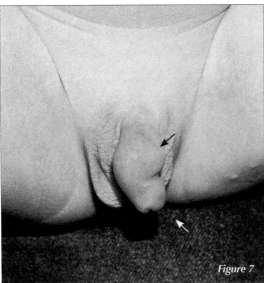

Figure 7

Balanitis

Case Study 7

This 2-year-old Native American male arrived from a reservation with ecchymosis on the dorsal surface of the shaft of the edematous penis and on the side of the foreskin. The child has been in the care of his parents. Neither parent suspected abuse of the child. However, his hygiene is poor. The pediatrician referred the child for a medical-legal examination. It was determined that the child has balanitis.

Figure 7. Ecchymosis on the dorsal surface of the shaft of the edematous penis and on the side of the foreskin (35 mm).

449

NORMAL FINDINGS
Annular Hymen

Case Study 8

This 2-year-old has a redundant, pink hymen.

Figure 8. A redundant hymen. The vascular pattern is not prominent. Labial traction, knee-chest position, or probing the hymenal edge with a swab may help to evaluate for continuity of the hymen. The arrow points to the hymenal opening.

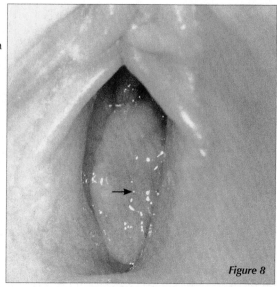

Figure 8

Crescentic Hymen

Case Study 9

This 3-year-old has a crescentic hymen.

Figure 9-a. The crescentic hymen is open in the supine frog-leg position. The left and posterior rim edges are smooth and uninterrupted, but the right rim cannot be clearly visualized.

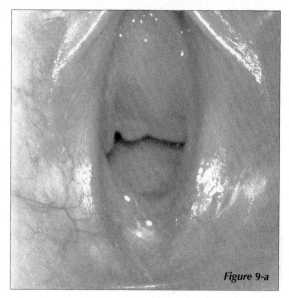

Figure 9-a

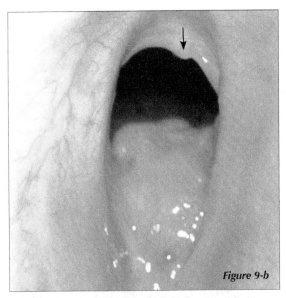

Figure 9-b. In the knee-chest position, a mound is visible.

Figure 9-b

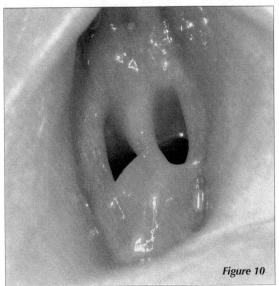

Figure 10

Septate Hymen

Case Study 10

This 3-year-old was referred for further gynecologic evaluation.

Figure 10. Septate hymen. Even the vascularity of the septum can be seen with increasing magnification.

YOUNG CHILD SEXUAL ABUSE: 4-8 YEARS OLD

HISTORY OF SEXUAL ABUSE

Acute Findings

Digital Penetration of the Vagina

Case Study 11

This 5-year-old Caucasian was kidnapped from a playground near her apartment by a stranger who put his finger in her vagina one time. She was examined within 48 hours of her abduction. The perpetrator pled innocent to charges of abduction and child molestation but was convicted.

Figure 11. *There is erythema and edema on the hymen from 1 to 7 o'clock.*

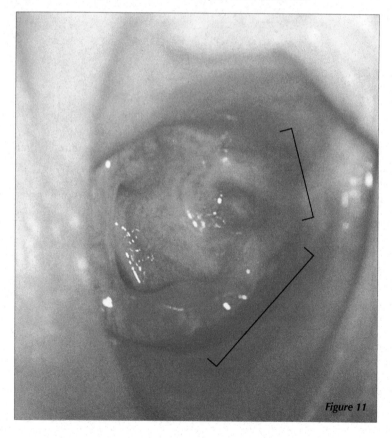

Figure 11

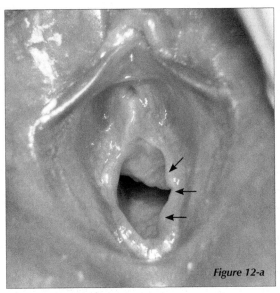

Figure 12-a

Normal and Nonspecific Findings
Penile Penetration of the Vagina

Case Study 12

This patient is 8 years old and African American. There is a history of beating with a belt and other physical abuse by her mother and stepfather. The stepfather's brother fondled the child over a period of 2 years and penetrated her vagina with his penis many times. The most recent is over 72 hours ago. She described bleeding during some of those times.

Figure 12-a. *Labial traction is used in this photo. There are mounds at 2 and 5 o'clock and a cleft at 3 o'clock.*

Figure 12-b. *This photo was taken with the child in knee-chest position. The mounds and cleft are still present in this thin, annular hymen.*

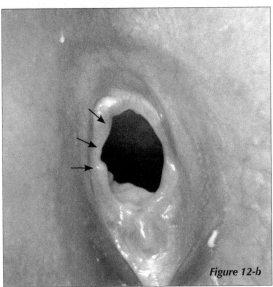

Figure 12-b

453

Special Cases
Males

Case Study 13

This 6-year-old male experienced penile-anal penetration by a 14-year-old male who lived in the same apartment building. The child stated "he used green lotion" as a lubricant. The 14-year-old called police to confess that he had forced anal penetration with several young male victims.

Figure 13-a. There is perianal erythema with stool in the anal folds. There is another ring of erythema closer to the anal orifice from 11 to 5 o'clock. This child is in knee-chest position (35 mm).

Figure 13-b. There is a laceration at 5 o'clock in the perianal folds. Toluidine blue dye would have made this laceration more evident.

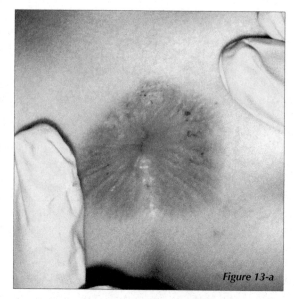

Figure 13-a

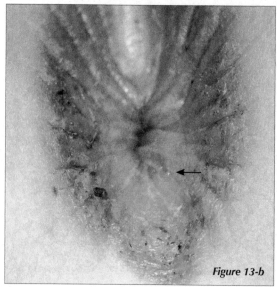

Figure 13-b

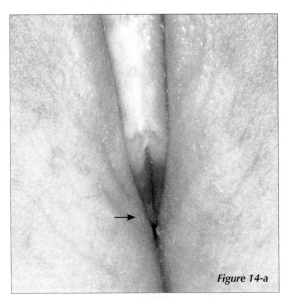

Figure 14-a

Incest

Case Study 14

This is an 8-year-old Caucasian female. She said, "My dad has bad touches." She would not reveal any details of the "bad touches." When she was being interviewed for potential abuse by her father, she explained that her "privates" were sore because she had recently fallen on the playground bars.

Figure 14-a. There is a bruise on the clitoral hood.

Figure 14-b. There is erythema of the anterior commissure and periurethral area with punctate erythema at 10 and 11 o'clock.

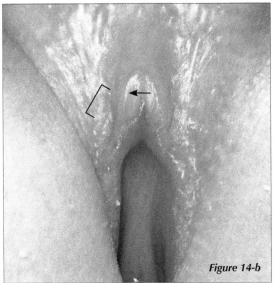

Figure 14-b

455

NONASSAULT
VARIANTS
Infections
Viral

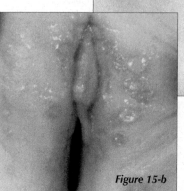

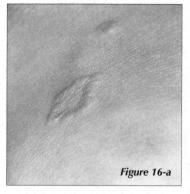

Figure 15-a

Figure 15-b

Case Study 15

This 6-year-old female was seen following a child protective services referral.

Figure 15-a. *Herpes simplex 2 vesicles on the labia majora (35 mm).*

Figure 15-b. *This photo shows vesicles on the medial aspect of the labia majora and around the introitus (35 mm).*

Case Study 16

This 4-year-old male presented for a physical exam. There was no history of molestation.

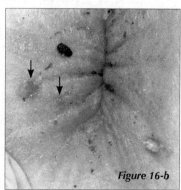

Figure 16-a

Figure 16-b

Figure 16-a. *Approximately 100 papular lesions were present in various places on this child, some in clusters. Some of the lesions were flat, others were raised.*

Figure 16-b. *There is perianal erythema with 3 papular lesions at 5 and 7 o'clock. There are brown stool particles around the anus.*

Parasitic

Case Study 17

This African American 7-year-old was referred for sexual abuse. She had pinworms.

Figure 17-a. A pinworm going into the perianal tissue; there is a laceration adjacent to the pinworm. Two nevi are present at 8 and 10 o'clock around the perianal tissue.

Figure 17-b. Pinworms on the perianal area.

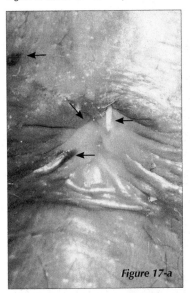

Figure 17-a

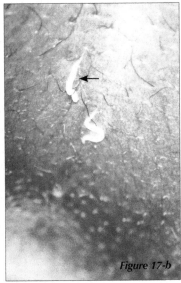

Figure 17-b

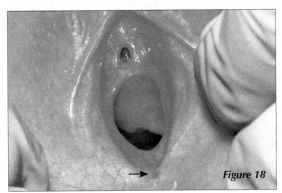

Figure 18

Friable Fourchette

Case Study 18

This is a 9-year-old Caucasian with no history of abuse.

Figure 18. An iatrogenic laceration of the posterior fourchette.

Anal Findings

Case Study 19

This is a 6-year-old Hispanic female with no history of molestation. She did have a history of hard stools.

Figure 19. Fissures at 6 and 11 o'clock.

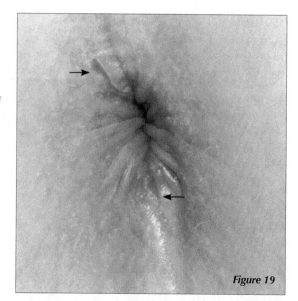

Figure 19

Normal Findings Annular Hymen

Case Study 20

This patient is 5 years old and Caucasian.

Figure 20. This annular hymen has mounds at 1 and 2 o'clock. The periurethral bands are distinct especially on the right side. There is baby powder on the labia creating a border for the vestibule.

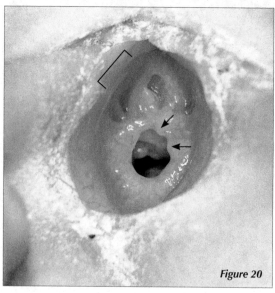

Figure 20

PREADOLESCENT SEXUAL ABUSE: 9-12 YEARS OLD

HISTORY OF SEXUAL ABUSE
Friend of the Family Perpetrator

Case Study 21

This 7-year-old African American female and her sister were 2 of 5 frequent visitors to a 56-year-old male neighbor. He gave them money for ice cream, took pictures of them "humping" each other, and touched their privates, according to the child's history.

Figure 21-a. This is a normal annular hymen with sharp edges. A nevus is noted at the left inferior labium minus. Periurethral bands are also visible.

Figure 21-b. Mild clitoral erythema is evident. There is a band inferior to the clitoris.

The suspect pled guilty and was sentenced to 18 years in prison and must register as a sex offender.

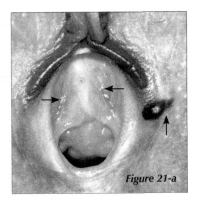

Figure 21-a

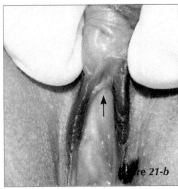

Figure 21-b

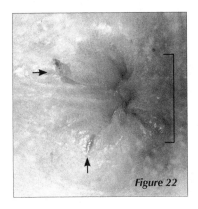

Figure 22

Adolescent Perpetrator

Case Study 22

This 9-year-old Hispanic male complained of anal pain and itching. He said a 16-year-old male forced penile-anal penetration many times. The examination was within 72 hours of the most recent incident.

Figure 22. The child is in knee-chest position. There are 2 healing lacerations at 7 and 10 o'clock and venous congestion from 1 to 4 o'clock. Erythema is present from 8 to 11 o'clock.

459

Nonassault Variants
Infection
Spirochetal

Case Study 23

This is a 12-year-old male.

Figure 23. There is a syphilitic chancre visible on the upper lip (35 mm).

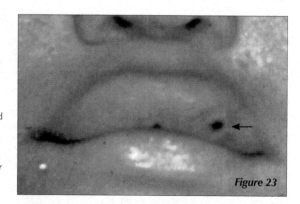

Figure 23

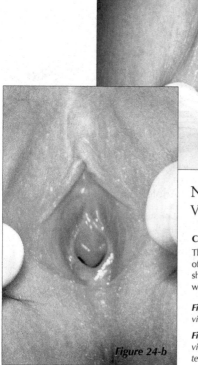

Figure 24-a

Normal Findings
Varied Examiner Technique

Case Study 24

This patient is an 11-year-old with no history of sexual abuse. This series of photographs shows the differences in visibility of anatomy with changes in examiner technique.

Figure 24-a. A normal crescentic hymen is visualized using labial separation.

Figure 24-b. The hymenal rim comes into view more clearly with the labial traction technique.

Figure 24-b

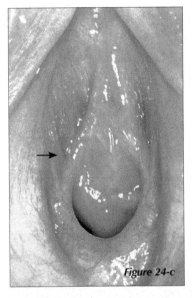

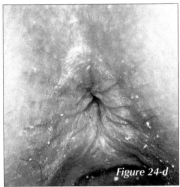

Case Study 24 *(continued)*

Figure 24-c. *With labial traction and greater magnification, the hymenal rim is more clearly visualized and perihymenal bands become evident.*

Figure 24-d. *A normal anus. Separation is used to visualize the perianal area.*

Hymen
Failure to Fuse

Case Study 25

This 12-year-old has a congenital anterior failure of the hymen to fuse.

Figure 25. *This hymen has failed to fuse. There is an intravaginal ridge at 3 o'clock.*

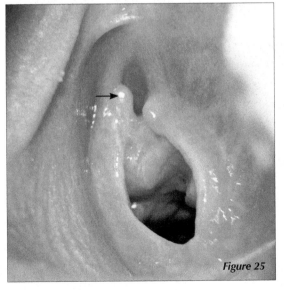

ADOLESCENT SEXUAL ABUSE AND ASSAULT: 13-17 YEARS OLD*

HISTORY OF SEXUAL ABUSE OR ASSAULT
Penile-Vaginal Penetration
Characteristics of the Injury—Acute Findings

Case Study 26

This 12-year-old Hispanic female has a recent history of 2-time penile-vaginal penetration with ejaculation, fondling of buttocks, and kissing by her natural father. The child was examined within 72 hours of the assault. There is domestic violence in the home, and the child is distressed and depressed. She is not sexually active.

Figure 26. *The vaginal wall can be easily seen through the opened hymen. Further evaluation is needed to determine the continuity of the hymen, especially at 3, 5, 7, and 9 o'clock. There is a thick white discharge. Cultures were negative.*

*Some cases in the adolescent group are younger than 13 years but are Tanner stage 2 or greater.

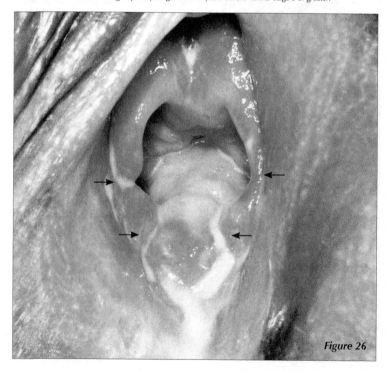

Figure 26

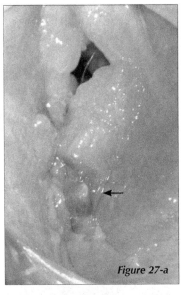

Figure 27-a

Characteristics of the Injury—Healing Injury

Case Study 27

This 12-year-old runaway was sexually assaulted by a 21-year-old male neighbor.

Figure 27-a. *There is acute bleeding from the laceration just below the hymen at 6 o'clock.*

Figure 27-b. *This photo shows more exposure of the same laceration. Exploring the hymen with a balloon-covered swab may have more clearly revealed the hymenal transection at 6 o'clock.*

Figure 27-c. *This photo was taken at a follow-up examination 2 weeks later and shows the healing laceration. Labial separation would help to better evaluate the hymen, fossa navicularis, and posterior fourchette.*

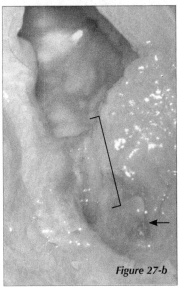

Figure 27-b

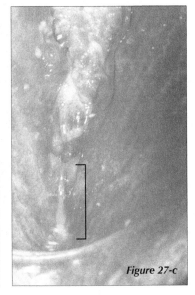

Figure 27-c

Characteristics of the Victim— Not Previously Sexually Active

Case Study 28

This 12-year-old Tanner stage 2 female has been postmenarchal for 1 year. She reported, "My parents beat and sexually abuse me." She reported forced fellatio, genital rubbing with penis, and penile-vaginal penetration with bleeding by her father. She was examined 2 weeks after the most recent episode of vaginal penetration.

Figure 28-a. There is anal hyperpigmentation visible (35 mm).

Figure 28-b. The hymen has a normal color and contour.

Figure 28-c. There is an anal tag at 6 o'clock.

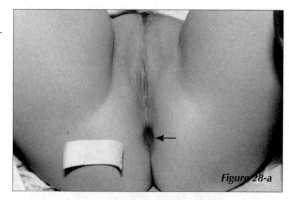

Figure 28-a

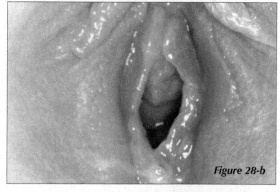

Figure 28-b

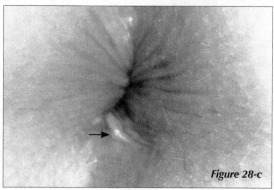

Figure 28-c

Photographic Appendix

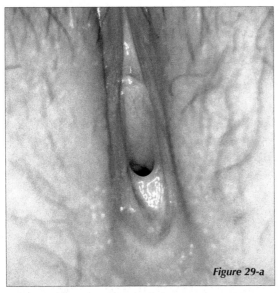

Figure 29-a

Characteristics of the Victim— Pregnant

Case Study 29

This Tanner stage 3 12-year-old female and her 13-year-old sister gave a history of fondling by their 17-year-old brother for the past year. Her urine test for HCG was positive on 2 occasions, supporting her pregnancy. She was not aware of being pregnant, nor could she provide any history of how it occurred.

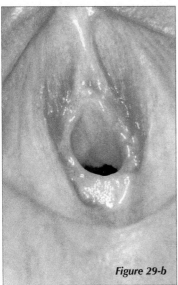

Figure 29-b

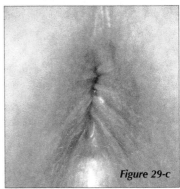

Figure 29-c

Figure 29-a. *The hymen is thin and has sharp edges. There is no separation being used here.*

Figure 29-b. *This is the same normal hymen, visualized with labial separation.*

Figure 29-c. *The perianal folds are asymmetrical in this normal anus.*

Digital-Vaginal Penetration

Case Study 30

This 15-year-old Tanner stage 3 female was molested by her 37-year-old stepfather but did not disclose the abuse to her mother because the mother was "fragile." The victim reported more than 75 incidents of fondling and digital penetration. The most recent incident took place 48 hours before the examination. The suspect pled guilty.

Figure 30-a. *The hymen is estrogenized and fimbriated. There is erythema at 6 o'clock in the fossa navicularis.*

Figure 30-b. *The pink cervix without injury. There is thick, white accumulation superior to the cervix, although the mucus in the cervical os is clear.*

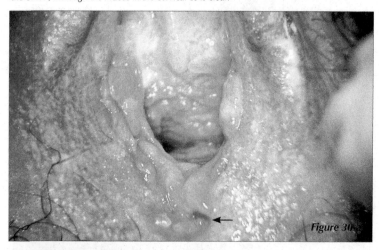

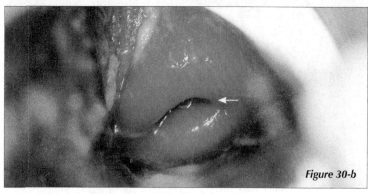

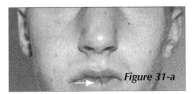

Figure 31-a

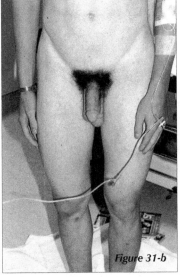

Figure 31-b

Sodomy

Case Study 31

This 15-year-old male was seen in the emergency department after having been brought in by ambulance. He explained that he was resting in his dorm room, and the next thing he remembers is the ambulance.

Figure 31-a. *There is ecchymosis below the right eye. The nose is swollen and a nasal fracture was confirmed by x-ray. There is also a laceration to the left of the midline on the lower, dry edematous lips (35 mm).*

Figure 31-b. *Abrasions of the lower legs. The genitalia appear to be normal, Tanner stage 4 (35 mm).*

Figure 31-c. *There is an abrasion on the glans penis, starting near the urethra at 4 o'clock and extending downward. Note the erythema of the fingernails from biting them (35 mm).*

Figure 31-d. *Erythema and edema of the anus (35 mm).*

Figure 31-e. *This broken-off pencil was retrieved from his anus; the eraser end was in first. The victim was not aware that there was a pencil in his rectum. The point of the pencil was not identified by anoscopic examination. It may have been broken off in order to make removal painful (35 mm).*

The case was inactivated because there were no suspects and no leads.

Figure 31-c

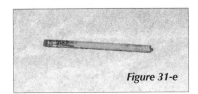

Figure 31-e

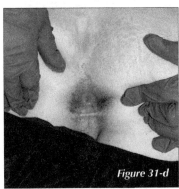

Figure 31-d

General Injuries

Case Study 32

This 14-year-old was beaten by her father because she was walking with a boy. She denied sexual assault by her father. Her father pled guilty.

Figure 32-a. This laceration to her upper lip was caused by a bracket of her braces when her father hit her mouth (35 mm).

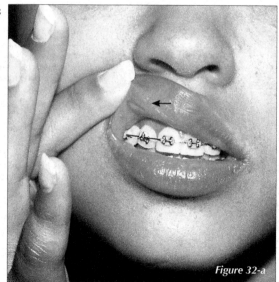

Figure 32-a

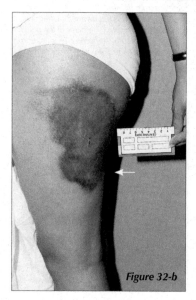

Figure 32-b

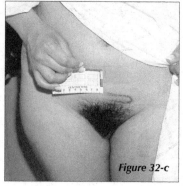

Figure 32-c

Figure 32-b. An ecchymosis where her father kicked her (35 mm).

Figure 32-c. An ecchymosis from the end of a belt (35 mm).

NONASSAULT VARIANTS
Skin-Related
Lichen Sclerosis

Case Study 33

This 9-year-old Tanner stage 2 female was reported to child protection because she wore no underwear to school and repeatedly touched her genitalia. She lives with both of her natural parents, and there was no history of sexual abuse.

Figure 33-a. A hypopigmented, thin friable area surrounding the genitalia. There is ecchymosis medial to the hypopigmentation, starting at the right labium minus and extending downward to the posterior fourchette. There is erythema lateral to the clitoral hood (35 mm).

Figure 33-b. A magnified view of the ecchymosis at the labium minus.

Figure 33-c. Ecchymosis at the posterior fourchette that ends in a hematoma. There are 2 lacerations evident. The hymen is pink, vascular, and has a continuous edge.

It was determined that this was lichen sclerosis. She was successfully treated with steroid cream.

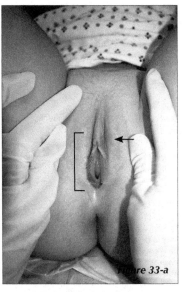

Figure 33-a

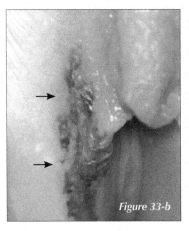

Figure 33-b

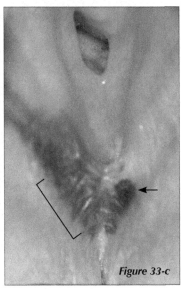

Figure 33-c

NORMAL
FINDINGS
Hymen
*Never Sexually
Active*

Case Study 34

This is a 14-year-old who has never been sexually active.

Figure 34-a. *The thick, pale hymen has an uninterrupted edge and thick, pale bands.*

Figure 34-b. *A balloon-covered swab is used to demonstrate the continuity of the lower border of the redundant hymenal edge.*

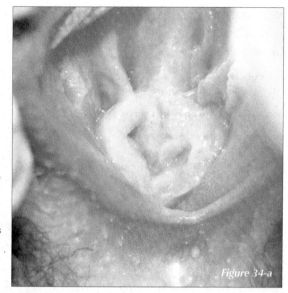

Figure 34-a

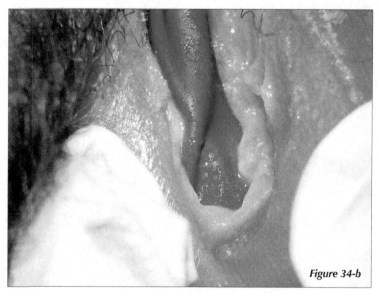

Figure 34-b

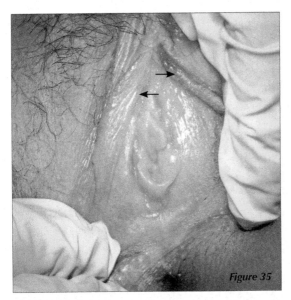

Figure 35

Asymmetrical Labia

Case Study 35

This is a 12-year-old Hispanic female.

Figure 35. *Asymmetrical labia minora with the left labium minus larger and more pigmented than the right.*

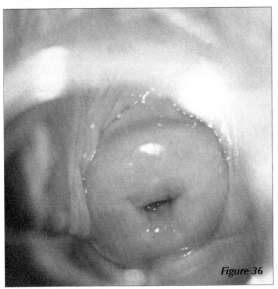

Figure 36

Cervix

Case Study 36

This 18-year-old female is 7 weeks postpartum.

Figure 36. *The os is opened and normally irregular. Mucus is flowing from the os.*

Anal/Rectal

Case Study 37

These 3 photographs show a normal rectum at 3 positions of the anoscope.

Figure 37-a. A view from 5 centimeters into the anus.

Figure 37-b. A view from half-way out of the anus. Yellow stool is present.

Figure 37-c. A view from just beyond the anal verge.

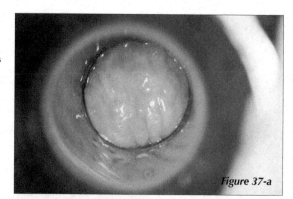

Figure 37-a

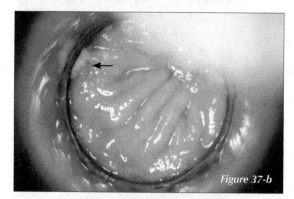

Figure 37-b

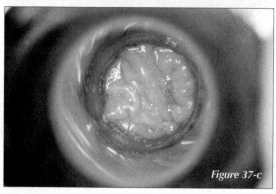

Figure 37-c

ADULT SEXUAL ASSAULT: 18-39 YEARS OLD

HISTORY OF SEXUAL ASSAULT

Case Study 38

This 35-year-old was in her apartment with her boyfriend when 2 African American males broke in, intending to rob her. The intruders forced the victim and her boyfriend into the bedroom. One of them threatened the victim with a kitchen knife. He held her prone and inserted a can of foot powder into her vagina 2 times. Then he pushed his penis into her vagina "for a couple of minutes." There was no ejaculation, but semen was found on the vaginal swabs. He attempted anal penetration.

Figures 38 a-d are of the crime scene.

Figure 38-a. The victim's bedroom. The assault occurred on the bed (35 mm).

Figure 38-b. The foot powder can used in the assault (35 mm).

Figure 38-c. Knives, one of which was missing, were used to threaten the victim (35 mm).

Figure 38-d. These items were found in the perpetrators' possession. The watch belonged to the victim, as did some collectable coins which are not present in the photograph (35 mm).

Figure 38-a

Figure 38-b

Figure 38-c

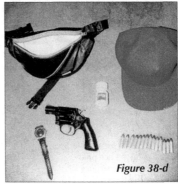

Figure 38-d

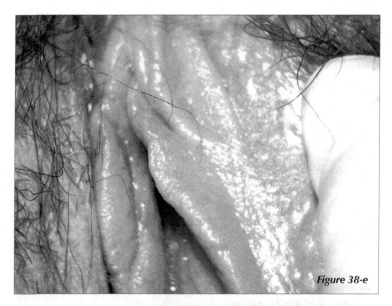

Figure 38-e

Case Study 38 *(continued)*

Figures 38-e *and* ***38-f*** *are of the victim.*

Figure 38-e. *There is ecchymosis of the labium minus at 9 to 11 o'clock.*

Figure 38-f. *Petechiae are visible on the cervix.*

The victim called the police and was able to describe the perpetrator's car, which was quickly identified, and the perpetrators were apprehended. They were convicted of conspiring forcible rape in concert, forcible sodomy and sodomy in concert, robbery, and residential burglary. Male 1 was sentenced to 61 years to life and male 2, who had prior convictions, was sentenced to 80 years to life.

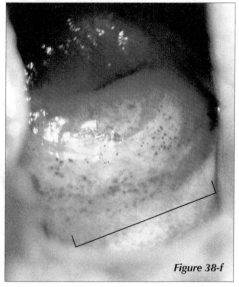

Figure 38-f

Disabled Victims

Case Study 39

This 19-year-old male is epileptic and autistic and lives at a residential facility. When he returned from a visit to his parents' house, he complained of anal pain to the care providers at the residential facility. He was examined 4 hours after his report of pain.

Figure 39-a. This is the victim. Note his posture is consisent with his disability (35 mm).

Figure 39-b. There is a laceration of the anus, and dried blood is present in the perianal area.

Figure 39-c. There is visible erythema and edema of the anus and a laceration at 6 o'clock. An external hemorrhoid is present at 12 o'clock.

Figure 39-d. There is venous pooling around the anus with a large laceration at 6 o'clock.

Investigation is being pursued.

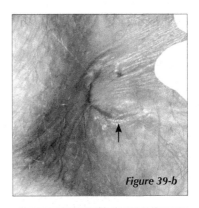

Figure 39-b

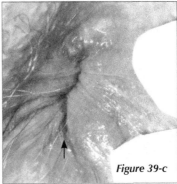

Figure 39-c

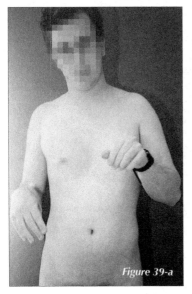

Figure 39-a

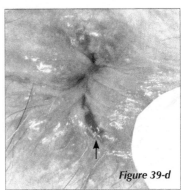

Figure 39-d

Oral Injury

Case Study 40

This 24-year-old female is a prostitute. Her pimp forced penile penetration of her mouth and then beat her because she wasn't making enough money. She was examined 17 hours after the assault.

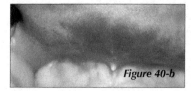

Figure 40-b

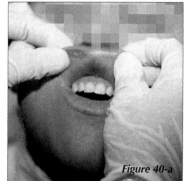

Figure 40-a

Figure 40-a. The victim with 2 sites of ecchymosis on the mucosal surface of the upper lip (35 mm).

Figure 40-b. A closer view of the ecchymosis of the lip. It extends to the gumline. There is also a split in the frenulum.

Figure 40-c. There is a laceration at the vermillion border of this ecchymotic area of the upper lip.

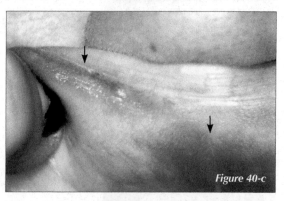

Figure 40-c

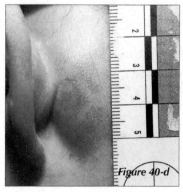

Figure 40-d

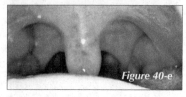

Figure 40-e

Figure 40-d. A site of ecchymosis behind the earlobe consistent with a history of forced penile penetration of the mouth. This may be called a "clapping" injury (35 mm).

Figure 40-e. There are petechiae on the uvula.

This case was accepted by the district attorney.

NONASSAULT VARIANTS
Skin-Related Findings
Irritation of the Medial Thighs

Case Study 41

This is a 300-pound Caucasian female.

Figure 41-a. *There is erythema and hyperpigmentation of the medial thighs extending to the buttocks. There is healing of the breakdown around the perimeter of the erythema. At the arrows, there are oozing abrasions and skin breakdown (35 mm).*

Figure 41-b. *A closer view of the area of open breakdown (35 mm).*

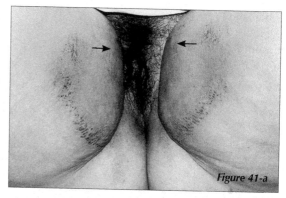

Figure 41-a

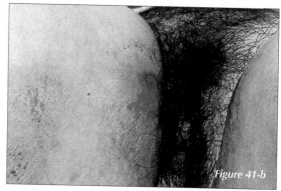

Figure 41-b

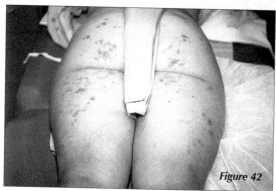

Figure 42

Folliculitis

Case Study 42

This is a 43-year-old female.

Figure 42. *She has had a history of folliculitis for over one year from an unknown cause. She was referred to a dermatologist for further examination (35 mm).*

477

Labial and Vaginal Findings
Lichenification

Case Study 43

Figure 43. *This 18-year-old has lichenification. Note the lack of pubic hair. She does not shave (35 mm).*

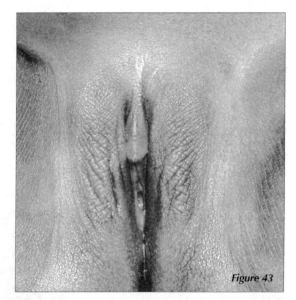

Figure 43

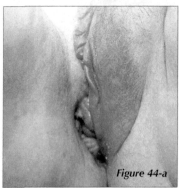

Figure 44-a

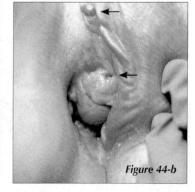

Figure 44-b

Vulvectomy

Case Study 44

This 40-year-old had vulvar cancer, and the right labium majus and labium minus were surgically removed. She remains sexually active. She is not taking estrogen.

Figure 44-a. *The labium majus and minus on the left are erythematous, as are 2 sites on the medial right thigh. There is thinning of the pubic hair (35 mm).*

Figure 44-b. *The vaginal orifice is visible with the labium majus pulled to the side. The clitoris and urethral opening are visible (35 mm).*

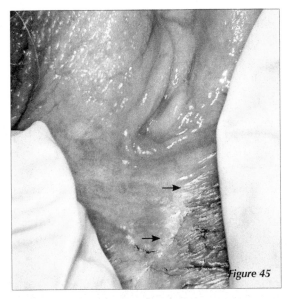

Figure 45

Episiotomy

Case Study 45

This 40-year-old female (gravida 2, para 2) has had 2 vaginal deliveries, both with term infants.

Figure 45. There is a medio-lateral episiotomy that is not easily visible. This photograph was taken 1 hour after consensual penile-vaginal intercourse. There is erythema of the left medial labium, posterior hymen and posterior fourchette.

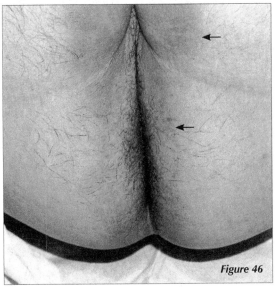

Figure 46

Perineum and Perianal Findings
Skin Irritation

Case Study 46

This 30-year-old heterosexual male has hyperpigmentation and skin thickening. He wears cotton briefs. This photograph was taken during the fall in a tropical climate.

Figure 46. The hyperpigmentation and skin thickening on the medial thighs and buttocks may be due to rubbing and moisture (35 mm).

Techniques
Genital Examination

Case Study 47

These 3 photographs demonstrate examination techniques. Although the shape of the hymen is not as significant in adults as it is in children, it is noteworthy to see how different techniques can alter the appearance of the anatomy.

Figure 47-a. *With labial separation, the hymen appears closed, and the posterior fourchette is uninjured.*

Figure 47-b. *With labial separation, the hymen begins to open and appears annular.*

Figure 47-c. *Using labial traction, the hymen now appears crescentic.*

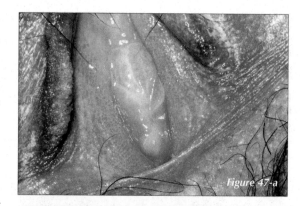

Figure 47-a

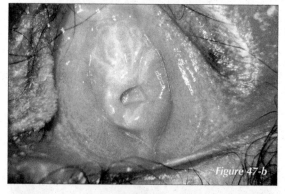

Figure 47-b

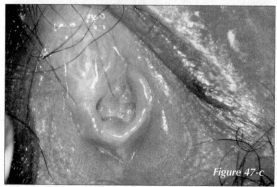

Figure 47-c

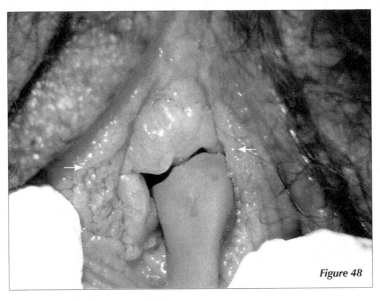

Figure 48

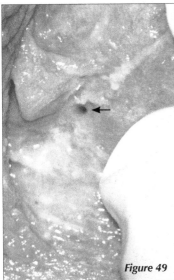

Figure 49

NORMAL FINDINGS
Vestibule
Vestibular Papillations

Case Study 48

This 27-year-old Caucasian female was unable to recall whether her mother took diethylstilbestrol or whether she had a difficult pregnancy.

Figure 48. There are vestibular papillations visible from 2 to 9 o'clock around the hymen. These papillations are seen most commonly in the vestibule in female offspring whose mothers took diethylstilbestrol during pregnancy.

Open Bartholin Duct

Case Study 49

A 27-year-old Caucasian gravida 0 female.

Figure 49. The open Bartholin duct is visible. Bartholin glands secrete mucus.

481

Periurethral Perihymenal Bands

Case Study 50

A sexually active 18-year-old Caucasian gravida 0.

Figure 50. There are periurethral bands bilaterally.

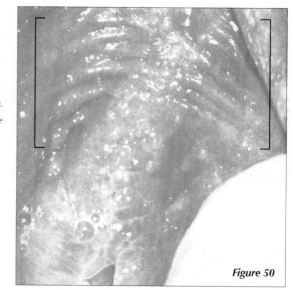

Figure 50

Hymens Related to Sexual Experience, Pregnancy, and Number of Vaginal Deliveries

Never Been Pregnant

Case Study 51

This 39-year-old female has been sexually active for 20 years but never pregnant.

Figure 51. The normally thick hymen has folds or clefts at 4 and 8 o'clock. These need to be more closely examined.

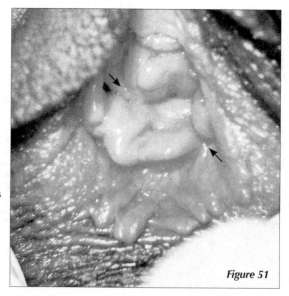

Figure 51

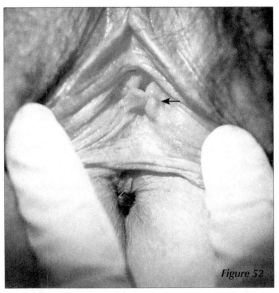

Figure 52

One Vaginal Delivery

Case Study 52

This 40-year-old obese female (gravida 1) has been sexually active and married for 20 years.

Figure 52. *The left lateral rim of the hymen is visible with a fold or cleft at 3 o'clock. There is a caruncula at 7 to 8 o'clock and a section of hymen visible from 9 to 11 o'clock. A more magnified view using a swab to explore the hymenal rim would be helpful.*

Vaginal Wall

Case Study 53

This 20-year-old has normal rugae on the left vaginal wall.

Figure 53. *The rugae are seen here through the side of the vaginal speculum. The most exterior tissue is the hymen.*

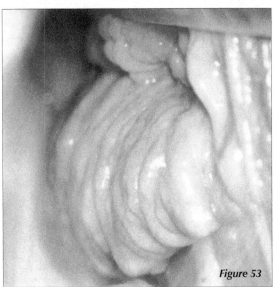

Figure 53

Cervix
Normal Findings

Case Study 54

This 23-year-old (gravida 0) has a normal cervix.

Figure 54. *The cervix is rose-colored and shiny, with a slit-like os.*

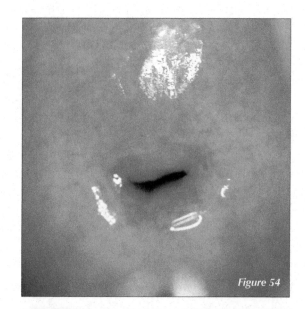

Figure 54

Intrauterine Device String

Case Study 55

This is a 25-year-old sexually active female with an intrauterine device (IUD).

Figure 55. *The IUD string in the cervical os has caused no apparent irritation to the cervix. The erythema right at the os may be ectropion. The tissue at 3 and 9 o'clock is the vaginal wall between the blades of the vaginal speculum.*

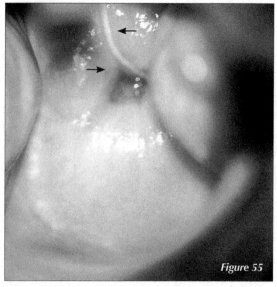

Figure 55

MIDDLE-AGED ADULT SEXUAL ASSAULT: 40-64 YEARS OLD

HISTORY OF SEXUAL ASSAULT
Characteristics of the Perpetrator

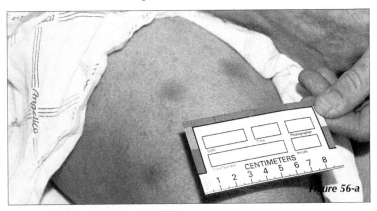

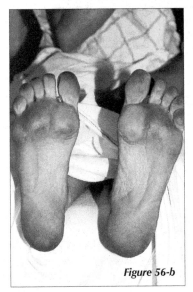

Figure 56-b

Case Study 56

This 47-year-old female (gravida 1, para 1) was assaulted by 2 strangers. She was picked up by the perpetrators, who then stopped in an empty lot and pushed her out of the car. At knifepoint, they took turns assaulting her, including forced fellatio, forced cunnilingus, and 15 incidents each of penetration of her vagina with penis and fingers. Her anus was penetrated by fingers 6 times and by a penis 15 times. She stated, "They couldn't get it very hard or couldn't come, so they kept trying. I was so scared I went along with it." When they were done, they pushed her back in the car and let her off where they picked her up. She was examined 6 hours after the assault.

Figure 56-a. *There are 3 fingertip-sized ecchymoses on the anterior thigh (35 mm).*

Figure 56-b. *The patient's dirty feet are consistent with the history of being barefoot outdoors.*

Case Study 56
(continued)

Figure 56-c. *The pink hymen is free of acute injury and erythema which might be expected with 15 incidents of forced vaginal penetration. The hymen is visible from 2 to 10 o'clock.*

Figure 56-d. *The posterior fourchette is free of injury.*

The case was inactivated because it was unsubstantiated and the perpetrators were not identified.

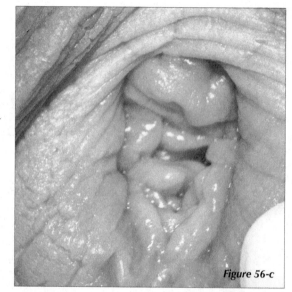

Figure 56-c

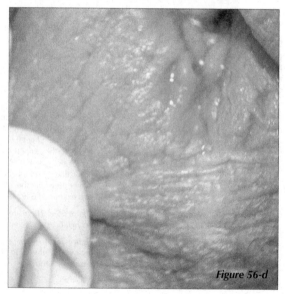

Figure 56-d

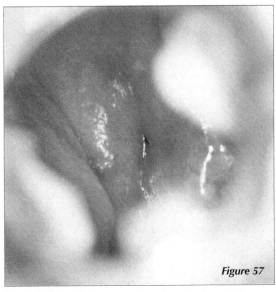

Figure 57

NONASSAULT VARIANTS
Nabothian Cyst

Case Study 57

This 45-year-old female (gravida 0) has had a nabothian cyst for several years. It is examined annually during her pap smears.

Figure 57. *The nabothian cyst.*

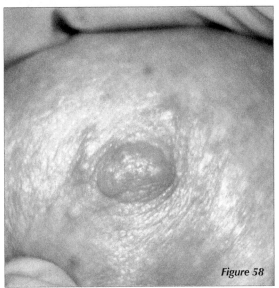

Figure 58

Breasts

Case Study 58

This 51-year-old is a sober alcoholic. She is on an estrogen-progesterone combination.

Figure 58. *The nipple. The color of the areola has lightened with aging and now blends into the surrounding breast tissue.*

487

Genital

Case Study 59

This 58-year-old female is a recovering alcohol abuser and a smoker. She is now a Tanner stage 3, having lost much of her pubic hair which is common with aging when exogeneous estrogen is not taken.

Figure 59. The pubic hair that remains is sparse.

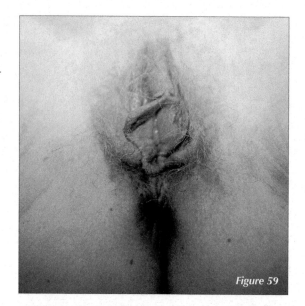

Figure 59

Case Study 60

This 50-year-old obese multiparous Hispanic female has been postmenarchal for 3 years and is on no estrogen.

Figure 60. The labia majora and thighs are sagging, and the labia minora are no longer visible. The pubic hair is thinning. There is erythema on the labia majora, which may be normal.

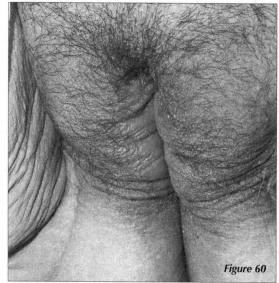

Figure 60

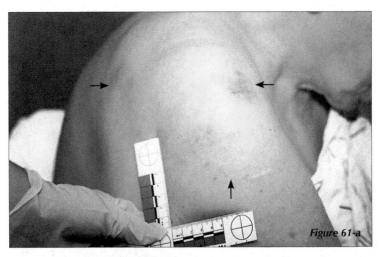

Figure 61-a

ELDERLY SEXUAL ASSAULT: 65 AND OLDER

HISTORY OF SEXUAL ASSAULT

Case Study 61

This 74-year-old female (gravida 6, para 6) is taking no estrogens. She went outside to empty the trash in the evening. Two men (one Caucasian, one Hispanic with a tattoo on his arm) pushed her back inside her house. They pushed her to the floor, kicked her in the abdomen, and hit her above the right eye. She lost consciousness. When she awoke, it was 7 o'clock in the morning and she was naked from the waist down. She arrived for her examination 20 hours after the assault. She was alert and answered direct questions but was hesitant to give details.

Figure 61-a. The ecchymoses of the right arm, shoulder, and back (35 mm).

Figure 61-b. The photograph shows the genital area, obscured by the obese medial thighs. The left leg is extended out, and the right leg is flexed up. The maceration on the inner thighs is related to moisture and obesity (35 mm).

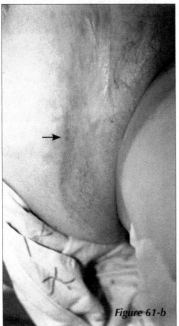

Figure 61-b

489

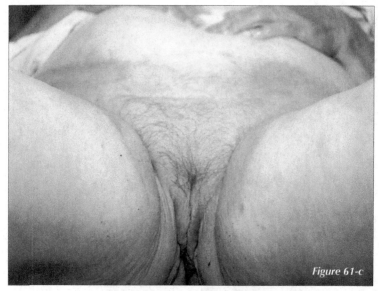

Figure 61-c

Case Study 61
(continued)

Figure 61-c. There is maceration on the abdomen and inner thighs. Pubic hair is sparse, consistent with the victim's age (35 mm).

Figure 61-d. The periurethral area is pink with no acute injury. There is a black lesion on the left labium minus. The color and borders of this lesion are irregular.

The victim was referred to gynecology for follow-up.

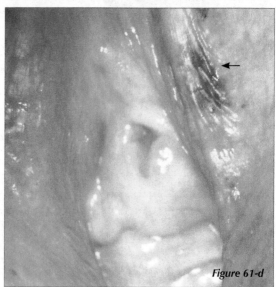

Figure 61-d

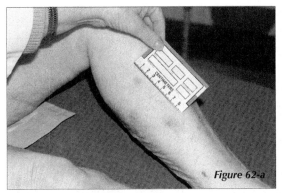

Figure 62-a

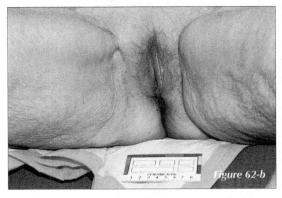

Figure 62-b

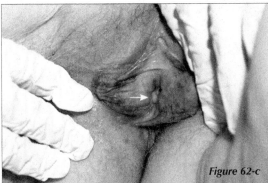

Figure 62-c

Case Study 62

This 79-year-old post-menopausal female (gravida 7, para 5) suffers from diverticulitis and constipation. She is able to stand and transfer but does not ambulate. She is incontinent and wears a diaper. Her diarrhea comes and goes. She lives in a skilled nursing facility and claimed that a male Middle-Eastern medication nurse gave her medication that made her go to sleep. When she woke up, she was naked from the waist down. She was unable to state what he did to her. She was examined in an emergency room 12 hours after she awoke. There was no photographic magnification available at the examination site.

Figure 62-a. Ecchymosis is visible on the left leg (35 mm).

Figure 62-b. The sparse pubic hair and sagging of subcutaneous tissue is consistent with the patient's age. The labia majora and minora are erythematous (35 mm).

Figure 62-c. Erythema is present on the right labium majus extending down to the medial thigh. It is also present on the right labium minus (35 mm).

Case Study 62 *(continued)*

Figure 62-d. *There is a hymenal tag protruding from the vaginal orifice. Further separation would allow for more complete evaluation of the vaginal introitus (35 mm).*

Figure 62-e. *The anus is erythematous. Anal tags are visible (35 mm).*

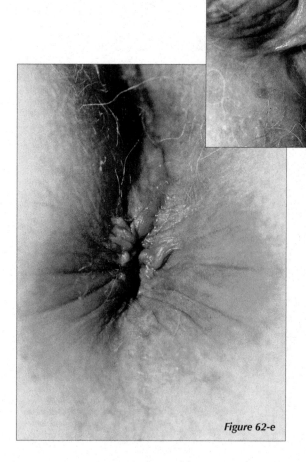

Figure 62-d

Figure 62-e

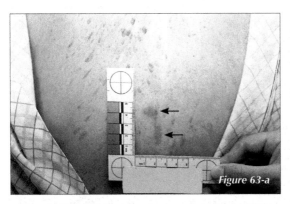

Figure 63-a

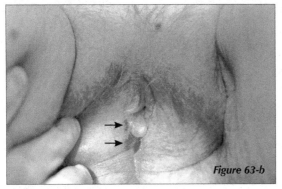

Figure 63-b

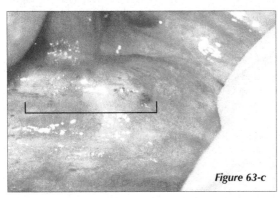

Figure 63-c

Case Study 63

This 94-year-old healthy white female lives in her own home. An unknown man came to the door wanting to use the telephone. She said she would make his call for him, but he pushed in through the door. He penetrated her vagina with his fingers and attempted to penetrate her vagina with his penis while she was on her back. He then put her on her abdomen and put his fingers in her anus and attempted to put his penis in her anus. He became frustrated and did not ejaculate. The victim was examined 2 hours after the assault.

Figure 63-a. The abrasions on the mid-back are consistent with the victim's story (35 mm).

Figure 63-b. There are lacerations on the right labium minus (35 mm).

Figure 63-c. There are abrasions on the posterior fourchette. There is white vaginal discharge present.

493

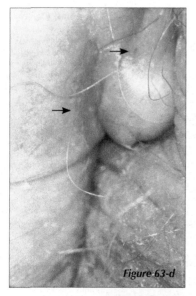

Figure 63-d

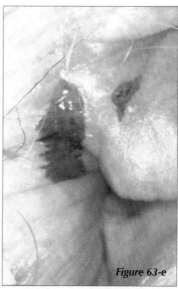

Figure 63-e

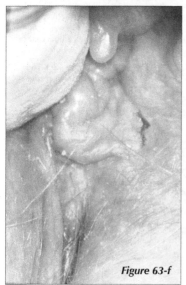

Figure 63-f

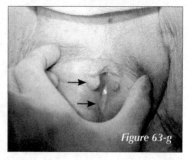

Figure 63-g

Case Study 63 *(continued)*

Figure 63-d. *There is a laceration lateral to the edematous right labium minus.*

Figure 63-e. *The dye uptake of the labial and hymenal lacerations.*

Figure 63-f. *This laceration of the perineum is oozing blood.*

Figure 63-g. *The labium minus laceration is resolved (35 mm).*

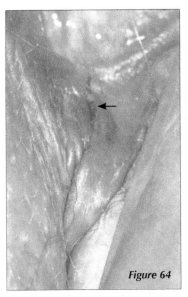

Figure 64

Nonassault Variants
Friable Fourchette

Case Study 64

This 94-year-old female has no ongoing vaginal infection and is not diabetic. She does not take estrogens.

Aged skin is less elastic and therefore less resilient to the separation technique and vaginal speculum exam.

Figure 64. This posterior fourchette laceration occurred during the speculum examination.

Rectal Polyp

Case Study 65

This 65-year-old female was seen for a report of sexual assault. She denies forced or consensual anal intercourse.

Figure 65. A rectal polyp is seen through the anoscope. She has no symptoms with this polyp, but she did with the previous one that started to bleed.

A polyp was removed previously because of bleeding. She was referred for diagnosis and treatment.

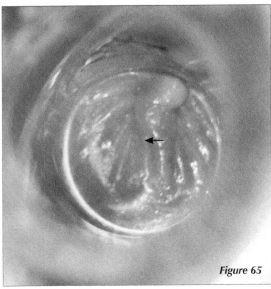

Figure 65

495

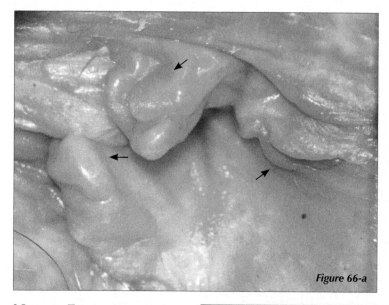

Figure 66-a

Normal Findings
Perianal Laxity

Case Study 66

This 88-year-old female states that she is "very healthy for her age." She explains that she has no constipation because of her diet, which includes 2 apples a day, and her daily walk of about 5 blocks.

Figure 66-a. There are perianal tags superior and lateral to the anus. The anus is beneath the sagging perineal tissue.

Figure 66-b. Using separation, the anus is revealed within the redundant perianal tissue.

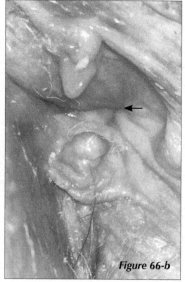

Figure 66-b

Index

A

W